PENGUIN BOOKS

# VENABLES

# THE AUTOBIOGRAPHY

Terry Venables, the current coach of the England football team, has the unique distinction of having been capped by England at every level in football, from schoolboy to full international. He joined Chelsea at the age of fifteen and has played for (and managed) Queen's Park Rangers, Spurs and Crystal Palace. In addition to his successful football career both on and off the pitch, he is known as an author, singer, television personality and businessman. In the 1960s he co-wrote *They Used to Play on Grass* with the author and journalist Gordon Williams. They also collaborated on three crime novels featuring the London private detective James Hazell, who formed the basis of the popular television series made in the late 1970s. *Venables: The Autobiography* won the William Hill jacket award in 1994.

Neil Hanson, the co-writer, has written many books, including the acclaimed *Mud, Blood and Glory* (1991). He lives in Ilkley, West Yorkshire, with his wife, Lynn, and their son, Jack.

D0773836

# Venables
## *The Autobiography*

TERRY VENABLES and NEIL HANSON

PENGUIN BOOKS

This book is dedicated to
my Mum and Dad

Thank you

PENGUIN BOOKS

Published by the Penguin Group
Penguin Books Ltd, 27 Wrights Lane, London W8 5TZ, England
Penguin Books USA Inc., 375 Hudson Street, New York, New York 10014, USA
Penguin Books Australia Ltd, Ringwood, Victoria, Australia
Penguin Books Canada Ltd, 10 Alcorn Avenue, Toronto, Ontario, Canada M4V 3B2
Penguin Books (NZ) Ltd, 182–190 Wairau Road, Auckland 10, New Zealand

Penguin Books Ltd, Registered Offices: Harmondsworth, Middlesex, England

First published by Michael Joseph 1994
Published in Penguin Books 1995
3 5 7 9 10 8 6 4 2

Copyright © Terry Venables, 1994
All rights reserved

The moral right of the author has been asserted

Printed in England by Clays Ltd, St Ives plc

# Contents

# *Acknowledgements*

THIS MAY BE AN AUTOBIOGRAPHY but writing this book has involved many people, apart from myself – too many to name individually – who have jogged my memory or given me useful insights. A few must be mentioned, however. Susan Watt and Louise Haines at my publishers Michael Joseph, Jonathan Harris, my literary agent, and my co-writer, Neil Hanson, have all worked tirelessly on the mammoth task of turning my often ramshackle recollections into a finished manuscript.

If the list of people who have helped with this book is large, the number I have cause to thank over the course of my life so far is endless. Looking back over my career, so many people have been important to me that it is impossible to thank them all. If I tried, I would be bound to miss someone out – like doing a speech at a wedding and forgetting to mention Auntie Nellie.

I have always admired loyalty and disliked fair-weather friends, but having gone through one of the darkest years of my life, prior to being appointed England coach, it has really come home to me who my true friends are. Above all, I must thank my wife Yvette, my Dad Fred and my daughters Nancy and Tracey, who have shared my troubles and never wavered in their love and support for me, no matter how bad things got. Eddie Ashby, Eric Hall, Jonathan Crystal and Ted Buxton have also shown me tremendous loyalty and friendship, standing by me and speaking up for me, and if I could single out one other friend from all those who have supported me, it would be Bobby Keetch, who phoned me almost every day during 'the troubles', with a word of encouragement.

I certainly needed it. In the period following my sacking from Tottenham, I was continually vilified in the media, as a barrage of press articles, television and radio programmes repeatedly called my character and honesty into question. Yet while those hostile to me had little apparent difficulty in getting their views aired, I was given very few opportunities to state my case. This book is the story of the whole of my life, not just a few months in 1993, but writing it has given me the chance to publish for the first time the whole truth about the events that led to my departure from Tottenham and to answer the many false allegations made against me. I have tried to do so in as even-handed a manner as possible, unlike much of the media at the time, which only appeared to be interested in one side of the story.

I am grateful to two journalists who led the counter-attack against the 'smear Venables campaign': Charlie Sale of the *Express*, the first journalist to believe my story and be willing to write it, and my old friend Jeff Powell of the *Mail*, who quickly followed up with a supportive piece. Many thousands of Tottenham supporters and other football fans also wrote wishing me well, and it was amazing how waking up to even the shortest letter of support was sometimes all the encouragement I needed to get through the trials of the day ahead. To all of these people, and to the many, many others who I have not mentioned by name, my heartfelt thanks.

Terry Venables
London, August 1994

# Photographic Acknowledgements

The Author and Publishers would like to thank the following people and organisations for permission to reproduce the photographs in this book:

SECTION I

Page 1: Author's collection. Page 2: Author's collection. Page 3: *above* Courtesy of the Evening Standard; *below* Author's collection. Page 4: Author's collection. Page 5: Bob Thomas Sports Photography. Page 6: *above* Mirror Syndication International; *below* Colorsport. Page 7: *above* Mirror Syndication International; *below* Bob Thomas Sports Photography. Page 8: Author's collection.

SECTION II

Page 9: *above* Mirror Syndication International; *below* Author's collection. Page 10: Author's collection. Page 11: *above* Courtesy of the Evening Standard; *below* Colorsport. Page 12: *above* Courtesy of the Evening Standard; *middle* By courtesy of The News Portsmouth; *below* Author's collection. Page 13: Bob Thomas Sports Photography. Page 14: *above* Bob Thomas Sports Photography; *middle* Author's collection; *below* Author's collection. Page 15: Courtesy of the Evening Standard. Page 16: Author's collection.

SECTION III

Page 17: Mirror Syndication International. Page 18: Author's collection. Page 19: Author's collection. Page 20: Courtesy of the Evening Standard. Page 21: *above* Courtesy of the Evening Standard; *below* Bob Thomas Sports Photography. Page 22: *above* Mirror Syndication International; *below* Courtesy of the Evening Standard. Page 23: Courtesy of Action Images. Page 24: Author's collection.

# Prologue: A Mexican Stand-off

'OH MY GOD, there's a woman on the roof over there. She's going to jump.'

I was halfway through the most important ninety minutes of my life, being interviewed for the job of England coach. For the past year I had been subjected to smear, innuendo and downright lie. Despite the provocations, and the times when I was bordering on complete despair, I had kept my nerve and my counsel, knowing that, whatever mud was flung at me, the truth would eventually come out. Now I had reached the final hurdle, believing that fate could not possibly have any further surprises in store. I should have known better.

FA chief executive Graham Kelly, who had been sitting on one side of me during the interview, had got up to stretch his legs and strolled to the window. To avoid the reporters 'door-stepping' the FA headquarters in Lancaster Gate, we were meeting in the Football League's Commercial Department in Winchester House, Old Marylebone Road. The seventh-floor room was directly opposite the roof of the building across the road. About twenty yards away from us, a dark-haired woman in a blue coat was perched on the parapet at the edge of the roof, with her legs dangling over the side of the building.

My first thought was an entirely selfish one: 'I don't believe this is happening to me. Of all the buildings in London, why did she have to pick this one, and this day of all days, to pull this stunt?' I was immediately ashamed of myself, for my lack of compassion. Despite everything that had happened to me in the previous few months, I had never felt desperate enough to want to throw myself off a roof.

The mere thought of the drop beneath the woman caused me to break out in a cold sweat, but she seemed to be facing the possibility of death with a certain nonchalance, swinging her legs as she gazed down into the street below. She had obviously been there for some time, for just a few yards beyond her, sitting with their backs tight against a wall, were two policemen. They were sitting deadly still, afraid of making the wrong move, not attempting to make conversation with her, but watching her intently.

She was also being studied equally closely from the seventh floor of Winchester House, where seven of us were now jammed into the width of the window, morbidly awaiting developments. It was a Mexican stand-off. The woman and the policemen remained motionless for several minutes, as if in suspended animation, while the FA viewing party was equally rooted to the spot.

Eventually, with no sign of either an imminent jump or rescue attempt, we reluctantly dragged ourselves away from the drama, back to the rather less life-threatening business in hand. 'It just goes to show,' said Graham, as we resumed our seats, 'I bet she's got more problems than all of us.'

I smiled and thought: Speak for yourself. If she had my problems she would have jumped twenty minutes ago.

# CHAPTER ONE

# East End Boy

### 1943–58

IT WAS NEARLY A VERY SHORT LIFE. The house in which my Mum had been living before I was born was bombed flat the night after she left to stay with my grandparents. Had she stayed twenty-four hours longer, or the Luftwaffe arrived twenty-four hours earlier, Alan Sugar's future life might well have been rather less complicated.

I was a war baby, born on 6 January 1943, in my grandparents' house at 313 Valence Avenue, Dagenham, the only child of Frederick Charles Venables and Myrtle Eileen Venables. For some reason numerous newspaper reports have said that I was actually born in Bethnal Green, but it is not true; I never went near the place until I had developed some muscles. My father, a petty officer in the Navy during the war, was actually in Halifax, Nova Scotia, when I was born, and did not get his first sight of his son and heir until he came home on leave several months later. My Dad's family were from Barking. He was one of six brothers and three sisters, so there was no shortage of cousins in the area. My Dad was twenty when he got married; Mum was eighteen.

When I was just six weeks old, my mother and I were evacuated to Wales, because of the bombing. Mum had moved to Dagenham with her parents when she was about fifteen years old, but any number of her other relatives still lived in the Rhondda, at Clydach Vale, a mining village high in the hills beyond Tonypandy. Even after the war ended and the bombs stopped dropping on the East End, my life was divided between Dagenham and Wales. I would spend the whole of the summer holidays in Wales every year and grew up thinking of myself as a Welshman, albeit one with a pronounced cockney accent. My mother always wanted me to play football for Wales, not England.

I was almost christened Duncan Venables, the name my Mum had originally chosen, but luckily my Auntie Mary talked her out of it. My Mum had been adamant about the name for a while, but when she was leaving Mary's house one day, with me in her arms, Mary called out 'Bye Dunc,' and that killed it for my Mum – Duncan was never mentioned again. My father came up with the name Terry, but not because it was an old family name or even a personal favourite. He decided on it when he was walking down the street and saw an advert for Terry's Chocolates on the side of a passing bus.

My earliest memories are of the house at 29 Park Street, Clydach Vale, part of a row of terraced houses dominated by the Cwmbran colliery at the end of the street. The whole family was as close-knit as the mining community; we lived with Auntie Olive and Uncle Fred at number 29, as did two more uncles, Dai and Joe. Albryn and Auntie Ivy lived at number 23 and 'young' Olive and Eddie at number 21.

My uncles used to work the night-shift down the pit, sleeping in the afternoons. I would get up in time to see them coming back off shift at seven-thirty in the morning, their eyes and teeth showing white in their coal-black faces. My Uncle Dai would often come home in the morning carrying a special treat for all the kids, a block of Wall's ice-cream, wrapped in plain paper. The pure, white ice-cream was clutched in his black, coal-dust covered fist, as we swarmed around him, eager for our share.

Like most of the houses, there was no bathroom at number 29, and we used to have to drag the tin bath in front of the fire, filling it up from the kettle, like Steptoe and Son. There were no pit-head showers then either, and my aunt had to scrub the coal-dust from my uncle's neck and back with a piece of coarse soap and a flannel that felt like a Brillo pad, as he hunched his powerful frame into the tiny tin bath. The other facilities were equally primitive. The toilet was right at the bottom of the yard, a journey that was no fun at all on a freezing winter's night when the wild Welsh wind whistled around my ears and howled through the gap under the toilet door. The houses opened straight on to the street and there were were no gardens, just back yards, but every family had a small allotment, where they would grow a few vegetables to eke out their wages from the pit.

The doors of the houses were always open and the children used to run freely in and out of each other's homes. It was a very stable, friendly and old-fashioned kind of community, quite unlike Dagenham with its docks and fast-expanding car factories and cement works, lining the north bank of the Thames. In Clydach Vale, coal-mining was the principal, almost the only, occupation.

My Grandad on my mother's side, Evan Oswald Evans – Ossie for short – had been a miner, but had also helped my Nan, Myrtle Amelia – known as Milly – to run a grocery shop in Clydach Vale in the years before they moved to Dagenham. Grandad was completely bald, apart from two tufts of hair sticking up from behind his ears and he had two dark blue marks on his bald pate, permanent mementos of gashing his head down the pit. Coal-dust in the wounds gave the scars their blue colour. Tommy Farr, later to become a world-famous boxer, had done the grocery deliveries for Nan and Grandad, and even when money was tight, with Tommy Farr calling round, none of the customers was ever late in settling the grocery bills.

There were plenty of sheep on the bracken-covered hillsides around the town – strange, exotic creatures to a boy who spent the rest of his childhood in Dagenham – but there was scarcely a car in the whole Clydach Valley in those days. Like kids everywhere then, we played in the street, and surprisingly for the heart of Wales, it was usually soccer we played, not rugby, using what was probably the only round ball in the whole of Wales. Even the adults played in the streets sometimes, though the annual athletics tournament was held in Cwmbran Welfare Park, opposite the Bush Hotel and a cinema called 'Dai Doots'.

There were competitors from all the local sports and social clubs, including Clydach Vale's 'Top Club' and 'Monkey Club', and my Auntie Ivy was always the star turn in the athletics, winning the sprints every year. The tournament was opened by a big parade, when the clubs would march down Park Street, accompanied by brass bands and the tootling of hundreds of kazoos. I can remember playing a comb and paper and strutting alongside the bands, as they went marching down the hill.

We were playing football in Park Street one day when the ball went through someone's window. Before the glass had even hit the ground, I did what every Dagenham boy instinctively does in such a situation – I ran for it. Surprisingly, I could not hear any footfalls from the other lads running after me, and when I slowed down and turned round to see what was going on, I saw them all still standing in the middle of the street, rummaging for enough pocket money to compensate Mrs Jones for her broken window. Very sheepishly, I walked back up the road and offered my share. It really was an old-fashioned community . . .

To avoid the risk of broken windows, we also played football in a field right on top of the mountain – or at least it seemed like a mountain to a small boy. We would be up there in all weathers, even when cloud shrouded the hillsides and the rain slanted down, shining the glistening slate rockfaces like glass. If someone kicked the ball too hard, it would disappear miles down the hillside. One of us would have to go all the way down to get it and then climb back up the mountain again. When we were playing up there, we would spend more time arguing about whose turn it was to go and get the ball than actually playing football.

Back in Dagenham, where it was flat as a punctured tyre and it would never have occurred to anyone to pay for a broken window, even if caught in the act, there was plenty of opportunity to play football too, either in the street outside our house or in Valence Park. Our Welsh relatives called Dagenham 'Corned Beef City', believing, not without some justification, that nobody ever ate anything else. It was not completely true, however, for some of the more adventurous eaters would sometimes have Spam for a change . . .

We lived on a huge 1930s estate, built to soak up the 'overspill' from the slum clearances of the East End, and the army of people lured into the area by the promise of regular work, for the memory of the 'Hungry 1930s' was still fresh in everybody's mind. The ranks of identical red-brick terraces marched towards the horizon, and you could easily have got lost on the estate, because many of the roads and houses were absolutely indistinguishable from each other. Valence Avenue was a rather grander road, though, with one distinguishing feature, a dual carriageway separated by a broad grass verge.

There were no hills and definitely no sheep around Dagenham. The sprawling growth of London and its urban satellites was slowly squeezing the life out of the last remnants of open country, and the closest most Dagenham kids came to the countryside was when playing football in Valence Park. Even if it was unashamedly urban, Dagenham holds nothing but happy memories for me. Looking back, I do not really think I could have been brought up anywhere better. We were never flush with money, but we never went without, and if I needed something, my Mum and Dad would do their best to get it for me. My childhood was wonderful and I was doubly lucky, because I was able to appreciate how fortunate I was at the time.

When my Dad came home after the war, we all lived with my grandparents for a while, before moving to our own house at 176 Bonham Road, just round the corner from Valence Avenue. My Dad, Fred, was a mean goalkeeper for Barking Town in his time, and also had some European experience – he played for the Navy against the RAF in Brussels. He can remember me kicking a football around as early as the age of three, but it was my grandfather, Ossie, rather than my Dad, who was the first big football influence on me. I idolised Milly and Ossie, who looked after me during the daytime, for my Dad drove lorries and my Mum worked full-time as well.

My Mum was in charge of all the Odeon restaurants in the area, at places like Chadwell Heath and Romford. In those days every Odeon cinema had a restaurant on the first floor. When people like Naunton Wayne would come to do personal appearances, she would always get their pictures signed 'For Terry'.

Mum would occasionally take me out to lunch at one of the restaurants, and on the way there, she would remind me about my manners. She always insisted on perfect table manners: hold your knife and fork properly, no elbows on the table, don't talk with your mouth full, always tip the bowl away from you when you eat soup, and so on. In addition there were strict little rules that she had obviously inherited from her parents. I would never be allowed a drink, for example, until I had completely finished my food – something I never understood.

When I was not lunching with my Mum, Ossie would take me over to the park every day and play football with me. He had been a football and rugby player and a professional athlete in his youth, his other claim to fame being that he had one brown eye and one blue one, which always fascinated me; I found it very difficult to stop staring at his eyes. He signed my first autograph book: 'Brown Eye, why are you so Blue?'

Ossie and Milly also looked after me later on, when my parents took over the running of a social club in Harold Hill. I did not want to move there because I was doing well in school, so I lived with my Nan and Grandad for a couple of years and just went over to stay with Mum and Dad at weekends, until they came back again.

Ossie had played football in the Rhondda with a man called Jimmy Seed, and they had both come to London together. Both men were determined that their sons should not have to go down the pit to earn a living, and had moved to London in search of work that did not involve scrabbling in filth in the bowels of the earth for a pittance of a wage. Jimmy played for Spurs and became a household name, going on to manage Charlton, but even though he was a fine player, Ossie soon gave up the game. He worked on the railways for the rest of his life. He used to walk home every day, a distance of several miles, and was still prodigiously fit, even as an older man.

My Mum's brother, Trev, was saved from a life down the pit by Ossie's move to London, and the closest he came to the coal industry was when he served as a stoker in the Navy during the war. Trev and his wife and daughter were also living with Ossie and Milly just after the war, and it was quite a houseful, with six adults and a child sleeping upstairs, while I slept on a put-you-up bed in the front room.

I can remember Trev coming back from the war, bringing me a bright red 'football', really a water-polo ball, which he had bought in the Far East. He got me out of bed to have a kickaround with it, even though it was three in the morning. It was one of my most prized possessions, for plastic footballs were unheard of then. Real leather footballs were horrendously expensive and far too precious to be scuffed to death in street football, even if anyone could have afforded one, so games in the street were almost always played with a tennis ball.

I needed little encouragement to play football, at three in the morning or any other time. I always had a tennis ball in my pocket, and in every spare moment, I would be off, kicking it against a wall and dribbling it down the pavement. My pals and I would play out in the street until it got dark, and I would still be out there, even when the other lads had gone home, practising in the pool of light from the streetlight. When my Mum called me in for tea, I would not go in until I had reached the target I had set for myself, like keeping the ball off the ground for fifty touches, with my head, feet and thighs. I just could not give in, there was something in me, that competitiveness, like someone who will not go to sleep until they have finished the crossword. It did not matter if I had reached forty-nine when I made a mistake, I would go back to one and start again, while my dinner went steadily colder on the table.

Even in Dagenham, the home of Ford Motors, there were not many cars around in those days, and playing football in the streets was not the dice with death that it would be today. As the former Spurs and Arsenal manager, Terry Neill, once said to me: 'We used to learn by kicking a ball in the streets, but now they're all full of cars. Were there any cars in your street, Terry?' 'No, only mine.'

There were one or two other dangers, however. We were playing in the street one day when I turned round and ran slap into a cast-iron pillar-box; I still have the scar to this day. Even when playing in the comparative safety of the park, the steel-toecapped boots we used to wear then remained another major health hazard. On one memorable occasion, I tried to head the ball just as another, bigger kid went to kick it, and he booted me in the face instead. I can even remember the name of the culprit, a boy called Harold White.

The whole of my face swelled up until it was inflated as much as our football. My mates had to carry me home and my parents nearly died of fright when they saw the state their little boy was in. There were no visible features at all – no ridge for my nose, no cheekbones and no eyebrows – just two thin slits for my eyes and another for my mouth, breaking the surface of a livid purple sphere. Looking in the mirror was like a horror movie; a black and purple watermelon from hell stared back at me. I have never seen anything as hideous in my life. My face slowly reappeared day by day, but I could not go to school until the swelling had gone down, because the look of it embarrassed me so much. Of course, the normal Venables face that emerged as the swelling went down was pretty frightening too.

There was no question of retaliating against Harold, not only because it was an accident, but, even more importantly, because he was the proud possessor of the only proper football that we had. 'I'll take my ball home' was enough of a threat to make sure that Harold was always given special consideration. It was a threat that he was ready to use at the drop of a hat, and was invoked every time one of us kicked the ball into the bandstand, which was frequently.

His parents must have had a few quid, because in addition to the luxury of a real leather football, he also came out to play every day wearing proper football kit – he even had creases in his shorts – whereas the rest of us had to make do with 'matched and patched gear' or played in our everyday clothes.

The goalposts were just jackets dropped on the ground, a fertile source of arguments about whether a shot had gone inside or outside the post. As many kids as turned up would play, and a game might involve twenty or even thirty a side. Harold White excepted, no one wore football shirts or any other insignia, and the teams changed every day, and yet astonishingly, even with sixty kids milling about, everyone always knew who was on their side. It was useful preparation for later in life, when it was not always clear who were friends or foes. If only they would wear red or blue shirts like football teams.

After the boot in my face, even football had to be put on hold for a few days, until the swelling went down, which was a major hardship, because I was always playing, often with boys a lot older than me. The Dagenham and Barking area was a real hotbed of football, and the sport was one of the recognised ways of avoiding a lifetime of 'penal servitude' in the Ford factory. Ford were still taking on workers, as car ownership began to be something that everyone could aspire to, but a job on the production line, knocking out 'Dagenham Dustbins' – the first mass-market Cortinas – never held any appeal for me. Football looked a much more attractive career option to me and the other Dagenham lads.

You could put together a pretty fair team, just from the boys who grew up around Dagenham and Barking. From Bonham Road alone, not even a particularly long road, running from Green Lane to Clifford's Corner, past the school, and then to St Martin's Lane, there was Kenny Brown, an FA Cup-winner with West Ham in 1964, and his brother Alan. The Allen brothers, Les – a member of the Spurs Double-winning side – and Dennis – who played for Charlton and Reading – have also fathered another generation of footballing Allens. I managed three of them, Clive at Crystal Palace, QPR and Spurs, Paul at Spurs, and Martin, whom I signed as a schoolboy at QPR. The youngest Allen, Bradley, is currently at QPR.

Further along Bonham Road, there was Dick Walker, who went on to captain West Ham, and David Coney, who was a real hero of mine, a good player and a great personality. He was captain of the Tottenham youth team for a while, but he veered away from the game towards the family plastering business. I would always be waiting for him when he came home from playing for the Spurs youth team, driving him mad with endless questions about the game. His son Dean has had spells at Fulham, QPR and Norwich.

Martin Peters grew up a few streets away and Jimmy Greaves was born nearby too, though he moved to Hainault as a child. In addition to all of these, Alan Holloway, Bill Adkins, Roy Stokes, Les Rix, Charlie Mussenden and my close friends Pete Auger, Ronnie Hanley and Jimmy Hazell, were all good enough to be signed by professional clubs. Jimmy, whose name I later borrowed for the 'Hazell' books, was in the same class as me at school and was an excellent footballer and cricketer; he and I were the two best players in the school.

As I grew bigger, instead of kickabouts in the street, our football games became more organised. If we were not at school, our entire day would be spent in Valence Park, between the ten tall trees and the bandstand, playing football from early morning until it was too dark to see. All the other boys were at least two or three years older than me, and most of them were four or five years older, but I was always trying to get a game with them. To begin with I was there only to make up the numbers, but the more I played against them, the more I noticed that my own play was improving. After dark, we would all go over to Weston's chip shop on Clifford's Corner, for fish and chips and a bottle of Tizer, before heading home to bed.

The only exceptions to my daily diet of football, fish and chips were when I was in trouble with my Mum, who would make me stay in my bedroom as a punishment, while everyone else played outside. I got so bored in there one day that I started climbing out of one back window, teetering along the windowledge and climbing back in through the other window.

A woman whose house backed on to ours saw me and came running round to report me to my Mum. Because of the lay-out of the houses, she had to run all the way up to the top of her road, along Valence Avenue for fifty yards, and then all the way down Bonham Road to our front door. She arrived puce-faced and in far greater danger of imminent death than me. She did it out of the kindness of her heart, of course, but just the same, she and her family were always known as 'The Smalls' from then on, named after Bertie Smalls, the first and most famous 'super-grass' of the era, who earned his notoriety by 'squealing' on a gang of armed robbers.

The incident did have one benefit for me because it gave my Mum and Dad such a fright that it put an end to me being sent to my room as a punishment. In any event, my Mum's strict discipline had often been subverted by my Dad, who could not bear to think of his little boy being sent to his room with no supper and would sneak snacks up to me when my Mum's back was turned.

My Dad always acted tough, but he was very soft-hearted. I remember having my tonsils and adenoids out when I must have been about five or six years old, and when they left me at the hospital, I was waving to them from the window and looking so sad and lonely that my Dad tried to persuade my Mum to go back and get me out of there.

My Dad was always more keen on amateur soccer than the professional game and, after he had given up playing himself, used to go to watch his former team, Barking Town, regularly; but his first attempt to interest me in them was a disastrous failure. I was too young to sit still for long, let alone ninety minutes, and after watching the game for a minute or so, thoroughly bored, I started clambering all over the seats and making a complete nuisance of myself. My Dad had to give up at half-time and take me home. As far as I was concerned, football was for playing, not for watching.

Ossie had the same trouble. He would take me round to the Winding Way Social Club with him and, while he played snooker, I would make a real nuisance of myself, running round, fiddling with things and clambering over the benches. In the end he stuck me in one of the broken benches, wedging me into a hole in it, so that I was trapped and unable to move until he had finished his game. It did not cure me, however; I cannot sit still for more than five minutes, even today.

My first school was Valence School in Bonham Road. I was already a useful footballer, helped by the fact that I was big for my age, and even in junior school I was always being told to concentrate more on my work and less on my football. I was not particularly aware of being a better footballer than other kids of the same age, but, consciously or unconsciously, I did tend to gravitate towards games involving older boys.

It was at my next school, Lymington, that I really began to get serious about the game, making my début for the school team when I was eleven. We were coached by a fair-haired teacher called George Jackson, who had played for Spurs as a young man, and had been a pilot in the war, but had lost a leg when he was only twenty-two, ending both his flying and footballing days at a tragically early age. He was an absolute perfectionist and a stern disciplinarian, who would stomp his way up and down the touchline on his wooden leg, yelling himself blue in the face and whacking his walking stick into the ground with rage when we did something wrong. One day we must have done something really awful, because George was hammering the ground so hard that the stick broke in two.

The school team had some very good players, but George was always particularly hard on me. It was a compliment in a way, because he was hardest on those he thought had the most talent, and despite the harsh words, he also had a soft spot for me. He was a good, solid man with great presence, and earned my respect – I even made him a spare wooden leg in woodwork class. I would have brought an apple for teacher instead, but the nearest apple tree to Dagenham was probably on the other side of the Thames, in Kent.

George was very tough and serious, but he had played for Tottenham, which cut a lot of ice with me. I decided that I had to play by his rules, because he knew a lot about football, and as the man who was going to set me on my way towards the football career I had already mapped out, I was not going to let him down. He always wanted me to play for Tottenham, too, and got his wish in the end. Although he moved away to the Midlands not long after I left school, we still keep in touch.

By now I had got over my dislike of watching football, but I was playing so much that I rarely went to games as a spectator. When I did, it was to see Tottenham, who had class players like Tommy Harmer, Johnny Brooks and Danny Blanchflower and played lovely football. I really thought that they were wonderful, and by the age of eleven, I had already made up my mind that I wanted to play for Tottenham . . . and manage them.

The first part of the ambition was normal enough for kids from Dagenham, but to be launching a career as a manager at the age of eleven was rather more unusual. I was already very much 'The General' on the field, a bit of a busybody, organising everyone and telling them where to go and what to do. I think you need that type of background to be a coach, and much as I wanted to be a player, my mother actually felt that I wanted to be a manager even more. She might have been right; I still have my autograph book from those days, its once lurid pink cover now faded with age, and among all the signatures of the Spurs stars of the day, I had added my own: 'Terry Venables, Manager of Tottenham'. The dream came true in the end, but it took another thirty-three years.

I occasionally collected the players' autographs by hanging around the main railway stations, especially Euston and King's Cross, on Saturdays, intercepting the teams as they set off or returned from away games. In those pre-motorway days, virtually every team travelled to games by train, because road travel was so slow. Thirty miles an hour was a good average speed at a time when major roads tended to run straight through town centres, and a journey from London to play Leeds United might have taken six or seven hours by bus. Things are very different now, of course, the journey from London to Leeds takes less than half the time, you just spend the other half waiting in traffic jams and crawling past bloody motorway cones.

The bulk of my autograph collection was assembled at White Hart Lane. In those days there were low, one-foot-high wooden benches running the length of both touchlines, where all the apprentices and promising young players from the area were invited to sit. Spurs' scout in my area had already passed on my name to them as a kid to keep an eye on, and as a result, they sent me a treasured 'green pass', which gave me free entry to White Hart Lane and the right to sit on the benches. I would arrive hours before the game and loiter in the car park to collect as many autographs as I could, before taking my seat on the bench for the game.

The first time I 'came on' for Tottenham from the bench was a disaster, however. I had just been given my first proper suit, in Donegal tweed, which my parents had saved long and hard to buy. There was a tear of pride in their eyes as I set off to the game, wearing my new suit for the first time. Spurs were playing Chelsea in front of a capacity crowd, and my moment of glory came when the ball rolled out of play towards me. I leapt to my feet and raced towards the touchline to kick it back, but as soon as my feet touched the wet grass, they slipped from under me, depositing me on my backside. The whole stadium erupted in laughter – not the last time by any means that a football crowd would laugh at me – and I had to go home to my parents with mud all over my brand-new suit.

Even though I was still doing fairly well in my schoolwork, by now I was completely obsessed with football and unshakeable in my belief that I would be a professional footballer when I grew up. My teachers did their best to persuade me to take an equal interest in academic work, but they were fighting a losing battle. There is a story that I never read a book all the time that I was at school, which is not true. I certainly read plenty of books, but none of them were school textbooks. I did try to read some textbooks, but after a few minutes' concentration, my mind would start to wander, drifting away on thoughts of a football flying through the air and crashing into the back of a billowing net.

When I was twelve, one teacher, Mr Warren, set us all an essay on 'What I want to be when I grow up'. The other boys in the class laboured long and hard to produce three- or four-page essays, but mine was very short and to the point: 'I am going to play professional football.'

Mr Warren was not impressed with either the length or the sentiments of my essay, telling me that only one boy in a million gets to be a professional footballer. As usual, I had an answer ready: 'That's me. I'm that one boy in a million.' Mr Warren was even less impressed after that arrogant reply. A stubborn streak is a necessary part of the make-up of a professional footballer, but it must have made my teachers' lives a misery.

He should have listened to a guy called Bert Myers, a local man, who was a very seasoned judge of younger players. When I was only eleven years old, he saw me playing in the park and told me that I would play for England Schoolboys one day. A lad called Eddie Speight, who had been selected about five years previously, had been the only Dagenham boy ever to play for England Schoolboys before, and I thought it highly unlikely that I would follow in his footsteps, but I struck a deal with my mother as a result of Bert Myers's comments.

My Dad just wanted me to do whatever I would be happy doing, but my Mum had always wanted me to have a good education and become a doctor. Like most mums, she was concerned that I should have 'a proper job' when I grew up, and she did not regard being a footballer as a proper job, unless I was going to be one of the best. In some ways, her attitude to football was no different than to any other potential career, however; she just did not want me to be mediocre at whatever I did. Her boy had to be the best.

She had no yardstick for judging my talents as a footballer, apart from people like Bert Myers, and she was not going to let just any old Tom, Dick or Terry decide her boy's future. After brooding on the problem for several days, she came downstairs one morning to announce her decision, like Moses descending from the mountain. The only way she would agree to me trying my luck as a professional footballer, was if I first convinced her that I had the talent and the dedication, by making the England Schoolboys team. If the England selectors thought I was good enough, then that would be good enough for her too. I had two years to prove to her and the England selectors that I had what it takes. If not, I could kiss a football career goodbye.

The other potential obstacle to a professional career was my height, for when I was younger, even though I was always powerfully built for my age, I was afraid that I would not be tall enough. I used to pester the life out of my Grandad, saying 'I've got to get bigger, Grandad, if I'm going to be a footballer', and he would measure me against the wall at the side of the fireplace, and put pencil marks up the wall to show how tall I was growing. He would only let me be measured once a week, and I would be in agonies of anticipation waiting for Friday to come round, so that I could see if I had grown at all. I only gave up the habit a couple of years ago when I realised I was not going to grow any more.

The strengths of my game as a boy were much as they were as a professional player later on – my passing and control of the ball, and reading of the game. I always played in more or less the same position, as a central midfield player, but I did not become a ball-winner until the latter part of my career, after taking several nasty knocks and seeing the need for a bit more aggression.

I was already playing for the under-15s team by the time I was thirteen. Just the same, England Schoolboys seemed a pretty tall order, but the only way to get out of plugging away at school, doing 'O' levels and 'A' levels, was to be good enough to play for England.

The first step on my own long road to the England School-boys team and a professional career, was to get myself selected for Dagenham Boys. I was already captaining the Lymington school side, and the following year, thanks in no small part to George Jackson's coaching, I was picked for the Dagenham team. Martin Peters played in the same side, although he was a year younger than me. We beat East Ham to win the Clark Cup, the first trophy I had ever won and – from the perspective of a small boy – the most massive one I have ever got my hands on, making the FA Cup look like an eggcup. It was as much as I could do to lift it up.

The school refused to keep the trophy on the premises, in case it got nicked, and no one knew what to do with it or wanted the responsibility of looking after it. In the end, the school asked my Dad to look after it and I took it back to our house. Instead of a place of honour on the mantelpiece, my Dad stashed the cup away under his bed, where it remained for the next twelve months, until it was time to hand it back.

The first year that I was playing for Dagenham Boys, 1956, I played against Jimmy Greaves, who was a couple of years older than me and already close to becoming a professional player. Jim was still in his local under-15s side, but was an awesome player even then. When the ball arrived at his feet, he would come alive, dancing around four or five players and scoring fantastic goals. I was so impressed by him that I actually followed him home on the bus one day, without talking to him, just staring at him, in the hope of getting some clues about how to become that good. I did not get any answers and had a long walk home, after travelling miles past my stop.

Apart from football, I played most other sports at school and I used to win a lot of medals at swimming, which made my Mum very proud, because she had taught me how to swim. I learned the breaststroke, which was the only one she could do, and I won the school gala doing breaststroke, even though everyone else was doing the crawl. I had cricket trials for Essex as well, and won the 'Star ball' on one occasion, an award made by one of the London evening newspapers for an outstanding cricket performance. I took seven wickets for nine runs and scored 49 not out, playing for Lymington against Bishop Ward. I even won the inter-schools cross-country race, which shows how slow the other boys must have been. Many of them ran in proper athletics gear, I just had my football kit, but still managed to beat them.

Despite the occasional taste of glory in other sports, however, I never had any doubts that football would be my career. I was completely dedicated to the game and would make any sacrifice to succeed, no matter how painful. I had wanted a bike for ages, and my Mum and Dad saved up really hard to buy me a lovely new bike for Christmas. It was a 'New Yorker', bright red, with drop-handlebars, and was the apple of my eye, but not for long. It was standing in the passageway when Chelsea scout Jimmy Thompson, one of the many club scouts who were by now keeping an eye on my progress, called in to see us one day.

'Whose bike is that out there?' asked Jimmy.

'It's Terry's,' said my mother.

'It's no good,' said Jimmy, 'not for footballers' legs. It develops the wrong muscles – it shortens the hamstrings.'

From that day on I never rode the bike again. It was put out in the shed and stayed there, rusting away for a few years until my parents finally gave it away. Looking back now, I am

ashamed to have been so churlish about the present my parents
had saved so hard to buy, but at the time, I could see no further
than the next step towards a football career, and if the bike was
in the way, then the bike had to go.

My recreations were football, football and more football,
and even when I went to the seaside with my mates, there was
usually a football connection. Jimmy Thompson took me and a
few other lads he was hoping to sign for Chelsea to the seaside
at Frinton one day. We did the usual things you do at the
seaside, skimming pebbles at the waves, eating ice-creams and
playing football on the beach. In the evening we went to a
funfair, under strict instructions from Jimmy to be back in time
for the last train. Ronnie and Allan Harris made it in time, but
Bert Murray, Ronnie Hanley and I stayed for one more go on
the Waltzer and missed the train. We finished up sleeping in the
waiting room and caught the first train back the next morning.

Not everyone shared my dedication to the game. I well
remember the first time I played for a proper park team, Edwin
Villa, with boys who were five or six years older than me. We
played at East Ham, with me on the right wing, and were
absolutely murdering the opposition. The score had got to
about 19–0, two of them scored by the débutant right-winger,
when one of the other lads pointed out that our goalkeeper,
Charlie Andrews, was sitting down between the posts reading
the latest paperback.

My Dad's goalkeeping days were numbered too, even in
kickabouts with me. We would often go over to the park
together, and he would go in goal while I practised shooting.
We were there one day with some of my mates, and much as I
wanted to impress my Dad with my shooting power, I also
desperately wanted my friends to be impressed with his goalkeeping. After a gentle warm-up, I set myself and hit a shot as hard
as I could. I caught it just right, the ball taking off like a rocket.
My Dad threw himself across the goal to make the save, but the

ball hit the ends of his fingers and bent them back at right angles. He has not had his hand in his pocket to buy a round ever since.

He got up and stalked off, clutching his hand under his arm and cursing under his breath. As his coach and manager, as well as his son, I was deeply disappointed with him, telling him, 'Come on, Dad, you can do better than that,' but he was having none of it. All I heard was 'Get lost' as he stormed off home, nursing his dislocated fingers. He was off work for a fortnight and never went in goal against me and my friends again.

Luckily, the abrupt retirement of my regular goalkeeper did not hamper my preparation for the England Schoolboys trials, but a foot injury proved a much more serious obstacle. After playing for Dagenham Boys, the natural progression was to play for Essex, London and then England. I played for Essex, but then missed the London trials because of the foot injury. I took a knock on the foot during a game and was in agony afterwards. I was absolutely desperate to play in the London trials, however, and when Jimmy Thompson came round and offered to sort my foot out, I was delighted. 'I've got to play for London, Jimmy. If I don't, the England selectors won't know me, and if I don't play for England, my Mum won't let me be a footballer.'

Jimmy took a look at my foot, frowned and tut-tutted, then nodded his head sagely and began to massage it vigorously with some oils that he swore were the ones 'the professionals use. I shouldn't really have this, it's the proper stuff, but I managed to get hold of some'. It was typical Jimmy Thompson cloak-and-dagger stuff, a complete load of nonsense, but I believed it at the time, my eyes like saucers at the thought of being treated with the stuff that 'the professionals use'.

He must have massaged the foot for half an hour, sweating buckets in the process, and as he worked on it, a livid black and purple bruise steadily appeared. I had never seen such a bruise, but it seemed to be the result that Jimmy wanted. When he had finished, Jimmy took me out into the garden to road-test his repair work, and told me to kick a football as hard as I could. When I did, I nearly fainted with the pain. Jimmy suddenly remembered some pressing business elsewhere, while I limped back into the house and went to hospital for some more conventional treatment, where an X-ray revealed that I had a broken bone in my foot, the only broken bone I suffered in the whole of my career.

By the time that I had recovered, I was afraid that my chance of an England Schools cap and a professional career might have gone for ever, but luckily some of the England selectors had already seen me play for Essex and I went straight from the Essex team into the England trials, eventually making my London début after I had already played for my country.

The first England trial, The North versus The South, was held at Doncaster on a freezing cold day, with snow-flurries blowing across the ground on a wind straight from Siberia. There were a lot of northern club scouts and coaches there, who had not seen me play before, but I was quite relaxed before the game; my parents were much more anxious than me. I was not generally nervous before matches anyway, because I was in too much of a hurry to get on with the game and as soon as I touched the ball, I forgot about everything else. I played a blinder at Doncaster, and had another good game in the second trial at Chesterfield, facing players like Peter Thompson, later to make his name with Liverpool.

When I was named in the England Schools team to face Scotland, I was ecstatic. Not only had I been chosen to play for my country, I had also achieved the target that my Mum had set for me. I could now leave school as soon as I was old enough, and pursue a career as a professional footballer, with her blessing.

I made my England Schoolboys début at Wembley, playing opposite a fiery, flame-haired character called Billy Bremner, whom I was to face many more times during my career. The match was shown live on television, and it was an incredible experience to be playing in the national stadium at fifteen years of age, in front of a capacity crowd of 100,000 people and a huge television audience. I can only vaguely remember coming out of the tunnel on to the Wembley turf for the first time, and I do not recall too much about the game itself. I did play very well in a 3–1 win, but the match passed in a blur.

I played six times in all for the England Schoolboys, and with the professional clubs also beginning to show a big interest in me, I suppose I must have thought of myself as a bit of a junior celebrity around Dagenham at the time, but I certainly did not use my new-found fame to impress the girls. Many of my pals were seventeen or eighteen years old and going to the Palais every weekend, drinking and carrying on, but I was not really into that scene. I would go down to the pub at the weekend with them, but I did not like it very much. I had been told that if I drank, I would not be a footballer, so I did not touch alcohol. Peter Auger and my other mates used to go and have a beer, and I was a bit of an outcast because I did not drink, but it did not matter to me, because I wanted my football more than a drink. I was very single-minded, and drinking did not feature in my priorities. It was not on the list at that stage, although I more than made up for my abstinence a little later in life . . .

As well as avoiding pubs like the plague, I did not smoke either, in fact I have only taken one puff of a cigarette in my life. I asked my Dad what smoking was like, one day, not because I wanted to start, but out of curiosity, because a lot of the other kids used to smoke. My Dad thought that the best way to put me off was to make me try one. I was not keen on the idea, but he lit one, and made me take a drag on it and inhale the smoke. I promptly went green in the face, and that was my first and last cigarette. I did start smoking cigars in my thirties, but that was more of an affectation than a genuine

desire to smoke; it was what football managers were supposed
to do . . . or so Malcolm Allison assured me, anyway.

Although I did not smoke, I did play cards, and there always
used to be a card-school at our house on Friday night, with my
pals, Peter Smith, Ronnie Hanley and Joey Jennings, and my
Dad, who was the biggest kid of the lot, always rowing with
everyone. Even when I became a professional, with a big game
every Saturday, the Friday night card games carried on. I would
go to bed about 10:30 p.m., preparing for the game the next
day, but I could never get to sleep because the rest of them
would all still be laughing and joking downstairs, my Dad's
voice twice as loud as everyone else's.

Joey Jennings lived next door to the school, but was always
late, because he would be running errands for his Dad, who was
a street bookie, taking bets on street corners in the days when
off-course betting was illegal. Joe left school without being too
clever at reading or writing, and became a jockey. Many years
later, I went with Allan Harris and his brother and father to the
Epsom races and saw Joe there. He is now a very wealthy man,
with a string of bookmaker's shops. As a Dagenham scrap
dealer once said about an illiterate, but very wealthy, rival: 'He
can't read or write, but by God, he can count.'

My friends say that I always had to win at everything –
football, tennis, cricket, even at cards – and I was, and still am,
a very bad loser, just like my Dad. We would have the most
ferocious arguments, but my Dad would always get it off his
chest and could not stay angry with me for very long. (I have
always been the same: I have to say what I think, but I never
bear grudges.) Ten minutes later we would be sorry, and were
mates again in no time.

If my competitive streak was one of my strengths on the
football field, I also worked very hard to eradicate weaknesses
in my game. I was not particularly quick, and used to spend a
lot of time sprint training in the park with Ronnie Hanley, who

later went to Chelsea with me. At Stamford Bridge, I put in even more time on sprinting, doing speed work with Johnny Hollins and Eddie McCreadie, even though the older players used to give us stick and call us 'Brownies' for 'creeping round the coach' by doing extra training.

Sadly things did not work out for Ronnie Hanley at Chelsea and he was not offered professional terms after his time on the ground staff. He was awfully disappointed, even though I think he realised himself that he was not quite up to professional standards. My Dad said he would get Ron a job with him at the docks, but he said, 'Don't bloody run away in a month or get the sack. At least stay there six months, to give me some credibility for recommending you.' I think he passed the credibility test, because he is still working there now, thirty-five years later.

Before I made the decision to sign for Chelsea, it seemed like half the football clubs in England were chasing me. It was a time when people were really starting to look for young players, especially in the East End, because lots of good players were coming out of there. Club scouts and managers were always watching me play and coming round to our house to tell me how much their club could do for me.

With the clubs showing so much interest, the press began to get excited as well. I was likened to 'a young Duncan Edwards' by some journalists, and Frank Butler, writing in the *Mirror*, called the chase for my signature 'The hottest hunt by soccer managers of a boy footballer, since Stoke City captured Stanley Matthews twenty-eight years ago'. It would have been easy to get carried away with all the press attention, but my family stopped me from getting too swollen-headed and kept my feet firmly on the ground. My mother was very solid and down-to-earth, and my Grandad, her father, was stingy with his praise, which of course spurred me on to even greater efforts.

I worked hard to get any praise out of them at all, but my

Nan was just the opposite, and was always boosting my confidence. As fast as my Mum or my Grandad would knock me down, she would say, 'Take no notice of them, everyone is saying that you're playing really well. They have been knocking on the door, just to tell me how well you're doing.' I lapped it up, of course, but if I had stopped to think for a moment, I would have realised that no one had said anything of the sort. No one had even been watching the school games, but to hear my Nan talk, you would have thought that the whole street had been there. Just as I began to get taken in by her descriptions of people flocking to tell her how great I was, my Grandad would come in and knock my confidence down again just as quickly, saying, 'The backstreets are full of people who thought they were good enough to be professional footballers, Terry. You've got a long way to go before you can call yourself a footballer.' They were a double-act as good as Brian Clough and Peter Taylor, and between them they did a good job.

By this time I was regularly going to train with several of the London clubs. West Ham had been the first to ask me along to training, when I was about fourteen. I went there on Tuesdays and Thursdays after school. Dick Walker, who was chief scout at West Ham then, and Kenny Brown, who was a senior player, took the training between them, and they were huge jokers, which made it good fun for the youngsters. My mother used to teach dancing classes at the time, to earn a bit of extra money, and Kenny, who was in the class, would start dancing with her every time he saw her out in the street.

My Mum was very attractive and a lot of the time would draw wolf-whistles in the street. She used to love dancing, and both she and my Dad were good dancers. I had learned to tap-dance very young, but like my mates, I needed lessons in 'proper dancing', before going to our first big dance. We all got a couple of lessons from my Mum in our tiny living room, four people jammed into a space about four foot square.

While on my way home from football training one evening in February 1958, I bought a paper to read on the bus and saw the news of the Munich air crash, and the death of so many great Manchester United stars, including Duncan Edwards. 'Busby's Babes' had been cut down, well before their prime. The impact of that disaster, not just on Manchester, but on the whole country, was devastating. Perhaps it reawoke memories of the senseless waste of young lives in the war, just as the scars were beginning to fade, but whatever the reason, it was seen as a national tragedy every bit as deep and traumatic as the Hillsborough disaster.

United swept to the Cup Final on a wave of emotion that year, only to lose at Wembley, and the loss of so many players made them redouble their efforts to sign new ones, but my own sights were still fixed firmly on a career with a London club. As well as West Ham, I was also training at Chelsea, Arsenal and Tottenham. When I started going to Tottenham, I used to think that White Hart Lane was a bit grand, but Arsenal was not like a football club at all. The marbled halls, bronze busts and aura of wealth made Highbury seem more like the Dorchester Hotel.

Stamford Bridge seemed more like a proper football ground should be, and Chelsea always felt more real because the players there were so young. Most of them had been schoolboys only a year or two ahead of me, and the route to the first team appeared to be much shorter than at other clubs, where the way was blocked by a queue of older players. That is what excited a lot of the young players and made them want to go to Chelsea. The big-time seemed so close there that you felt you could almost reach out and touch it. Much later, that was the atmosphere that I wanted to recreate at Tottenham. People usually think that schoolboy footballers sign for the club that throws the most money at them, but while that is a consideration, other, less tangible, factors also play a part. Some clubs, in some eras, just seem to have a buzz about them, and that is what attracts young players as much as the money.

All the clubs tried very hard to persuade me to sign, advancing good reasons why I should join them and offering both my parents and me various inducements ... usually folding ones. My Mum and Dad would have nothing to do with the cash offers that came their way, however, telling the clubs what they had already told me: that it was my decision alone. Arsenal had made me a good offer and I liked Spurs as well, because I used to go and see them play, and Dave Mackay and Danny Blanch-flower were two of my heroes, the sort of skilful ball-players and on-field leaders that I hoped to become myself, but Tottenham and Arsenal very rarely gave young lads the chance to play first team football in those days, and would buy in players over the top of you. In the end my choice came down to two clubs – West Ham and Chelsea.

Malcolm Allison was captain of West Ham at the time, and I was impressed with his passion for football. He talked about the game in a way that excited and inspired people, which was one of the reasons why he became such a good coach later on. His appetite for life was also as great as his love for football. I will never forget my first sight of him: I was fourteen, training with West Ham, and watching saucer-eyed, as the first-team players walked off the field after training, when Malcolm raised his arms to the sky and shouted: 'What a wonderful life ... look at that blue sky.'

Even the loss of a lung following an attack of tuberculosis did not affect Malcolm's appetite for life. He has lost neither his love of football nor his zest for the finer things in life, over the years, remaining true to a creed that he acquired while lying flat on the ground after a collision with the original irresistible force, Derek Dooley of Sheffield Wednesday. 'I thought I was dying,' said Malcolm. 'It came into my mind that I was going to die and I still had £200 in the dressing room that I hadn't spent.'

Malcolm's taste for flamboyant dressing has also stayed with him. I can visualise him now, coming round to our house, wearing a big, loud, checked jacket. The chairman of West Ham, Reg Pratt, had asked him who the best young players were in the East End, and Malcolm told him that they already had two of them, Bobby Moore and John Cartwright, but said that the other one was a boy called Terry Venables. Malcolm and Reg came round to our house that night to ask me to join West Ham, but I told them that I had already promised to go to Chelsea and there was no shaking me from that. West Ham had a lot of young players, like Bobby Moore, Geoff Hurst and Martin Peters, coming through, but as much as I liked the club, my final choice was always going to be Chelsea.

Malcolm has claimed that there were 10,000 reasons why I wanted to join Chelsea rather than West Ham, but that is simply not true. My decision had nothing to do with money, because all the clubs were offering much the same terms. The maximum-wage system was still in operation until 1961, three years after I joined Chelsea. My Dad got a part-time job scouting for them as part of the deal, and he actually ended up being paid more for scouting for Chelsea than I was for playing for them. I had to take some part-time jobs to earn extra cash and keep body and soul together, working as a swimming pool attendant at the baths in Barking Park every summer. Even when I became a member of the Chelsea first-team squad, my wages were only £20 a week in the season and £18 a week in the summer.

The choice between Chelsea and West Ham was the first really hard decision I had ever had to make. Chelsea seemed a bit more glamorous than West Ham, which inevitably suffered by comparison, just because it was my local club. I had also become very friendly with a few of the players in the England Schoolboys team, and three of them, Bert Murray, Terry More and Allan Harris, had already signed for Chelsea, but the decisive factor was probably that I thought that I could replace the guy playing in my position in the Chelsea first team, quite quickly. It came down to that cold-blooded decision in the end; I just thought that I would make the first team quicker at Chelsea than anywhere else. I was only just seventeen when I did get into the side, so the plan worked out pretty well.

Jimmy Thompson, the Chelsea chief scout, who had taken Jimmy Greaves and several other good young players to Chelsea, was another big factor in my deciding to sign for them. He was a hell of a man, and a tremendous character, who loved nothing better than to make a melodrama out of his job. He was unabashed by the failure of his 'professional treatment' of my broken foot, and often called round at our house to chat and offer advice, but he never wanted any of the other club scouts to know what he was doing. On one occasion, he was sitting in our kitchen when one of the other scouts came to the door, and Jimmy went and hid in the bathroom for an hour, until the other man had gone, rather than be spotted by his rival.

My Dad saw him one day, watching a game in which I was playing, lying on his stomach in the long grass behind the goalposts. When Jimmy saw him, he whispered, 'Fred, get down here quick. Don't let anyone know I'm here.' Only when my Dad was safely down in the long grass alongside him, did Jimmy relax enough to indulge in some polite conversation. He also arranged to meet me at Waterloo Station once, under the four-sided clock. I stood there for twenty minutes and could not see him anywhere, and I was about to give up and go home when I heard someone going 'Psst, psst.' I finally spotted him hiding behind a pillar and beckoning to me. When I asked him what was going on, he just said, 'You can't be too careful. You can't be too careful.'

For a man obsessed with secrecy, he was ridiculously conspicuous, well over six foot tall and invariably clad in his trademark bowler hat, pinstripe trousers, and furled umbrella.

The bowler hat was probably the only one in the whole of Dagenham; he might as well have gone round with a neon sign on his head, saying 'Jimmy Thompson, Football Scout'.

Jimmy was also into racing in a big way, and would place bets for the 'racing aristocracy', the lords and the ladies. He always had good tips as well; I am sure it was just bad luck that none of them seemed to win, though Jimmy had a sure-fire winning system himself. He would place bets of £1000 and more for his noble punters – an astronomical sum then. If they won, he would get a slice of their winnings, and if they lost, he would get a back-hander from the bookmaker for giving him the business.

With all the other club scouts promising me the earth to sign, Jimmy was not to be outdone. He promised the earth, moon, planets and stars, as he always did to youngsters he was keen to sign, but no one ever got anything in the end. His persuasion and my own feelings about the club did the trick, however, and I became a Chelsea player on my fifteenth birthday, 6 January 1958 – school-leaving age then – my mother having long since resigned herself to the fact that a football, not a stethoscope, would be the tool of my trade.

Young players normally sign professional forms when they join a club, but I actually signed as an amateur, because I was hoping to play for England in the 1960 Olympic Games in Rome. I had already moved up from the England Schoolboys to the England Youth team and I was also selected to play for England Amateurs against West Germany at Dulwich Hamlet, but when the Olympic squad was named, I was not included, even though I was a Chelsea first-team player by then. A guy called Roy Sleap was chosen instead of me, and at that point I signed professional forms.

Despite her original hopes of a more stable career for her son, my mother was a loyal supporter of my football. She and Fred came to watch every game I played, carrying as a talisman

a tiny pair of boots that I had worn as a child. Both my parents
and my tiny boots followed me throughout my playing career,
but when I hung up my own full-size boots, the tiny ones also
went into honourable retirement, and now hang on the wall of
my Dad's pub in Chingford.

# CHAPTER TWO

# Chelsea and England

## 1958–66

I ARRIVED AT CHELSEA with a big reputation, boosted by the press ballyhoo about the chase for my signature, and one or two people at Stamford Bridge were keen to knock 'the new Duncan Edwards' down a peg or two. On my first day, the head groundsman, Harry Winston, lined all the new boys up together and said, 'Right, which one's Venables?' When I told him, he said, 'Okay, I've got a right shit job for you.'

The capacity of Stamford Bridge was enormous at that time, holding 80,000, with huge stands and vast expanses of terracing. One of the jobs that the ground staff were given was to sweep the rubbish off the terraces. We started at the top and went along the rows, brushing the rubbish down to the step below. The next guy then came along and swept it down to the next level, and so on. While the rest of the boys were sent off to clean some of the terraces together, Harry gave me the whole of the biggest stand to sweep on my own. The others finished about an hour before me and were sitting on the opposite side of the ground, killing themselves laughing, while I struggled on, covered in dust and sweat.

One or two of the senior players were not keen on cocky young kids either. When I first got to train with the first-team squad I was desperate to do well and I set off round the running track like a rocket. As I came level with the club captain, Peter Sillett, however, he growled at me, 'You trying to show us all up, are you? Get to the back and don't run faster than me or I'll smash your chest in.' I still had much to learn.

Even that could not dampen my enthusiasm. I lay back on the grass at the end of my first training session, with the hot sun shining on me, chewing on a grass-stem and savouring the intoxicating smell of new-mown grass, and thought how lucky I was to be alive, and to be a footballer. The smell of new-mown grass still fills me with a sense of anticipation. To most people the smell probably means gardening and mowing the lawn, but to me it means football and the promise of a new season.

Professional training was a severe shock to the system. For the first time I came up against something so demanding and powerful that it could make me physically sick. The worst part of training was the sprint-training, known as 'doggies'. We would do a set of four forty-yard sprints, then break for thirty seconds, then do another set, then break, and so on. The time allowed was cut each time, forcing you to sprint faster or lose the recovery time, and in the end you were sprinting almost continually, lungs gasping for air, blood pounding in your ears, praying for the end. After the pain of 'doggies', the footballer's worst friend, anything that happened in a game seemed a picnic by comparison.

Not everyone took training quite as seriously. One player, whom I later fictionalised in a football novel as Jock Toms, the goalie, was a quick-change artist, who would sometimes leave his shirt and tie on under his tracksuit, so that he could get away from the ground quicker than anybody else after training. He used to boast that he could leave the dressing room, do his laps of the pitch and be back before the door had stopped banging. He also claimed that after a game, he could be washed, changed and in the pub across the road having his first pint before any of the fans got through the pub door.

Spurs' winger Cliff Jones was similarly quick off the mark. I remember having an argument with him one day when I came out of the showers and found him already standing there, bone-dry with his shirt and tie on. I gave him a hard time about his insanitary habit of getting dressed without even bothering to have a shower, but Cliff insisted that he had already had a shower. We began one of those 'No, you haven't' – 'Yes, I have' kind of arguments, which ended when I told him to look down. When he did so, he noticed that, along with his shirt and tie, he was still wearing his football socks.

I came into a tremendously talented youth team at Chelsea. Manchester United had their 'Busby's Babes', and under Ted Drake, we became known as 'Drake's Ducklings', though our youth-team coach, Dick Foss, really deserved much of the credit. If Jimmy Thompson was the man who made sure a lot of the best youngsters came to Chelsea, Dick was the man who got the best out of them. He had great charisma and an aura of authority, but he was the first man I had seen who showed me that you could still have that authority with a relaxed and friendly atmosphere, and he certainly got the results. We used to win our South-East Counties games by 10–0, 12–0 and 14–0, and won the FA Youth Cup twice in succession, beating Preston, who included two former England Schoolboys, Peter Thompson and David Wilson, the first year, and Everton the following season. After that, it was not long before a number of us made the transition to the first team.

Apart from the joy of achieving my ambition of first-team football, it was a great relief to leave the youth-team tea behind. We used to train out at Hendon, where the groundsman, a dour Scot, inevitably called Jock, would make tea for everybody. I used to drink gallons of it, until I happened to wander into the gloomy cubby-hole that was Jock's kingdom, one day, and saw him stirring the tea with the filthiest stick I have ever seen in my life. We made him promise that he would only use a spoon from then on, but I could never again bring myself to drink the tea, without first suppressing a shudder and scanning it for bits of floating mud and bark.

Surprisingly, I found that the move up through the Chelsea teams became progressively easier rather than more difficult. The change from schoolboy to youth football was the biggest shock that I ever had. It was an under-18 competition, so most of the players were a couple of years older than me when I started, but they were also so physical, quick and aggressive that I never seemed to get into the game. At that stage, after imagining that I was going to be a young superstar, I began to wonder if I could cope with it at all, but the others were experiencing the same problems. The moves up from youth to A team – which no longer exists, but was then another rung on the ladder – then to the reserves, and finally to the first team, were much easier in some ways. Paradoxically, I seemed to have more time on the ball in the first team than there had been in the youth side.

My first-team début for Chelsea came soon after my seventeenth birthday, in February 1960, and the 'new Duncan Edwards' comparisons continued to haunt me. Ian Wooldridge wrote menacingly in his column: 'They have dared to compare him to the late, great Duncan Edwards, and now – two years to the day after the air crash in which Edwards lost his life – we shall see.' Unfortunately I did not have the happiest of débuts. We lost 3–1 and Ian Wooldridge was able to gloat the next day: 'A star is launched with a resounding tinkle'.

That first appearance was against West Ham in front of a capacity Upton Park crowd. The noise was deafening as we ran out and I was filled with a tremendous excitement as we kicked off. This was the moment I had been dreaming about all my life, for I was now a 'proper' professional footballer. A few minutes later, the excitement had given way to unease, for I was absolutely all at sea. By the end of the game, Malcolm Allison must have been relieved that I had chosen Chelsea instead of West Ham. By a miracle, Chelsea held a 1–0 lead at half-time, but as I sat in the dressing room, staring at my boots, I was far from happy with my own performance and desperate for some advice from one of the senior players. My prayers were soon answered . . . in a sense.

There are plenty of players in football, like Jimmy Hill for example, who lack the ability of the great players, but who have bags of self-confidence, which helps them to get by. Equally, there are others, brim-full of natural talent, who are often fatally undermined by a lack of self-confidence. It is not something that I have ever been accused of, but even so, sitting nervously in the dressing room, halfway through my début, I would have been grateful for a word of encouragement or a piece of advice from anyone.

I looked up and saw another of my heroes, Johnny Brooks, the finest footballer in the team, heading across the room towards me. Johnny was a sensational player, an England international, built like an Adonis, with two good feet and a great body-swerve. In short, he had everything . . . except self-confidence. Just seventeen years old, barely aware of what I was doing on the field, let alone anybody else, I waited expectantly for his words of help. He sat down next to me, put an arm around my shoulders and said, 'How do you think I'm playing, Terry?' I learned the lesson quickly. Football may be a team game, but when the chips are down, it is every man for himself.

After my inauspicious start in the full glare of the media spotlight, the 'new Duncan Edwards' tag was mercifully laid to rest, enabling me to concentrate on just living up to the name of Terry Venables. That proved to be a rather easier task and before long I was established as a first-team regular. The man who had given me my first crack at the big-time was Ted Drake, then the manager at Chelsea. Even without that debt of gratitude, it would have been very hard not to like Ted, who was a lovely man. He was also a great centre-forward in his time, a national hero for England, and scored a record seven goals for Arsenal against Aston Villa. He had been a rugged, hard, tough player, but you would not have dreamed it when you met him. He did not seem like a footballer at all, because he was such an elegant, worldly, charming person.

It was almost as if he was in the wrong business, and should have been in rugby instead, but the older players like Peter Sillett, Peter Brabrook, Derek Saunders and Bill Robertson, were also a little bit like that. I did not notice that at West Ham or other clubs, but at Chelsea, the older players seemed slightly more middle class. Ted got on particularly well with the older players at Chelsea, but while the younger players also liked him, a split was developing between the old and new generations.

The game was beginning to change. Coaching had never had a high profile before – it was just a matter of running a few laps around the pitch and then playing football – but a number of guys like Malcolm Allison, Phil Woosnam and Malcolm Musgrove became involved at Lilleshall, where the FA ran their coaching courses, and for the first time coaching ceased to be seen as just something for the academic-type footballer and became open to the more 'rough-and-ready' guys, who bridged the class gap. The trauma of 1953, when the Hungarians had shown us football from another planet, had also helped to foster an interest in the coaching of the game.

When Tommy Docherty came to Chelsea as a player-coach during the 1960–61 season, complete with his FA coaching badge and a head full of new ideas, he encouraged his players to express themselves, and the younger ones responded and took to Docherty's new approach. It split the camp in two, however, because the older players resented Docherty and his new ideas. They just came in, did their job and went home, whereas, like the 'West Ham Academy' under Malcolm Allison at the same time, the younger ones were really interested in the coaching of the game. I was always asking Docherty questions, because I had such a thirst for knowledge about the game. Later on, he began regretting his encouragement, because my constant questions became a bit of a bugbear for him. I think he felt that I was testing him or querying his methods.

Ted Drake often seemed as interested in the theory and practice of golf as football. Part of his daily routine involved practising his golf shots with the club secretary, John Battersby. They used to open the connecting door between their offices, put a waste-paper basket on the desk and chip plastic golf balls into it from the other office. They would follow that with a bit of putting practice, tapping golf balls into a glass laid on the carpet, and in the afternoons, they would usually be out on the course itself, seeing if the practice had had any beneficial effect.

As Chelsea slipped towards the bottom of the table, however, Ted became more preoccupied with football problems than golfing ones. Peter Sillett, who was a golfing buddy of Ted, accepted a lift home after training one day, when Ted was unusually silent, turning something over and over in his mind. He stopped at a traffic light and gazed into space as the lights changed from red to green and back again. Peter sat quietly in the passenger seat, waiting for Ted to come out of his trance. Finally, he was interrupted by a tap on the window. 'Is there a problem, sir?' asked a policeman. 'The lights have changed to green half a dozen times, while you've been sitting here.'

'My God, Peter,' said Ted, 'I thought you were driving.'

Years later, managing Crystal Palace, I told that story to Kenny Sansom, as I was dropping him off at the Elephant and Castle. 'Boss,' said Kenny, 'you did exactly the same thing with me the other day.' I was not sure if that was just a wind-up, or if it was true, but I would not have been surprised; I had already discovered that the rigours of management were much greater than I used to think when I was a cocky young player.

Ted Drake also got the red light from the Chelsea board, as the split between the old guard and the new came to a head. When Ted was sacked, Tommy Docherty took over as caretaker-manager. Tommy brought in as coach Dave Sexton, a student of the game, whose life was football. I have been friends with him ever since and coaching remains the same labour of love for him today. He was and is a good coach, but I do not know if he was as good at the psychology and man-management. He himself said that he was more of a coach than a manager, but because the coaches were always paid a lower wage, everyone was pushed into being a manager in the end, Dave included.

After Ted's laid-back approach, the older players' resentment at Tom's abrasive management style was understandable, particularly when he also decided to give the younger players our opportunity, a chance we were to grab with both hands. We were dedicated in those days, in bed early and up early for training. Things were rather different later on, when Alan Hudson, David Webb and Peter Osgood were around and the King's Road became a vibrant place, but the Swinging Sixties at Chelsea really only started after I had left the club.

My one brush with the 'celebrity life style' came a couple of years later, after I was voted Young Player of the Year, and invited to one of Harold Wilson's famous Downing Street soirées. It was a typical cocktail party, in which everyone came up and talked to you for precisely two minutes, while constantly looking over your shoulder, in case someone more important came in. People clearly assumed that a footballer would be unable to talk about anything else, and after a perfunctory word about the game, they would pass on. The guests gravitated towards Harold Wilson and his charmed circle at the centre of the room, but once there, you soon discovered that it was really not that wonderful after all and gradually drifted back out to the fringes again.

In the 1960s, just like the 1990s, there were claims that Britain was becoming a classless society, and quite a few working class 'heroes', like David Bailey, Michael Caine, Twiggy and an assortment of pop stars and footballers, were not only invited round to Downing Street for drinks, but were also fêted by the media and gently patronised by the aristocracy. Nineteen-sixties British society was no more and no less open to stupendously rich people than it has always been, whatever their origins, and I always had the feeling that the 1960s' fascination with the working class was going to be fairly temporary. It was as if the Establishment was saying, 'Look, aren't we nice and open-minded to let the normal people come in and have a little bit now and again.'

The 1960s 'fashion' for working class people proved to be just a passing fad, and while a few of the landed gentry may have thought it was terribly chic to hob-nob with 'ordinary people' for a while, there was also plenty of resentment of the new working class 'upstarts' who did not know their place.

There was plenty of resentment on my side too, that condescending upper class twits should have the nerve to criticise working people whose only crime was to want a better life for themselves and their families. Even more horrendous in their eyes, was that we should be able to earn a living 'just by playing football'. Expensive lawyers and highly paid company directors who had just spent four or five hours on the golf course, or three hours on a 'working lunch', would complain about 'lazy, working class oiks' getting paid an alleged fortune for kicking a football around.

'Working class' may be a rather old-fashioned expression these days, but the working people and communities are still there, and the values of 'Essex man', the symbol of the Thatcher years, have not taken over completely. Dagenham has not changed that much and it remains as much a hotbed of football as it was when I was growing up. Three of the present England side, Tony Adams, Paul Ince and Paul Parker, are all from the area, and if you take a walk through Dagenham you will still see hundreds of kids – the next generation – kicking footballs around.

If you have not been brought up in a football culture, you cannot begin to understand what the game means to us. Football is our magic, our culture and our history; it is even our version of nationality.

It infuriated me then and it still annoys me now, that football is seen as all easy money and glamorous living. For every well-paid star, there are a thousand kids who dream of a career in football, and give themselves up to it completely, only for a marginal lack of talent, pace, commitment, courage or just plain luck, to shatter those dreams. At the age of sixteen or seventeen, they have to throw away their hopes and start again, finding a job if they are lucky, or going on the dole. Even the ones who make it may be stuck on the bottom rungs of the ladder, playing out careers in the lower divisions or in non-league football, providing only local fame and only modest fortune. Injuries, too, reap their harvest, ending careers early or leaving old footballers with painful legacies of their careers. The battering taken by footballers' legs means that few avoid rheumatism or arthritis in later life.

If most football injuries are accidental, however, a few are deliberately inflicted. One of England's greatest footballers of the modern age had one testicle surgically removed, early in his career, after he had been kicked in the vitals by an opponent. It was by no means unknown in the game. Another great name from a previous era, the legendary centre-forward 'Dixie' Dean, told a newspaperman that when he was just starting in the game as a seventeen-year-old, a defender came up to him after he had scored a goal and told him that he would make sure he did not score any more. He kept his promise, kicking the young legend-in-the-making so brutally that one testicle had to be removed.

I was perhaps lucky to avoid similarly savage treatment after my early publicity in the game. There is nothing you can do to prepare for that kind of brutality, but I did my best to ensure that I was ready in every other way for each game of football. I worked hard to maintain peak physical and mental condition, and always prepared myself meticulously for games, as I had even as a boy. I would be in bed early the night before a match and was also very careful about my diet, particularly on the day of the game, when I would eat only light, easily digestible food. For one home game, against West Bromwich Albion, I scrounged a lift from my Chelsea team-mate Jimmy Greaves, who lived not far from me. At the time, it was still very rare for players to own luxury items like cars, but Jim was the proud owner of a pale blue Ford Popular, and picked me up at twelve, telling me that we were going via his favourite pre-match lunching spot, the Dinner Gong at Gants Hill.

I was probably not the best company on the day, for I was very preoccupied by the match, in which I was to be directly opposite Derek Kevan, a colossus of a bloke, six foot three inches tall and built like the proverbial 'brick shithouse'. I sat there, worrying about how I was going to fare against him and determined to make sure that every aspect of my pre-match preparation was perfect. When we got to the Dinner Gong, I scanned the menu for suitable food.

'What are you having, Terry?' asked Jim.

'I think I'll just a have a piece of grilled chicken breast,' I said, maintaining my stringent pre-match routine.

'Damn good idea,' said Jim. 'I'll have soup, roast beef and Yorkshire pudding.'

While I nibbled daintily on my morsel of chicken, Jim disappeared behind a mound of roast beef, Yorkshire pudding, carrots, peas, cauliflower, three roast potatoes and three huge boiled potatoes.

'You're never going to eat all that, are you?' I asked. 'We kick off in two and a half hours.'

'Just watch me,' said Greavesie, returning to his plate.

Half an hour later we were on our way to Stamford Bridge, with Jim wiping the last traces of his dessert – steamed pudding and custard – from his chin. I gazed at him in disbelief. Was this any way for a professional sportsman to carry on? Evidently it was. We won 6–1 that afternoon and Jim scored five of the goals.

Jim never seemed to take football seriously and never appeared to do any practice, although he must have done a bit somewhere along the line to have acquired that level of skill. Even when he played in five-a-sides in training, he would always go in goal, yet when it came to matches, Jim really delivered. He was a natural ball-player and the game just seemed to come easily to him. Nothing seemed to bother him on the pitch. He would never query referees' decisions, unlike a certain young team-mate of his, who was always arguing with them. Jim would just say, 'Leave it, Terry, it doesn't matter. Forget it and get on with the game.' It was only much later in his career, when he was a part-timer at Barnet, that he began to get into a great deal of trouble with referees and other players.

I have often wondered if that was because Jim realised that his time in football was slipping away from him and belatedly discovered that the game was more important to him than he had thought. Missing out on the 1966 World Cup final, when Alf Ramsey left him out, was also a really big blow. It was an enormously brave decision for Ramsey to make, for if England had lost, he would never have heard the end of it.

Jim had been injured and Geoff Hurst and Roger Hunt had looked a good combination in his absence and worked very hard for the team. You knew before the game what you would get from them, whereas you were not always sure with Jim. There was a universal belief that one of them would be left out to make way for his return, however, and the only speculation was whether it would be Hunt or Hurst. In the event, Ramsey left out Greaves, which amazed English football fans and must have hurt Jim badly, although only he himself can say that for sure. Ramsey's decision was vindicated when England won the

Cup, with Hurst scoring a hat-trick, though Jim's supporters would doubtless argue that England would have won even more convincingly if he had been playing. The contrary view was that Jim would score a lot of goals against weaker opposition, but would not necessarily do it at the highest level. I am left to wonder how much better Jimmy Greaves, already one of the greats of the game, could actually have been.

His career at Chelsea ended as mine was really beginning. The abolition of the maximum wage came too late to stop Jimmy taking the lira trail to Italy. He was transferred to AC Milan for about £100,000, a fee that would not even buy a Third Division full-back these days, and it was not a happy move for Jimmy, Milan or Chelsea. A lot of players went to Italy at the time, earning wages light-years beyond those offered in the English League. Even today, as Paul Gascoigne and David Platt have discovered, Italian clubs can still offer cash rewards that even the richest British clubs cannot match, but for British footballers then it was a straight choice between £20 a week and a fortune. John Charles went from Leeds, Greaves went from Chelsea, Denis Law from Manchester City and Joe Baker from Hibs. Only John Charles, alone in being willing to learn the language, settled there. The rest were homesick and back in Britain fairly quickly.

Jimmy left Chelsea before the 1961–62 season and, without his goals, we were always struggling. Tommy Docherty even came out of playing retirement to try and stop the rot, taking my place in the side for four matches, which did not do much to endear him to me. The Doc's magic touch either as player or caretaker-manager had no immediate impact on the team's fortunes and we stayed rooted to the bottom of the table and dropped into Division Two.

Perhaps surprisingly, Docherty was confirmed as manager despite our demotion, and it was to be a short stay in Division Two, for we were promoted straight back at the first attempt. It

took a last-gasp victory at Sunderland and a home win against
Portsmouth in our last two matches to make sure, 55,000 fans
packing into Stamford Bridge for the final game of the 1962–63
season.

Ninety per cent of the playing squad was under the age of
twenty-five, but with a little more experience to go with our
youth, we rapidly became one of the best sides in the top flight.
Even at twenty, I was now one of the veterans of a side
containing quite a few teenagers. We finished fifth at the end of
the 1963–64 season, our first back in Division One, and went on
to win the League Cup in 1965, reaching the semi-finals of the
FA Cup in both 1965 and 1966, and the semi-final of the
European Fairs Cup in 1966.

Even then, we were still a very young side, but Tommy
Docherty was impatient for even greater success. He was a
mercurial character and my relationship with him was certainly
pretty fiery. At times he would make you so angry that you
would swear you would never speak to him again, but ten
minutes later he would be cracking jokes and making you laugh,
and he could be hysterically funny.

One Christmas we were staying at the Norbeck Hydro
in Blackpool, our normal base for games in the North-West.
A black-tie function was being held, and we stood around the
edge of the ballroom watching the dancers, just to pass away
the evening until it was time to go to bed. Tommy was in
a mischievous mood, however. He was talking to a woman
who had bad breath, and he made no secret of the fact, turning
his head away ostentatiously whenever she spoke and putting
his hand over his nose. Despite this unsubtle approach, the
poor woman did not even appear to realise what he was doing.
After a few minutes, he asked her to dance. The floor was
packed, and they quickly disappeared into the crowd as they
waltzed away. By the time they came round again, Tom had
tied a handkerchief over his nose and mouth, like a bandit

in a Western. All you could see were his eyes, while his partner kept dancing away, staring at him with a puzzled smile on her face.

Later the same evening, a guy who was as drunk as a skunk started button-holing Docherty about football, in an aggressive way. Tom took the drunk's tedious opinions and insulting comments for a while, but eventually had had enough. The drunk was smoking a cigarette, which 'The Doc' pushed back towards his face with the palm of his hand. The guy zig-zagged backwards, stumbled and fell over, ending up face-down on the floor, with the crumpled cigarette in his mouth, and his legs stretched out behind him. Before he could blink, Tom got hold of his legs and was off, running him across the dance-floor, as if it was a wheelbarrow race, while the drunk kept his arms moving as fast as he could, still with the squashed cigarette in his mouth.

The Doc was more of a kid than the young players, in those moods. If we lost a couple of games, he would have a team meeting, and say, 'Now, no more fooling around, you've messed around too much and you're not concentrating. Get serious, the main thing is the game', while we stared at him in disbelief, for he would fool around more than anybody. Straight after the meeting, he would start pulling stunts and making us laugh. When Allan Harris told him to stop, because he had just told us we were supposed to be taking things more seriously, all Tom would say was, 'Oh, never mind all that, look at that bloke in the ridiculous wig over there.' On another occasion, he ended a lecture on the need to get serious by diving on Marvin Hinton and planting a huge love-bite on his neck. 'Go home and tell your wife that Tommy Docherty gave you that,' said Tom, 'and see if she believes you.' Marvin's expression showed that he thought his chances were pretty thin.

It was by no means all laughs with Tommy. Mickey Harrison was another practical joker, but his jokes would often be a bit too strong, and Docherty got rid of him, because he thought he was a disruptive influence. Mickey went to Blackburn, settled down wonderfully well and was very popular up there, with everyone except Keith Newton. Keith had a pair of crocodile-skin shoes that he had bought on an England trip to Bogota, and he practically worshipped them. He was always shouting at everyone, 'What do you think of these?'

The dressing rooms were very big then, with high ceilings and parquet floors, almost like ballrooms. One day, while Keith was out training, Mickey Harrison drove two six-inch nails through the soles of his crocodile-skin shoes into the parquet floor. When Keith came back, he went to pick up his shoes and they would not budge. He tugged harder and harder at them but they still would not move. When he looked inside, he saw the nails, but he must have thought that they were only short ones, for he gave another jerk on the shoes, and the uppers tore away from the soles, leaving them still nailed to the floor. Everyone else thought it was hugely funny, but Keith was beside himself at the loss of his most prized possessions and would probably have killed Mickey if his mates had not dragged him off him.

Docherty changed his opinions as often as Keith Newton changed his shoes. One minute you would be a favourite, the next, someone else would be flavour of the month and you were on the outer. I was one of his favourites when he first took over as manager, and he even made me captain when I was just nineteen, but things changed dramatically later on, and we clashed over quite a few things. I think the resentment between us arose largely because we both had strong personalities and senses of humour. He would always knock someone down with his humour and make them laugh, but if I came back with a comment that made the players laugh, he would be furious.

We would sometimes row over football too, and I am sure

there were lots of times when it was my fault. I was a very young and inexperienced player, but then he was also a very young and inexperienced coach. A more seasoned coach would either have taken me to one side and straightened me out or given me a dressing-down in front of the group. Tom did neither, which allowed the friction between us to grow worse.

Captaincy was an honour, but the role of a captain in football is not like that in a cricket team. In cricket the captain has time to stand and watch what's going on; in football everything happens too quickly for the captain to have quite the same role. Someone has to carry the ball out, however, and a captain can have a powerful influence on a side, whether, like Tony Adams, it is through his fighting spirit and never-say-die attitude, or, like David Platt, through his awareness of tactics and his ability to spot things going wrong and correct them.

Captains tend to have plenty to say, and I was always quite 'mouthy' on the field, though not in a nasty way – I was just chatty like little Johnnie Byrne, who was called 'Budgie' for the same reason. Being in central midfield, I was close enough to chat to the referee quite a lot, especially to a non-mobile referee, and if he was as non-mobile as me, we would be like Siamese twins.

In those days the referees used to love a joke, perhaps because we were not running around as much. I can remember Jim Finney, who I thought was a very good referee, coming back at me after I queried a decision, 'What are you complaining about? Look at the scoreboard, and you'll see if that was a goal or not', and when I said, 'Cor, you're having a nightmare, ref,' he would snap back, 'You're not playing too well yourself' . . . and he was quite often right. It is much more high-pressure now. All of a sudden, you cannot swear and if you do, you have to be booked. It is unfortunate, because I think humour takes the sting out of many things, and I do not think that element should be taken away. The humour can remind you that it is

not a referee, it is not a press man, it is just another guy, trying
to do his job.

The Doc's way of trying to do his job included a fair
measure of paranoia. Mickey Harrison always believed that
Docherty was hiding outside the door, trying to hear what we
were saying about him, but for a while we thought that Mickey
was the paranoid one. He would whisper, 'Keep talking,' then
tiptoe to the door and suddenly throw it open, to reveal nothing
but an empty corridor.

We realised that it was more than just Mickey's paranoia
when we heard a noise from a cupboard in the changing rooms
one morning and found Docherty hiding inside it. A few days
later, Mickey, Allan Harris and I were in the showers, and
Mickey did his usual act, miming to us to keep talking while he
wrapped a towel round himself and sneaked over to the door.
This time when he opened it, Docherty, who had his ear pressed
against the door, half-fell into the room.

The Doc's idiosyncrasies were as nothing compared to some
football characters, though. Cliff Lloyd, the chairman of the
PFA at the time, told me about a chairman he had played
under, who fully deserved his honorary title of 'the meanest
man in football'. Cliff injured his ankle badly during the first
half of a game and was carried off on a stretcher, with the
physio fearing that the ankle was broken. They put him on the
treatment table, but then left him there while they went back to
watch the rest of the game. The manager gave his half-time talk
across Cliff's prostrate body and then they all filed out for the
second half, leaving Cliff on his own for a further forty-five
minutes, while his ankle swelled up like a balloon.

Finally, when the game was over, the club doctor came in to
examine Cliff's ankle, and told the chairman, 'It's so swollen
that I'll have to cut the laces to get the boot off.' The chairman
blinked, turned to the coach and said, 'How are we off for
laces?'

The manager at another club produced the weirdest and least appreciated end-of-season bonus in Football League history. The team, which had better remain nameless, had just escaped relegation. On the following Monday, the players were finishing training when the manager said, 'Lads, we've escaped relegation and I'm proud of you. As soon as you've dressed, come into my office, I've got a special bonus for you.'

The players had never been in and out of the bath so quickly in their lives, scrambling into their clothes, dreaming of the fat cash bonuses that were about to be theirs. When they all filed into the manager's office, however, he pointed to a crate of apples in the corner of the room and said, 'There you are, lads, help yourselves, there's enough for three a man.'

Charlie Mitten at Fulham was another eccentric manager, who was a big greyhound man. A couple of his injured players went into the treatment room one morning and found Charlie there giving one of his dogs deep-heat treatment under the lamp. They had to hang around for half an hour until he had finished, because he would not get the dog off the couch to make room for them. He told them the dog had a bad hock, but when one of them said, 'Sure he isn't just putting it on to miss training?' he went all serious and said, 'I never thought of that.'

Treating greyhounds was not in Tommy Docherty's repertoire, but he definitely saw himself as a saviour of lost football careers. George Graham and Tommy Docherty had a few run-ins together, mostly starting from Tommy's claims that he had saved George from oblivion. Docherty had seen George play for the Scottish Youth side and brought him to Chelsea from Aston Villa, where he had been 'doomed', until Tommy rescued him, as he never ceased to remind him. We promptly christened him 'Doomed George', a name he hated.

Just after he joined Chelsea, we went to Sweden on a pre-season tour, and all the way there, George said not a word to anyone. He was not particularly shy, just keeping himself to himself, while he weighed everything up. About the second day there, while staying at a place called Kindus training camp, where the Brazilians had trained when they won the World Cup in 1958, Tom gave us a day off and we all went into Gothenburg.

Six of us caught the train into the city and as it rattled through the forest, everyone was fooling around and doing their Frankie Howerd and Tommy Cooper impressions, except for George, who just sat quietly in the corner. All of a sudden he burst into song, doing a serious and exaggerated impersonation of a singer called Billy Eckstine, 'We seem like passing strangers now . . .' Everyone turned round to look at him, but he just kept gazing out of the window, singing the song. When he had finished, he said to me, 'What do you think of that, then?'

I said, 'Well that's great for Sarah Vaughan, but how about giving us Billy Eckstine?'

From then on, we became very good friends, so good that I was best man at George's wedding a few years later. By that time, he was at Arsenal and I was at Spurs, and for some reason he chose the morning of the Arsenal–Spurs derby to get married. After the service, everyone else went to the reception, while we went off to play football. It was a happy day for George in all sorts of ways, for Arsenal thrashed us and he played a blinder, which was a bit of a surprise, because I was expecting him to save his energy for the wedding night.

I beat George to the altar by a couple of years, for I had married my girlfriend Christine McCann, just before I left Chelsea. I met Christine at a wedding when we were both sixteen. Her mum and dad were friends of one of my uncles and aunts, Ernie and Mary Yuill. Ernie was a real cracker, one of those great lovely uncles that kids adore, always full of fun.

He worked at the docks and knew Christine's dad from there, and when we went to the wedding of Ernie and Mary's son, Christine was also there with her mum and dad.

We got friendly, and began going out together, though it was something of a long-distance relationship for a while. We rarely saw each other more than once or twice a week, because she lived in Canning Town, a long haul from Dagenham. I had had a few casual girlfriends before, but Christine was my first 'steady girl' – six hours of football a day did not leave too much spare time for romance.

Our own wedding had its bizarre moments, for the vicar who married us was a West Ham fanatic. After pronouncing us man and wife, he followed us out of the church and had his Hammers' scarf and bobble hat on over his cassock and surplice by the time they started taking the photographs outside the church. He later christened our daughters Nancy and Tracey, even coming out of retirement to christen Tracey, still wearing his Hammers' hat and scarf.

The vicar would have been delighted with our choice of neighbours, for our first house together was at 82 Beechwood Gardens, Gants Hill, right around the corner from Bobby Moore. I had known Bobby since I had gone training at West Ham. He was usually there as well, trying to learn from Malcolm Allison, who, with Noel Cantwell, helped with the West Ham coaching then, and a hero to Bobby. Bobby was a couple of years older than me and I looked up to him. He was an imposing figure, a fair-haired, good-looking, all-English boy, in contrast to the crew-cut, gum-chewing all-American boys we would see around London in summer. He was warm-hearted and friendly. He was also incredibly generous and if we had a sandwich or a coffee at the little restaurant round the corner from the ground, he would always pay for it. He put a tremendous value on being a professional footballer and had that quality that showed you he was a born leader. He was also one of those players who seemed to grow bigger when he put his football shirt on.

Nothing made him flap, for he was always in control. In League games, you knew that he would give you a chance, but he made mistakes so rarely that it would shake you when he did. He was an outstanding passer of the ball for a defender, and such a good player that it became popular to look for his faults. People would criticise his pace and his heading, but his reading of the game was so good that he never got outstripped and he would be in a position where the centre-forward would have trouble. With or without pressure, his passing was as good as any English player I have seen. The higher he went, the better he became, and the more he enjoyed it. In England's game against Brazil during the 1970 World Cup he gave a quite outstanding display, timing his tackling and interceptions to perfection and using them as the springboard to turn defence into attack.

Becoming one of Bobby's neighbours strengthened what was to become a lifelong friendship. Having lived in Gants Hill for some time, he was also able to mark my card about which pubs to go to and which to avoid. After growing up in a council house, the house in Gants Hill was the first one that was all our own . . . apart from the mortgage. We sold it a couple of years later after the birth of our eldest daughter Nancy, and with our second child, Tracey, already on the way, we moved to Loughton, deep in Essex suburbia. We had seen a lovely house there, much more expensive than we should have been considering, but I knew that I could be really lazy or a real workaholic, and I thought that a mortgage I could barely afford might just be the whip on my back that I needed. I made an offer, half hoping that it would be turned down, but it was accepted.

Peter Lorenzo, one of the first television football commentators, lived near by. After we had moved in, he came round for a cup of tea and told me that I had made the most horrendous mistake in paying so much for the house, but three months later the property boom took off and the house doubled in value in a very short time. Peter was straight round again, saying, 'You knew something,' but I really did not, it was just luck.

It took me quite a while to settle in Loughton as it seemed very impersonal. I did not feel that I knew the neighbours as I had in Dagenham, and I spent a long time agonising about the move, wanting to be sure that it would not change me as a person. Although it is natural to want to better your living standards, I really had guilt pangs about turning my back on my upbringing and felt that I had left my roots behind me. I was reminded of that, every time I went out. There were a lot of cars in the road, and playing football in the streets Dagenham-style would have been impossible.

I was soon to discover how different the people in Loughton could be. The police were just beginning to clamp down on drink-driving and I was caught coming home a bit the worse for wear from a Christmas party. It was a stupid thing to do, something I would never do today, and I could have no complaints when I was caught. I was doing under thirty in a thirty-mile-an-hour limit, but was stopped and breathalysed for going too slow. As a result, I was banned for a year, but I decided to take it on the chin and get trains or taxis, naively thinking that I might even enjoy it.

A couple of months into the ban, Ron Jones, who was the athletic coach to QPR and a former Great Britain Olympic captain, was coming to my house for a very early breakfast, before another friend picked us up to take us to the ground, ready for a club tour of Sweden. Christine was not dressed when Ron phoned from the station, and as it was a long walk and we were a bit pushed for time, I jumped into Christine's car to go and pick him up. That was the only time I drove during the year, and I quickly forgot all about it.

A few months later, I was having a quiet drink at my Dad's pub, when a policeman came up to me and said, 'By the way, make sure you don't drive your car again.'

I said, 'I haven't driven it.'

'Yes you have,' he replied. 'It was about six o'clock one morning. One of your neighbours rang the police station and told them that you were driving your car.' I had genuinely forgotten all about it by then, but I could not believe that I had been 'shopped' to the police by a neighbour – the Smalls had obviously moved to Loughton as well . . . If you did something like that in Dagenham, you would be tarred and feathered and run out of town on a rail. Rule One for East Enders is that you never grass on your own. The obvious corollary to that is that you are loyal to your friends and family, and that is one thing that I have never swerved from throughout my life.

Such neighbourly types were the exception in Loughton but I still felt that I had lost something in making the move. Even after leaving Dagenham behind, I never felt ashamed of who I was or where I came from. I loved my upbringing in Clydach Vale and Dagenham, I still have my old friends there, and still love to go back.

Some people do not realise the value of what they have, until it is gone, but even as a kid, I always thought how lucky I was to live in that environment. I had a family life that could not have been better, good friends, and top-quality, young football players around me, with whom I could develop my skills and against whom I could compete. I have been very fortunate in many ways, even though the decision to throw in my lot with another East End boy, Alan Sugar, paid back some of that luck. I suppose you always have to pay for it in the end.

I do not believe that people are born to be footballers. Some people are born with an innate ability at ball-games, but which game you pursue depends very much on your environment. Kids born in Weybridge do not become good footballers. Like boxers, footballers need to be 'hungry', but it is no good having a hunger for the game if no one else in your street is playing it – you cannot learn it on your own. If you had taken Bobby Charlton to Australia when he was three months old, he might have finished up as a great tennis player or cricketer, but it is hard to imagine him becoming a great footballer. You also need the role models, which these days you are as likely to see on television as in the flesh. American kids might aspire to be a golfer like John Daly, a tennis player like Pete Sampras or an American footballer like Joe Montana, but they will not grow up dreaming of becoming a top footballer. There are no role models to inspire their dreams.

As well as the environment in which I grew up, I was also very lucky to have such a special bond with my parents. Everyone always said that being an only child must be lonely, but I never found it so, because my relationship with my parents was so active. As an only child, I was even closer to my parents than most children are, and if my Mum and Dad argued, which did not happen often, I used to feel terribly insecure and worried until they had made it up again. When I was old enough to be left at home without a baby-sitter, I also used to worry whenever they went to the pub with their friends, and would imagine all sorts of dire accidents befalling them as they were coming home.

They would ask me if I wanted to go with them and I would put on a bold front, not wanting them to think that I was not grown-up enough to be left and say, 'No, I'll be fine here, no problem.' After they had gone, I would sit on the window-sill, looking for them, and could not go to bed until I heard the car in the drive, and was sure that they were all right. As soon as they were home, I would jump into bed and pretend to be asleep, as if I had not really been bothered about them at all – real macho-man stuff which fooled nobody. I have remained

especially close to my parents throughout my adult life. I still
meet my Dad at least once a week and we speak on the phone
every day. He has always been a joker and great fun to be
around, and his outlook on life taught me never to take myself
too seriously, only the work I was pursuing at the time. I believe
that attitude has helped me through some of my tougher times
in football.

My mother was more serious than my Dad and had the
better business head. She was such a steady person, and a great
influence on me. She died of lung cancer on Tuesday, 7 August
1990. My Mum was the one who played the greatest part in
pointing me in the right direction. Her business acumen gave me
a really solid point of view on what I should be doing with my
life and where I should be going. Her attitudes and beliefs
shaped the person I am today and my greatest sadness is that
she is no longer here to guide me.

My Dad would be mates with anyone straight away, but my
Mum would never take to people quickly, they had to win her
respect, and she urged me not to take people at face value. She
always told me to keep my feet on the ground as well, and not
get carried away by whatever success I was enjoying. She also
encouraged me to find an alternative long-term career, so that if
anything went wrong in football, I would still be able to make a
living.

I have a grandson now and if he wanted to be a footballer, I
certainly would not discourage him, but I would give him the
same advice that my parents gave me. If you make the right
moves, and take the right precautions to protect yourself, it is a
great life, but you have got to do something else as well. I can
remember seeing a few famous footballers from previous generations when I was growing up, and most of them were on their
uppers after their careers were over. That was not the exception,
it was the rule, and I hate to think of that happening to any
footballers now, let alone my own grandson.

Soon after I moved to Loughton, my Mum and Dad left Dagenham as well. My Dad had been working in the docks as a lorry driver and 'meat-runner' for twenty years, and was ready for a change. He took early retirement, while my Mum sold the café she had bought after leaving the job with the Odeon cinemas, and together they took on the tenancy of the Royal Oak in Chingford. They had been trying to get a pub together for ages, but kept missing out. They went for so many, only to be let down, that they had decided the Royal Oak was going to be their last effort. If they had missed out, they were not going to try again. I helped behind the bar on their opening night, when all of my team-mates came along, and the place was packed.

It was a big gamble for them, for while Mum knew the catering business, their only previous experience in the licensed trade had been when I was very young, and Mum and Dad had worked in a club called the Red House in Harold Hill. The Royal Oak was a tiny pub, but it had tremendous potential and plenty of room for expansion, with a huge car park and six acres at the back. Dad bought a couple of horses, Rebel and Tinkerbell the Shetland pony, for his granddaughters to ride, and Rebel was still around over twenty years later to be ridden by Dad's great-grandson as well.

Sadly, like so many other people who go into the pub trade, Mum and Dad found the stresses proved too great for their marriage. The pub business is probably the worst possible one for marriage break-ups, for if there is a weakness anywhere, running a pub will flush it out. You work very long hours, in each other's company seven days a week and twenty-four hours a day, and you are working while everyone else is relaxing and having a good time. You have to be nice to everyone too, even if they are sometimes less than nice to you, and it often ends up that the only person you can vent your frustrations on is your partner.

Mum and Dad were still close and there was never any real

acrimony or anyone else involved, but they eventually reached the point where, as they could no longer live together, they would have to live apart. Dad liked it where he was, but Mum had always wanted to go back to Wales, and in the end they went their separate ways.

The Royal Oak grew into a thriving business, and Fred and I went on to buy a number of other pubs, but if I am the boss in the football business, Fred is definitely the 'guv'nor' in the pub trade. Myrtle also branched out on her own in the end, and she and I bought the Farmers' Arms in Upper Church Village, Tonteg, just outside Pontypridd, in the Rhondda Valley. It had been owned by three old ladies, who were aged ninety-one, ninety-three and ninety-five when they decided to retire. They used to serve rough cider, the strong stuff, which they kept in the back, and they had the names of the cider drinkers on a blackboard. Every time you ordered a glass, they would mark it on the board, and once you had had two pints, they sent you home because they said it made you go funny in the head.

There was a tiny snug bar at the back, where you had to ring a bell for service, but at the front was a very basic, spit-and-sawdust bar, for men only, apart from the three old ladies who were serving them. The whole pub did not appear to have been redecorated since the Boer War, but Mum fell in love with it straight away and was determined to have it. She also bought the cottage next door, and we extended the pub into half of it, while Mum kept the other half as her living quarters.

She quickly showed that she was a very strong personality, with her own ideas on how to run the pub, which did not include a men-only bar. After redecorating throughout, she made women as welcome as men in the front bar, which went down like a lead balloon with the men. They said that she would go out of business, because they would walk out and never come back, but it proved an empty threat. My Mum stuck to her guns, the men soon sheepishly shuffled back in and she built a good business there. My cousin, Alan Watts, and his wife, Jean, had helped my mother out a lot, and after her death they took the pub over.

My own licensed premises are a bit more expensive to run than the Farmers' Arms. I bought Scribes West, a private dining club in Kensington, a few years back and it has become something of a family business, with my second wife, Yvette, also known as 'Toots', running it, and my daughter Nancy helping out on Saturday nights.

The 'landlord' of my football club also had a pretty strong personality and my football career was not being helped by the growing hostility between Tommy Docherty and me. The tensions occasionally erupted into a full-scale row, although the success that the team was beginning to enjoy helped to paper over the cracks for a while. By the early 1960s, Chelsea had become a good side and a tremendously exciting team to watch, playing some fabulous football.

Yet it was also a time when the game was getting very dirty, with 'over the top' tackles almost routine. It was not always easy for a bystander – or even a referee – to spot if the tackle was deliberately vicious or just an innocent, mistimed effort, but the effect of 'showing six' – the six studs on the sole of the boot – and kicking or stabbing downwards over the top of the ball into the shins, would put ball-players off their game, and could even put them out of the game altogether. Talented players, who wanted to play football, spent a lot of the time being carried off, because the others spent most of their time stopping them from doing so.

Chelsea were not the worst side by a long chalk, but we were by no means entirely blameless. I was about four yards from Leeds' Johnny Giles, when my Chelsea team-mate, Eddie McCreadie, launched himself at him and went straight through his shin pads. Giles was carried off. After it had happened to him a few more times, Johnny said that it would not happen again; he was going to protect himself in future, and many of the talented players decided that they were going to have to be tough, just to survive.

Alec Young, 'the Golden Vision' to Everton fans, was a beautiful player, but he could also handle himself. He put in a particularly vicious challenge on Johnny Hollins when we played Everton in 1963. Fresh to the game, Johnny was an exuberant boy, full of running and smiles. When he went into a tackle with Young, however, Alec really 'did' him. Johnny was lying on the ground, writhing in agony, and Alec just stood there, hands on hips, looking down at him. While our physio was trying to put Johnny back together, I said to Alec, 'Come on, what's your game? He's a great kid, what did you do that for?'

'I know he's a good kid,' said Alec. 'That's why I only gave him half of it.'

Another Leeds player, Bobby Collins, was a good footballer, but an extremely aggressive one, part of a team, including Norman Hunter, Paul Reaney and Billy Bremner, that, to put it mildly, was famous for its aggression. Every era has its hard men, of course, but whether every team needs a hard man is questionable. It really depends on what players you have. If you have a number of skilful players, you may need a hard man to win the ball for them, just as Nobby Stiles used to do for Law, Best and Charlton at Manchester United.

If you have three midfielders who are willing to do their bit in defence, even if all they do is close down space and work to win the ball, you may not need a hard man. It is important to have a blend of skill and hardness, and if you can find players who themselves are a blend of the two, then you are very fortunate. Denis Law, for example, was one such player, and Desailly of AC Milan, who had such an outstanding European Cup final against Barcelona in 1994, is another, but it is unusual.

Fans love to argue about who was the hardest hard man, and though Norman Hunter and Liverpool's Tommy Smith were particularly famed in my own playing era, I thought that Chelsea's Ron Harris was the toughest of the lot. Ron was extremely quiet when he played. He never said much, and kept a poker-face whatever happened, but he was very, very tough. I do not think that Jimmy Greaves ever played well against him, and not many did, in fact. Rodney Marsh played in a Cup quarter-final for QPR against Chelsea, at a time when Rodney was playing particularly well, but he got snuffed right out – he never had a kick all match, except from Ron, who kicked him a couple of times, which did not please him very much.

Ron seemed to be absolutely impervious to pain. We went to Jamaica on tour one year and were under strict instructions not to overdo the sunbathing, but Ron promptly fell asleep in the sun and was there for hours, waking up with a blister the size of a table-tennis bat, right in the middle of his chest. Ron did not say anything to the team doctor, and played in our game that night.

We all helped him to get on his shirt over his terrible blister, but in the first minutes of the game, the ball was booted skywards and we knew with a terrible inevitability that it was going to land smack in the middle of Ron's chest. There was a sickening 'squelch' as the blister burst, but Ron's expression did not change. His shirt was wet through from all the pus and he must have been in agony throughout the game, but you would never have known it, for he still had that same impassive look on his face.

As a rule, Ron was not a dirty player, he was just a tough one. He would not disappoint you; if there was a hard man coming towards him, he would get the better of him every time. Roy Barry came to Coventry with the reputation of having been the hardest man in Scotland. They played Chelsea in his first game and what he was not going to do to Ron Harris was nobody's business. When he tried it, he ended up on the floor, and for good measure, Ron walked all over him, treading on his hand and his head.

There were worse fates than being fouled, however, especially for George Graham, who saw himself very much as a man-about-town. In one game, George was involved in a mix-up in the opposition goalmouth, and next thing, he was flat on the deck, blood gushing down his face, as he groaned and twisted in agony. I ran over and said, 'Is it bad, George?' He just gasped, sounding as if he was going to breathe his last at any moment.

'You've got a kick in the head, George,' I said.

'Where?' he moaned.

'Just above the hairline.'

He opened his eyes and asked, 'Can you see it?'

'No, it's above the hairline.'

He sighed with relief: 'Thank Christ for that, I'm going dancing tonight.'

If on-field violence was the dark side of the game then, there was also some beautiful football being played. One of our best victories, and one of my great memories at Stamford Bridge, was beating Manchester United 3–1. Law, Best and Charlton were all in the United side, but we played them off the park. I was a particular fan of Denis Law, whom I thought was terrific, and rated him even ahead of George Best, though there was very little in it. Denis would play football and score his goals, whether it was a battle on a wet Tuesday night in Oldham or a sun-drenched Saturday at the San Siro. He was a footballer for all seasons, an exceptional player, which made the pleasure of beating the pants off his team even greater. Denis and George are still friends today and often come into Scribes together.

Not all Chelsea's successes were achieved by good football. Tommy Docherty pulled an outrageous stroke to get a European Fairs Cup tie postponed, for example. We had a barrow-load of injuries and were struggling to put together a team, so Tom decided that our best hope was to postpone the game and give the walking wounded a week or two to recover. But postponements are not granted for injuries and what we needed was a tropical downpour to wash out the match.

There had been a fair bit of rain, but nowhere near enough to threaten the match, at least until the Doc decided to give Mother Nature a helping hand. He organised the ground staff to run hosepipes out on to the pitch from every available tap and they were left running all night. The next morning, just to make doubly sure, Tommy had us playing a six-a-side on the pitch, turning it from a swamp into a quagmire. Unsurprisingly after all this, the referee took one look and called off the game.

Some rather puzzled-looking reporters, who had passed through the bone-dry streets of Chelsea on their way to Stamford Bridge, were summoned to a press conference to explain the decision. 'How bad was it, Tom?' asked one of them. The Doc was casting around for a suitable analogy, when he caught sight of chairman Joe Mears's house, just outside the ground. 'It was so bad this morning,' said Tom, 'that Mrs Mears couldn't even shave.' In the stunned silence that followed, Docherty barked, 'Good morning,' and left the room.

My playing career reached its zenith in 1964, when I won my two caps for England, under Alf Ramsey. It completed a full set of English honours for me, at every level from schoolboy to senior international, a record that has never been equalled, and now never will be, since amateur internationals are no longer played. When I heard on the radio that I was in the team to play Belgium at Wembley, my first thought was that I had to tell my Mum, before she heard it from anybody else. I drove straight up to her café to break the news and she was so excited about it that she even forgave me for being chosen for England instead of Wales.

I played reasonably well in a 2-2 draw with Belgium and was selected for the next match, against Holland in Amsterdam, which we also drew, 1-1, and I made the equalising goal in both games, but I was never to play for England again. If only Bobby Tambling and Barry Bridges, who had been getting on the end of my passes since we were kids, had been in the same side, we might have all had long England careers ...

Ironically, sharing the same Dagenham roots as Alf Ramsey may not have helped my fledgling international career. I held him in very high esteem, because he had done a particularly good job with the England team, but he was not a man who was easy to know.

I still have the accent of the people I grew up with in the streets of Dagenham. Alf came from three streets away, but you could not tell that from the way he spoke. I can understand why Ramsey may have felt a need to moderate his accent, for even now, the attitude summed up by 'It's not for the likes of thee', is still invoked to baulk the ambitions of working people. It is an age-old, working-class problem, I suppose, about barriers. Are you going to accept that barrier and stay behind it, or are you going to try to fight it?

In Europe, society seems less stratified. When John Toshack was coach of Real Sociedad, for example, he had a player called Arcanada as his goalkeeper. Toshack went to be manager of Real Madrid, before returning to Real Sociedad, where the club president, the equivalent of an English club chairman, was now Arcanada. These things are possible when people open their minds. I cannot resist attempting something that I think might be achievable, whatever the obstacles in my path. That attitude probably has a lot to do with where I come from.

My father was a good mate of a man called Sid, who had lived next door to Alf Ramsey in Dagenham for many years, and Sid asked me to say 'Hello' from him when I met Ramsey.

At a pause in my first England training session, Ramsey approached me and I said to him, 'Sid, your old next-door neighbour from Dagenham, sends his regards.' There was a pregnant pause. He looked at me as if he had just stepped in something unpleasant, turned on his heel without a word, and marched off to the other side of the ground. For some reason, I got the feeling that Alf's Dagenham roots were not a subject that he was keen to discuss.

Ramsey did choose me for a third game for England, but I was injured and had to withdraw. John 'Budgie' Byrne took my place, did particularly well, and as a result, I could not get back into the team. Shortly afterwards, I was transferred to Spurs, where I did not play as well as I had been doing at Chelsea. I made Ramsey's forty-man squad for the 1966 World Cup, but missed out when the number was reduced to twenty-two. My England international career was over.

Relations with my club manager were also going downhill fast. A couple of months after my international début, we won the League Cup, beating Leicester City 3–2 over two legs. I captained the side and scored one of the goals, but within a month of that, I had been stripped of the captaincy and dropped from the team. The source of the trouble was the infamous incident in Blackpool.

The reports that we had been indulging in some late-night boozing the evening before a game were completely untrue. The night out was on a Tuesday, and our next game was not until the Saturday. Docherty had previously said that we could all have an evening out, which most of us had made arrangements to do, but when we returned from our game at Liverpool that day, he changed his mind. We were third in the League at the time and, had we won there, would still have been in with an outside chance of the Championship, although it was a tough run-in – away to Liverpool, Burnley and Blackpool. We did not play badly at Anfield by any means, but we lost by the odd goal, and as a result Docherty cancelled our night out. That incident alone would not have been enough to provoke a mutiny, but it was the culmination of a number of disagreements between Tom and the players, the straw that broke the camel's back. As a result, we decided to ignore him and go on our night out anyway, making a confrontation inevitable.

It was not the first run-in between Tom and I over breaking his curfews but it was the most serious, because the previous one had only involved a night-in, rather than a night-out. We were staying at a hotel in Kensington preparing for a game and were given a strict curfew by Tommy, who ordered us all to be in our rooms by nine o'clock. Knowing that he was going out for the evening, however, the whole team got together in the hotel ballroom. As usual, I could not resist the lure of a microphone and was soon up on stage, 'guesting' with the band.

I was halfway through singing 'Winter Wonderland' when one of the players spotted the Doc making his way through the hotel lobby. The rest of the team scattered like birds before a sparrowhawk and were probably all tucked up in bed before he even reached the ballroom, but I was oblivious to the commotion, still singing my heart out. Tommy's eyes swept the room. He smiled, happy that his players had obeyed his orders. He was about to turn and go when he spotted something familiar about the vocalist with the band. Our eyes met across a crowded room . . .

Perhaps that was the reason why Docherty was so eager to believe that I must have been the ring-leader of the 'late-night boozing' in Blackpool, after which eight of us – Barry Bridges, George Graham, Eddie McCreadie, John Hollins, Joe Fascione, Bert Murray, Marvin Hinton and me – were all sent home in disgrace, giving the tabloids a field day.

I heard nothing more from Docherty until the following Friday night. I had already gone to bed, getting an early night as usual before the Saturday game, when the phone rang. My Dad, who was staying with us that evening, took the call. 'This is Tommy Docherty. Tell Terry he's not playing tomorrow and he's not captain any more.' There was a click as Docherty hung up. His principled stand proved rather expensive, for without the eight of us Chelsea were thrashed 6–2 by Burnley.

The Blackpool incident was only the last of a number of things that had widened the gap between us into an unbridgeable gulf, but the most frequently quoted cause of friction was Docherty's complaint that I was changing his tactics out on the field. This was given a lot of publicity, and it did have some justification, for it certainly did happen in a European Fairs Cup tie against Roma in the 1965–66 season, but the change of tactics was very much a team decision and was a far less serious breach of the coach's authority than it might at first appear – the system we used, after all, was one of Docherty's. We had won the home leg against Roma 4–1, a night made even more memorable for me, because I scored three of the goals. I was carried off in the first half, but returned after half-time to score my third goal.

There was a lot of controversy surrounding the game, with Eddie McCreadie getting sent off and Tommy Docherty having a very public row with the Roma manager. The incidents were blown up in a predictably lurid way by the Italian papers, ensuring us of a hot reception in Rome, when we played the second leg.

We were blissfully unaware of what lay in store, as we set off for Rome, kitted out in some new, powder-blue club blazers. A flight delay left us hanging around the departure lounge at Heathrow, always a fairly tedious place to be, and to make it worse, there was a severe shortage of seats. I spotted a few check-in desks that were not in use, and John Dunn, Eddie McCreadie and I hopped behind the counter of one and sat down for a chat.

The combination of the pale blue blazers and a check-in desk had an immediate effect. People kept coming up to the desk and asking for information, mistaking us for airline staff. Eddie, John and I exchanged meaningful glances; footballers love practical jokes more than life itself and this was a God-given opportunity. The first few passengers were simply des-patched to far-flung corners of Heathrow, but then I found a cardboard box under the counter, with some particularly long and impenetrable-looking forms inside it. When the next passen-gers arrived, asking, 'Which gate is our flight?' I said, 'Well, first you have to fill in this form.'

After they had laboriously completed the form, I passed it to Eddie, who put it on his desk and banged his fist down, as if he was stamping it. He then handed it to John, who studied it intently, nodded briskly and said, 'Gate 98.' Our fame spread rapidly, and within minutes a long queue of eager passengers had formed, all filling out forms as if their lives depended on it. We kept straight faces, but things were beginning to get a bit out of hand. The queue stretched further and further back towards the entrance doors, and one or two faces towards the end of it were starting to look ominously familiar; the founder-members of the Gate 98 club were back and not looking too pleased. It was time to disappear, and John, Eddie and I slipped quietly away. Funnily enough, I never wear pale blue blazers these days. You can't be too careful, as Jimmy Thompson always used to remind me.

It was to be one of the few laughs on the whole trip. By the time we arrived in Rome, the hate campaign in the Italian media had done its work, and the whole population hated our guts. About 10,000 people turned up just to watch us train, booing, whistling and spitting abuse at us. When the crowd had a go at Tommy Docherty, he did not improve the situation by dropping his shorts to them.

There was a fundamental difference of opinion between

Tom and the players about the way we should approach the game. Tom had been swayed by a respected football journalist who had said to him, 'You don't need to use a sweeper, you were playing well in the last game without one.' Tom replied, 'Yeah, you're right, we'll play our own way,' and that became his instruction to the team.

The players had a different view, however, and were saying to me, 'We could get done here. With the fans behind them, if we lose an early goal, we could be in trouble.' As a result, we had played with a sweeper in previous away legs in Europe. Marvin Hinton, a very polished defender, tended to drop a bit deeper in his natural game anyway and I told him, 'If you sense danger, just drop out like you normally do.' Although we did not play a formal sweeper system, instead of going in with a flat back four, we left him to drop out into a sweeper position. But if I took the lead in organising things there is no doubt that I was just reflecting the views of all the players. The whole team felt much more secure about protecting a three-goal lead, playing that way.

The home side were trying every trick in the book to put us off our game. The match had been switched from the Olympic stadium to a smaller ground, where the crowd was right on top of us. It was a seven-thirty kick-off and we went out early to have a warm-up, planning to return to the dressing room for a few minutes before the game. As we came out of the tunnel, we realised exactly what sort of night it was going to be. We were not just facing the normal hostility to visiting teams, the atmosphere was absolutely terrifying and the crowd looked capable of any lunacy. We were greeted by a fusillade of tomatoes and every other kind of fruit and vegetable, eggs, coins and lighted cigarettes. More worryingly, there was a barrage of stones and pieces of concrete, and even a huge piece of ice, as big as a boulder, though God knows how they got it there. One of the stand seats was also ripped out, exposing a jagged steel edge, and thrown on to the pitch. Paul Boyne, the club's medical officer, was hit by a container full of something warm and wet, which he fervently hoped had been coffee.

We warmed up, keeping a wary eye out for missiles, but when we tried to go back to the dressing rooms, we found that the doors at the entrance to the tunnel had been locked against us, leaving us stranded out on the pitch. To no one's great surprise, the scheduled kick-off time came and went without any sign of the home team. We were forced to stay out on the pitch for half an hour before Roma finally appeared and the game got under way.

Despite all the psychological warfare, we kept our nerve and did the job, drawing o–o, to take the tie 4–1 on aggregate. We left the field to a storm of booing and a fresh hail of missiles, and there was worse to come when we actually left the stadium. It seemed as if the whole city had turned out to throw stones and bottles at us, despite the presence of riot police and armoured vehicles.

Roma were banned from European competition for three years after the riot, but that was not much help to us at the time. Many of the lads were lying down on the floor of the coach, in the aisle between the seats, with their bags over their faces to protect them from rocks and flying glass, but one of the directors' wives had her face cut by broken glass after a fan threw a brick through the window. It was terrifying, for the hate that was out there that night was immense. I have seen a few similar scenes since, but nothing quite as vicious and angry as that mob. There was one moment of light relief, when we reached the relative safety of the team hotel. The same journalist came up to the Doc and said, 'See, I told you you didn't need to play a sweeper.'

We had a good European run that year, including a terrific game against the German team Munchen 1860, an exceptionally good side at the time. We also beat Rapid Vienna and AC

Milan, and then met Barcelona in the semi-finals. I played in the first game, but was transferred to Tottenham before the second leg. The scores were tied after the two legs and it went to a third game. By then, I was travelling to New York with Spurs on an end-of-season tour and heard on the radio on the way to the airport, that Chelsea had been beaten 6–0 in the decider.

Docherty had gone to the Chelsea chairman Joe Mears and made the classic 'It's him or me' speech. With his chairman's backing, the Doc signed Charlie Cooke, and I knew immediately that the writing was on the wall for me at Chelsea. The Doc had signed him to replace me and was quickly singing Charlie's praises and saying what a good player he was. That was true, of course, and he was also a great one for the fans, very good entertainment value, able to do really clever things and go past people. He was a completely different type of player from me, however. I was a long-ball passer, who did not hang on to the ball, but played it early. I had grown up with Barry Bridges and Bobby Tambling, who were runners off the ball. If people make early runs, you have got to pass it early. We had built a blend over the years, and our games were tailored to each other's strengths. When Cooke arrived, Tambling and Bridges would be off and running and the ball would not come. They would go again, and again it would not come, and inevitably they would get frustrated. Later on, people like Osgood seemed better suited to Charlie's game.

A week after our FA Cup semi-final defeat by Sheffield Wednesday at Villa Park, I was on my way, followed soon after by Barry Bridges, Bert Murray and George Graham. The year before, we had lost to Liverpool at the same ground, at the same stage of the competition. Liverpool had played a midweek European Cup game in an Iron Curtain country and had then travelled back through the night. They must have been awfully tired and we were confident that we would run the legs off them, but perhaps we were over-confident, because Liverpool, with Ian St John and Roger Hunt in full flow, beat us 2–0. A year later, we went down to Sheffield Wednesday, in a game we were again confident of winning.

Ironically, my last game for Chelsea, four days later, was the Fairs Cup tie against Barcelona. Docherty brought Charlie Cooke into the dressing room before the game, to introduce him to the team. I knew that Charlie and I would have only the briefest of acquaintances. I went out to play my final game in Chelsea colours in the cavernous Nou Camp stadium. My next appearance there, eighteen years later, would be in very different circumstances.

Two FA Cup semi-final defeats in a row were too much for Docherty, who decided to dismantle the team and start again. Yet that Chelsea side, also including Ron and Allan Harris, John Hollins, Bobby Tambling, and my hero Johnny Brooks, was a tremendous combination, brim-full of talent, young and constantly developing as a team. It was more like a family than a football team to me, and I still find myself thinking about those Chelsea lads. Although I had some good friends at Tottenham and QPR, there was a closeness at Chelsea that I never found anywhere else.

I will always believe that if Docherty had kept that side together, we would have gone on to be as dominant as Leeds or Liverpool in that era. We nearly always seemed to have the beating of Leeds at the time, and Don Revie's players were the same age as us. They also suffered similar disappointments. The only difference was that Revie kept patience with his side, whereas Docherty lost patience with us. He simply gave up too soon, wrecking a potentially great side. The premature splitting-up of that Chelsea side still rankles, even after all these years.

Yet when I look back now at why Tommy Docherty and I fell out, it all seems so irrelevant. Tom and I had our arguments and fights, and sometimes I would even have a go at him in front of the players, which embarrassed him and was wrong of me. He would then have a go back at me, giving the wheel another turn.

The split may have been mostly my fault; I did not like losing at anything and I used to get really annoyed if we were having a bad run, because I wanted to win so badly. With the wisdom of age, I am sure both us would handle the situation very differently, but perhaps we were both too young then, doing and saying silly things, which we would regret later, when the damage had already been done. We were definitely not on each other's Christmas card list for a few years, but the split has not left any permanent scars. I see Tom regularly at football functions and he can still have me in fits of laughter.

Chelsea had accepted offers from both Spurs and West Ham, but left the decision up to me, and for the second time in my career, I decided against West Ham. Spurs manager Bill Nicholson, one of my idols, had been on the phone to me just minutes before Ron Greenwood called up to ask me to go to West Ham, but even if Ron had got in first, my decision would have been the same. Bobby Moore almost went to Tottenham at the same time, and was excited about joining Spurs, but his move fell through and Tottenham eventually bought Mike England instead.

If I was sad to be leaving Stamford Bridge, I was elated that the move was to be to White Hart Lane. Tottenham was close to home, my favourite team, and Dave Mackay was another of my heroes, so I thought to myself, That's it. That will do nicely. There was not much negotiating for money in those days, you really had to just take what they gave you, so the signing was completed quickly, with Spurs paying Chelsea £80,000.

# CHAPTER THREE

# Spurs and QPR

## 1966–74

FOR A LONG TIME, it did not seem as if my move to Spurs was real. Even when I had been there for weeks, I kept thinking that I was on loan and would be back at Chelsea quite soon. I had been there from the age of fifteen to twenty-three and I just could not believe that I would not be going back. Although I had been a Tottenham supporter since I was a boy, there was something unique about being at Chelsea with all those great young players. Chelsea was like a family, whereas Spurs was just football – being a professional.

Your first club is always your best one, of course. It comes as a bit of a shock when they do not want you any more, and your second club suffers as a result. Finally, I snapped out of it. The old cliché says that the club is bigger than the player, but suddenly it dawned on me that the game is bigger than the club as well. I was playing the game long before any club came for me, and my first loyalty was to football. I loved the game for itself. It did not matter what strip I was wearing, I went out to play football and to win. It was the only way I knew.

That feeling helped me to accept that I would not be going back to Stamford Bridge, and buckle down to the job at White Hart Lane, but it did not take long for me to realise that things would not be quite the same at Tottenham as they had been at Chelsea. There was a formality and grandeur at Tottenham that spread right down into the wood-panelled dressing room, which could have been the boardroom at some other clubs.

Bill Nicholson reinforced the feeling of formality, seeming to be a dour, stiff and unbending personality, but his wife 'Darkie', whom we would always see pedalling her bike around Tottenham, doing the shopping, was such a contrast, always laughing and joking, that I eventually realised that there must be another side to Bill. When I got to know him better, I found that Bill was a very warm, but shy man, who used his gruff exterior as self-protection, but in my early days at White Hart Lane, he seemed a forbidding figure.

At the start, friendly faces were in very short supply. On my very first day there, I clashed with Dave Mackay in the gymnasium. Dave had a technique out on the pitch of coming at you very fast and going on the ground, spreading his legs as he came in, so that whichever way you went, he would either get the ball or knock it away somewhere. You could not put it through his legs, because he was on the ground, and you could not put it to either side, because his splayed legs stopped you.

He did not have the same facility in the gym, because he could not go on the floor, so you could either put it through his legs or pull it wide of him early. I did that very successfully the first time that I tried it in the gym, only to be forcibly reminded of the old adage 'You might go past me, the ball might go past me, but you won't both go past me together'. As I tried to go by him, Dave hit me right in the balls with his fist. I folded over in agony and fought to get my breath, but when I had recovered, I thought to myself, I won't make a big deal about it, that could have been an accident.

The next time I got the ball, I slid it past him again as he came in to challenge me, and once more he whacked me in the balls. This time I was sure it was not an accident; I turned round and punched him smack in the face. Unfortunately, I had a ring on my middle finger and it sliced his cheek open and damaged my knuckle. He had a scar on his face for a few days and it was quite a while before I could get the ring off my finger, because the knuckle swelled up so badly.

All the boys jumped in to break us up, but by then honours were about even – he had belted me in the balls, but I had punched him in the face. Things remained a little strained between us for a couple of days, because we were both strong characters and he was obviously determined to sort me out and find out what I was made of, but we went over the road to the pub for a shandy after training one day, had a chat, and were fine from then on.

I had first come up against Dave when I was seventeen. The Tottenham side was the 'Double' team of 1961, full of quality footballers, and playing with a confidence and skill that left every other team trailing in their wake. I had not played many games for Chelsea at that stage, but had been given a lot of publicity, which Dave had obviously noticed. I was warming up near the tunnel, when Tottenham came out. Dave ran out, holding the ball above his head, looked across at me and shouted, 'Oi, Venables!' He tossed the ball over to me and said, 'Have a kick now, 'cos you won't get one once the game's started.' Sure enough, he was right.

That was the sort of bloke he was, with an unshakeable confidence in himself and his team. He was also a superbly talented footballer, far more gifted than many people, who regarded him as simply a destroyer – a Nobby Stiles type of player – would imagine. He was a rough, tough cavalier, of course, but he was never given credit for his skill; Dave could make everything look so simple.

He was phenomenally skilful with a coin, never mind a football. He could toss a coin, catch it on his foot, flick it up and catch it on the back of his neck, then let the coin slide off his neck and catch it on his foot again and walk away. He could also toss the coin high in the air, catch it on his forehead, and then begin twitching his face, until the coin started to slip sideways into the socket of his right eye, and he would suddenly straighten up, with the coin fixed like a monocle in his eye. After a dramatic pause, the coin would drop out of his eye and back on to his foot, and for the grand finale, he would flick it high into the air, letting it spiral down into the breast-pocket of his jacket. Then he would shake his head, as if to say, 'That was so bloody easy,' and walk off.

Dave was also a real larger-than-life character and his duels with Eddie Bailey, who was on the Spurs coaching staff, kept us constantly entertained. Eddie was like Alf Garnett; he had a good sense of humour, but was always moaning, especially at his 'Scottish soldiers' as he called them – Robertson, Gilzean and Mackay.

We often used to train in the gymnasium, which was a bit of a rarity for football clubs in those days. We would line up with a ball at our feet, backs to one wall, facing across the gym to the opposite side, which had different coloured lines, painted at various heights, on the wall. Eddie would shout commands to practise various skills, improvising as he went along: 'I want you to kick the ball against that blue line. When it comes back, bounce it up on your foot, then volley it against the yellow line. As it comes back, thump it up on to your chest, then volley it against the green line. When it comes back, get it up on your head once, then volley it against the white line. When it comes back, kill it stone dead with your foot.' When he had finished, Dave Mackay would say, 'Do you mean like this, Ed?' and proceed to do exactly what Eddie had told us to do, carrying out the skill drill to perfection. We would all stand around and applaud, while Eddie muttered, 'Bloody footballers – they make you sick.'

Eddie would have been equally unimpressed by the display of skills practised by another of Spurs' greats, Cliff Jones, in an away game at Notts Forest. An hour before kick-off, as the ground was just beginning to fill up, there was a display of police dog-handling, with Alsatians going through barrels, jumping through hoops, leaping over barricades and walking planks. The Spurs team were watching and somebody said, 'I wouldn't do what those dogs do, for love or money.'

'I would, I'll do it for a quid from each of you,' said Cliff. Next minute, he was out on the pitch, in his ordinary clothes, and he did the whole dog assault course, wriggling through the barrels, crawling under a sheet of canvas pegged out on the ground and shinning up the barricade, while the Spurs lads cheered him all the way.

There were few cheers for me from the Tottenham fans, however. I had thought that the move to Spurs would be terrific for my career, and might help me to win back my place in the England side, but although Spurs were very successful while I was there, always in the top three, playing in Europe and winning the FA Cup in my first year, I did not play as well as I had done at Chelsea and invariably got some barracking from the Tottenham crowd.

Jimmy Hill, then presenting *The Big Match*, thought that the Spurs fans were being a bit unfair to me and put together a segment on the programme, highlighting two beautiful passes I had put through in a game against Manchester City. The way my luck was running, though, I should have know that something would go wrong. Just as they were about to reach that bit of the programme, *The Big Match* was faded out to show pictures of Concorde taking off on its maiden flight. By the time they returned to *The Big Match*, the segment on my contribution to Spurs was over, unseen by anyone but a handful of technicians.

The fans continued to give me a hard time. I had been bought to replace John White, who had died so tragically, killed by lightning on a golf course, and the fans may have been heckling me just for not being John White, although I was never a similar style of player anyway. In any event, while Spurs fans look back now and think of John as a football genius, at the time he was playing they were not quite so enthusiastic. He regularly used to get the bird from the fans too, for being a bit lightweight and not getting stuck in, something which people have forgotten now, but I never had any doubts about his ability, for he was an exceptional player. When I played against him, he used to run me off my feet.

My biggest mistake at Spurs was in not remaining the same on-field personality and the same type of player that I had been at Chelsea. Docherty had always given me stick for wanting the ball all the time and being too overpowering, but that was the way I was and what got me to Spurs in the first place. I should have stuck with that, but instead, I started thinking too much about my game and worrying about not appearing to be 'the big shot'. I was now playing alongside Alan Mullery, Dave Mackay and Mike England, and I thought, Well, I'll just slot in here and be part of the team.

I was always in the team, so I must have done something right, but at the same time, I did not play to my strengths. That was a big mistake. Whatever happened, whatever personality clashes might have ensued, I should have gone into the team and been myself. I would have been better for it, one way or another. It surprised me that Bill Nicholson never really called me in throughout my three years at Spurs, to say what I was doing wrong; not that I hold it against him, I always got on well with him and have a lot of admiration for him.

If my time at Spurs as a whole was not the happiest part of my playing career, appearing in the 1967 FA Cup final at the end of my first season was certainly one of the highlights. Our opponents, almost inevitably, were Chelsea, in the first-ever all-London final. If I needed any extra motivation apart from facing my old side, Tommy Docherty thoughtfully provided it in a newspaper interview:

I think Terry Venables is a first-class player, he knows the game and he's dedicated to it, BUT I don't think he's as good now as he was when he was playing for Chelsea. At Chelsea he was a recognised star. He was a big fish in a young pool. In fact this was the only trouble I had with Terry. In training he thought he was the boss – I knew I was.

Now he's just another player in a team of stars. He's got people around him who aren't perhaps prepared to run for him like the Chelsea players used to. I don't anticipate too much trouble from Terry Venables in the Cup final, my men know his game too well. At one time I used to think Terry was as good as any inside forward in Europe. I don't think so today.

Like Chelsea, Tottenham had also had the disappointment of losing two previous semi-finals, but we cruised through the semi-final at Hillsborough, with Frank Saul and Jimmy Greaves scoring two cracking goals. Jim had never settled in Italy after being sold by Chelsea to AC Milan, and had been brought back to England by Tottenham, who paid the bizarre price of £99,999 for him. The transfer was actually set in motion in a toilet, not the most obvious place to open negotiations of a footballing nature, but Bill Nicholson bumped into Jim in the gents at a football function, and after learning how eager he was to get back to England, Bill rapidly persuaded the Spurs board to find the cash.

You start playing football as a young boy with a head full of dreams of glory, then one day you find yourself playing in the FA Cup final – the dream come true. Everybody always says that the Cup final is over so fast, that you wish you could go back and do it again, just to savour the atmosphere, but my memories of it are crystal-clear. As we walked up the tunnel, I thought to myself, I must look around and savour every moment of this, because I remembered virtually nothing of my England Schoolboys games at Wembley. I made sure I enjoyed the atmosphere to the full, but as soon as the whistle went, I was so absorbed in the game, that before I knew it, I was back in the dressing room, admiring my winner's medal.

Looking back on the Spurs–Chelsea final now, what stands out was the absolute confidence of Dave Mackay; there was no question in his mind about the result. I walked along Piccadilly with him on the Saturday morning, on the way to buy a new pair of shoes, and he kept saying that we would slaughter them, there was not a chance that we would lose. Nor was he saying it just to give the rest of us confidence, he was genuinely convinced that we would win. As usual, he was right.

The game was not the great showpiece that everyone was hoping for, and the neutrals in the crowd must have found it a bit disappointing, because it was a far-from-dramatic match. Tottenham played so well that the issue was never in doubt. We were winning 2–0 until right at the end, when Bobby Tambling got a headed consolation goal. Like most FA Cup finals, there had been tremendous optimism and anticipation before the event, and like many things, the anticipation was better than the reality. The Tottenham–Chelsea final was a rather tame affair, but it did not make putting one over the man who had sacked me from Chelsea any the less sweet.

I was also the only member of either side who could not lose financially, whatever the result of the game. I do not normally bet at all – on horses, dogs, or anything else – and do not even do the football pools, but two of Tottenham's 'Scottish mafia' – Dave Mackay and Alan Gilzean – would have a bet on anything that moved. They went over to the betting shop in Tottenham High Road after training one December day, before the FA Cup had even started, and I went along with them, for something to do. The FA Cup odds had been published and while Spurs were short odds to win the Cup, Chelsea were listed at 25–1. As I looked at the odds, I thought that it would be just my luck for Chelsea to win the Cup that year, after getting knocked out in the semi-finals for the last two years that I was there. I walked over to the counter and put a £20 bet on them, the first and last time I have ever placed a bet on football in my life.

With both Tottenham and Chelsea reaching the final, I was in financial clover. Spurs were offering a £500 winning bonus, but if Chelsea had beaten us, I would have picked up £500 from the bookies. Financially, that would have been a better result for me, because the winnings would have been tax-free, but I was willing to forgo the extra few quid, for the pleasure of having a Cup-winners' medal. The only reason I feel safe in telling this story even now, is because Tottenham won. If Chelsea had beaten us, I would have sent someone else to pick up the money from the bookies for me and taken the dark secret of my bet on the opposition with me to my grave.

With the job done and the FA Cup won, Dave Mackay went on the booze for three or four days. As soon as he had showered and changed, he was knocking back everything he could lay his hands on and drinking champagne out of beer mugs. He was already half-cut, laughing and singing, before we even got to the official banquet on the Saturday night. As we sat down to eat, one of the club directors, Arthur Richardson, came over to us, proudly bearing a big tray of commemorative medals, but Dave just laughed and knocked them all up in the air. They rolled underneath the table, as Arthur Richardson stood there, rooted to the spot, unable to believe his eyes. We crawled about under the table, trying to retrieve them, while Dave sat there and laughed till he cried.

Whatever we might do to them when drunk, medals were far too precious to throw away or damage. At the end of your career, your medals are the only solid evidence of your time and achievements in the game. Contrary to the popular assumption that players are interested only in money, medals are as cherished by footballers as they are by war heroes, and for similar reasons; they remind you, your family and friends, 'I was there and this is what I did.'

Mum and Dad on their wedding day in 1941

Me, aged five years old, with my Mum and Dad wearing my first cap

Me trying to look dapper at the
local Winding Way Social Club

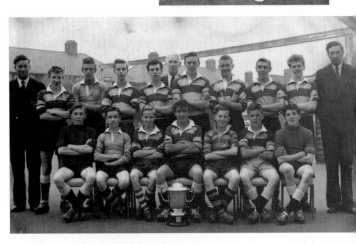

The Dagenham boys ... where are they now? Answers on a postcard please?
Ronnie Hanley is second from the left in the back row, Peter Auger fifth and
Jimmy Hazell seventh. I'm centre, first row

Me as a giant England schoolboy at fifteen in 1958 – why didn't I grow?

At Butlin's, Clacton, July 1959. *Clockwise, from left to right:* Allan Harris, Dennis Butler, Terry More, me and Ronnie Hanley

A pre-show warm-up before going on to do a miming act at Butlin's

Singing for England with Joe Loss at the Hammersmith Palais, 1959

Two Dagenham boys, two England managers: Sir Alf Ramsey and me

Me in my young international days riding an Austrian tackle

*From left to right:* Tommy Doc, Eddie McCreadie, me, Johnny Hollins and Ken Shellito after an important FA Cup draw: Johnny wants to take five while the rest of us are happy with two!

Me with George Graham (left) in our Chelsea days as teenagers

Over his dead body. The first leg of Chelsea v Roma at Stamford Bridge, 1965. We won 4–1 and I surpassed myself by scoring three of them

A grand old man shows the kids how to do it. Stoke City's Stanley Matthews dances past Ron 'Chopper' Harris as I look on

The snow must go on. The Doc and me in sombre mood after a game is cancelled

Football is my living because I had the ability and the determination to be a footballer – but the ambition was to play the game, not to make money from it; that came afterwards. Of course, like everyone else, footballers are out for as much money as we can make, and we have to be quick about it. In most jobs, a man is just beginning to earn good wages at the age of thirty, but that is when our earning days are coming to an end. Money is a fact of life, the stuff they give us for being good at the game, but a medal is different.

When we finish playing, we think back over all the games and all the seasons and ask ourselves, 'What was it all about? Did it mean anything at all?' One pound coin is exactly the same as another, but you cannot find a medal in the gutter. Two years after we have given up playing, we are still young men, but the fans are already cheering other stars. A medal is proof that they once cheered for you and that you counted for something, once. It says, 'I was there and I was one of the best.'

When we had retrieved our medals from under the table where Dave Mackay had knocked them, Bill Nicholson gave a serious speech about winning the Cup final, saying that we had not played that well, putting us all down, which was not necessarily what we wanted to hear at that particular moment, and Dave shouted out, 'Sit down, Bill, you're pissed!' It was typical of Bill, that he was unable to relax and unwind, even on the night of the Cup final, but was already thinking and worrying about the next season instead. I spoke to him later that evening and asked him if he was pleased, but all he could say was that he thought we should go into the transfer market before the next season. Bill's enjoyment was always the football, and nothing but the football, unlike Dave Mackay, who was enjoying himself hugely. By eight o'clock he had shot his bolt, however, and had to be carried off to bed, before the night had really started.

Even without Dave's drunken pranks, the rest of the evening was not all sweetness and light, for there was a furious row with the directors over the players' preference for an unofficial Cup celebration at the Hilton, hosted by a supporter, Maurice Keston, to the club's official banquet at the Savoy, which many of us found a bit too stuffy for our tastes. Maurice Keston was a big supporter of Spurs, but was not particularly liked by the directors, who felt he was a hanger-on, attaching himself to the players. I thought that, if anything, it was more the other way round, with some of the players hanging on him, exploiting his good nature and generosity.

There may be hangers-on who do it for the wrong reasons, getting close to players in order to take advantage of them, but there are also those who do it for no other reason than their enjoyment of the sport. Nor is it as easy as some people think, to ingratiate yourself with footballers. The game is a closed world and outsiders are viewed with suspicion and not accepted easily. Maurice Keston was accepted, mainly because there was never any harm in him at all, he was very kind-hearted, and the one thing he loved above all others was Tottenham Hotspur.

He loved the club so much that he even changed his religion for Spurs. Tottenham were playing a friendly in Egypt in 1963, a time when no Jewish people were allowed into the country. In order to see the game, Maurice put 'Christian' rather than 'Jewish' in the space for religion on his visa form and was able to get into Egypt for the match. He also laid on a fleet of taxis so that the players could see the Pyramids; if that is being a hanger-on, most players would like to see more of them.

If footballers were in a normal job, so-called 'hangers-on' would simply be regarded as friends. As you grow older, you have to decide who your friends really are, but you often do not discover that until you have been through a rocky patch in your life. Maurice Keston has more than passed the test of time, as far as I am concerned.

Footballers also frequently hear the suggestion that they have turned their backs on their 'real friends' after becoming successful. People say accusingly, 'You've changed,' as if it was a crime. Of course, I have changed, as has everybody; I would hate to think I was still the same person I was at ten years old. That does not mean that I have turned my back on people since I have got a bit of fame and fortune, however. I have made plenty of new friends, but I still have my old mates – Billy Atkins, Peter Auger and Ronnie Hanley – from the days when I was growing up in Dagenham, as well. They are still good friends today.

As well as my old friends from Dagenham and the new friends I had made through football – or 'hangers-on' as the Spurs directors would probably have called them – I also used to enjoy the company of the journalists who covered the game. I would often go out for an evening with people like Ken Jones, Brian James and Peter Lorenzo. To an extent, I still do socialise with journalists, but there is much more nervousness now than there used to be, a feeling that whatever you say, whatever the circumstances, will go in the paper the next day.

When I was out with Ken, Brian and Peter, I could relax with them, without worrying that any off-the-cuff remark I might make would be taken down and used in evidence against me in the papers the following day. Unlike some of their counterparts now, those guys got by on the quality of their writing, and did not have to sell newspapers on crap and side-issues; not that I blame the guys today, because the pressure they are under nowadays is enormous . . . almost as much as football managers.

That is still the case in Spain, to some extent. The Spanish press run acres of stories and there is never any shortage of copy, because one or two Barcelona directors, for example, would give stories to their favourite journalists. They would soften them up by feeding them bits of information, in the hope of stopping the press from writing about them and slaughtering them, at some stage. Over there, it is a simple system. If the team is winning, you are the best, and if it is losing, you are the worst. That is how you are judged. While that is also true in Britain, the journalists who cover football in Barcelona are not interested in your private life or outside activities.

Things are very different here, but in their defence, journalists are under intense pressure from their editors to meet a deadline or beat their rivals, and inaccuracies do occur. That is understandable, but I have less sympathy for journalists who have already made up their minds before a ball has been kicked. They are supposed to be unbiased, and cannot do a good job if they are carting barrow-loads of prejudice around with them. There is no value in having a wide vocabulary or in being an excellent writer, if you merely use your skills to demonstrate your prejudices.

My one-time co-writer Gordon Williams used to tell me that he believed the sporting press did not actually like the athletes they wrote about. 'There they are, writing about people they think don't have the intelligence to string two words together,' said Gordon, 'and it offends them. They hate even more the fact that the athletes have achieved the success in their sport, that deep down, the journalists believe they could also have had if circumstances had been different. Why did Norman Mailer want to fight in the streets? Because he wasn't Mohammed Ali, he just wrote about him. That made him feel inferior and he had to prove that he could also be a fighter if he wanted to be.' It was an interesting point, but whether it is right or wrong, I could not say.

Football managers must have an attitude towards the press, however. It is no good saying that they are all bad and we are all good. There are good and bad journalists just as there are good and bad footballers and managers. Some journalists are remarkably ignorant about the game, but others are knowledgeable, without necessarily having all the information at their fingertips and if you have not got the information, you cannot always make the right judgement.

That applies to supporters just as much as journalists, as a QPR fan was to discover, when he sent me a letter, which read:

Dear Mr Venables,

Why is Tony Currie not playing in the team? You must be one of the biggest idiots I've ever come across. Tony Currie is an international, he can play short passes and never give the ball away, he can hit long passes forty yards on the dot, and he is so strong that you can't get the ball off him.

All these things were absolutely correct. He ended by saying:

Come on, you can't be as big a fool as you look. I just want to know one thing. Tell me, tell me, tell me, why isn't he in the team?

I wrote back, a very short letter, saying:

Dear Sir,
He's got a broken leg.
Yours faithfully,
Terry Venables

Journalists like Ken Jones and Brian James used to complain that managers then were very dour, never showing any humour. I vowed to myself that if I ever became a manager, I would show that side of myself to the press, but when I did, I was immediately accused of being glib. Sometimes you just cannot win with the media, which is a shame, because although there are inevitably going to be things that you want to play down and they want to play up, we still do have a lot in common.

I did not seem to have too much in common with the Spurs

fans, however, and the FA Cup success did not make any difference to their attitude towards me. From the first game of the next season to the last, they were back on my case in a big way. Bill Nicholson was very supportive, but it often got me down, and after three years at Tottenham, I had had enough. During the summer of 1969, Queens Park Rangers made an approach for me, and Spurs agreed a fee of £70,000, only £10,000 less than they had paid for me three years before.

Even though it meant dropping down to the Second Division, I jumped at the chance to get away, because it did not look like I would ever win over the crowd at Spurs. It proved to be one of the best decisions I ever made. I had one of my finest spells as a player at QPR, and it was also one of the most satisfying times of my career as well.

The move to QPR was the beginning of a long relationship with Rangers' ebullient chairman, Jim Gregory. I had first met him during the previous season, when QPR played Tottenham. I injured Bobby Keetch during the game and he was carried off. I went into their dressing room afterwards to apologise and Jim Gregory turned to the manager, Les Allen, and said, 'He's got some front, we'll have to sign him!' A few months later, he did.

There was a much warmer and more homely atmosphere at QPR than there had been for me at Spurs. The dressing rooms were especially homely – if you lived in a very small house. The rooms were no bigger than fifteen foot by twenty, and when empty it was hard to imagine how the players, coaches, physio and kit man could all fit in there together.

I also particularly liked Jim Gregory, and struck up a rapport with him straight away. Jim liked having the players up to the boardroom after a game, which was far from normal behaviour for a chairman, but he liked the banter with the players. He was also game for anything. One night at Sunderland, he challenged one of the players to a 100-yard race, even though it was freezing cold, one o'clock in the morning and Jim must have been about forty-eight at the time. Even more surprisingly, he won. He earned himself a bit of a reputation as a man who was hard on his managers, but he was a good supporter of the players, and a good judge, who really knew his football. When I was manager at QPR later on, I really looked forward to going up to his office once or twice a week, just to talk about football for hours.

Les Allen and I also had plenty in common. He came from the same street in Dagenham as me, Bonham Road, and I had always liked him. He had trained as an architect and played a lot of different sports, but was not 'spotted' by a football club until relatively late. He went to Chelsea, and did reasonably well there, but was then transferred to Tottenham, becoming a key member of the Double-winning team. Bill Nicholson was talented at finding players like Les and Bobby Smith, who were good, but by no means outstanding, at other clubs, but became very special players at Spurs, under Bill's guidance.

Things did not go particularly well for Les as a manager, however, and he was eventually sacked by Jim Gregory, adding to his reputation for a fast turnover of managers. Les felt that he was unfortunate to get the sack, and became disenchanted with football as a result, although the success of his sons later rekindled his enthusiasm.

When Les was sacked, Gordon Jago took over. Gordon was very much an FA type of coach – a gentleman amateur rather than a hard-nosed professional. He quickly earned the nickname 'High Heels' from the players, because he had an odd running style, exactly like a woman in high heels sprinting for a bus. He was more of a schoolteacher than the 'mud and bullets' type, but he was quite willing for the players to express themselves.

His own attempts at self-expression were not always well

received. Poor Gordon kept trying to make long, Churchillian speeches calling for blood, sweat and tears, and inspiring us to greater efforts, but just as he was about to reach the climax, a wisecrack from one of the players would reduce us to fits of laughter and leave him completely deflated.

At his first team meeting, he started to explain his plans, and just talked, and talked, and talked. We soon worked out how to cut him short. At that time Rodney Marsh was both the captain and the main character of the team. Gordon kept droning on and on, and it was just getting to the stage where we were falling asleep from boredom, when Rodney leapt to his feet and said, 'On behalf of all the players, Boss, I want you to know that we're all behind you, forty per cent.'

When Gordon came into the dressing room the next day with our mail, Rodney called out, 'Good morning, Postie, did you knock on the door?'

Gordon said, 'No, I'm the manager with the mail.'

'Well, you better start as you mean to go on. If you want to come into our dressing room, you have to knock on the door!'

Gordon needed some change one morning and I lent him £5, which must have slipped his mind later on, as I did not get it back. I bided my time and during one of his long speeches at training, he started going on about not being happy until we had reached the very top and every one of us had a Rolls Royce in the car park. I chirped up, 'Never mind the Rolls Royce, any chance of that fiver back?'

Gordon was a nice sort of bloke and it was not his way to answer back, but he paid for it sometimes, with Rodney giving him a really hard time. His revenge did not come until many years later, when Rodney was playing for the Tampa Bay Rowdies in the United States, with Gordon as their coach.

It was the last game of the season, the Championship decider, in front of 40,000 fans, and it was also Rodney's last game

before retiring. Tampa were losing 2–1, and with thirteen minutes
to go, Gordon called across to Ted Buxton, who was working
as his assistant, 'Get Rodney off.'

'You've got to be joking,' said Ted. 'It's Rodney's last
match.'

'I know that, but he has got to come off.'

Ted signalled to Rodney, showing him two fingers to signify
two minutes. Rodney scowled at him and responded by getting
the ball and dribbling past five defenders before unleashing a
shot that the goalkeeper just managed to save.

Ted looked enquiringly at Gordon, but there was no change
of plan. Ted held Rodney's number up, and he came off the
field with eleven minutes left in the last match of his career. He
tore his shirt off and threw it on the ground in disgust. 'I'm
sorry, Rodney,' said Gordon, 'but I want to inject some pace up
front.'

'Bloody hell, Gordon. I've been playing in your teams for
seven years and you wait until eleven minutes from the end of
my career to tell me I'm too slow.'

Gordon may not have improved Rodney's speed much, but
he did wonders for the rest of us. He brought Ron Jones to the
club to work on our fitness. Ron had been a sprinter and
Olympic athletics captain, and introduced us to the delights of
220-yard 'power running'. Ron said that, for athletes, a 440 was
the hardest run, because it was a sprint all the way round, but
footballers, who develop a different sort of fitness, could not
maintain a sprint for that distance, and he felt that the hardest
run for us would be a 220-yard sprint. He was absolutely right,
it made 'doggies' seem like 'walkies'.

We ran a series of 220s flat out against the clock, in rapid
succession. I would manage, say, twenty-three seconds for the
first one, twenty-five for the second, then twenty-eight for the
third, becoming slower and more exhausted all the time. It was
so demanding that we would be physically sick, but we found

we benefited greatly from it, and it made a football match seem like an afternoon stroll.

I nicked the idea and used it at Crystal Palace, QPR, Barcelona and Tottenham and it always produced results. The running of Vinnie Samways and Justin Edinburgh developed tremendously at Tottenham, for example. They hated the training and it was really horrible for them, but they were much more powerful over the full ninety minutes of a game as a result, while Neil Ruddock, who was not a particularly good runner before, was transformed by it.

Nevertheless, I was a bit deflated when I spoke to Fatima Whitbread one day. I proudly told her that we had built our footballers up to four 220s against the clock in succession, but she laughed and said top athletes were doing ten or twelve. That does not necessarily mean that athletes are fitter all round than footballers, for every sport demands a different blend of speed, power and endurance. I can remember the distance runner Gordon Pirie playing a charity football game and being shattered after five minutes, because football made unusual demands on him – short runs, falling over, jumping, taking a physical challenge, getting knocked over, sprinting, checking and turning – another type of stamina and fitness.

While Gordon Jago was often the butt of our wisecracks, luckily he never really took offence, whatever the provocation, which was just as well. His life would have been a misery, for there was certainly no shortage of characters in the side, with Rodney, Gerry Francis, Don Shanks, Frank McLintock, Terry Mancini and the inimitable Stanley Bowles.

Some of the 'journeyman' professionals at QPR did not always take kindly to the way the 'stars' treated them. Rodney Marsh was often inclined to rub their faces in it, taking the mickey out of the other players, saying, 'I'm the one that earns your money'. He was winding them up on purpose, of course, but just the same, they used to be fuming about it, at least until Rodney produced a bit of skill to win a game.

Stan Bowles was game for a wind-up as well and formed a double act with Don Shanks, which was in a different class altogether. They never had any money – the famous saying about Stan was absolutely true: 'He could pass a football, but he could never pass a bookie's' – and they always used to be borrowing money or wanting an advance from the club secretary, Ron Phillips. Ron was such a lovely guy that he could never say no, and if they managed to get into his office, that was it. They would put the squeeze on him, until he gave in and handed over some money. Jim Gregory would then give him a bollocking for being so soft – he could not win.

As a result, every time Stan and Don came near Ron's office, his secretary would give him a secret knock to let him know that they were coming, and he would then hide, or lock his door and pretend to be out. One day, just like Major Major in *Catch 22*, he actually climbed through the window and ran down the road to get away from them.

Stan and Don also did pretty well out of a slick operator called 'The Colonel', who was a runner at the horse-track, putting on bets for the top punters, like Arab sheikhs. The Colonel, Stan and Don used to play cards and talk about everything except football on a Friday night, but Stan and Don used to lose at cards every single time. They could not work out why, but were convinced that the Colonel was up to something, and came up with a scheme to get their own back. If Don needed a five to make up a winning hand, he would say, 'Frank McLintock must be one of the best centre-halves in the game,' and since Frank was always number 5, Stan knew that Don wanted him to discard a five if he had one. Stan would then say something like, 'Yes, but Ian Gillard [number 3] was a good left-back,' and Don would chuck in a three.

The Colonel would get caught up in the conversation and

start enthusing about Frank McLintock and other centre-halves he admired, much to the amusement of the other two, who would have been willing to describe Norman Wisdom as a good centre-half, if it helped to beat the Colonel at cards. They ended up taking him to the cleaners, while he sat there losing all his money, but unable to understand why.

Stan showed some similar skills when playing his first international for England in Rome. It was a highly publicised game and an agent approached him before the match, suggesting that if he wore Puma boots, he would be paid £250. Stan agreed like a shot, and was in the dressing room, lacing up his boots, when another player told him, 'You shouldn't have got those boots, Adidas pay much more.' Next minute, Stan was sprinting out of the dressing room in search of the Adidas agent. When he found him, he signed up with Adidas as well. Having reached agreement with two different firms, there was only one thing for Stan to do; in a truly British compromise, he ended up making his international début wearing one Puma boot and one Adidas.

As well as being quite a character, Stan was quite a footballer too. He and Gerry Francis were an unbelievable combination. People say players take a long time to settle into a team, but Gerry and Stan had an incredible rapport, from the first six-a-side game on the very first day. They were so good at playing one-twos, it was as if they had a radar. It was uncanny, they just connected somehow. Even though Gerry did become captain of England, neither of them was really given the recognition that their talent merited – except at Loftus Road, where they were idolised.

Not all the players were larger than life, but the quiet, stay-at-home types used to get a pretty hard time from the others. Ian Watson was a really nice fellow, but kept himself to himself, and did not enjoy being 'in with the gang'. He much preferred being at home to hitting the town with the lads, and whenever we had anything lined up, Ian would suddenly remember a prior engagement. On one particular night, Rodney Marsh was organising a big night-out for the whole team. He went round taking the names of the people who were going, but when he asked Ian Watson, true to form, Ian said, 'I'm sorry, Rodney, I can't make it that night.'

Rodney laughed and said, 'Let me tell you which night it is first.'

Although there were some outrageous characters in the team and we were always laughing and joking, we were also very serious about wanting to do well. I was playing some of the best football of my career and we started winning, and doing so in style. The team began to get the reputation of being a very entertaining side to watch and crowds at Loftus Road grew as we climbed the table, heading for Division One.

Although I was enjoying my football at QPR, I also had an occasional reminder that, in a young man's game, I was no longer quite as young as I used to be. We played Chelsea in an FA Cup quarter-final, and they had a strong side, with some good youngsters coming through, like Alan Hudson, Peter Osgood and David Webb. I was marking Hudson, who was then only eighteen. I used to coach him on Tuesdays and Thursdays at Chelsea, when I was a player there and he was about eleven years old, but this was no time to be nice to a former pupil. I thought to myself, It's the FA Cup, I'll 'bosh' him early doors.

Unfortunately, when the game started, it turned out that I could not get near enough to bosh him. He never stopped running and passing, had me all over the place and I could not get anywhere near him or the ball. When I finally did arrive in time to challenge him, he was a lot stronger than he looked – it was like hitting a barn door. He gave me 'a right seeing-to' that day, and I weighed up my chances against eighteen-year-old footballers a bit more carefully after that.

Off the field, I had taken on another new role. I had been elected vice-chairman of the Professional Footballers' Association – the PFA. My insatiable curiosity about the game extended to the way it was run and I felt that the experience I gained on the PFA would stand me in good stead for a managerial career when my playing days were over. I became something of a 'Rumpole of the Bush' at the PFA, representing my fellow-players in disputes and disciplinary hearings with the FA. In those days you could cross-examine the referee and the linesmen, if there was a disagreement about a decision they had made, and you could sometimes get it reversed.

Players often found the atmosphere of the marbled halls of Lancaster Gate rather intimidating, let alone the hostile questioning of indomitable characters like Burnley chairman Bob Lord. I found it quite nerve-wracking myself, because I was still just a twenty-seven-year-old player, but there was great satisfaction in winning a case and seeing a player who might have been banned for several weeks, if the verdict had gone the other way, turning out for his team on the following Saturday.

I had just fought a successful case for Mike Summerbee, who was at Manchester City at the time, when Dave Thomas, who had joined QPR from Burnley, approached me about a problem. Burnley had a bonus system, whereby if they won promotion, the players would receive, say, £100 for every game they had played that season.

When Dave came to QPR, he had already played twelve games for Burnley, who were eventually promoted to the First Division, along with QPR, at the end of the 1972–73 season. Dave got his bonus from QPR, but was still owed £1200 by Burnley. Bob Lord disagreed, saying, 'He's left the club, so the contract is void,' but on my reading of the contract, if Dave had played the games, he was entitled to the bonus, wherever he moved afterwards.

Dave asked me to represent him at the FA hearing, and when we got to Lancaster Gate, across the table was the well-respected – and feared – Bob Lord, the tyrant of Burnley. Bob was a throwback to an earlier age, a Victorian businessman who thought that players should know their place and take what they were given, without argument. He looked like a bulldog chewing a wasp, with a haircut from hell, two cauliflower ears, a complexion like raw meat, and eyes that stared right through you.

He was definitely trying to frighten me before we started, and did a pretty good job, but I stood my ground during the hearing and did not let him intimidate me. Bob Lord stated Burnley's case forcibly to the FA panel hearing the case, but I was equally forceful in stating Dave's claim to the money. Dave kept pulling at my sleeve and whispering, 'You can't talk to him like that, it's Bob Lord!' and I kept saying, 'I know it is. It's all right.' In the end we won the case. Burnley immediately appealed, but we won again. They appealed once more, and yet again the verdict went our way. Bob Lord was forced to concede defeat, not something he was fond of doing. As we left, he gave Dave a look that probably still has him waking, screaming in the night, but Dave had his £1200 bonus. Dave waited till we got outside and round the corner, safely out of Bob's way, before jumping up and down, punching the air and shouting, 'Yes! We won!'

Dave wanted to take my wife and me out to dinner to thank me for my help, and took us to The Sportsman, a casino with a restaurant at the back, which was used by a lot of footballers and other sportsmen. The choice of venue must have been for our benefit, for Dave was not much of a party animal. He did not really approve of drinking and gambling, and rarely went out. His wife was quite a lively person, who liked to go out and enjoy herself, but Dave was a fanatical gardener, whose idea of a pleasant evening was to do some gardening and then watch TV.

By ten o'clock, Dave was ready to go home, just as his wife was warming up. She did not want to leave and had a row with him about it, while Christine and I took a sudden interest in the flower arrangements, but he insisted that they had to go. I walked with them through the casino towards the exit, but just as we were about to go through the door, he looked over my shoulder, stopped dead and said, 'It's him, it's him.'

With all the enthusiasm that he was showing, I thought, that at the least, Frank Sinatra must have walked into the room, but when I looked round, there was Dave's idol, the television gardener Percy Thrower. I had never met Percy, but I offered to introduce Dave anyway and was leading him over, when Dave stopped dead and said he was going home and did not want to meet him after all. He had seen that Percy was playing blackjack and drinking a large Scotch, and Dave was so strait-laced that he could not bear to see his idol's feet of clay. He probably went straight home and burned all his gardening books.

My other reward from Dave was rather less welcome. I was playing in a six-a-side when Dave, who was very muscular and strong, hit me with his elbow and broke my cheekbone. It felt like I had been hit with a sledgehammer and I actually did see stars, which I had always thought was a myth until then. It was a complete accident and he was really upset about it, though not quite as upset as me.

Luckily the injury did not keep me out for too long and I was back in the Rangers side as we clinched promotion to Division One. Before our next home game, we all lined up in front of the crowd to celebrate promotion. Terry Mancini, nicknamed 'Henry' in honour of the composer, was as bald as a coot, but had always said that if we went up, he would take the field wearing a wig. As we lined up to wave to the crowd, there was Henry with a luxuriant thatch of black hair. The fans always said afterwards that something was missing, but no one could work out what it was until, just before kick-off, Henry suddenly doffed his 'syrup', to reveal his familiar bald dome.

Henry was another major character in the Rangers side. At one point, we realised that someone from QPR kept leaking stories about the club to the *Daily Mirror*. We suspected that the culprit might be Henry, who would not have done it for any nasty motive, but simply to do a friend a favour. To test the theory, we decided to play a trick on him. Henry always got to training a little later than us, and as he came into the dressing room one day, I said to Mike Ferguson, 'Well, Fergy, all the best, son. I hope it goes well for you at Oxford.'

Mike played along with me, and when Terry wanted to know what was going on, I said, 'Didn't you hear? Fergy's going to Oxford for £60,000. He heard last night and he's a bit sick about it.' Sure enough, the following day, the story was all over the back page of the *Mirror*. When Henry came in for training, we were killing ourselves laughing and told him that Fergy was not going anywhere. He called us a few names, but saw the funny side of it in the end.

He also called Jim Gregory a few choice names after a very public row with him. As a result, Henry was put on the transfer list, but he was determined to have the last word. Shortly before kick-off in a home game, he ran across to the directors' box, turned his back, pulled his shorts down and waggled his arse in Jim's direction. After that, relations between them deteriorated still further and his transfer to Arsenal was just about inevitable.

Frank McLintock had made the journey in the opposite direction after falling out with Arsenal coach Steve Burkenshaw. When our coach, Bobby Campbell, left to go to the Arsenal, everyone was speculating about who would be appointed to replace him. We were told to go to the tea-bar, and wait for the new coach to show up. While we waited, Frank was telling me his likes and dislikes in coaches.

Over Frank's shoulder, I saw the door open as he was saying, 'As long as we don't get Steve Burkenshaw, we'll be all right. I've just had him for a few years at Arsenal and he drove me round the bend.' I said, 'In that case, I think I've got some bad news for you, Frank. Steve Burkenshaw has just walked through the door.'

He thought I was joking, and started to do his impersonation of Steve. When he finally looked round, wondering why everyone else had fallen silent, he nearly collapsed, because sure enough, our new coach, Steve Burkenshaw, was standing right behind him.

After the order and discipline of Highbury, Steve must have wondered what kind of place he had wandered into at Loftus Road. We put plenty of energy into our football, but we still had plenty left for incessant pranks and practical jokes as well. Tony Hazell was frequently the butt of my jokes. He was a good footballer and a great character to have around, but he was also a very argumentative guy, and would not give way, whatever the evidence against him, though to be fair, he was often right.

He had a card trick in which he claimed that he could tell which card you had touched just by the 'vibrations' in it. He would lay out the cards and then turn his back, while someone touched one of them. As he rubbed the cards, to 'feel the vibration', I would cough to indicate the one and he would move on a few cards and then go back to it and do a little act, before picking out the right card. He thought the other lads did not know that I was in cahoots with him, but in fact I had told them as soon as we started the trick. They all went along with it, however, pretending that they thought he was looking to see which one to pick, and piling loads of cushions on his head, so that he could not see. He would emerge, red-faced, with his hair all over the place and do the trick right, because I was still coughing.

The next refinement was to let him go up and down the cards, trying to get 'the vibration', while I sat there, silent as the grave. He kept looking at me, in panic, waiting for me to cough. Eventually he just touched any card at random, but everyone cheered and said he had found the right one again. He was ecstatic, thinking that he had got it right without any help from me. When the lads had gone, he asked what had happened, and I told him that they had suspected something and were watching me, but he could obviously now do it without my help. He did the trick another five or six times and got it right every time, with no help from me, because every time he touched a card, all the lads would cheer and congratulate him. By now he was actually convinced that he had some mystical talent and really could do the trick. When we finally let him in on the secret, he did not know which one of us he wanted to kill first, but I was probably the favourite.

Tony was quite an aggressive character out on the pitch, and had a series of fights in training, without ever landing a punch, though he got knocked out three times himself. One Christmas, I and the whole of the QPR squad appeared on *The Russell Harty Show*, celebrating twenty-five years of Independent Television. I had featured on the credits of *The Big Match* when it first started. After being booked by the referee in a game at Derby County, I turned to the crowd, shrugged my shoulders, rolled my eyes and waggled my eyebrows up and down. The eyebrow-waggling was captured on camera and became part of *The Big Match* credits every week. They showed the old footage on the programme and Harty got me on to mime to, 'What do you want to make those eyes at me for?', a record I had cut a few years before. I was backed by all the players and their wives, sitting in the studio, wearing blue and white hooped QPR scarves.

I sang the song, quite oblivious of any trouble behind me and was back in the hospitality area, having a drink, when one of the programme staff told me that there had been a fight between some of the players. Ian Evans had taken the mickey out of Tony Hazell, right in front of his wife. Never one to hesitate, Tony leaned across Ian's wife and boshed him right on the chin. Next minute it was all on, with footballers grappling with each other, while the wives, done up to the nines, sat there pleading with them to stop. It was all captured on camera, but luckily they did not show it on TV at the time, otherwise the entire QPR playing-staff would have been facing an FA disrepute charge.

Tony also became involved in a punch-up with Mark Lazarus, who was just as stubborn as he was, after Tony told him that he would never play for England because he was Jewish. Tony said it as a joke, but Mark boshed him right on the chin and knocked him to the ground. 'That will teach you a lesson,' said Mark. Tony got up, dusted himself down and said, 'No it won't. You still won't get in, because you're still Jewish,' so Mark knocked him down again. If they had not pulled the two of them apart, they would probably have been scrapping now, because Tony insisted on having the last word and Mark was equally insistent about having the last punch.

QPR did well in our first season back in Division One, 1973–74, finishing high enough to qualify for Europe the following season, though I was not destined to take part in that campaign. As well as captaining the side, I had also been contributing to the coaching at Loftus Road and in many ways I was already a player-coach, but my first formal coaching appointment did not come until after my transfer from QPR to Crystal Palace. That move came as a complete surprise to me. It was September 1974, and the new season had only just started, when Jim Gregory called me into his office and told me that he had negotiated a deal with Crystal Palace, in which Don Rogers would be coming to QPR, in exchange for Ian Evans and me.

I was upset, both about the decision itself and the fact that Gordon Jago had said nothing to me about it. Although I was thirty-one by then, if the legs had lost a little of their speed, I felt that my experience more than compensated for that, a feeling shared by my fellow-players, who were as baffled as me by the suddenness of the move.

We were having a bad run, and perhaps Jago thought that a change was necessary, with me nearing the end of my career. Other people felt that I was sold because I had a very strong personality. Although we did get on quite well and I used to take some training sessions for him, we felt very differently about football.

Whatever the reasons, at the third attempt, Malcolm Allison was at last able to persuade me to sign for him. It was the final move of my playing career and it turned out to be the shortest. There was one irony for Rangers. One of my fitness problems was arthritis of the ankle, which did not hamper me in matches, but did require a lengthy warm-up before each training session and game. If I tried to run from cold I would be in agony, but if I went out half an hour before the other players and began walking, then jogging and then running, by the time the rest of them came out, I could run flat out and the pain had disappeared . . . until the next morning. Although it was Gordon Jago's wish to sell me, Jim Gregory did the deal with Malcolm, and if Jim thought that he had got rid of a potential 'crock', he must have been chastened to discover after the transfer that Don Rogers had arthritis too, in his knee . . .

As well as two players, Malcolm also netted £20,000 in cash, which was not a bad deal. Typically, I had not even been there a week when Jim Gregory had second thoughts. After selling me on Thursday, Jim rang Malcolm at eight o'clock on Sunday morning, having sacked Jago in the meantime, saying he wanted to buy me back, to make me manager.

Malcolm cheekily replied, 'It'll cost you another £10,000.'

Jim went berserk at the idea, but Malcolm offered to drive me over to see him for a chat. By the time we got there, even more typically, Jim had changed his mind yet again. I had already been a professional footballer for fifteen years, five of them at QPR, but when I sat down with him, Jim told me, 'You don't have enough experience, I don't want you.' I went back outside and relayed the conversation to Malcolm, who told me not to worry, adding, 'He'll have to pay £100,000 for you next time.' Sure enough, he did, a few years later, when he brought me back from Palace to be manager of QPR.

# CHAPTER FOUR

# *From Player to Coach: Crystal Palace*

## 1974–80

IF I WAS DISAPPOINTED to be leaving Loftus Road for a Third Division club, I was delighted to be linking up with Malcolm at last. We had kept in touch, ever since I went training at West Ham as a fourteen-year-old. After he finished playing football, Malcolm became a professional gambler for a while and then bought a little club in London, the A & R, where a few of the other Chelsea players and I used to spend some time. Jimmy Greaves actually signed the contract to go to Milan there.

Malcolm and I stayed friends all the way through his coaching career and I always valued his views, on football and everything else. He was the first person to see the football novel that I wrote with Gordon Williams, for example, when I asked him to give me his opinion.

Writing novels is only one of many alternative careers that I have taken a sideways look at along the way, with varying degrees of success. My first 'day-job', as an attendant at Barking Baths, earned the money to buy my first car, a green Hillman. It was brand-new when I bought it, but was a pretty ill-fated car; one theft and three crashes later, I sold it. The crashes were partly a result of the speed at which I drove, and though the crashes are less frequent these days, the speed has not dropped very much.

I am a quick driver, to say the least, which may explain why my friends prefer to give me a lift in their cars, rather than accept a lift in mine. If they do travel with me, they usually arrive at the far end with their knuckles white from hanging on to the dashboard and with cramp in their legs from pushing on an imaginary brake pedal all the way.

The state of my car interiors – not very well organised, rather untidy and jammed to capacity – reflects the state of my mind to some extent. I do have a good memory, but I am also a bit absent-minded. When I was a kid my Mum used to pin a ten-bob note to the inside of my jacket, because I would often wander out of the house to go training, without taking any money with me. I always seem to be under such time-pressure these days, that I tend to be already thinking about the next thing before I have finished tidying up the one before, and the minor details can get forgotten. My office desk and my car reveal that aspect of my personality. Each of my cars is immaculately clean only twice in its life – the day I buy it and the day I sell it – and I am sometimes knee-deep in bits of paper with messages and telephone numbers scrawled on them.

I did not seem to be very lucky with my cars in the early days. After the Hillman, I bought a blue Ford Consul, which was my pride and joy. I used to park it at Barking Station and catch the tube to Fulham Broadway, the nearest station to Stamford Bridge. After training, I would travel back to Barking with Ken Shellito, who lived three or four stops further down the line at Elm Park.

I was always playing jokes on Ken, who was easily embarrassed and would blush crimson at the slightest provocation. In the rush hour, when the train was packed, my favourite prank was to throw my arms around him and hug and kiss him, just as we got to Barking. I would get off the train, but Ken had to go another few stops with everyone staring at him. In those days gay people were not as visible as they are now, and he would have to sit there, writhing with embarrassment, while the ranks of shocked commuters stared at him in disgust. In the end he would get off the train with me at Barking and wait for the next one, rather than endure the glares of his fellow-passengers all the way to Elm Park.

I had to learn to endure a few glares myself as I wanted to go into football management if I could, and had already started an FA coaching course, but I was also well aware of how few actually make it. If, in my old teacher's words, only one in a million star-struck schoolboys gets to be a professional foot-baller, only one in a hundred footballers gets the chance to become a professional coach, and only one in a hundred of those goes on to be a successful manager.

I was determined to ensure that I had an alternative career to fall back on and tried several to see if they would work. Some people said that I was in danger of falling between different stools, which was a valid criticism, but football would not go on for ever and I was looking ahead. I knew too many footballers who had put their life-savings into busi-nesses, only to be stung, losing everything. I was prepared to give plenty of things a go, and if the down side of them was that I risked losing three or four hundred quid, that was a price I was perfectly happy to pay. I am sometimes accused of having a butterfly mind and to some extent that may be right, but the only way to find out if things are right for you is to try them. I have learned from my mistakes, and I would rather die ruing the things that I did, than the things that I did not do.

I was always interested in business and had formed myself into a limited company when I was eighteen, the first footballer to do so, which attracted a certain amount of notoriety at the time, of the 'Just who the hell does this Terry Venables think he is?' variety. The idea was recommended to me by an eager accountant, who had noticed that a number of motor-racing drivers had done the same thing, and thought that it might have tax advantages for me too. My earnings were not so stratospheric that it made a huge difference at the time, but later on, when I began doing endorsements for football boots and a number of other products, it proved valuable.

One of my early business ventures was in partnership with my Chelsea team-mates George Graham and Ron Harris, and football writer, Ken Jones. We set up a tailoring business in Old Compton Street, Soho, hoping to capitalise on the number of showbusiness people who came to Chelsea games, but while they loved watching Chelsea and loved the clothes we sold, unfortunately they were rather less enthusiastic about paying their bills.

Norman Wisdom was one of our celebrity clients, and I had been a huge fan of his as a child, but his patronage was a very double-edged sword. The fact that we clothed him was not necessarily the best endorsement for our goods. When I told some people that we made Norman Wisdom's suits, they said, 'Well, that's not much of an advert for a tailoring business,' and walked out of the shop. I only realised after they had left, that they thought I meant the crumpled ones, two sizes too small, that he wore on stage. The tailoring business did not survive for long.

At least we did not make Norman Wisdom's flat caps, though I had previously tried my hand at another sort of headgear in a business called Thingummywigs. These were hats with wigs already attached, that women could wear to hide their Hilda Ogden-style curlers. It might sound pretty bizarre now, but it seemed like a good idea at a time when ninety per cent of women wore curlers and would not be seen dead without a hat or a headscarf when they went out.

Thingummywigs was not a great success, but it did not cost me much, because I did not have any real financial involvement, and it did introduce me to one of the funniest guys I have ever met, a manic super-salesman, whom I christened 'Bilko' after the Phil Silvers character. His product may not have been the biggest success in the world, but his resemblance to Bilko was enough to endear him to me, for I loved the programmes more than anything on TV. I have fifteen hours of Bilko programmes on videotape and I know them practically by heart, but they still make me laugh till I cry, even forty years after they were made. Like Laurel and Hardy, who also reduce me to tears of laughter, Bilko has stood the test of time; it is the difference between just being good and being special.

I also spent a fair bit of time around Tin Pan Alley – Denmark Street in Soho – while I was at Chelsea. My infatuation with showbusiness had begun early: I was tap-dancing with a group called 'The Happy Tappers' at the age of four, and learned a mime act later on, which I used to do for charity, performing at a local disabled people's home. Emboldened by this modest success, I eventually did my act in a talent contest at Butlin's holiday camp.

Allan Harris, Bert Murray, Ronnie Hanley and I went to Butlin's every year when we were in our teens, and we always used to watch the talent contests. I was convinced that I could do better than most of the acts on show, but even if I was proved wrong, I was still willing to give it a try. At the time the Butlin's talent contests were the largest in Britain – the 'Opportunity Knocks' of that era – with contests held at every Butlin's camp and an end-of-summer grand final.

I was seventeen when I finally made my stage début. I had to do an audition first, held in an unnervingly big theatre, just to get into the show, but got through the audition and then won the contest, miming to Spike Jones's 'I Went to Your Wedding'. I was supposed to go back in September for the 'All-Winners' final', but, understandably, Tommy Docherty would not give me a weekend off from the Chelsea first team. While I played football, the Bachelors won the competition.

I also sang with the Joe Loss Orchestra several times at the

Hammersmith Palais, before Docherty put a stop to that as well, telling me to choose between football and showbiz, because there was not room for both. That was the last time I sang with Joe, a super bloke, who always kept in touch, even years later, sending me a card or a note when something that I had done was publicised in the press.

I had met a few people in the music business by then, and even tried writing songs with help from a man called Tony Hiller, who later wrote a Eurovision Song Contest winner, 'Save All Your Kisses For Me'. I would do my football training and then go to Tony's office at Mills Music in Denmark Street; it was somewhere for me to go, rather than hanging round the streets in the afternoons, even though I was clearly never going to make my fortune as a songwriter.

I sat in with Tony, listening to the jam sessions and demos, and met some real characters. I first met Adam Faith there, and also got to know two cheeky young lads in brown overalls, who worked in the packaging department. I was always giving the two of them a hard time and sending them out to get coffees, from the café along the street. One was Eric Hall, who later became the 'infamous' football agent and friend of my family and me. The other one, a very funny kid who did impressions all the time, was called Reg Dwight. He eventually became rather more famous as Elton John.

Years later, I met Elton, in all his regalia, at the Room at the Top in Ilford, where Watford were holding a function to honour the Morgan twins. He came over, said 'Hello', and asked if I remembered him. I did not recognise him at all, even when he reminded me that he had worked in the packaging department in Denmark Street, with Eric Hall. I would not believe him at first, because Reggie Dwight had been a very fat kid, and I thought that Elton was pulling my leg. When I told him that I remembered Reggie doing a great Kenneth Williams impression, however, Elton launched straight into it, and I thought, Oh my

God, it really is him. If only I had started managing Elton instead of football clubs; I would have made ten times as much money with one-tenth of the aggravation.

Not all my activities were aimed at making money for myself. A business partner of mine, Geoff Bradley, had a five-year-old son called Ricky, who had a serious eye complaint. His sight was saved only by the skill of doctors at the Institute of Ophthalmology in London. One of the doctors there mentioned that the research unit was chronically underfunded, and in gratitude for what they had done for Ricky, Geoff and I decided to do what we could to help.

We launched a charity, Fight For Sight, raising money through recycling newspapers. At the time, it was a relatively new idea and proved very successful. My Dad drove a big Albion van, picking up papers in bulk; my grandparents, Ossie and Millie, went round with an old pram, collecting door to door; and we also recruited the local Boy Scout troops to make their own collections. The papers were stacked from floor to ceiling in my garage and every time we had a full load, we would sell them for recycling to paper mills. That simple idea raised over £100,000, an enormous sum in those days.

Like Fight For Sight, the most successful of my business sidelines involved little investment. I started writing when I was still at Chelsea, and carried it on throughout my time at Spurs and Queens Park Rangers. I was first contacted by my co-writer, Gordon Williams, when he was working for a press agency in Fleet Street, which had people like Denis Law, Tommy Docherty, Bobby Moore and Bobby Tambling on their books. A lot of the other Chelsea players were also being approached to write newspaper columns at the time. The money on offer was £100 for a small article, but the players would have to find an agent to negotiate the deal and a 'ghost' to write the copy for them, and would finish up with only forty per cent of the money.

At the age of sixteen, I had rejected the approaches of an

agent, for I could not see why some guy in a camel hair overcoat, standing on the sidelines, should take ten per cent of my earnings, and I was no more keen on doing so a few years later. Gordon told us that most footballers were much more intelligent than the reporters who wrote their stories for them, and asked us why we did not write our own articles and keep 100 per cent of the money. Peter Osgood told him, 'I couldn't keep still that long, it would be too boring,' but I was all for the idea. I watched Gordon typing and it seemed easy enough, so I went straight out and bought a small, pale blue, Brother typewriter. Gordon could type amazingly quickly with two fingers, but I went to a school to learn to do it properly, the only man in a class of about forty women, which made the class very enjoyable. I got up to a speed of about twenty-five words a minute, but after I finished the course, I soon reverted back to two-finger typing, like my mentor.

Few players followed my lead. Out of all those in the Spurs–Chelsea FA Cup final in 1967, for example, I was the only one who wrote his own profile in the programme. The first proper article that I wrote was called 'Jokes the Fans Don't Hear', about the banter that happens out on the pitch. I sold it to a newspaper for considerably more money than I earned in a week playing football and it was used, almost unaltered. From then on, I was hooked on the writing bug in a big way.

Gordon next suggested that I think about writing a soccer novel, but at that stage I did not have the confidence to do it, and by way of breaking me in gently, he asked me to have a try at a short story instead. I wrote 'Sammy Small', a so-far unpublished story about a Londoner who went to Newcastle and got caught up in a murky world of ticket touts and other dubious characters. I was a bit shy about showing it to Gordon, but I eventually found the courage to let him see it. He obviously found it funny, although he could have been laughing at the grammatical errors. When he had finished it, he told me it was one of the best Damon Runyan pastiches he had ever seen, which was news to me. I had never heard of Damon Runyan, and did not even know which team he played for . . .

Gordon then disappeared from London for a while, living in a very isolated farmhouse on Dartmoor while he wrote a novel. Having finished it, he came up to London for three days to see his publisher, but when he got back to Devon, he found his wife, Claerwyn, a nervous wreck. A dangerous criminal had escaped from Dartmoor prison and was on the run, and his wife, alone in that farmhouse on the moor, with no phone and no car, had been absolutely terrified, too scared even to go outside. The good writer turns every experience into source material and Gordon immediately began thinking about how you would protect your home against an intruder in a situation like that.

He wrote a novel, *The Siege of Trencher's Farm*, based on that idea, in precisely ten days. The film rights were sold almost as quickly and the book became Sam Peckinpah's film *Straw Dogs*, starring Dustin Hoffman and Susan George. Gordon did not even publish the book under his own name, because it was so different from his normal work, and when I suggested that he should have his name associated with it, after the release of the film, he was absolutely horrified. The film was notorious for its violence and for an explicit rape scene, and Gordon may have felt that his other work would be taken less seriously if he was known to be the author of *Straw Dogs*.

As a result of its success, Gordon made a good deal of money and moved back to London, buying a house in Notting Hill Gate. By now I was playing at QPR and had not clapped eyes on him in ages, until he phoned up out of the blue and said, 'Remember me? I went to see you play the other day and at one point, when you were taking a throw-in, I almost reached out, tapped you on the shoulder, and said "What about that novel we were thinking of doing?" So what about it?'

By then, I was ready to give it a try and we began work immediately. I finished training at half-past twelve every day, and used to go straight to Gordon's little office in Soho, where we spent every afternoon for about nine months, working on *They Used to Play on Grass*, which was published in 1971. I found that writing the novel was a little easier than finding a parking meter in Soho Square; I would often drive round and round for up to half an hour, until I found a parking space.

As a good East End boy, feeding copper coins into a parking meter, instead of silver ones, was an almost automatic action, but it got me into some trouble one day, when a twopenny piece jammed in the meter. I tried to free it with my Yale key, which was on a length of chain fixed to my trouser waistband. I had to stand on tiptoe to get the key into the coin slot and in trying to ram the two pence in, the key got jammed as well.

I was now trapped by the trousers, standing on tiptoe, with my right foot almost off the ground. The only way I could release the key-chain was to take my trousers off, but quite apart from the embarrassment of stripping off in Soho Square, I would have had to stand on my head to get them off at all. Luckily Gordon had spotted me from his office window, and after controlling his laughter, he phoned up the head traffic warden and said, 'My friend is stuck by the trousers in a meter in Soho Square.'

'I have never heard of this before. We do not have any method of dealing with this.'

'His name happens to be Terry Venables.'

There was a pause.

'I will set wheels in motion for Mr Venables. I will be there in person, tell him to hang on.'

'He hasn't got much choice.'

When the head warden appeared, I was sure that I was going to get done for stuffing two pences in the slot, but he just unlocked the meter, extracted my key, asked for my autograph and wished me good luck in the weekend game. Gordon was speechless at this latest example of preferential treatment for footballers.

Writing *They Used to Play on Grass* was incredibly exhilarating for me. When describing an imaginary match, I found that I could not get the words down fast enough to keep pace with the mental images. I was writing about something that really excited me and it was like turning on a tap, the words just began to flow. The adrenalin was flowing equally fast and Gordon was as excited as me. As I was writing, he kept hovering behind me, wanting to know the score. It was so vivid and intense that a night never passed without dreaming of the characters. They would complain to me in my sleep that their lines were not funny enough, or I had not made them handsome enough – the book began to take me over completely.

When the book was published, it was immediately assumed that Gordon had actually written it, and that my involvement was just a publicity stunt. That was unfair, and made Gordon as angry as me, because the book was a genuine co-operation between us. Gordon was such a good writer of narrative but he said I was good on dialogue, and though I owed so much to him, I wrote thirty-five to forty per cent of the book myself.

Even now, *They Used to Play on Grass* still seems ahead of its times in some ways. A lot of the things we wrote about did materialise, like 'plastic' pitches, colour in the newspapers, changes to the points-scoring system and all-seater stadia, but I am still waiting for a few, like the British Cup competition we predicted.

Unfortunately the book tended to get gimmicky publicity, and was only reviewed by sports reporters, on sports pages. We were keen to work together on other books, but after this experience, we decided to use a pseudonym in future. To disguise our identities, we chose 'P.B. Yuill', coincidentally the surname of an uncle of both of us, reasoning that if the books did not succeed, no one would be any the wiser, and if they did, it would not be as the result of using my name for publicity. It was a dumb choice of pseudonym, for Gordon had pointed out to me only a few months before, that our surnames – Williams and Venables – meant that any book by us would always be towards the bottom right-hand corner of a bookshop's shelves. Both of us had forgotten that lesson almost immediately, however, and instead of a sensible name like 'Aardvark', we finished up with a pseudonym beginning with Y – even closer to the bottom right-hand corner.

I turned my back on football for the subject-matter of the next novel. My second daughter, Tracey, had just been born, and she was the inadvertent source of the idea. When I went to the maternity ward to see her for the first time, the name tag from her wrist was lying on the floor. If it happened nowadays there would be public inquiries and all sorts of trouble, but I complained to the nurse that the tags were a bit flimsy and that Tracey should have had 'Venables' written all over her.

Later that evening, I was at home on my own, sitting down having a glass of wine, when I started to think about the incident. It was the time when the film *Love Story* was an enormous success, making millions, with not a dry eye in the house. I sat there thinking about potential tear-jerkers, and began to wonder what would happen if you found out that the child you were bringing up was not your own, three or four years after its birth. I started to ask all my friends how they would feel, and began to write a straight tear-jerker with Gordon, about an East End couple and their child. They moved to Los Angeles, and when they had a car crash four years later, blood tests taken in the hospital proved that the man could not be the real father of their child. He accused his wife of having an affair, which she knew was not true. It eventually dawned on her that there was only one logical explanation, and she came back to London to find the proof.

The story was fine in theory, but Gordon and I rapidly realised that it was just not going to work in practice. We were two deeply cynical guys, trying to write a sensitive, romantic story about love and babies, and it just did not ring true. We decided that we had to put a hard-boiled, cynical character into the story to represent us, and that did the trick. The character was a private detective called James Hazell.

That first Hazell novel, *Hazell Plays Solomon*, was followed by two others, *Hazell and the Three-Card Trick* and *Hazell and the Menacing Jester*. Four years after they were first published, they were picked up by Thames TV, which made a pilot show and then released a series in 1978, starring Nicholas Ball in the title role. Hazell topped the ratings in Britain and the books even sold well in Spain, years later, translated into Catalan, after one of its authors got himself a job over there. By then, we were happy to reveal the real identities behind 'P.B. Yuill'. BBC's *Arena* later gave Gordon and me the chance to cast our own choice of actor for Hazell, in a programme about our creation. We conducted the auditions for the lead role in my Dad's pub in Chingford, with Gordon choosing Michael Elphick, while I opted for John Bindon.

As well as being a fine writer, Gordon was extremely good and lively company – sometimes too lively. He was the most entertaining raconteur you could wish to meet, up to about eight beers; after that he could land you in hot water. In the early stages, I would sometimes suggest having a lager on the way home, but Gordon could never stop at one, he would be off and running for the night. This would invariably lead to arguments, because I would want to drink up and go home, but he would want to drink up and then drink some more. In the end we decided to abandon the 'one lager' idea; and if the choice was either none at all or an all-night session, I preferred none at all.

When we finished the book, however, Gordon convinced me

that we had to celebrate the completion, just like 'wetting the baby's head' after a birth. I was prepared for the worst, but went along with him, as we set off on a pub-crawl around Fleet Street. After about half an hour in one particular pub, I went to the toilet, returning to discover that we had been barred. I asked Gordon what had happened, but he refused to say. The landlord was equally uninformative, merely pointing to the door and advising us of the best way of opening it and placing ourselves on the far side of it.

We carried on to the next pub, where the same thing happened again, and the next pub, and the next. As the evening wore on, we were close to being barred from every pub in the area. To this day I still have no idea what Gordon did to get us banned with such monotonous regularity. Gordon was not saying at the time and he now claims that he cannot remember.

Malcolm Allison has also shared some interesting nights with Gordon. Malcolm likes a glass of champagne, as everyone knows, and was not averse to an occasional drink with us. One night I escaped early, leaving the two of them to their fate. Unusually, Malcolm was not even drinking, but was concentrating on looking after Gordon, who had already put a fair quantity away. After a long and liquid evening, he then decided that he wanted something to eat and took Malcolm along to his local restaurant. When the first course arrived, Gordon immediately slumped forward on to the table, face down in the vichyssoise. Malcolm hauled Gordon's face out of the soup, dried him off a bit and was wondering what on earth to do, when the waiter came over and said, 'Don't worry, it's quite normal.'

Malcolm could get no sense out of Gordon, but finally discovered what he hoped was the right address and took him home in a taxi. As Malcolm half-carried and half-dragged him through the door, the lights came on in the house, to reveal

Claerwyn, standing at the top of the stairs, hands on hips, looking daggers at them. Gordon opened his eyes for the first time in two hours and said, 'My God, it's Lady Macbeth.' Malcolm, who was totally sober after struggling for two hours to get Gordon home, was trying to steer him to a chair, when Claerwyn started yelling at Gordon, 'What do you think you're doing, bringing your drunken friends home at this time in the morning? Get him out.' Malcolm sighed, made his excuses and left.

Gordon also had a long-running feud with the sports writer Hugh McIlvenny. It went way back and they were always at each other's throats. We went to Bobby Moore's testimonial dinner together, all in our tuxedos, and by the end of the evening, the two of them were swinging at each other. All the 'sweaty footballers' were behaving impeccably and there were these two highly regarded writers, grappling on the floor, though neither of them could land a punch. Eventually they retired to the bar for a drink.

Gordon obviously had a bit of an alcohol problem, but to his credit, he went on to beat it and has not had a drink in a long time. Whatever his minor faults, he taught me a tremendous amount, not just about writing, but about life. Footballers can be very naïve in lots of ways; it is such a closed world, and Gordon made me realise that there is a bigger world than football out there.

Out in the big world of South London, Crystal Palace was very different from QPR. I had left a successful First Division side to join one struggling in the lower reaches of the Third Division and the atmosphere at Selhurst Park was not particularly good. If Loftus Road had the flavour of a smart, young, upwardly mobile football ground, Selhurst Park was more of a slightly dowdy and down-at-heel South London auntie when I first went there, but the supporters' 'Save the Palace' campaign did a power of good. They spruced the place up, painted everything that did not move red and blue and made it a much nicer and more welcoming place.

Having Malcolm at the helm always made life interesting, for the public, the press and for us. At the same time that the fans were giving the ground a face-lift, Malcolm was rejuvenating the team, bringing through the first of the string of young players who would send Palace soaring up the League in the next few years. The groundwork for the 'Team of the 80s' was all laid by Malcolm, and he was not given enough credit for it at the time.

When he took me to Palace, Malcolm already had a vague idea that I might at some stage join the coaching staff. Players who have the gift of being able to instruct and organise other players out on the pitch tend to make decent coaches, and organising the team had been a part of my game since I was a kid, but neither Malcolm nor I realised quite how quickly the switch to the coaching side was going to be made. I had played just fourteen games for Palace when he summoned me to his office on the morning of New Year's Eve. I thought he was going to wish me a Happy New Year, but instead he came straight to the point, 'You're finished. Playing in the Third Division, with the players we have at the moment, you are not going to be able to give of your best on the field, particularly as you've also lost a bit of your pace, so you're going to stop playing and work with me on the coaching side instead.'

I could hardly believe my ears. Here I was, a mere youth, still a week short of my thirty-second birthday, being told I was too old to play any more. I glowered at Malcolm, 'I wouldn't take this from anybody else. I'm not even sure I'm going to take it from you. I might, but I definitely wouldn't take it from anybody else.'

Malcolm was taking no prisoners, however, 'Listen, never mind you might, you're finished. Come on the coaching side and you'll be of more benefit to us than you will as a player. You're going to be a good coach. Go away and think about it and then come back and start doing it in the morning.'

I did not like that at all. I walked out of the room, but a moment later, I knocked on the door and went back in. Malcolm looked up, expecting a big argument about whether I should carry on playing, but I just said, 'Happy New Year.' He looked at me blankly, so preoccupied by his football problems that he had forgotten the date. He later told me that the two most difficult things he had had to do in his life were to tell Colin Bell and me that we were finished as players.

Coaching had always been one of my ambitions. As far back as I could remember, I had wanted to be first a player, then a coach and then a manager, and I knew how few players were actually given that chance. To stay in the game was the player's dream, but only one in a hundred achieved it, and only one per cent of those who were lucky enough to get jobs as coaches or physiotherapists or managers, made a success of them. Every player swore blind that if he became a manager he would do it properly, avoiding all the mistakes and tricks managers had pulled on him, yet the funny thing was that they changed as soon as they became managers. I was determined to be different.

It was not the thought of coaching that deterred me, quite the reverse, it was the idea of giving up playing the game that I had played and loved since I was old enough to walk. I had no fitness problems, for the arthritis in my ankle had improved a lot following the move to Selhurst Park; indeed, since I stopped playing, I have never been bothered by it. Like all players, I knew in my head that the day I dreaded would come some time, but I secretly felt in my heart that I would be immortal and play for ever.

That night I went out for a drink with Frank McLintock and Bobby Moore and told them what Malcolm had said. They were both older than me and still playing, and were encouraging me to play on, either at Palace or somewhere else, saying, 'You don't want to pack in playing, keep going as long as you can.' I was not so sure, however. I knew that I was not going to get better as a player, but I might get better as a coach. I was also unsure why they felt it was so essential for us to carry on playing. 'What do we want? If it is to play, well, we can do that in training. To play in front of crowds of people? I've done that, maybe it's time for a new career.' By the time I had finished, I had almost convinced myself that Malcolm was right, but Bobby and Frank could not understand and gave me a pretty hard time about it. We shifted quite a few drinks while we talked, and I had probably lost another half yard of pace by the time I got home.

Before I went to bed, I sat down with a nightcap in the silent, darkened house and thought back over my playing career. It could not have begun better, playing for the England Youth team, making the Chelsea first team at just seventeen and becoming captain at nineteen. Chelsea were a successful side and I had been the hub of the team. The side needed a delivery of passes to suit the young front players, Tambling and Bridges, and I did not feel I could have done a much better job, although Tommy Docherty claimed that 'it was not a healthy thing for the team to rely too much on Venables' and said I was too big for my boots. He was probably right. That is the way I had to be to fill that role in the team, but I was probably a bit insensitive.

When Docherty sold me to Tottenham, I was surrounded by the best collection of players I ever had as team-mates. There was much less emphasis on coaching than there had been at Chelsea, with Dave Mackay embodying the team attitude of 'Never mind that, just leave it to us'. We were successful, but I was only ever a piece in the jigsaw, rather than the hub, for to attract the ball, you have to curse, cajole, threaten and demand,

and I never did that at Tottenham. The style of play was different too. At Chelsea I used to play it over the top for Bridges and Tambling, whereas at Spurs it was always to feet – push and run – which was not my forte.

By the time I joined QPR, dropping down a division, I had more of a mixture in my game, and the players looked to me to set a lead, much as I had done at Chelsea. I felt I played my best football at Loftus Road, a view I later discovered had been shared by Alf Ramsey, who would have brought me back into the England team, had he not felt that, pushing thirty, I was a bit too old to recall.

My strengths remained the same – good control, touch, passing and awareness, and I had also become a lot stronger in the tackle, with more aggression in my game. My weaknesses were the same too. I was always a poor header of the ball, and my pace was never blinding, though I was quick enough and worked hard at it throughout my career.

Pundits at the start of my career might have expected more from 'the new Duncan Edwards' than three England caps, and I had a personal regret that I had not played well enough to make the England World Cup squad in 1966, but it was hard to argue with Alf Ramsey's choice – you cannot do much better than win the World Cup, after all. Overall, I felt that I had got as much out of my natural ability as I could. I was never going to be a Glenn Hoddle or a Bryan Robson, but I had won my share of medals, caps and plaudits, and had a stack of great memories and good friends as well. It had been a pretty good career, and on that happy thought, I drained my glass and made my rather unsteady way upstairs to bed.

The next day I was late for work, the first time I had ever been late, and Malcolm greeted me warily, waiting to see which way I would jump. I was still not completely convinced, but I respected Malcolm enough to accept his opinion. I hung up my boots and joined the coaching staff, and the more I thought about it, the more I knew that it would work out. There are a lot of genuine and dedicated people making a living out of the game, but there are con-men too, guys who do not have real ambition. They drift within the game. I want to be the best at anything I do – if I was a waiter, I would want my restaurant to be the best in the district – and if you have the self-belief, then you have a chance. I had heard all the stuff about the mystique of coaching, but when I looked at some of the people who were doing it, I had a sneaking fancy that I would be okay.

The combination between us worked well. Malcolm was a very successful coach, and his Manchester City team in the late 1960s and early 1970s, with Bell, Summerbee, Lee, Young, Coleman and all those guys, was one of the best teams I have ever played against. It had everything – power, strength, finesse, imagination – an excellent side, but he had become bored with Manchester City winning, strange though that sounds, and was looking for a fresh challenge.

He went to Crystal Palace, where he told me a lot of the players were confused by what he was doing, which is surprising, because Malcolm is very good at simplifying things. After seeing me coach them, he realised that he had made a big mistake. I started off with very basic things, and it reminded him that he should have started at Palace, as he started at Manchester City, by building from the same basic principles. Instead he started at Palace as he had ended at Manchester City, and without the basics, his progressive ideas were all too much for the players. After he put me in charge of the team at Palace, he was able to concentrate on handling the off-field activities, doing the promotion and 'front-of-house' stuff, which, with his natural showmanship, he did so well, while leaving most of the coaching of the side to me.

When I first joined the coaching staff, however, I would wait for instructions from Malcolm before beginning the day's training. This could take some time, because Malcolm's legendary difficulty with time keeping often meant that he was hours late and sometimes would not turn up at all.

A couple of years later, with Malcolm about to take charge at Plymouth Argyle, we were at Bisham Abbey on a coaching course together. Rodney Marsh, Don Howe, Ron Atkinson, Allan Harris, John Bond, Malcolm and I were all sitting in my very small room, drinking and talking football one evening, when Don Howe started telling Malcolm that he was throwing away his talent, and had to make sure that he did not not go out on the tiles any more. He must not oversleep and take days off, he had to be more consistent, because he had so much to offer.

All of a sudden, Malcolm launched himself into a great speech, saying, 'You're right, I've got to start pulling myself together. I'm one of the best coaches there is, and I'm going to prove it. I'm going to get myself fit during the summer. I'm not going to have a holiday, I'm going to go to fitness camps and I'm going to do special weight training. When I go to Plymouth, I'm going to get them back for pre-season training, not four or five weeks early, but seven weeks early. Never again will I lie in. I'm going to be up every morning at seven-thirty and I'm going to make sure that I never break that regime right the way through the whole season. I will be the first one on patrol. Not one day will go by, through wind, snow, sleet, hail – no matter what the weather – I'll be there. This is a new Malcolm Allison. I'll mould and motivate that Plymouth team into a promotion-winning side.'

It was a great speech, and by the end of it, he had us all thinking that we would like to be at Plymouth ourselves, to see this incredible transformation, but when I tried to wake him up for training the next morning, he just put his head under the covers and said, 'Oh, piss off, I'm too tired to get up,' and finally appeared for the nine-thirty session at eleven-thirty.

He has not changed at all. I had a note from his wife, Lynn, recently, after I had asked her, in desperation, to set a time for a much-postponed meeting with Malcolm. The reply came back, 'Malcolm looks forward to seeing you on Wednesday or Thursday next week,' which is as precise an arrangement as you are ever likely to get with him.

Malcolm's assistant at Palace, Frank Lord, and I would wait around for a while, but Frank, who had seen Malcolm's 'punctuality' many times before, always came prepared with sets of his own training plans in his pocket, which he had sweated blood to produce the previous evening. We would start training with these, but as soon as Malcolm appeared, he would stride over to us, and say, 'I've got this great new idea for training today,' and Frank would sigh, roll his eyes to heaven, and after glancing through his carefully penned plans one last time, would smile bravely and rip them into pieces, scattering them to the winds.

If that was cruel, Frank was not above pulling rank himself sometimes. He played for Plymouth at one time, and was on hand when a young lad playing his very first senior game, got past the centre-half and went round the goalkeeper. He was just going to knock it into the net for a début goal when Frank shoved him in the chest, pushed him over and side-footed it into the net himself. Frank was back at the halfway line by the time the lad overhauled him, saying, 'That was my goal.' 'Read the paper in the morning,' said Frank, 'and you'll see whose goal it was.'

Coaching Palace was a real challenge, for it was not a good team then, though Malcolm had already laid the groundwork and cut out some dead wood. When he first went to Selhurst Park, there were about fifty-five professionals on the books, a ridiculous number for a top side, let alone one languishing in the Third Division. They went along to the athletics stadium to do some sprint work one day, and there were so many players that the last few had still not set off when the first ones came round to complete their first lap.

Malcolm did some drastic pruning of the playing staff, and between us, we got Palace really buzzing. In 1976 we began a Cup run that was to take us all the way to the semi-finals. We beat non-League Walton & Hersham in the first round and saw off Millwall after a replay in the second, earning a crack at the giants in the third round ... who turned out to be Scarborough.

Footballers are a superstitious lot, and Malcolm made his trademark fedora hat the team's talisman on that Cup run. It made its first appearance as we were standing at the station, on our way to play at Scarborough. The players were about fifty yards away, further down the platform, when Malcolm un-zipped his bag, pulled out the big fedora hat and put it on. When the lads noticed, they called out, 'That'll do for us, Boss,' but Malcolm just said, 'Never mind that, we're going to win the Cup with this hat.' He told me that he learned the trick from a manager called Jack Timm, who led Portsmouth all the way to a Wembley victory, wearing a pair of 'lucky' spats.

The hat did the job at Scarborough, where we had to kick off at two o'clock, because the club did not have any floodlights. We were already travelling back on our chartered train, packed full of Palace supporters, directors and players, when the draw for the next round was made. Malcolm and I were sitting in the first carriage with the players, facing back down the train. We could see a bloke coming towards us, who had obviously heard the Cup draw on his radio. He was stopping to talk to everybody as he came down the aisle, and had a very long face. Malcolm said to me, 'From the look of this bloke, we've drawn a First Division side away. When he tells us which team it is, get very excited, say what a lucky ground it is for you, and really give it some hype.'

The bloke came up to us and said, 'It's Leeds United, away.' Malcolm leapt straight out of his seat, punching the air and

going, 'You beauty! What a great draw for us,' and I was up on
my feet as well, saying, 'Yes, I always played well at Elland
Road, I love the atmosphere there, we couldn't have had a
better draw if we'd done it ourselves.' The players sat there
open-mouthed, staring at us as if we were completely mad,
because Leeds had not lost a home game for something like two
years at that time. Later, as Malcolm and I sat and chatted
about the game, he looked at me and said, 'It's true, you always
have played well at Leeds, do you fancy playing?' It had obviously not taken me long to get used to the idea of retirement,
because my answer was immediate, 'No chance.' In some ways I
was tempted, because I could have been out there organising the
team, but I felt that as coach I ought to take a step back and not
be seen to be muscling in, just as the team was starting to have
some success.

Our bravado paid off, and our 'spontaneous' display of
confidence rubbed off on the players. They went to Elland Road
genuinely believing that they could beat Leeds and were re-
warded with a 1–0 win. The self-belief of the whole side was
graphically illustrated by Stuart Jump, a very quiet person, who,
as a rule, was not the most confident player in the team. He
looked across at me on the bench with about twenty minutes to
go and feigned smoking a cigar, as if it was so bloody easy. It
was never that simple, but we beat them fair and square, and
did it by playing some fine football, not by hacking them off the
park. As I said after the game, 'I've always compared Leeds
with the gunfighter who moves into town, does a job with cold
efficiency and then leaves without a smile. We smiled a bit
today.'

We also smiled a bit at training one day when Malcolm
turned up with 1970s sex symbol Fiona Richmond in tow. We
were out at the training ground, when a Rolls Royce pulled up.
Malcolm got out, wearing his tracksuit, followed by Fiona
Richmond in a fur coat. Her arrival had obviously been stage-

managed by Malcolm, because a photographer appeared from nowhere and started clicking away for all he was worth.

When we had finished training, we went back to the ground to get changed. We were sitting in the communal bath in the first-team dressing room, when Malcolm appeared and hopped in, closely followed by Fiona Richmond, who stripped off and jumped in the bath too. I was out of the bath like lightning when I saw the photographer lurking around. Malcolm later told me he had never seen me move as fast on the football field. No one else noticed him and certainly no one appeared to be complaining about sharing the bath water with Ms Richmond, until the photographer leapt out and started clicking away again, taking pictures that were to cause some of the players no end of trouble with their wives. Some of them had told their wives the story, but many of them kept quiet about it, hoping that the photographs would not be published. When the pictures were splashed all over the tabloids, however, they had some serious explaining to do.

Fiona Richmond could not be blamed for our exit from the Cup. We reached the semi-finals by beating Chelsea 3–2 in the fifth round at Stamford Bridge and then saw off Sunderland in the quarter-finals. That was the end of the road, for in the semi-final we were beaten by Southampton, who went on to a famous victory over Manchester United at Wembley. Perhaps distracted by the Cup run, Palace missed out on promotion as well, finishing fifth, three points adrift of Millwall. They came to play us at Palace in a game we had to win to beat them to promotion. We were level when Peter Taylor missed a penalty that would have given us the win, and our chance was gone.

It was a bitter blow, but I felt sure that it was only a temporary set-back, because a string of talented young players like Kenny Sansom, Terry Fenwick, Billy Gilbert, Peter Nicholas, Vince Hillaire and Jerry Murphy, were beginning to come through, and I knew that Palace's future was very bright. The future was apparently less rosy for Malcolm, however, despite the tremendous work he had put in with the younger players. His reward was to be sacked by Palace chairman Ray Bloye at the end of the 1975–76 season; perhaps the Fiona Richmond caper had come home to roost.

Malcolm and I went out for a drink together and I told him that I would leave with him, but he would not hear of it, saying, 'Don't be daft, Terry, why should someone else get the benefit of all the work we've done? Stay on and complete what we've started, bringing on the kids who are coming through from the youth team.' That remark showed the real Malcolm, kind and warm-hearted, a big man in every way.

Malcolm nominated me as his successor, and despite their differences with him, the Palace board accepted his recommendation. They wanted me to sign a contract straight away, but I was going away on holiday to Majorca with my family the next day, and after making a verbal commitment to Ray Bloye, it was left that we would agree terms and sign a contract when I got back. About the third day in Majorca, I fancied having a go at the para-sailing on the beach. I had watched children and old men do it and thought that it could not be too difficult or dangerous. I put the harness on, ran down the beach as the boat moved off and I was soon soaring up into the air. When I reached the highest point, however, something went wrong. I still do not know what happened, but the next thing I knew, I was dropping like a brick, and went crashing into the sea seconds later.

There was a momentary flash of pain but nothing worse and I was congratulating myself on a lucky escape, when I noticed a gaping hole between my thumb and first finger. I could see right into the inside of my hand. The impact had also ripped my ear half off, leaving it dangling by a thread, but I was so preoccupied with the injury to my hand that I did not notice the ear until a few minutes later. I needed ten stitches to reattach my ear and another eighteen to close the wound in my hand.

Water sports did not seem to be my forte, because I was pretty average on water-skis too. I had tried that a couple of years earlier, when we went on holiday to Malta with Allan Harris and Dave Webb and their wives. All the way out on the flight, we were talking about going water-skiing. Allan and I had never done it, but Dave Webb reckoned to have done it lots of times, and was giving us the full SP, saying, 'Strength comes into it, but you've got to bend your knees and keep your arms straight, make sure you don't bend too far back.'

The first morning, we went down to the beach and had a go at it. I got up and fell down twice, but the third time I managed to get up and stay up. I was not really enjoying it wobbling about all over the place, but I managed to get all the way round. Allan Harris went next, got up straight away, and in his first attempt, went all the way round. Dave Webb, the man who knew all about it, came next, and he could not get up to save his life. He must have made thirty attempts to get up and did not manage it once. More and more people were coming out of the hotel to watch him falling over time and time again. He swallowed half the Mediterranean in the process and had water coming down his nose and out of his ears.

We went back the next day, and a large, expectant crowd had turned up for the free entertainment. Allan and I did the circuit again, but Dave again kept falling over. Once he managed to get up and stay up for about six yards and had just started waving to everybody in triumph, as if to say, 'By George, I've got it,' but as his arm went up, he fell head-first straight into the water again.

In desperation, the guy running the water-skiing produced a thing like a round table top, saying, 'You can't go wrong, we put the kids on this,' but Dave still could not do it, even falling off that. In the end, I found the perfect solution: 'Just stand on the beach Dave, we'll get them to tow the island around.'

I was not quite so quick with the clever remarks after my fall from grace on the para-sailing, and I was told not to go swimming for the rest of the holiday, because of the wounds, but as it turned out, my holiday was to be rudely interrupted anyway. That night I took a phone call from a friend of mine who, out of the blue, asked me if I would contemplate managing Arsenal. I was absolutely staggered, I had never managed anyone before and had only just been offered my first job with a Third Division club, yet apparently one of the greatest and proudest clubs in the country, a giant of the First Division, was about to approach me to manage them.

Sure enough, the Arsenal secretary, Ken Friar, rang me later in the evening. I told him that I had made a commitment to Crystal Palace but had not yet signed a contract, and he immediately arranged a flight back to England, to discuss the Arsenal job with their board of directors. I flew out of Majorca at dawn the next morning and Ken picked me up from the airport and drove us over to the chairman's house, to meet the Arsenal board. After a one hour interview, in which the chairman, Denis Hill-Wood, explained Arsenal's problems and asked for my ideas of solutions, they then asked if I would take a walk in the garden for ten minutes. I did so, almost getting lost, for it was big enough to land a plane in, and they then called me back in and offered me the job.

I was genuinely amazed that someone at Highbury had spotted me, when I had not even managed a club, and have never got over the fact that they offered one of the top jobs in English football to me as an untried manager. They obviously have a very good managerial talent-spotting policy, because they did pretty much the same with George Graham later on, snapping him up after only a couple of years in the lower divisions with Millwall. I said that I thought that it was a bit early in my managerial career, and I was not sure if I was ready for such a prestigious first job. They clearly had confidence in me, but I told them that I would have to think about it, and in any event, could only take the job if Raymond Bloye would agree to release me from my verbal agreement with Crystal Palace, which I expected him to do.

I phoned Raymond from Denis Hill-Wood's house, told him about the Arsenal offer, and arranged to meet and talk about it. By this time, I was more worried about my wounds than the job. The bandage on my hand was getting dirty and needed changing, the wound in my ear was throbbing like mad and I was imagining all sorts of dire consequences, up to and including lockjaw and gangrene. I met Ray and he drove me to five different hospitals around London, while I explained the Arsenal offer and asked if he would be willing to release me, in between my unsuccessful attempts to get someone to change the bandage and have a look at my hand and ear. We ended up at the old St George's Hospital at Hyde Park Corner, which is now a hotel, and finally managed to get it done there.

All the time we were driving from hospital to hospital, Raymond remained absolutely insistent that he would not release me from my agreement. If Denis Hill-Wood had been driving me around, I might have finished up at Highbury instead of Selhurst Park, but Raymond left me with two choices: to sign a contract with Palace as agreed, or to break my word and go to Arsenal.

I was torn between the lure of a dream job with Arsenal and the need to keep faith with Raymond Bloye, but to break my word was no way to start in management. Many people in a similar position have broken their word without a second thought, but I have seen so much bad faith and destruction in football that I did not want to start my managerial career on a broken promise. I also had at the back of my mind the belief that if you deal honestly with people, what you lose in the short term, you will get back in the long run. I called Arsenal and told them that I could not join because Raymond Bloye would not release me. They were disappointed, but understood and wished me well.

Even if I had not given my word to Raymond Bloye, there were good reasons for beginning my managerial career with Palace rather than Arsenal. There are no formal qualifications for being a football manager. You cannot take a course at university or spend three years as an indentured apprentice, learning the trade. Apart from a three-week course that the PFA used to run, there is nothing to prepare you at all. Your only qualification is what you have observed as a player and what you feel about football tactics, and you have so few chances of being a manager that if you get the opportunity, you simply have to learn on the job, by trial and error. Clubs usually want the security of having someone with a track record, and if you go into it as a new coach/manager and make a hash of it, you will not be given a second chance, at that club or anywhere else.

I had tried to prepare myself as well as I could for a coaching career, by gaining knowledge and learning from other people while I was still playing. I had been on all the coaching courses when I was quite young, and passed my full and advanced licences. I also went to St Helens on the first ever PFA management course. Ian St John, Ron Yeats, Bobby Charlton, Bobby Campbell, Ritchie Barker, and a lot of other players who went on to become managers, also went there and it was very helpful. Don Revie was one of the speakers, and I nearly drove him mad afterwards with my incessant questions. Don told me I reminded him of himself at the same age, because he had gone to see Matt Busby and done the same thing to him.

I also used to go to watch every game possible. I would go and see a match four or five nights a week, just to observe and get to know people and the game better. I remember Bernard Joy of the *Evening Standard*, telling me that he had seen me at more games than any coach or manager. I was ready for the Palace job, and even after the Arsenal offer came along, I felt that I would be better off learning my trade lower down the ladder, than going to a big club like that too soon.

I went back to finish my holiday in Majorca. It was still boiling hot, and as the thought of not being able to swim and of spending more time trailing around hospitals to get the stitches taken out was too awful to face, I sneaked into the bathroom, out of sight of Christine, found some scissors and cut the stitches out. It proved to be easy – I just snipped the end and pulled them out with a pair of tweezers. I managed to have two days of swimming before going home, without gangrene setting in, and when I got home the hand was sufficiently healed to sign the contract that Raymond Bloye had prepared.

When I became Crystal Palace manager, John Cartwright, who coached the youth team there, said, 'If you can get this right, you can get anything right.' In a seventy-four-year history, Palace had never won anything, and never looked likely to, but I was full of confidence about our prospects. With every passing month, the team was growing stronger.

People in the game had always given me two warnings about going into management. The first was not to become a player-manager, because while it is hard enough to play, and hard enough to manage, to do the two together is just about impossible. The second was never to become the manager of a club where you were a player, because it is impossible to get the necessary respect from players who were team-mates a little while before. I heeded the first warning, but ignored the second, without coming to any great harm, although I was fortunate in not having been a player at Palace long, before hanging up my boots, so the players did not know me particularly well.

Meeting with the players for the first time as a manager was a little strange; it seemed weird to be sitting facing them instead of alongside them. I told them that I wanted to have a good atmosphere at the club but at the same time to be professional, and that they would have to respect my right to make decisions for the good of the club, and that would not necessarily always be popular with individual players.

I could not have achieved success at Palace if I had not had such an excellent apprenticeship under Malcolm Allison. Malcolm remembered the things that had upset him at Manchester City, when Joe Mercer was manager and Malcolm his coach, and had made sure that they did not happen to me. I was equally determined that my experiences under Tommy Docherty at Chelsea would not be repeated by the young players under me at Palace. At thirty-three years old, I was one of the youngest managers in the League, the same age as Docherty when he had taken over at Chelsea, but unlike Docherty, I wanted my players to express themselves on the field and off. That did not mean that they would be running the club, but their opinions would be heard and respected. A democratic system like that is the hardest to organise, but once established, it is the easiest to operate. Everyone can have their say, but in the end, the decision rests with the manager.

It took a while for the younger Palace players to develop the confidence to express their views in front of their peers, but gradually they responded. Everyone had an equal right to contribute, whether it was to tactics, team discussions or the sing-song on the bus coming home from a match. We took the football seriously, but we had some great laughs too and the results were there for everyone to see on the pitch.

We went from strength to strength, despite a cash crisis that made me question the wisdom of my decision to turn down Arsenal. On my fourth day as manager, the phones were cut off, because the bill had not been paid. Since money had been promised for team strengthening, this was not a particularly encouraging sign, and when I confronted Raymond Bloye, he admitted that the club was in some financial trouble, but promised me that half of the transfer fee we received for Peter Taylor could be spent on new players. Promises, promises . . .

Peter had already won England honours as a Third Division player, but wanted to move to a more glamorous club to 'improve his England prospects'. I was at a loss to understand how he could improve his prospects when he was already being selected anyway, and tried to talk him into staying, but he was insistent on a move to a First Division club. My helpful reminder, 'If you hadn't missed that penalty against Millwall, you'd already be playing in the Second Division, and that's close enough,' went down like a lead balloon.

Leeds offered £160,000 for Taylor and the directors wanted me to snatch their hands off, because they desperately needed the money, but I held out for more, even though the Palace directors came to see me, one at a time, to try and persuade me to take Leeds' money. They were panicking in a big way, because the alternative to selling Taylor was for them to put some money in to pay the bills. One thing I have always believed, however, is that if you are trying to sell a player, and you really believe that he is the genuine article, you do not accept anyone else's opinion on his worth. If you hold your nerve, you will get your price in the end, no matter how long it takes. That certainly paid off with Peter Taylor. While Jimmy Armfield at Leeds was hesitating about whether to go higher and the Palace directors were pressing me to take his first offer, Tottenham came in for Peter and paid £200,000 for him. The Palace directors were all doing cartwheels then, of course.

Ironically, after leaving Palace for Spurs, seeking to enhance his England career prospects, Peter never played for England again. He was exceptional for Palace, but – like T. Venables before him – did not do as well at Tottenham as he should have done, which can often happen to a good player when he changes clubs, for reasons no one really understands.

The Palace debts, which eventually turned out to total £1.4

million, swallowed all the £200,000 and, despite Ray Bloye's promise, virtually nothing was left. I felt terribly let down by the board, who after all, would have had £40,000 less if I had not insisted that Taylor was worth more than the Leeds offer, but I just had to make the best of it.

I badly needed to replace Peter Taylor, so I signed two absolute bargain basement players – Barry Silkman from Plymouth on a free transfer and Rashid Harkouk for about £1500 from Feltham – and it was a struggle to get the £1500 from the Palace directors. I hoped that one of the players would do the job for us, and as it turned out, they both did very well. I ended up selling Silkman to Manchester City for £35,000 and Harkouk for £95,000 to QPR, so Palace did not do badly out of an investment of £1500. Jim Gregory tried to get Harkouk for £30,000 and I would not sell him for that. We did a deal in the end, but Jim was not very happy about the price he ultimately had to pay. He was even less happy after Harkouk failed to show the same form for them. He did really well for us and had plenty of ability, but was a bit of a rascal, and rather wayward, which made him unreliable.

Several months later, he was not even in the QPR first team. When I went over to Loftus Road to watch our reserves play QPR reserves, I looked round and could see Jim Gregory about four rows behind me, and scowling ferociously at me. I called out, 'Hello, Jim,' and, still scowling, he said, 'Thanks for that Harkouk. If I had wanted a bleeding clown, I would have gone to Bertram Mills' Circus.'

My other signing proved to be significant both on the field and off it. My old mate George Graham had been in the doldrums when I signed him for Palace, after sharing relegation with both Manchester United and Portsmouth, but he did a tremendous job on the field for us, his experience proving invaluable to the youngsters in the side. Injuries forced him to pack in playing at the end of the season, but I then gave him a break into coaching that was ultimately to lead him to one of the top jobs in the game.

I also gave Bobby Moore a chance to coach, after he had stopped playing. It seemed incredible that no one had snapped up a man who had such stature in the game and he worked with the youth team at Palace for a while before getting a chance to coach at first team level with Cambridge. He was desperately close to getting the Watford job, but missed out and went on to Southend, and he did not enjoy the success that I and many others might have expected.

He did not have the luck that any new coach – including me – needed, but the transition from captaincy to coaching is also more difficult than many people imagine. Some think that all you have to do is put a suit on a good captain and he will automatically be transformed into a good manager, but it is not quite that simple. Two of the best captains of my own generation were Bobby Moore and Frank McLintock, but coaching never worked for them, yet in the team that McLintock had captained was George Graham, who has become a fabulously successful coach.

Before the start of the 1976–77 season, I took the Palace players to Sweden, for a few days' intensive training. Every little town in Sweden had great sports facilities and the football pitches were beautiful. Our hotel had several running tracks radiating out through the pine forests and up into the hills. The different tracks were colour-coded; the green run stayed at low level, following the edge of the nearby lake, while the yellow track was moderately steep and the red one was a punishing high-level run.

As soon as we got to the hotel, I went to take a look at the tracks, to see which one we would use the next day. Along the yellow route, I walked past an old fort, deep in the forest, with its wooden palisades still virtually intact. The logs from which it was built were so close together that you could scarcely see between them, but it was clear that the fort had been unoccupied for many, many years. I went back to the hotel for a meeting with the players before dinner.

I told them that we had checked out the runs, which all looked pretty difficult, and said that they would be starting on the yellow route and that I would decide in the morning if they would have to run the circuit once or twice, at which they all groaned. They wanted to know a bit more about the route, so to put a spring in their step, I told them that it went past a nudist camp. 'You can't miss it,' I said helpfully, 'it's inside an old fort in the middle of the forest. You can't see much, but if you squint through the fencing, you can just about see what's going on.'

As I spoke, I could see them all exchanging glances and nudging each other, and as soon as the meeting was over, groups of two or three players gathered in the lobby, had a sly look round to see if I was watching, and then sneaked out of the hotel. From my vantage point in the bar, I watched them disappear up the track towards the old fort at high speed, and saw them return again half an hour later, sweaty and not at all amused, though I am sure the exercise did them a power of good. The Swedish fresh air obviously had the right effect, for with only the three additions to the squad, to compensate for the loss of our best player, Palace stormed up the table that season, while our youth team won the FA Youth Cup.

The Palace 'seniors', who, George Graham excepted, were little more than youths themselves, also ran Liverpool desperately close in the FA Cup, drawing at Anfield and only losing the replay 3–2. At the time of those Liverpool matches, I stated the Venables football philosophy, which remains unaltered today:

> I would like to think that Palace are becoming the Liverpool of the
> Third Division, but in the long term I am looking to emulate what

they have to offer; I want my team to be as complete. I believe we are one of no more than six clubs who improve players and help them understand the game that they are playing. When I see some of the West German teams playing, and consider how much nearer they are to perfection than anything we have in England, I want not only to win games like Liverpool, but also to play football that is visually exciting, which can stimulate the senses.

That pronouncement might have seemed a little grandiose from someone whose side was still in the Third Division, but Palace's play was beginning to attract attention from all over the country. The phrase 'The Team of the Eighties', which hung around us like a millstone when we reached the First Division, was already being used when we were in the Second.

In the short term our ambition was the more prosaic one of gaining promotion from the Third Division, however, an aim which we achieved, although it was a desperately close thing. We made a late run through the second half of the season and went to our last game at our promotion rivals, Wrexham, knowing that we had to beat them by two goals, and then pray that Mansfield, who were already promoted along with Brighton, would also beat them in their last game.

If one game in my long playing and managerial career stands out in my mind over the years, it is not any of the big ones – the Cup finals and top of the table clashes in London or Barcelona – but that Third Division game at Wrexham. There was a capacity crowd, a tremendous atmosphere and, with twenty-five minutes to go, we were winning 2–0 and cruising. Silkman had played despite a heavy cold, but looked tired, and I called him off and sent Harkouk on. Before I knew it, there were five minutes to go and the score was suddenly 2–2. Ray Bloye told me later that he was already penning notes for a consolation speech in the dressing room: 'So near and yet so far. Congratulations on what you've achieved this year, and better luck next season.'

Jeff Bourne, whom I had signed for a bargain £30,000 just before the transfer deadline, scored in the dying seconds of normal time to put us 3–2 ahead. I can still see the drama that followed as clearly as if it was yesterday. Deep in injury time, with the referee staring at his watch, the ball went out of play for a throw-in well inside the Wrexham half. Wrexham's centre back, Roberts, had gone down injured, needing the trainer, and the delay gave Kenny Sansom time to come all the way across from left-back to take the throw from the right. Kenny took one of his speciality long throws, the ball was flicked on into the area and Rashid Harkouk volleyed the ball from around head-high into the back of the net. Like Frank Lord before him, Ray Bloye ripped his notes into shreds and scattered them to the winds, as the rest of us went berserk.

We had done all that we could, but our fate still rested on Mansfield beating Wrexham away, to send us up in their place. Poor Wrexham fell at the final hurdle again, as an eighty-ninth-minute goal by Mansfield's Ernie Moss did the trick, giving us promotion instead of Wrexham, on goal difference.

One of our keenest rivals all season had been Brighton, where Alan Mullery had just taken over as manager. Alan and I were more or less the same age, had played in the same midfield position, the '2' in Spurs' 4–2–4 formation, and had even roomed together for a while at Tottenham, and the media made much of our rivalry. There was an undeniable edge between us, and we both wanted to beat each other, but we took it in good part and it was by no means nasty . . . even when I read a quote from Alan saying that he 'longed to see the super-successful Venables fall flat on his back for once'.

He had to wait a while. We had a lot of games against Brighton in League and Cup, and each one was a real grudge match. We won nearly all of them, which made me very happy, but did not do a great deal for Alan's composure. There was a great Cup exchange between us which went to a second replay.

We drew down at Brighton, thanks to Harkouk. We were losing 1–0 when he got the ball and dribbled it down the wing to the by-line. Instead of crossing it, he dribbled it all the way back again and, on the turn, hit a left-foot shot right into the top corner of the net. It was one of the most brilliant goals I have ever seen and gave us a 1–1 draw.

We fought out another draw at Palace, and in the third game, although Brighton played really well, we won the match against the run of play. Alan Mullery was naturally upset and went mad at the final whistle, running on to the pitch to have a go at the referee. When the press went into the Brighton dressing room after the game, he threw a £5 note on the floor saying, 'Palace are not worth that much.' When the press asked for my reaction to the incident, I just asked them if the £5 note was still on the floor.

The two clubs matched each other stride for stride, rising from the Third to the Second Division together and being locked together in the race for promotion to the First Division as well. By then, I had begun the managerial partnership with Allan Harris that was to last fourteen years and take us from Selhurst Park all the way to the Nou Camp in Barcelona. When Allan had first come to Palace, he had done some scouting for Malcolm, and then worked with the youth team for a while, succeeding John Cartwright. I had known Allan since the England Schoolboys days, and soon moved him up to work alongside me.

His replacement with the youth team was George Graham. George had been thinking of giving up the game altogether and taking a pub, and he took some persuading to give coaching a try. After some discussion, I said to him, 'You've got a lot to offer. Try it for a year. If you don't like it, you can leave and get a pub then.' George agreed to give it a go and was a revelation to himself, though not to me, for I had seen the same coaching ability in George that Malcolm Allison had seen in me.

Some parts of the job had nothing to do with coaching ability, however. I had always heard stories of mad-keen supporters having their ashes scattered on the pitch, but I have come across it only twice, both at Crystal Palace in the space of about three months. It was the first winter I had been manager there when I had a letter from a woman whose father had recently died who had wanted his ashes spread where he used to stand, by a barrier behind the goal.

On the appointed day, the woman turned up with her mother, her little girl and boy, who used to go with his grandad to games. They had asked if I would stand with them while they scattered the ashes, and I was wearing my black suit, white shirt and black tie. The boy led us out and said, 'There it is, that's where Grandad used to take me.' We found the exact crash barrier, and were standing there as she proceeded to walk up and down, emptying the ashes.

It was windy and absolutely bitter cold – I could not feel my fingers – and I had not realised how much ash there would be. There must have been the ash from the coffin as well as the body; there was heaps of it. The woman kept pacing to and fro, scattering ashes, while everyone complained about how cold it was. She had only got halfway through when she suddenly said, 'Bloody hell, it's too cold for this,' and dumped the rest in a heap on the concrete underneath the barrier, and everyone shuffled off in double-quick time.

Three months later there was another ashes ceremony. By now it was April and the sun was out, but it was windy. This time I had to spread the ashes on the centre circle, while the dead man's wife and sister stood and watched. We chatted and had a cup of tea, and then went outside, me once more in my black suit, white shirt and black tie. I started to pour out the ashes, but the widow said, 'No, no, you've got to swish them around.' As I did my best to oblige, the wind changed, and I finished up with all these pink ashes, the earthly remains of her husband, all over my face and my almost new black suit. They stared at me and did not know whether to laugh or cry.

I was near tears myself when we only finished ninth in our first season in the Second Division, 1977–78, but I knew that I had to be patient with my team. The players were very young, and nothing would be achieved by pressuring them; with an average age of just twenty, they had already achieved results beyond their years.

Ron Greenwood had obviously been keeping an eye on my coaching, for he called me up in January 1978, to form part of his England set-up, working with Dave Sexton coaching the Under-21s. I was also beginning to attract a number of offers from other teams. Jimmy Armfield offered me the chance to work with him at Leeds United; Birmingham City expressed interest in signing me; Jim Gregory at QPR made the first of several approaches; and there were also offers from two rather more exotic destinations when I was given the chance to manage the Australian national team and then told I could pick up £200,000 tax-free by 'doing a Don Revie' and coaching in the Middle East.

Flattering though all these approaches were, however, I had worked too hard at Palace to leave the club just as we were on the brink of even bigger things. Only two players had been with the club when I first joined Malcolm Allison there, the rest had been developed by my coaching team of Allan Harris, George Graham and John Cartwright. Despite the frustrations caused by Palace's financial problems, and the resulting restrictions on transfer-dealing, there was no way that I could turn my back on one of the strongest foundations in English football. It was my team and I wanted to see how high we could fly.

The following season, 1978-79, both we and Brighton were again pushing for promotion. We made a hesitant start, drawing our first six games, but when it counted most, the players responded, winning five and drawing one of our last six games to guarantee promotion and the title. Brighton had been long-time leaders of the table, but we arrived at our last game of the season with everything to play for. Brighton had finished their programme and had already left on an end-of-season tour of America as we faced our other promotion rivals, Burnley, in our final match. If we won, we were champions, if we drew we went up, but if we lost, we did not even get promoted.

Crowds had steadily been increasing all season, and for this final showdown there were 52,000 people jammed into Selhurst Park. Ian Walsh and Dave Swindlehurst scored the goals that gave us the 2–0 victory that made us champions, while Brighton were actually in the air heading for America, so neither Alan nor his team were very happy with us again.

I was very proud of the side, for as well as playing football of great skill and excitement, they had also shown the heart to fight for the ball when they had to. The Palace victory celebrations began on the pitch and carried on in the dressing rooms, before we moved on to a hotel for the Championship drinks, but somehow I was not in the mood to party the night away. I slipped away for a while, leaving the players to their well earned celebrations, and Gordon Williams found me later on, pacing up and down a dark corridor with a face as long as a wet weekend in February. 'What's up, Terry, what's on your mind?' asked Gordon. 'Next season,' I replied.

As I said it, memories of Bill Nicholson at the Spurs FA Cup final banquet came flooding back. I had thought then how bizarre it was that he could not relax and forget football even for one night, yet here I was falling into the same trap. I went back into the bar with Gordon and by the end of the evening I had almost forgotten my own name, never mind football. The planning for Palace's first ever season in Division One did not begin until the hangover cleared.

It had been a meteoric rise for Palace. We were lucky enough to have had a wave of good players coming through at the right time, but we worked for that luck – the scouts, the coaches, everyone at the club sweated to get it right. The atmosphere we had created was similar to the one at Chelsea when I started my career. The players were always receptive to ideas, genuinely wanting to learn and there was always a tremendously competitive atmosphere about the place. If you did something well, you would immediately find someone else trying to do it better. That is how players progress and improve.

The progressive ideas on the playing side were carried over into the rest of the club. Palace was the first club in the country to introduce family enclosures, where only children accompanied by adults were admitted. At a time when terrace violence was much in the news and on everybody's minds, the family enclosures provided a reassuring safe haven for people with young children. Parents who had stopped taking their children to the football because of the fear of violence began to return.

I wanted the principles behind the family enclosures to be more widely applied as well, writing in newspaper articles at the time:

> It might help to have grounds with seating only, so we can get rid of the obscene fences, which look like something out of Auschwitz. We are still too rooted in tradition. In America, if they want a new stadium, they build a brand new one outside of town with plenty of parking spaces and all the facilities you could want. All our stadiums are in the middle of towns and have been there for a hundred years, but the supporters would not hear of you moving away from the ground that they and their fathers have been going to for years. What are we supporting – the team or the stadium?

I was also campaigning for two changes to improve the game on the pitch – more points for a win, and fewer matches, with the income from shirt sponsorship – then a very new idea in the game – making up for the loss of income. Both were eventually introduced by the League, although inevitably, the greed of the clubs meant that most wanted to have their sponsorship cake and still eat as many fixtures as they could swallow, irrespective of the effect on the players or the entertainment value for the fans.

I also felt a great responsibility for the welfare of our squad, particularly as so many of them were very young. Having persuaded all the club's vice-presidents to take at least one player under their wing and teach them about the business that they were involved in, I then held a meeting with the players to convince them that they should think about their lives after football. When you grow older, you realise that ten years is not long, but as a youngster, the day when you give up playing seems a million years away; you cannot imagine a time when you will not be a footballer – thirty-two never comes.

When I first took over at Palace, quite a few of the team, like Ian Evans, Peter Wald, Alan Whittle, Tony Burns and Stuart Jump, were at that sort of age. I told the Palace players that I would not be doing my job properly if I did not point these things out to them, and for a short time, I managed to convince them that football was not eternal. I got them very motivated and quite excited about doing something different, having reassured them that there was no need for it to interfere with their football at all. They would normally go and play snooker or something after training anyway, so I just asked them to do something positive instead for a while.

The vice-presidents, who were very active in the club, jumped at the chance to show the lads how to be architectural draughtsmen, commodities brokers, scrap-metal dealers, or whatever they were involved in. The players started off full of enthusiasm too, but sadly, one by one, they all fell away and did not last the course. None of them really stuck at it long enough to acquire some genuine experience or qualifications, because the lure of football was just too strong and appealing for them. Despite our efforts, they still could not see the point in working at other things when they were young and could earn money playing football for ever. I did not even mind that they were not building a business or a post-football career, I was just concerned, as I still am today, that footballers do not blow it all in a short career and finish up penniless, on the dole.

The vast majority of footballers form a cross-section of the working class. They obviously have different levels of intelligence, but contrary to the popular 'sick as a parrot/over the moon' image of footballers, I have always found that someone who plays football has a sharp and lively mind and is quite receptive to ideas. Footballers are not sweaty, moronic oafs, but decent human beings.

That does not necessarily mean that they will pursue academic studies, however. There is potential there, but it is not often sparked. If you leave school at fifteen or sixteen and go out into the real world, you have to find a job to earn money on which to live. As a professional footballer, you do not enter that world. Your club is almost an extension of school, where many of your worries are taken care of and you are left to do what you enjoy, without thinking about the future.

People call footballers 'lucky' to be able to do that, but I do not see them as lucky, I see them as fortunate, which is a different thing. Luck is like the spin of a wheel or the toss of a coin, over which you have no control, whereas while you are fortunate to have been born with a latent talent, it is up to you whether you build on it or throw it away. I have seen many talented players who have just squandered their gift and finished up spending the rest of their lives saying, 'I could have been a contender.'

The reality is that, even for the most gifted player, it takes hard work to become a footballer and make the best of your talent. It hurts when you are training, but you want success so badly that you go on. Some people fall by the wayside when it hurts; they do not want the training because it is too tough, but you have to extend yourself in training to succeed.

Training excepted, football can also make you lazy and unreliable, however. You finish training, have a bite of lunch, play snooker, talk football, and a lot of players go on doing that until they are in their thirties. At twenty years old, a footballer may be at the top of his profession, but by the time, in the mid-thirties, when most people are beginning to know about their trade, footballers are finished. It is suddenly all over, and they then have to start again from scratch, as if they were leaving school at thirty-four or thirty-five. It is only then that they panic.

Before 1960, when there was a maximum wage, the change from being a £30-a-week footballer to a steady £20-a-week job was not too difficult an adjustment, but in these days when players earn big money, the change is a dramatic one. The higher division players have given themselves and their families a very good standard of living, but when they leave football, they have to maintain it, which is not easy. The ones in the lower divisions have never been paid that much in the first place and they can have a real struggle to get by.

I was as street-wise as any East End kid when I was young, but there was also a naïvety about me, as there is about all footballers. It is very easy to get on that football roller-coaster and treat everything as a bit of a laugh, but you are not insulated from the harsh side of life for ever. Despite the failure of my scheme at Palace, I still believe that footballers should be sparked off early to do other things with their lives, so that the end of football is not the end of everything for them, but I have to say that clubs do not do as much as they could, to acquaint players with the harsh realities they will face after their playing careers are over.

The game has changed so much since the introduction of freedom of contract, however. In the days when you signed a ten-year contract, the players were the club's responsibilities and they did try to meet these responsibilities to some extent. Today the contracts are so short that players and clubs are like ships in the night and there is precious little loyalty on either side.

Not all players are the same. Some like to stay at one club, even though they might not get quite as much money. They like the club, the management, and where they are living, and they do not want to go and live in Blagthorpe or Inverdoon instead, but in the main turnover has become very fast – a money business. I'm in, I play well, I'm out, I go somewhere else, I play well for the next one, then zap, I'm thirty-two, I've saved all that money, what do I do with it? By the same token, clubs now tend to feel that there is no real incentive for them to interest themselves in their players' long-term futures. I think they are wrong, however, because you can build up responsibility and loyalty over time.

My own loyalty to Palace was further tested when, during the summer, just as I was getting down to serious preparation for our first season in the top flight, I received an approach that was to lead to an incredible offer to work abroad. The attempt to launch football in the United States was in full swing and some very serious money was being offered to star players and coaches. The New York Cosmos made contact out of the blue, and offered to make me a millionaire if I would join them as manager. They were offering £250,000 a year plus bonuses, for a four-year contract, and several of my friends urged me to take the money and set myself up for life. While I was tempted by the cash, however, and the chance to work with some of the greatest names in the game, like Franz Beckenbauer, Carlos Alberto, Giorgio Chinaglia and Johan Neeskens, I had reservations about the game in the States and felt that I could easily lose my edge – as so many players seemed to have done over there – as a coach, as well as becoming a forgotten man in English football.

When I told Raymond Bloye of the offer, he responded by offering a four-year deal of his own. The money was far less than the Cosmos were waving at me, but it still made me one of the best-paid managers in the British game, and it was the deciding factor; I stayed with Palace. There was also an emotional reason. When Palace won the Second Division title, I saw middle-aged men singing and waving their scarves above their heads, with tears in their eyes. They had endured years of being second-best, years of taking stick from their mates about their team; now they were on top and possibly as happy as they had ever been in their lives.

That is something that many people do not realise about football – quite how much it means to so many people. Sometimes it means a bit too much, of course. I was sitting in the dug-out at one Palace game when a row flared up in the stand behind us. Two middle-aged supporters had become so wound up that they started exchanging blows, and the police went into the crowd and led out the two miscreants. As the second one was frog-marched past the bench, with blood pouring from his nose and his eye already closing, he turned to me and said wearily, 'The fings I do for you, Tel.'

There was an occasional brawl on the pitch too, one of which inspired the funniest sporting headline I have ever seen. Ian Philip, a fiery Scot, and a player called Queen were both involved in a punch-up on the pitch. The next day the *Evening Standard* had the headline QUEEN AND PHILIP IN PALACE BRAWL.

I signed Gerry Francis and Mike Flanagan to spearhead our challenge to the royalty of the First Division and we made a dazzling start the following season, 1979–80. Ironically, our first game in the top flight was away at Manchester City, managed by Malcolm Allison, who had returned to Maine Road. We got over that hurdle safely, beginning a ten-match unbeaten run, including a 4–1 thrashing of the powerful Ipswich side, that saw us top the table for the first time in Palace's history.

For a while it seemed that Palace might live up to the tag of 'The Team of the Eighties' that the press had saddled us with, but after all the early promise, we faded badly to finish in a respectable, but disappointing thirteenth place. There was just not enough stability and experience in the squad to keep us at the top throughout the long haul of an English season. When things became tough, there were not enough old heads there to help pull the young ones through.

It is a problem that a number of other football clubs have had. In many ways we seem to be too bothered by age in this country, feeling that we have to give youth its head. That can sometimes pay dividends, but looking around the Premier League today, you can see that there is no substitute for experience. Chris Waddle, Peter Beardsley, Ray Wilkins and Gordon Strachan are all old heads, still showing people how to play football. Every player eventually reaches a point where he has to give the game up, but there are plenty of players who still have much to offer when they are scrapped just because they have a few miles on the clock. Three or four bad games at twenty-three years old, are just three or four bad games, but at thirty-three, everybody immediately decides that it is the end of your career.

We signed Clive Allen in a controversial deal before the start of the 1980–81 season, in a straight swap for Kenny Sansom. Clive had been bought by Arsenal from QPR for £1 million, during the close season, but without Clive kicking a ball for them in a League game, Terry Neill decided that he needed a full-back even more. When he came in for Kenny, I saw a way of solving our shortage of strikers, without laying out any hard cash. There were suggestions that Arsenal had just been 'warehousing' Allen for us, since QPR would not have sold him to us direct, but the stories were not true, and swap deals were one

way to bring in some fresh blood at a club like Palace, which
had no money to spend at all.

The season began in precisely the opposite way to the
previous one. We put together a dismal opening run, losing nine
of our first ten games, and hit the bottom of the table in
October. The financial position of the club was no better. We
arrived at the station for one away game to find that the club
had not paid the bill for previous travel and we had to have a
whip-round among the players and me to buy the tickets. At the
next board meeting, my request for money for expenses, to
avoid such embarrassments occurring in the future, was met
with a stony silence. I had the feeling then that I would have to
leave by the end of the season, but I did not want to go with
Palace at the bottom of the table. Events forced my hand,
however, and within weeks I had left the club. Managers have
been sacked for shorter losing streaks than the one with which
we had begun the season, and if the Palace board had come to
me and told me that they wanted to make a change, I could
have had few complaints. On the record, they remained committed to me but behind the scenes things were very different.

Not long after the boardroom incident, I heard rumours on
the grapevine that Palace had approached two other managers,
one of them Howard Kendall, who was then at Blackburn. I
phoned Howard, who confirmed the story, and one of the
Palace directors also privately told me that it was true. Yet
when I confronted the whole Palace board, they still denied any
approach. I said to them, 'One of the managers involved has
confirmed that you have approached him. If you want a change,
there's no point in going to other managers behind my back.
Perhaps it's time for a change for you and for me.' Far better to
join a new club that wants you than stay at one that clearly
does not.

They still refused to admit it, and I left the room with the
matter still unresolved. When you discover something like that

is going on, however, you do not hang around waiting for the chop – it is better to move before you are pushed. QPR chairman Jim Gregory had obviously heard the rumours too, because he contacted me to ask if I would join them as manager. It was the second time in five months that Jim had approached me; the previous May I had turned him down, after he had sacked Tommy Docherty. It was the second time he had done that as well, for the Doc had been signed and sacked by Gregory inside a month back in 1969. Docherty returned to Loftus Road in 1979, but was again sacked by Gregory at the end of the season. Nine days later, pressure from the players and fans made him swallow his pride and reappoint Docherty, but now matters had again come to a head and the Doc had been sacked for the third and last time – at QPR at least.

Jim Gregory never wasted much time when he decided on something – the call to offer me the manager's job came just after dawn – and this time I said that I would join him if he agreed compensation with Palace. I also told the Palace board that I would leave only if they received acceptable compensation from QPR. That gave them a way out, a chance to show what they really thought, for if they wanted me to stay, they had only to turn down the compensation as unsatisfactory.

Jim offered Palace £100,000, the first 'transfer fee' that had been paid for a manager, and a great deal of money at the time, and Palace snapped his hand off and made the decision for me. In fact, Jim should have been paying the money directly to me, for Palace owed me the same amount. When I became manager, they had promised me a £100,000 bonus if I could take Palace into Division One. At the earliest, it would only be payable two years down the track, but when it came to it, the money was not forthcoming.

Despite that and their furtive negotiations with another manager, I still had mixed feelings about leaving Palace, but the board had decided to find another manager and they gladly accepted the money to buy out my contract. When there were complaints from their fans and players, however, they tried to make out that I had been the one to go behind their backs, even though they had already made an offer to Howard Kendall.

I had a lump in my throat and could not help shedding a tear as I left Selhurst Park for the last time. Embarrassingly, on my way out I bumped into goalkeeper Paul Barron who saw the tear glistening in my eye, and asked, 'What's the matter?' but I was too choked to speak to him, and jumped in my car and drove off.

......................................................................................................

# CHAPTER FIVE

# *Manager at QPR*

## 1980–84

FOOTBALL IS FULL OF IRONIES and my move to QPR provided one to savour. Tommy Docherty, the manager who had sacked me from Chelsea, was now himself getting the boot, to be replaced by the man he had dumped at Chelsea ten years before. All I had to do was avoid the same fate at the hands of the most 'sack-happy' chairman in the League.

When your football career is finished, if you are very lucky, you might then become a manager. You can do that for a few years, but if you are not very good, or not very successful, you are out – 'You've had your chance, cheerio, next one please.' It is the guy who owns the town and owns the football club, who sits there for ever.

Directors and chairmen are criticised these days for being greedy, but they are not a patch on the robber-barons of old. Today everyone talks about football as a business, and the need to make profits to reinvest in facilities and players, but what happened to all the money, years ago? There were 80,000 crowds in those days, yet they never spent a penny on the grounds, transfer fees were minimal and the maximum wage was £20. The price of admission was admittedly not that big, but even 80,000 sixpences – whatever they amount to – is pretty big money.

These days, in my experience, there are far more people putting money in than taking it out, and they are in a no-win position. Everyone blames the chairman – he should invest more money, buy more players, sack more managers. Being chairman, the man at the top, is a difficult business. It is a lot easier being Denis Hill-Wood or Martin Edwards, when the actual investment was made many years before, and the club is something that you inherited and can enjoy, but when you put fresh money into a club, you have really got to be on top of your game.

Yet football is like no other business. When you are the chairman of a company, more often than not you have worked your way up through the ranks and got to know every aspect of how that company works. It does not happen like that in football, which is a business that the chairman may not understand at all. If you are successful in building, or wood-chopping, or whatever, for some strange reason that makes you qualified to run a football club . . . unless it is just handed down to you by Daddy.

To run a club successfully is a big problem, which is made more complex by the need to find a manager whose football decision-making the chairmen and directors can trust. I am sure that most chairmen – with one or two exceptions – always have the good of their clubs in mind, and if they feel that the club is not in good hands, it must be a nightmare for them.

The best relationship I ever had with a chairman of a British club was with Jim Gregory at QPR, despite his reputation of being a very tough man to work for. Only two of his many managers – Dave Sexton and me – left his employment voluntarily, the rest were sacked. In his early days as chairman, he was undoubtedly very impatient with his managers, but he did desperately want success for the club and he built a fine stadium from nothing.

Jim, a Rangers fanatic all his life, went to school in Shepherd's Bush. He needed every bit of his enthusiasm for the club, for the first game after his takeover in 1965 produced a crowd of only 3500, and for many years, it was only Jim's enthusiasm, commitment – and money – that kept the club afloat. His enthusiasm sometimes caused problems, however. In his early days in charge, Jim wanted to get to know his players and would go into the dressing room, but he found himself cutting across the duties of the manager. Players would come to know Jim personally and go straight to him with any problems. That inevitably causes friction between chairman and manager, which usually ends up with the manager getting the sack.

My dealings with Jim were never dull, but I would have loved to have been a fly on the wall during some of his confrontations with Tommy Docherty. Tom tells a story about having a few drinks one day with Jim, who then invited him into his office for a glass of champagne. Jim opened a bottle, poured each of them a glass, and then told Tom that things were not going well and that it was about time they parted company. 'I don't think you should go, Mr Chairman,' said Tom. 'I think you are doing a great job. I would like you to reconsider.' I wish I could have seen the look on Jim Gregory's face.

Perhaps he was mellowing with age, or perhaps he was beginning to have the success that he craved, but unlike a few of my predecessors, I cannot really remember ever having a row with Jim until I finally left the club. I had heard all about his reputation, but I found him open and straightforward. He had a 'dome' as bald as Terry Mancini, craggy features and a twinkling eye, and if his manner was sometimes brusque, it concealed a genuinely warm and kindly man.

He had begun his career selling second-hand cars, before building up his property business, but he was a fishmonger at heart, a trade which he had learned at his father's knee. He had a yacht in the South of France, formerly owned by Sophia Loren. He bought it after saying to one of his sons, 'Would you rather have that yacht or Martin Chivers for Rangers?' His son did not share his father's whole-hearted passion for QPR and opted for the yacht. When I went to stay with him in the South of France, Jim loved nothing more than taking me round the fish market early in the morning, giving me the benefit of his expertise.

He was also available to lend his expertise in the business of football whenever I needed it, either from his airy, wood-pan-elled office or his home overlooking Wimbledon Common. He reckoned to spend twenty per cent of his working time running QPR: 'I moved my office to the ground and spent fifty per cent of my time there one year and we got relegated, so it didn't do a lot of good,' Jim told me, with his characteristically self-deprecating humour.

In truth, where Rangers were concerned, Jim gave himself 100 per cent to the club. His emotional involvement in the game was as great as any player and there was no question of Jim adopting a chairmanly, lofty detachment when Rangers were playing. He was so tense during the games that he admitted that he never really enjoyed them, and afterwards would often have to retreat to his inner sanctum until he had control of his emotions, for fear of 'diplomatic incidents' with the officials of the visiting club. He would travel round the country, following not just the first team, but the junior teams too, and went all the way to Ipswich once, just to watch the boys' team in the Floodlit Cup.

When I was just starting at Crystal Palace, Brian Jupp, a psychologist brought in by Malcolm Allison to build a positive mental attitude in us, told us, 'You cannot have the power and the glory in this game.' As I carried on in football, I came to appreciate the truth of that remark. When I look at clubs like Manchester United or Blackburn today, it is Martin Edwards and Jack Walker who have the power, but the glory goes to Alex Ferguson or Kenny Dalglish. It is something that Alan Sugar could never understand at Tottenham; he wanted the power, but he wanted the glory too.

Jim Gregory understood it, however, in a way that few

chairmen do. He would say, 'If you're struggling, son, I'm by your side, but if you're winning, go up there and take the accolades, I'll be back here.' He had what he wanted, he had the power and he had a different type of satisfaction. I came and I went, as did Rodney Marsh, Stan Bowles, Frank McLintock and Dave Sexton. We all played our little parts, but it would not have been QPR as it is today, without Jim Gregory. He had the power, while the manager had the glory – or the sack.

I would go to Jim's office two or three times a week and we would discuss every aspect of the progress of the club together. Progress was needed swiftly, for when I joined them, QPR were about fourth from bottom of the Second Division and in danger of relegation. The club was not exactly awash with cash either, and I had to sell players before I could buy. We had two goalkeepers, Chris Woods and Peter Hucker. I had offers for both of them, but the one for Chris Woods, from Norwich, was for £200,000 and the offer for Hucker was only £12,000. At that time, I did not think that there was anything between them, as they were both very good goalkeepers, so I sold Woods and kept Hucker, who did particularly well for us.

I then went back to Palace on a shopping spree – it was like a January sale. I bought Gerry Francis, Mike Flanagan, Terry Fenwick and Clive Allen from Palace, picking up the first three players in a package deal that caused some controversy at the time. Palace complained I was taking unfair advantage of them, but the players could see the club's parlous financial state as well as I could, and shared my view that QPR were going places, while Palace were going nowhere fast. I originally swapped Steve Wicks for Allen, but later I bought him back again as well. Simon Stainrod also arrived as I tried to strengthen areas of the team that looked weak around players whom I thought were good enough.

One player who was definitely good enough was Tony Currie, who enjoyed the same sort of adulation from the Rangers fans that they had reserved for Rodney Marsh when I had been a player at Loftus Road. Currie had the same skills as Rodney, but was a very different player. He was very strong and much tougher than Rodney, who, though he could be aggressive on occasions, did not have that as part of his normal game.

Tony played slightly further back than Rodney and took a more responsible role, and if Marsh had scored more goals, Currie had more of an all-round game. He had any amount of individual ability, but he was a team player and popular with his team-mates, and like Stan Bowles, should certainly have played for England much more often than he did.

It seemed a shame that Rodney had had to show his abilities in a team game, because he really wanted to play one-man football, although, as he grew older, he came to appreciate the team side of the game more. His skills were extraordinary, however, and he could keep an orange or a bar of soap in the air as easily as a football. He would always be seeking ways to challenge his own skill and I can remember him once trying to hit the ball into a basketball net when we were training in the gym. Most of us would have been content to try and chip it in, but Rodney found that too easy and kept trying to knock it in on the half-volley. His greatest problem was that he recognised his own talent too much; he saw himself as the leading light and everyone else as bit players ... though there were plenty of QPR fans who seemed to share his opinion. Gerry Francis also had a huge amount of talent, but it was at the service of the team. He was quick, with a devastating change of pace, strong and skilful, a good passer and finisher and a powerful tackler – he had the lot as a player, and is turning out to be a pretty fair coach too.

Allan Harris, who had always been a good worker, honest and very loyal, joined the exodus from Palace to QPR, and it was not long before George Graham also left the Palace coaching staff to join us. Frank McLintock was on the coaching staff at

QPR for a while too. George had been very good with the youth team at Palace, probably too good for his immediate promotion prospects, for I was a bit against taking him away from the kids, when, like John Cartwright, he was so successful with them. John eventually graduated to the reserves at the same time as a lot of the young players he had been coaching, but I really felt that, on ability, they should both have been higher up, working with the first team.

I have always been happy to employ strong, opinionated characters; it has never worried me, because getting opinions from each other makes us all better coaches. I would learn from them as much as they from me, and you learn with your ears, not your tongue. Malcolm Allison said that the key was to try and surround yourself with people who were as good, if not better, than you, because then everyone would stretch each other to their limit.

The rise of Rangers was not quite as meteoric as that of Palace, but it proved to be more durable. We climbed the table rapidly to finish eighth in the Second Division during my first season, were fifth the next one and then won promotion in my third year, 1982–83, taking the Second Division Championship by the length of a street.

Just as at Palace, QPR also had a tremendous FA Cup run, reaching the 1981–82 final as a Second Division team, only to lose to Tottenham. We needed replays to dispose of Middlesbrough and Blackpool in the third and fourth rounds, beat Grimsby at Selhurst Park in the fifth and then faced Crystal Palace in the quarter-finals. Clive Allen scored the only goal to put us into the semi-final against West Bromwich Albion, a very good team at the time.

We were complete underdogs, but a couple of tactical changes swung things our way. I played our two strikers, Clive Allen and Simon Stainrod, out of position, one wide and one pulled right back and we also went into the game using a

sweeper. The changes were introduced on the Monday before
the game and, unusually, I told the squad what the team was
going to be at the same time. That is not always ideal, because
players who know they are definitely in the team may ease off
in training, but for a big match it is worth it and may help to
relax them in the run-up to the game. Our players worked hard
in training to become used to the system, which worked perfectly. West Brom could not make head nor tail of us and we
won 1–0, thanks to another Clive Allen goal.

My old mate from Spurs, Maurice Keston, had asked me
years before if he could have a seat on the bench if I ever
managed a side at Wembley. He phoned up when we reached
the final and said 'How about that seat on the bench?'

'Will you stand up and cheer if Spurs score?'

'Of course I will.'

'Well, you can't sit on our bench, then.'

Perhaps I should have let him, because watching someone
cheering a Spurs goal from the QPR bench would at least have
given someone a laugh. We did not have much else to laugh
about because, sadly, I could only add a loser's medal to my
collection of Wembley trophies. Spurs beat us, though only
after a replay. The next time I returned to Wembley it would be
as a winner, but it would once more be with Tottenham, not
QPR.

We were outplayed, and fortunate to draw the first game 1–
1, Terry Fenwick scoring our equaliser, heading in a long throw
that Bob Hazell flicked on at the near post, after Glenn Hoddle
had brought Maurice Keston to his feet by giving Spurs the lead.
We had very much the better of the replay, however, only to
lose 1–0 to a Hoddle penalty, awarded after Tony Currie had
brought Graham Roberts down. We had what looked a good
goal disallowed, after Simon Stainrod had allegedly impeded the
Spurs goalkeeper, but Jim Gregory and I watched that incident
on video at least twenty times, and the goal looked perfectly all

right to our totally unbiased eyes. It completed a frustrating final for Jim, who then smoked eighty to a hundred cigarettes a day, although he has since given up. The two club chairmen sit next to the royal guest of honour for half the game each during a Wembley final. Jim smoked like a chimney in the first half, but then had to go 'cold turkey', spending the second half and the whole of extra time sitting next to Princess Anne, wound up with tension about the game, and unable to ease it with a cigarette.

Despite the disappointment of a Cup final defeat, my working relationship with Jim blossomed alongside the QPR team. We would discuss things for hours; I had a tremendous thirst for knowledge, while Jim was a great encourager and had a talent for looking at problems in a different way, turning them on their head. He gave me a lot of room to manoeuvre, and as I enjoyed the business of football, Jim took me under his wing, and brought me on to the board in November 1981, making me managing director.

Managers always complain that they do not have enough money to spend, but as managing director, I now had to balance the books, as well as the team. In time, I became the second-biggest shareholder in QPR, after Jim himself. When I later left QPR for Barcelona, he insisted that I sell him my shares. I would have preferred to have kept them, but to avoid a major row with Jim, I agreed to do so.

What most impressed me about Jim was his vision. When he took over QPR, Loftus Road was little more than a dirt-heap and he worked tirelessly for twenty years to transform the ground and the club. The 25,000-capacity ground had an intimate feel, with its stands grouped cosily around the pitch, but it was also one of the most modern and well equipped in the League, and at the time, the only new soccer stadium to be created in the country since the Second World War. Jim began the move to all-seater stadiums, which Gordon Williams and I had prophesied long before the Taylor Report dragged the rest of the clubs kicking and screaming into the twentieth century.

What I wrote in a newspaper column in the early 1980s should have been engraved on the hearts of a few other club directors: 'Money should be spent on improving the grounds and the disgusting facilities, instead of inflating transfer fees.' Most football grounds at the time were virtually unaltered from the era a few years either side of the Great War, when they were built. Much of the terracing was open to the elements and even covered accommodation was in cavernous, draughty, tin-roofed sheds, furnished with nothing but concrete terracing and a few ageing crash barriers. Stands were little more luxurious, with uncomfortable seats, insufficient leg-room and pillars that invariably seemed to be right in your line of sight whenever a goal was scored. There were hardly any refreshment facilities, while the toilets were filthy and pitifully inadequate for the numbers trying to use them. Many spectators simply urinated against the back of the stand or relieved themselves where they stood, on the terraces.

Apart from the new stands and facilities at Loftus Road, Jim Gregory also invested heavily in one other ground improvement, which was to be far less popular, a 'plastic' pitch. I flew to Holland during the summer of 1981, at the invitation of a Canadian company, to look at a new kind of artificial turf. Jim did not come with me, for he would not even fly to Barking, such is his dislike of planes. He prefers to go by boat, perhaps because he is closer to the fish . . .

I liked what I saw in Holland and ten years after the publication of *They Used to Play on Grass*, with its apparently futuristic view of football played on synthetic turf, Jim made QPR the first club in Britain to install an artificial pitch, at a cost of £350,000. While some praised him for his vision, however, many more lined up to complain about the pitch and the allegedly unfair advantage we would gain from constantly playing on it. We let visiting teams use it the day before matches, to familiarise themselves with it, but few went home happy after the game, unless they had taken the points, of course.

The major complaint about the pitch concerned the unnaturally high bounce of the ball on the Omniturf. We could solve that problem by increasing the amount of sand in the pitch, but that led in turn to players grazing their legs on the abrasive surface. If there were some problems, though, there were also many advantages to the artificial 'grass'. It provided a true, consistent surface on which players had the confidence to practise their skills and to display them in matches. There were no more games snowed off, no more 'ice football' on a pitch like a skating rink, no more 'swamp football' on mud-heap pitches and no more 'desert football', after a long season and a dry spell combined to bake a grassless pitch into a brown, arid dust-bowl.

If we could get men to the moon, surely we could find decent artificial turf. The manufacturers told us that we would not know the difference between an Omniturf pitch and grass, and in time everyone would have one, but while that was certainly never true, its faults were greatly magnified. I am sure that many clubs were put off both because it was new and because it was expensive to install, enough to strike terror into the hearts of plenty of club directors – spending money on the ground, whatever next? The shock of the new is always a potent force, however, and artificial pitches were eventually outlawed by the Football League.

When we introduced the Omniturf pitch, I did a TV interview parodying the Bob Newhart sketch about Sir Walter Raleigh trying to explain his new discovery, tobacco: 'So let me get this straight, Walt. You get this weed, you roll it up and put it in your mouth, right? And then what do you do? You do what? You set fire to it? That's what I thought you said.' Listeners to my speeches praising Omniturf often showed similar scepticism, but I asked them to imagine the situation if we had been playing on artificial pitches for years and then someone told them they had discovered grass: 'It has to be cut twice a week, reseeded every summer, and costs a fortune to maintain? After a few weeks it turns to mud, then it freezes solid, then it gets covered in snow, then it turns back to mud, and finally it gets baked as hard as concrete? Sounds great, but tell you what, don't call us, we'll call you.'

Our away form was pretty impressive too, suggesting that it was not the pitch that gave our opponents most difficulty, but the team. Rangers finished the 1982–83 season ten points clear of runners-up Wolverhampton, with Leicester another five points back in third – and it was only two points for a win in those days. Not even the most hostile critic of the 'plastic pitch' could use it as an excuse for that kind of margin. Our junior teams were doing equally well, for we also won the Football Combination and the South-East Counties League, the first time that particular double had been achieved in thirty-four years.

We clinched the Second Division title in a game against Leeds, but the sight of the London 'Flash Harrys' being promoted was too much for some Leeds fans, and at one stage police horses charged on to the pitch to deter them from coming over the barriers. There were a number of arrests for fighting on the terraces, too, but newspaper reports later suggested that most of the Londoners arrested had actually been Chelsea fans, travelling under false colours for the chance of a confrontation with their hated rivals from Leeds.

Just after the Leeds game, Jim Gregory dropped a bombshell by announcing to me that he intended to retire as chairman. 'I'm fifty-five and I had made up my mind to do this when Rangers were back in the First Division,' he told me. 'I want to help arrange for it to be all right when I leave. I don't want to die in the chair, leaving everyone not knowing what is going to happen to the club.' The news was broken to the public after the game. Literally hundreds of Rangers fans wrote to him asking him to reconsider, and Jim eventually allowed himself to be persuaded to carry on. He insisted that he would only remain as non-executive chairman, however, while he began shaping plans for Loftus Road that were as innovative as its artificial turf.

Promotion to the First Division made no difference to the number of moans from our opponents about the artificial pitch. The only difference was that, being the First Division, we got a better class of complaint, but the surface encouraged skilful, entertaining football, and whatever our opponents thought of it, the Rangers fans had no complaints at all.

Alongside our success, we also kept the reputation for entertainment – both on and off the field – that we had enjoyed when I was a player at QPR ten years before. Some observers thought we were too much the entertainers, too lightweight to make it in the fiercely competitive world of the First Division. One commented, 'The only way this lot will qualify for Europe is through the Eurovision Song Contest.' The writer obviously knew more about light entertainment than he did about football, because at the end of our first season in Division One, we finished fifth and qualified for the UEFA Cup. Both the team and its manager would be competing in Europe the next season, but as things turned out, it would not be in the same side, the same competition, or the same country.

My contract with QPR expired at the end of the season, but Jim and I had already been discussing a new and unique arrangement, in effect a buy-out, in which Jim would continue to own the ground but I would take over and run the footballing side on a twenty-year contract, leasing the ground from him for about fifty days a year.

Arsenal and Spurs had been sniffing around while I had been at QPR and although Jim gave both of them short shrift, he was using the prospect of ownership as a way of keeping me at the club. As Jim put it, 'If he owns the gaff, no other club can come and nick him off us.' Had it happened, Jim would then have been free from his other duties to develop the stadium for other uses. His plans included fitting a roof over it, allowing it to be used as an all-weather venue for rock concerts, boxing promotions and a host of other non-football activities.

While I was excited by the idea and was actively seeking finance, however, I knew Jim well enough to be aware that nothing was ever definite until the contracts had actually been signed. On one occasion when I was at Crystal Palace and we were negotiating the transfer of a new player, we had a long and liquid lunch together, a further hour of 'light refreshments' afterwards, and after all that, we agreed what I thought was a great deal.

There was always a nagging doubt in deals with Jim, one final hurdle to be overcome. I knew that if I could get through the rest of the evening and up to the start of training the next morning, without Jim phoning up to cancel the agreement, I was home and dry. I got through the evening, but the next morning, I was sitting in my office at nine o'clock when the phone rang. I knew it would be Jim before I even picked it up. 'Hello, Terry,' said Jim, speaking in the dopey voice that he reserved for such occasions. 'Now, what was that deal we agreed yesterday?' I explained it, with a sinking heart. When I had finished, Jim sighed and said, 'I don't think so. I must have had too much to drink,' and put the phone down.

Negotiations on the deal to take over from Jim at QPR had been even more protracted, to say the least, for the idea had first been floated twelve months before and it could easily have been another twelve months . . . or even twelve years . . . before the takeover materialised.

I started to find my backers, and I had already put the deal together when Jim began to look as if he was having second thoughts about it. He took an instant dislike to an Arsenal supporter who was proposing to put up most of the money, and I was sitting in Jim's office when he had a row with the Arsenal supporter on the phone, and finished up telling him, 'Sod off, we don't need your bloody money.' I could not believe my ears, and tried to grab the phone from him, but it was too late. Jim may not have needed the money, but I certainly did, and Jim had just ruined the deal I had been working on for months. I knew that he had changed his mind and had picked a fight with the guy on purpose to scupper the deal, but I went along with it, because I just could not get angry with Jim, even though we were now back to being chairman and managing director again.

In the meantime, Jim was also talking about renewing my managerial contract, but kept umming and aahing about it. I had already told the supporters that I was going to stay at QPR, but I could not agree a deal with Jim.

We were still friends, but he was always hard with me over money. I was on £30,000 a year at the time, and Jim offered £40,000, but I thought that with everything I had done at QPR, it was not enough. While we were at loggerheads, Barcelona, who were about to part company from their Argentinian World Cup-winning coach, Cesar Menotti, made contact and offered me an interview.

I was flattered that a club of Barcelona's profile had even heard of me, let alone thought sufficiently of my work to consider me for their coaching job, but when I told Jim that Barcelona wanted me to go for an interview, he started laughing. He thought that I was bluffing, inventing the approach to try and get him to increase his offer. When I asked him if he minded me going for the interview, he said, 'Of course not. That's fine, Terry. Go for the interview, and good luck with it.'

# CHAPTER SIX

# In the Nou Camp: Barcelona

## 1984–87

I FLEW INTO BARCELONA on 21 May 1984, the night before my interview, and after showering and changing, I took a stroll along the Ramblas, the broad tree-lined boulevard in the heart of the old city. It was thronged with people, crowding the flower and bird stalls and gathering around the chess players at tables in the open air.

Lottery-ticket sellers hawked tickets for 'El Gordo' – the fat one – the state lottery, which ranks second only to football in the list of Spanish obsessions, and news stands bristled with papers from every country under the sun. I bought an English paper and sat at a pavement bar in the cool of the evening, a habit I was to continue throughout my time in the city, catching up on the news from home, drinking a glass of wine and watching the endless parade of people passing by. Later, I chose a restaurant at random, and ate a beautiful dinner of seafood, before strolling back to my hotel, through the crowds in the streets. I was entranced; if this was Barcelona, I wanted to be part of it.

It was to be the only relaxing part of the trip, however, for when I got back to my hotel, I discovered that the media pack was in full cry. They pursued me through the lobby, into the lift and would have all piled into my room with me, given half a chance. After a couple of hours of incessant phone calls, knocks at the door and notes pushed underneath it, I decided the only way that I was going to get any peace was to change hotels. I packed and climbed out of the window. The last time I had been teetering on a window-ledge was when I had been a kid in Dagenham, but this time there was no 'Bertie Smalls' to shop me, and there was a fire escape rather than a sheer drop to the ground. I tiptoed down the fire escape, leaving the press still knocking on my door and mounting guard in reception. When I reached the ground, I walked round the corner, hailed a passing taxi and finally ensured a good night's sleep by checking into another hotel, under a false name.

The next day, I took a taxi to the home of Barcelona FC – the Nou Camp stadium – where, after side-stepping the inevitable press hordes, I was met by one of the club's vice-presidents, Juan Gaspart, the right-hand man to the club president, with special responsibilities for footballing matters, who was also one of its only English-speakers. He took me on a guided tour of the Nou Camp, which is actually a double arena, for alongside the main, 120,000 capacity, stadium, is the original one, now used as a training ground. Its 'modest' 25,000 capacity is greater than many English League grounds, but was woefully inadequate for Barcelona, who sell 110,000 season tickets every year, which entitle supporters to attend all sporting activities and parts of the complex. There are four football pitches in the Nou Camp complex, as well as an ice hockey arena, a roller-skating rink, bars, restaurants, a medical centre and a residential 'farmhouse' for young players.

The scale of the organisation matches that of the stadium. Barcelona run eight teams and have 200 players and eighteen directors. The club even owns its own bank, which is perhaps not too surprising, with gate receipts alone of over £1 million from a single home game. In addition to the 120,000 fans who pack the stadium, there are 750 supporters' clubs scattered across the globe, the largest membership of any club in the world.

The club's care extends to the supporters, who enjoy facilities that would make most English fans weep – from the 'basics' such as good food and clean, new toilets, to 'luxuries' like a crèche where supporters can safely leave their young children in the care of trained helpers, to be collected after the game – or games, for the Sunday match days are a football fiesta. They begin with the Under-19s, who kick off at three-thirty; the reserves play at six; and the first team take the field at eight-thirty to a roar that can be heard in Cadiz.

Juan Gaspart reeled off the mind-boggling statistics as he led me through the offices and down into the vast dressing rooms, as well equipped and luxuriously furnished as a leisure club in a top hotel, with the players all having their own private cubicles, showers and jacuzzis. Off the passageway leading towards the pitch is the chapel, large enough to accommodate the entire team and all its officials. The underside of the terracing forms its roof, and the whitewashed walls are decorated with the pennants of the teams who have played here over the years, like emblems of the saints.

The chapel, and the whole dressing-room area, cocooned below the terracing, are thoroughly sound-proofed; there is no advance warning for visiting teams of the intimidation by decibel that is to come. The passage dips and then begins to rise, ending in a spiral ramp, which lifts you up out of cathedral calm into an inferno.

When we reached the top of the ramp, we stood there blinking in the bright sunlight. The five-tiered terracing of the cavernous stadium towered above us, the sound made by a workman high in one of the stands, echoing eerily in an arena that boils on match days into a cauldron of noise.

It was the second time I had stood on this spot. The first had been almost twenty years earlier, under the glare of the floodlights, as thunder-flashes thrown from the crowd exploded around the pitch. Smoke and the smell of cordite hung in the air, the deafening pounding of drums and the baying of

100,000 voices making us feel like a team of Christians about to be thrown to the lions. That European Fairs Cup tie turned out to be my last appearance for Chelsea. I hoped that this visit to the Nou Camp would not end in a similar disappointment.

Having shown me the kingdom, Juan Gaspart took me to meet the men who would decide if I was to ascend to the throne. I was interviewed by the club president, Josip-Luis Nuñez, the senior vice-president Nicolau Casaus and two other directors. The men, all with heavy tans and gold watch-chains stretched across their waistcoats, sat in a room reeking of wealth – oak panelling, high ceilings, deep-pile carpeting and fine oil paintings.

Señor Nuñez is a fabulously wealthy construction tycoon, while Señor Casaus, also a very successful businessman, is a Catalonian hero, who was sentenced to death by Franco during the Civil War. The sentence was later commuted to life imprisonment and he served six years in gaol, before being released in an amnesty for Franco's political opponents. Señor Casaus personified the way that all Catalonia's aspirations had been channelled into the one activity that even Franco could not suppress – football. During the Civil War, the Nou Camp was the only place where they were able to speak their own Catalan language, and even now, to defeat Real Madrid, the capital of Castilian Spain and the power base of the hated General Franco, is like winning another battle in the Civil War to them. 'For forty years, all political expression was forbidden here,' said Señor Casaus. 'Our only means of self-expression was through football.'

When the means of self-expression failed to achieve the ends that Catalonians desired – the Spanish League title – the Barcelona directors could act with a ruthlessness that General Franco might have admired. In its entire history, the club had never had a coach who had lasted more than three years, and in the previous five years alone, there had been eight coaches: including Rife, Menotti, Kubalas, Herrera and Romero.

Barcelona was not even the most ruthless club, however. Atletico Madrid's intemperate owner, Jesus Gil, had run through nineteen coaches in six years. Luis Aragones was the longest-serving, lasting twenty-two months, but he paid the price with some sort of breakdown. When Gil brought in a Dallas psychiatrist to analyse the problem, his diagnosis was unsurprising – 'phobic anxiety'.

I was pretty sure that I would not reach the same point, but eight coaches in five years at Barcelona gave me pause for thought. If that was an unpromising pedigree for me to consider, it is fair to say that I was scarcely a household name in England at the time, let alone in Spain. The Barcelona directors wanted to try and blend some of the virtues of the North-European style of football into their side, however. They had come to the conclusion that Barcelona's footballing problems were partly due to their players not being fit enough and believed that British coaches were tougher and made players fit.

In fact, directors everywhere never know why teams are not playing well. They always think that it is because they are not fit enough and do not run as much as the other teams. The real reason is often because they lack organisation or have lost their spirit and do not have the same hunger; it is much more a state of mind than of body. That opinion was confirmed when I actually met the Barcelona players, who turned out to be the fittest bunch of players I had ever seen, and did not need any extra physical training at all.

If the directors felt that an English coach might be the answer, though, I was certainly not going to disabuse them of the idea at this stage. They had approached Bobby Robson in 1981, when his polished Ipswich side had been regularly qualifying for Europe, but he had turned them down, fearing that the language problem would be an insuperable barrier.

Bobby had told me of the offer while we were at the World Cup in Spain in 1982. I had been in Valencia, doing reports on the group there for Ron Greenwood, while England were in Bilbao. Bobby Robson, Dave Sexton and Howard Wilkinson were also checking potential opposition. When it got to the finals, Bobby and I met up in Madrid to do some reports together. While we were having a coffee, he said, 'I would have been manager at Barcelona for a year today, if I had signed for them.' I asked him why he had turned them down. He said, 'Because I didn't know the language.'

'Was that all?'

'Yes, that's all it was really.'

The memory was obviously bothering him, because he mentioned it three times in rapid succession, and I had to tell him to change the subject in the end, but I thought then that if I ever had the chance to work abroad, it would take more than a language problem to put me off. Unlike Bobby, I already spoke a little Spanish, but not as part of any long-term strategy to manage the club, as some people have suggested. I spent my holidays in Spain every year, liked the place very much and felt that learning the language would be useful. There was no hidden agenda involved; if there had been, I would have been learning Catalan instead of Castilian Spanish.

I was on a shortlist of three, with two of the heavyweights of the European game at the time, Helmut Benthaus of Stuttgart, who had just won the German Championship – the Bundesliga – and Michel Hidalgo, who was about to take the European Championship with France. If I was the outsider in the betting, however, I soon got the impression that I was the favourite with the board. Juan Gaspart was the only man who spoke English, and he interpreted for me, as my limited Spanish was of no use to me at all in the detailed questioning of the interview.

Juan kept asking me questions and then telling them my answers, but I wondered if his grasp of English was quite as good as he had claimed. Not that it mattered, for Juan appeared to be on my side, and to this day I am sure that he was giving the directors the answers that he knew they wanted to hear. If so, he certainly did a good job, for I later heard that they had not even bothered to interview Benthaus and Hidalgo, though that rumour may have been started by the Barcelona directors, just to boost my confidence.

After the interview, held in Juan Gaspart's office and lasting five hours, we had dinner in the oak-panelled boardroom. Señor Casaus, who never stopped smoking throughout the interview and the dinner as well, asked me if I would like a cigar. He brought out a great oak box, but much to his embarrassment, when he raised the lid, it was empty. Undaunted, he produced a smaller, silver box, but that was empty as well. To spare his blushes, I offered him one of my cigars.

If you keep cigars in your pocket, they always get broken. The only place you can guarantee that they will be kept straight is down your sock. So I lifted up my trouser leg and pulled two Monte Cristo Number Ones out of my sock. Señor Casaus could not believe his eyes – I think that one incident got me the job. As a devoted cigar-lover, Señor Casaus was sold on me.

The interview resumed the next morning, but after a ninety-minute session, the directors adjourned for a brief discussion, while I smoked another cigar, and then returned to offer me the job. I asked them the same question that almost everyone in Barcelona would soon be asking, 'Why me, instead of Hidalgo or Benthaus?'

'Because we want a coach who is still hungry,' said Señor Nuñez. 'We try to spot young coaches, the way that coaches try to spot young players. We do not necessarily want to sign coaches who have done everything and won everything, because the fire that once burned in their bellies may have gone out. We have had coaches like Menotti, who came to us after winning the World Cup. They have not done well for us. We decided it was time to appoint a coach who was still on his way up, not resting on his laurels.'

As is common in Spanish football, the job was purely to be a coach, not a manager. Few teams have managers in the English sense, with all the negotiation of contracts with players being done by club directors and chief executives. I would be expected to deal with team affairs only, selecting and coaching the players, but with no involvement in contracts or any of the financial side of the job, which was the province of the directors and the chief executive. Although I greatly fancied the idea, I asked for forty-eight hours to think it over, for I still had to talk to my family . . . and Jim Gregory.

I flew back to London the next morning, and told my family that I was likely to be going to Spain. Christine received the news with resignation. Our marriage had been in difficulties for some time. There was no acrimony between Christine and me, no drama, but we had slowly drifted apart over the years. If anyone was to blame for that, it was me. I had been very fortunate to have a great relationship with my daughters and I was determined that I would not lose that or neglect my responsibilities to Christine, but it seemed unlikely that our already rocky marriage would survive the separation. The only person going to Barcelona with me would be Allan Harris as my assistant.

I then went to see Fred and phoned Myrtle in Wales with the news, before going to see Jim Gregory. I told him that Barcelona had offered me the job, but he may still have thought I was bluffing, because he said he was fed up with 'all this nonsense' and, for the first time ever, we really got annoyed with each other. When I told him that I thought I deserved better than he was offering, Jim just said, 'Fair enough, I won't go beyond £40,000 a year to keep you here. That's the offer, take it or leave it.' So I said, 'I'm going to leave it, then,' and walked off.

Jim would sometimes let you leave the office after an argument and then ring down to reception as you were on your way out and tell the receptionist that he wanted to see you again, or call you up the next morning to bring you back; it was part of his managerial style, to keep people on their toes and keep them guessing. If he was trying a bit of brinkmanship this time, however, it backfired. I was fuming and did not wait to see if it would happen this time. When the receptionist called to me, I ignored her, walked straight out, jumped in the car and drove off.

I could not leave it that way, however, because I liked him too much to part on angry terms, so I went back a couple of days later and spoke to him again. We were both choked, because in many ways I did not want to leave and he did not really want me to go, but I put an arm round his shoulders and said, 'I'm going. I've made up my mind and I'm going.' I think there was a tear in both our eyes, and it was a very sad moment, because we had made so many plans for the future of the club, but there was to be no back-tracking. My decision was made and the die was cast. Twenty-four hours later, I had signed for Barcelona.

When the news broke that I had been given the job, people in England were queuing up to claim the credit for getting me there. Jeff Powell, of the *Daily Mail*, said that he had been asked to recommend a British coach to Barcelona and had named me. The football agent Dennis Roach claimed that Barcelona had phoned him and asked whom they should get. Juan Gaspart said that he was a very good friend of Doug Ellis, the chairman of Aston Villa, and had also spoken to Bobby Robson, both of whom recommended me, as did another couple of people. I am not sure which of the stories was accurate, but there was probably a bit of truth in all of them.

My Dad was all for me taking the job, and was thrilled for me, but I could tell that he was also a bit down about it. I usually dropped in on him or called him on the phone every day. He felt that my going to Barcelona was like going to the ends of the earth, and that he would never see or hear from me. I wanted to prove to him that Barcelona was not that far away from Chingford at all, and the day that I was due to go back to Spain, I went into his pub to see him for a farewell drink, leaving it very tight to catch my plane. I told him that I would phone him as soon as I got to Barcelona, but left him very upset.

I drove like a maniac to Heathrow and caught the flight by the skin of my teeth. To save time, I had made sure that I did not have any luggage to check in or collect. The flight took an hour and forty-five minutes, and it took another fifteen minutes to reach my hotel. As soon as I got there, only three and a half hours after I had left the pub, I rang my Dad. He thought that I must have missed the flight, and would not believe that I was calling from Spain. I insisted on him ringing me straight back to make sure, and when he heard my voice again, it made him see that I really was not that far away, and he was much happier.

Once he became used to the idea, he came out to see me all the time. He absolutely loved it out there, and I think he misses it now. He would always arrive, insisting that he could only stay for a week, but would end up staying at least two or three instead. The last time, he stayed for six weeks, after telling me he could only stay for a few days.

When I started in Barcelona, my Dad was nearly sixty-five, and only a tenant in his pub, the Royal Oak in Chingford. At that age, the brewery could have thrown him out if they had wished. It was something that worried me, for the pub was his life as well as his living, so I made contact with the brewery and bought the freehold for him. With his future assured and his worries about the distance from Chingford to Barcelona eased, I turned my whole attention to the task of steering Barcelona to the one thing they craved above all others, the Spanish League Championship.

Almost immediately I had to break off to rebuff yet another

approach from Jim Gregory, however. He came to stay with me while I was in Spain and we remain very good friends to this day. He had appointed my old rival Alan Mullery to succeed me, but things did not work out for him. He left the club after only six weeks, complaining that the players would not play for him as they had for me. As a result, Jim was straight on the phone to me in Barcelona, in a vain attempt to persuade me to return, saying, 'Why don't you come back? They don't take football seriously over there.'

Nothing could be further from the truth. If football was much more important than a matter of life or death to Bill Shankly, he would have found plenty to agree with him in Barcelona, for football is all of that – and the moon and stars as well – to the Catalan people. They are perhaps the most fervent football supporters in the world, their dreams centred on one of the most magnificent stadiums anywhere, the Nou Camp, and while my assistant, Allan Harris, and I did not share their culture or history, we fully understood the passion that drove them, and the problem that the football club faced. It was possibly the biggest club in the world and they were hiring us for one thing alone – to fulfil their expectations by winning the Championship.

Despite all their famous coaches and players, they had not won the Spanish League in eleven years. To finish behind Real Madrid, year after year, was more than the public could bear. All they wanted was for Barcelona to win the League. We knew exactly what to expect, canonisation if we won the title, the sack if we did not. In case we had any doubts, the club's only previous English coach, Vic Buckingham, who had been at Barcelona fifteen years earlier, spelt it out for us, 'If you win here, you're a king; if you lose, they'll set fire to your car.'

The club directors were heavily criticised in the Barcelona press for appointing me. It was said that they had found their new coach among the English tourists on the beach, a belief that was evidently shared by one or two of the Barcelona players. 'He will be some English coach, out in Spain for a holiday, wanting a few beers on the beach,' according to Bernd Schuster, one of Barcelona's biggest stars. The biggest star of all, Diego Maradona, was equally unimpressed: 'I don't think the English style of play will suit me.' What to do about Diego would be one of the first decisions I had to make. Minutes before I signed my contract with the club, Maradona had a furious confrontation with the board.

Although I had not formally taken over from Menotti, who was seeing out the last few weeks of his contract at the fag-end of the season, I did see him at a training session. He looked very relaxed, but the players were wandering around and not looking particularly interested. Jeff Powell, a mutual friend, arranged for Menotti and me to have dinner together, and before we had even sat down, Menotti was saying, 'The players are concerned, they know you are taking over, they've read it in the papers, wouldn't it be better for you to get involved now? You'll have time to get to know them and they'll be far happier.'

It took me all of a second to spot the sub-text to this – Menotti wanted to get home to Argentina and was trying to con me into taking over at a time when there was nothing in it for me. I was fortunate to see it coming, and just said, 'Well, it's very kind of you, Cesar, and I appreciate you thinking about me this way, but if it's all the same to you, I'll continue with the plans originally devised.'

Over dinner, he told me that he thought there were only three players in the whole squad – Maradona, Miguelli and Schuster. The next year, after I had taken them to the top of the table, he came back for a short holiday in Barcelona, and told all the press that he had left me with 'a giant of a side and, without doubt, every player was an expert'.

His initial opinion about the players did concern me, and I had my first chance to judge for myself when I went to see

Barcelona play in one of their last games of the season, a League Cup semi-final in San Sebastian. It took seven or eight hours to drive there, and the game against Real Sociedad was a depressing experience. Several Barcelona players were playing in an international, and with practically a reserve side out, Barcelona gave an awful performance and were well beaten. Even more depressingly, there was a guy in front of me who kept turning round and having a go at me, saying, 'Why have you come here, Terry? What makes you think you can win? You cannot possibly win.'

On the journey back, his words, and Menotti's opinion of his team, kept echoing in my ears, and I wanted to know exactly how rosy my future in Barcelona would be. I was living at the Princess Sofia Hotel until I found an apartment, and for the next week, I scarcely put my nose outside, sitting in the gloom of my darkened room, endlessly watching the videos of Barcelona's first and second division games during the previous season, because I knew nothing about the players.

At the end of the week, I was much less depressed, for I had seen enough talented players to give me hope. The situation with the most talented player among them, on the other hand, seemed more hopeless than hopeful. If Maradona stayed with Barcelona, he would miss the first three months of the season because of a suspension imposed after brutal clashes at the end of the Spanish Cup final the previous season. He was also costing the club a fortune, not only with his own contract, but through the bills being run up all over Barcelona by his enormous entourage. He had a huge house with about thirty-six guys living in it, who were clubbing and drinking round town and signing his name for things, leaving the club to pick up the tab.

Much as I had been looking forward to coaching one of the world's great footballers, when the board explained the nature of the problems with Maradona and asked me for a decision on his future, I could give only one answer: 'Sell him.' He had to go, so that we could make a fresh start right away. Within a week the 'Hand of God' was packing its owner's suitcase for the one-way trip to Napoli, while Barcelona were banking a cheque for £5.5 million.

When I was asked whom I wanted to replace Maradona, I said, 'Steve Archibald.' I had tried to sign Steve from Aberdeen when I was at Crystal Palace, only to lose out when he chose Tottenham instead, and he was a player who consistently worried me when we played against him. I really felt he was a top player, a fine goal-scorer, intelligent, quick, good with his head, and nearly always on target. The directors preferred a Mexican player, Hugo Sanchez, who was then at Atletico Madrid, and though the money was a bit more for Sanchez, it did not matter, because we had a lot to spend. I thought that he was a good player too, but I knew Archibald better, and I felt confident in him.

There were one or two suggestions that Archibald was a loner, but I thought that criticism was actually in his favour. Players who like to be 'one of the lads' may miss that when they move to a foreign club, but if you are a loner anyway, it does not really matter where you are. Steve can be a little aloof at times, but I met him and liked him immediately, as I still do today. He is a solid guy, with a good approach to the game.

The directors were much more keen on signing Sanchez than Steve Who? to play under Terry Who?, but my mind was made up and I felt that I had to assert my authority in playing matters from the start. It was a battle I could not afford to lose, because the directors had a reputation of going over their coaches' heads, and if I lost the first round, I would lose all the rest too.

I eventually persuaded the directors to back my judgement, but they were careful to distance themselves from the decision. I even had to sign a contract, at the directors' request, saying that the decision to sign Archibald was mine alone. Had the signing not worked out, the directors were making sure that I, not they, would carry the can. In the event he proved to be outstanding, playing a huge part in our successes, and the contract 'blaming' me for the signing was not referred to again.

I was presented to the Barcelona public in the traditional way there. The first training session of the season is a public affair and 50,000 fans turned up on 1 July, to run the rule over the players and take a look at the new coach. I had learned enough Catalan by then to be able to make a short speech to the crowd in their own language. It was scarcely Henry V before Agincourt, little more than 'If we all work together, we can do it. Let's go'. No other foreign coach had bothered to learn their language before, however, and after a moment's shocked silence, every one of the 50,000 was on their feet cheering their heads off. I kept up my daily Spanish and Catalan lessons throughout my time in Barcelona, but I did not kid myself; without success on the field, no amount of good PR in Catalan or any other language would save my hide.

There was a rather less enthusiastic reaction in other quarters. I received three death threats early in the season, all postmarked Madrid, but I did not worry about them too much, for that sort of thing just went with the territory – it was almost a compliment. The club took the threats seriously enough to assign a 'minder' to me, however, a genial, seventeen-stone giant called José Ceballos.

There was a further chance to assess the strengths and weaknesses of all the players on the books during a training session in Andorra, high in the Pyrenees, where Barcelona went for pre-season training every year, and by the end, I was even more pleased with what I had seen. There were three or four players who had not been picked for first-team duty by Menotti, who really caught my eye.

The teams were organised differently from those at English clubs. We had about thirty-six professionals in the first team squad, but if you did not play in the first team, you did not play at all. Many of those players would not play a single game during the year, because they simply did not play in the lower teams; it was below their category once they had played for the first team. People could be out for months with an injury, but once they got fit, they would go straight back into the first team, whereas in England they would play in the reserves until they were fit. I was never convinced about this particular aspect of the Spanish way of doing things, and felt that the English way was best.

Barcelona Athletic was the second team, effectively an under-23 side, although there was no formal age limit, and if you had not graduated to the first-team squad by the time you were twenty-four, you would probably never make it. Once you had made the first-team squad, you would not go back. Barcelona Athletic, like Castillon, which is the Real Madrid second team, and Bilbao Athletic, are three of the biggest sides in Spain, but are permanently in the Second Division and cannot be promoted. Even if they finished first, second and third in the table, the fourth, fifth and sixth teams would be promoted.

Players seemed to have to go through a lengthy 'apprenticeship' in the second team, and as a result, they were not coming through to the first team at eighteen or twenty. They only tended to come through at twenty-three or twenty-four, which made their span in the first team relatively short. I thought that some of the young players in the reserve squad were terrific, easily good enough to strengthen the first team immediately, and I promoted them straight away. Two young players, in particular, really impressed me: Caldere and Rocco. Rocco had been number two in the world to Maradona in an under-19 tournament in Japan a few years before, but then had a period in the wilderness and was stuck in the reserve squad.

I brought him into the first team and he was sensational, the best and most consistent player I had. There were other consist-

ent players, like Miguelli and Archibald, but for Rocco, a guy
who was virtually unknown, to have such a fantastic year was
incredible. He was badly injured early in my second year, never
really recovered, and we missed him more than anyone; everyone
had underrated his presence and his ability to contribute.

Both Rocco and Ramon Caldere, a twenty-four-year-old
midfielder, made the national team that year. Mohammed Ali
Amar – also known as Nayim – who was later to follow me to
Tottenham, was another player pulled straight from the obscu-
rity of the shadow squad to begin training with the first team.
Esteban too, was only on the fringes of the team, but I brought
him in and he had a very good spell.

Menotti had been much too quick to dismiss their abilities,
but he was right to praise Miguelli, who was a clever defender
and possibly the strongest, bravest and best centre-half I have
ever worked with – although Tony Adams is improving so fast
that I may soon have to revise my opinion. Miguelli was
outstanding and should have been the captain, but he would not
do it, because he was superstitious and felt that captaincy had
been unlucky for him before. The other centre-half, Alessanco,
also had a terrific year, and scored about twelve goals from set-
pieces. He is now one of the coaches at Barcelona.

The left-back, Julio Alberto, also played for Spain, and was
another outstanding footballer. He was very quick, and reminded me of Kenny Sansom. Like the rest of his team-mates,
he had some initial doubts about my coaching, as he confessed
later in the year. 'We all thought you were an absolute head-
case when you took us to Andorra, because you did the exact
opposite of everything we had been taught, all our lives. Instead
of dropping back deep to the box, you pushed us up; instead of
showing wide players the outside, you showed them the inside.
We really were concerned, but when we won a few games, we
began to think that you might have something after all.' Winning
the early games was the biggest thing that went for me, because

if you train something new into players, you have got to have success early on, otherwise they do not believe in it.

After all the build-up, it was a relief finally to begin serious work with the players, and I immediately had another very pleasant surprise. We hear plenty about the temperament of European footballers, but we hear very little about their thoroughgoing professionalism. I quickly realised that the players there took a great pride in being professionals. It is a different attitude from here in England, where we too often think of professionalism as simply being paid to do something that we enjoy doing anyway. The footballers at Barcelona and elsewhere in Europe know that they only have a certain amount of time to play and always make the best of it.

In football your body is your business. If you had a corner shop you could not smash the windows or throw the stock away. A footballer has to look after his body and keep it in the best condition he possibly can for the period he plays football, which is probably less than half his life. Footballers abroad appreciate this far more than their British counterparts. At Barcelona, we would travel to San Sebastian by coach, a journey of seven or eight hours and the players would just drink water, all the way there and back. In England, the players would drink water and Coca-Cola on the way to a match, but on the way back they would be swilling beer. In Spain, I did not see a single player smoke or drink until we won the League, and then they all got absolutely smashed. They were professionals and the job was done. In England we do it every Saturday, after the match.

The Spanish footballers care about their condition, their fitness and their behaviour. They enjoy showing off their skills. The British are more functional, they get the job done, and are professionals from that point of view, and if they lack the technical ability of the Spanish players, they do have resilience. If the Latin teams are one– or two–nil down, then as a rule, you can forget it, but the British will fight to the death. We both have our strengths and weaknesses, but the sight of a squad of highly skilled, motivated and disciplined footballers waiting for me at my first training session with Barcelona, was a very welcome one.

The professionalism of the club and its players extended to the young players, who came to Barcelona from all over Spain, and lived in a 'farmhouse' called La Masea, just behind the training pitch, at the side of the stadium. La Masea provided a homely atmosphere, an extension of the close family life in Spain. The youngsters also had a year's national service, which helped to give them a good basis for their lives as football players. They were very well-behaved boys and there was a discipline about their approach, even at such a young age.

For the first few weeks, I met the directors for lunch at La Masea on Mondays to talk about progress, but the press were very strong in Barcelona and always got to know what went on at the meetings. In the end Josip-Luis Nuñez, Juan Gaspart and I used to go to a restaurant instead, to try and keep things to ourselves and stop the leaks to the media.

After the total involvement in England, it was a refreshing change to be back as a coach pure and simple, dealing solely with the training, tactics, and players, and finishing work at the same time as the players, being on my way home by 12:30 p.m. When I had first joined Crystal Palace as a manager, Ron Greenwood told me to be careful, because it was a tough job, with responsibility for so many things. Ron told me that your responsibilities went out like the spokes of a wheel, to your players, your own staff, your directors, the youth team, the mums and dads, the press, and on and on.

In England I had tried to delegate a lot of those things to other people, who would report back to me, leaving me freer to concentrate on the playing side of the game. In Barcelona, that had already been done for me. None of the other aspects of management would affect me, for my responsibilities were to one thing alone, the football, while other people dealt with the rest. Nor did my coaching duties extend beyond the first team, and I had nothing to do with the youth policy of the club.

The pre-season training went well despite the language difficulties. Those were not helped by my translator, José. My suspicions about his lack of knowledge of English hardened into certainty as I watched the players' puzzled faces while he laboured to translate my instructions. In the end, I had to ask the club to replace him, and got in Graham Turner, an Englishman living over there, who was fluent in Spanish and Catalan. After that, the blank looks on the players' faces disappeared. I could actually speak Spanish better than I often let on, but I found the presence of an interpreter gave me valuable thinking time in press conferences. Occasionally I had to reveal my knowledge, however, notably in one press conference when I interrupted Graham's translation to say, 'Don't give them your version of what I said, just tell them mine.'

One change was brought in straight away. Under Cesar Menotti, training had been switched to the late afternoon. Everyone had always trained at ten in the morning, but he wanted to train at five in the afternoon because, he said, that was the time when the body was most perfectly attuned. He was a great talker and could romance everyone – directors, players and even the press. He claimed that it was good for the players' biorhythms to train at the same time of day that they were going to play, but switching the time of training would be just as handy if the coach wanted to be out dancing till dawn the night before.

When I had first met him, his opening words, delivered through a cloud of smoke from his habitual cigarette, had been, 'If you like women, Terry, welcome to paradise.' Five o'clock training gave him enough time to recover from the rigours of the night before, but the new English coach had brought with him English attitudes to organisation, punctuality and discipline. Training sessions were moved back to the morning, beginning at ten o'clock sharp, and a house rule of 'No more *mañana*' was introduced.

Some of the players were wary of me at first, fearing that long-ball 'Route One' football was about to be introduced along with the English discipline. Most were quickly won over, but it took me all of a month to convince Bernd Schuster that the club had not lumbered him with a coach who wanted to play kick-and-rush. I needed no convincing of Schuster's talents. He was probably the best player I have ever dealt with, and could do absolutely anything with the ball. He was not only gifted, he was prepared to work hard at his game, and you do not get too many like that.

It is sometimes difficult to convince players at the highest level that they can still improve further, because they are already stars in their own right. They might say 'Why should I need more?' but I believe that, however good you are, you should stretch yourself further, just as Jack Nicklaus has done in golf. You can keep improving; Gary Lineker did it, because he was smart; and Bernd Schuster did it, too.

After training, he would often stay out on the pitch for another hour, firing in shots from all over the place. He could hit the ball like a rocket, chip it with the delicacy of a professional golfer, and bend a shot around any wall you could build. He would even go and stand out by the corner flag and curl shot after shot into the net from what would have been an impossible angle for almost anybody else. He had been practising the whole of his life, for his wealthy parents had erected a set of goals in the large garden of their home, when he was a kid.

He believed that there were two ways to get the ball, from your own team-mates or from the opposition, and he was prepared to work hard to take it from the opposition. He attracted the ball and when it was given to him, he had the ability to deliver the killing pass. With such skills, Schuster should never have been out of the team, but he was also a difficult guy, and dominated by his wife. The endless ribbing his German team-mates had given him about her was one of the reasons he left the country to come to Barcelona. Despite his natural talent, at one stage he was playing so poorly that I never picked him for the first team for a whole year.

Such problems lay a long way in the future, however, when I made him team captain at the start of my first season. While I learned Spanish and Catalan, and got used to being called 'Meester' – which Spanish players call their coach as routinely as English ones say 'Boss' – the players soon picked up on my cockney accent and one or two of my swear-words. When the goalkeeper, Andoni Zubizarreta, played in a friendly for Spain against England, Gary Lineker put four goals past him. I met Andoni coming out of the dressing room, and started to commiserate with him, but he just shrugged his shoulders and said, 'Facking 'ell, Meester.'

The message was getting through to the Barcelona public too, albeit in rather less explicit terms. We had our first serious test with a four-club, pre-season tournament, held at the Nou Camp in August, in which we beat the Argentine side Boca Juniors 9–1. Steve Archibald, wearing Maradona's number-ten shirt, scored two of the goals, which immediately took much of the pressure off him. The newspapers promptly christened him 'Archi-goles'. We then saw off Bayern Munich 3–1 in the final. Cesar Menotti had been sitting in the stands, having earlier given an interview to the Spanish press, telling them that he would soon be back in charge at the club. After the tournament, he was forced to issue another statement, withdrawing his previous remarks.

The English coach known as 'Mister Who?' who Barcelona 'had found on the beach' and the Scottish striker who no one had ever heard of, were suddenly two of the most popular men in Barcelona. Every time I stopped my car at a traffic-light, people were coming up, smiling, waving and chanting the local version of my name: 'Benabless, Benabless.' Steve was also popular with his team-mates; if they gave him the ball there was every chance that they would get it back, which made a refreshing change for many of them. He was not worried about making himself look good by going past opponents. If he could pass, get into the box and take a return pass in a scoring position, that suited him fine. He could compete with the hard men if he needed to, but he also had the ability to keep his cool and make the right decision in front of goal. If he could not get a powerful header in himself, he would look to knock it back across goal to give someone else a chance of scoring.

The real test for me, Steve and the rest of the side came in the first League game, on 2 September. It could not have been a harder first hurdle – away at the Bernabeu Stadium, against Barcelona's most hated rivals, Real Madrid. The excitement in both cities was palpable. The match was sold out weeks in advance, with tickets changing hands on the black market for £125. I had raised my personal stakes by dropping Marcos Alonso, the leading scorer from the previous season, for a game that we had to win. A defeat at the Bernabeu, followed by two or three more bad results, could easily have seen me on my way out of Barcelona; coaches had been sacked after as little as half-a-dozen games.

If winning the title was the club's first priority, beating Real Madrid came a very close second. 'I don't care what else happens,' said a venerable Barcelona supporter, accosting me in a restaurant the night before the game. 'Just make damn sure we beat Real Madrid.' We did.

Allan and I had worked hard with the team to drill them into the way we wanted them to play. The players were top-class, but they liked to show off their talents in areas of the pitch where it could do us the most harm. I asked them to keep their ball skills up their sleeves, so that they could suddenly produce them in areas where they could do the most damage to the other side. I had to drum into them that there are times and places on the field where passing the ball is more productive than trying to beat people.

I also stressed that they should 'press' the ball, hustling the man in possession with three or four players at a time and trying to rob him in parts of the field from where we could counter-attack quickly and effectively, instead of falling back and only winning it when their entire team was in front of us. If you can win it when you only have five players between you and the goal, life becomes a lot easier. It sounds obvious, but it was not the way that they were used to playing.

I had given the team my final instructions in the relative calm of the dressing room, and as they took the field in the searing, ninety-degree heat, with 93,000 Real Madrid fans baying for their blood, I tried to reach my seat in the stand. There was such a mob of people that I could not get within miles of it, however, and had to settle for a place in the dug-out, which is not my preferred location for watching the game. It is much easier to see the patterns of play from a higher vantage point, but with the Bernabeu crowd spilling all over the seats and the gangways, in the end I was grateful to be able to see any of the game.

Most of the Real Madrid fans must have been wishing that they did not have such a good view, for we cruised to a 3–0 victory, with Steve Archibald laying the ghost of Maradona to rest, as he scored a vital goal and had a hand in the others, to make the number-ten shirt his own. By half-time, the Madrid crowd already knew the game was lost and vented their frustration on the visiting dug-out. I had to call for police protection after vollies of coins, crushed beer-cans and broken bottles rained down around our ears, and at the end, we sprinted for the tunnel, under a screen of police riot shields, with missiles rattling like hailstones on them.

As we boarded the coach for the drive to the airport, I could
see a mob of Madrid fans howling at us from beyond the gates.
I had a flash-back to the terrifying night when the Chelsea
coach had been pelted with rocks after we had beaten Roma. I
told the players to pull down the shades over the windows, and
as the coach moved off, I called out to them to get down on the
floor. The warning came only just in time, for as we sped
through the gates, the windows were smashed by a fusillade of
rocks, one going straight through the space that had been
occupied by Allan Harris's head until a couple of seconds
before. Luckily the players were unhurt, but the coach-driver
was badly cut on the face by flying glass. I was beginning to
realise why not one of the Barcelona directors had made the
journey to Madrid for the match.

When we landed at Barcelona, there were thousands of
people there to greet us, chanting, shouting greetings and waving
Barcelona banners. In the city itself, although it is the oldest
cliché in the book, the crowds really were dancing in the streets,
and an impromptu fireworks display was lighting up the night
sky. As we surveyed the scene, one of the club officials turned to
me, winked and said, 'Terry, take my advice, you have twenty-
four hours to ask the club president for anything you want –
double your contract and double your wages – Barcelona is
yours.'

The next morning, I had almost as big a treat, English
sausages for breakfast, delivered by Malcolm Allison on a flying
visit. I ate them on the terrace, looking out over the city, where
according to one excitable radio journalist, they would shortly
be erecting a statue of me. On the same programme, a former
Championship coach with Barcelona, Helenio Herrera, who had
earlier predicted that I would be 'gone by Christmas', was now
saying that he was the man who had recommended me to the
club.

That first game set the pattern for a season that could

scarcely have gone better. We opened with a twelve-match unbeaten run, the longest in Barcelona's history. With twelve games to go, we were nine points clear of Atletico Madrid in second place, and we secured the Championship by the end of March, with games in hand. By then the 'Englishman off the beach' was so popular in Barcelona that I could make time stand still. To my great embarrassment the restaurant where I went for a New Year's party held back midnight by sixty minutes to celebrate it by Greenwich Mean Time.

We even survived a players' strike before my third game in charge. It was nothing personal against me, and was not even confined to Barcelona, being a national players' strike, but it was a worrying disruption, just as we had got off to a flyer. As a manager in England I would have been at the heart of negotiations with the players, but as a new coach – and only the coach – in Barcelona, I was sidelined, completely out of the ring, while Señor Nuñez and the players argued it out. The dispute looked like it could run and run, because the players were holding the clubs to ransom, but the clubs would not shift. There was no emotion about it at all; both players and clubs had made cold, business decisions and were determined to stick to them.

If the players had succeeded in disrupting the fixtures, the pressure to settle from the fans would have been enormous, but the clubs put up a united front and all fulfilled their fixtures by playing their youth teams in place of the seniors. It was an arrangement that suited me down to the ground. Our youth team beat Zaragossa 4–0, continuing our superb start, and played so well that it would not have bothered me if we had carried on like that for the rest of the season. In fact the strike was settled that week and normal service was restored, with the first team playing equally well.

Before his sacking, my social life for the first few weeks was in the hands of my driver and translator José, who would often take me to his local bar. He also asked me, on behalf of the

owner, if I would act as a judge at a beauty contest being held
at his favourite night-club. My impressions of Spain remained
very much as they had been on my first visit, a country still
feeling the effects of Franco's long reign, rather repressed and
moralistic, with its young women strictly chaperoned and not
allowed skirts above the ankle, never mind the knee. The idea
of a beauty contest was in itself something of a surprise, which
just shows how out of touch with the reality of modern Spain I
had become.

José drove me to his club on the night of the contest, after I
had dressed in Barcelona blazer and tie, determined to look
good, as I was representing the football club. The club was
packed, with a compère and a comedian warming up the audience for the main event. The girls came out in swimsuits and
did the usual bland question-and-answer sessions and then they
all disappeared behind a curtain stretched across the stage. I
noticed a hole cut in the curtain, about two foot across, and I
was just wondering why it was there, when the girls began
supplying the answer. Each one had removed her swimsuit and
in turn they began poking their backsides through the hole in
the curtain. I could not believe my eyes; so much for my ideas
about repressed, moralistic Spain.

The compère then bet the comedian that he would not do
the same, but he disappeared behind the curtain and went one
better, revealing his entire 'three-piece suite' instead. At that
point, I decided that discretion was the better part of valour and
before anyone had the bright idea of getting 'Benabless' up on
stage to show what he was made of, I quietly drank up and
slipped away.

The only set-back in an almost uninterrupted run of success
that first season came in the European Cup-Winners' Cup, when
we were beaten 4–1 at home by Metz, after we had won the first
leg 4–2 in France. That defeat was probably the best thing that
could have happened to us, however. Persuading talented foot-

ballers to play for the team and not themselves, is as much of a problem in Spain as it is in England. The players thought that they could go out and indulge themselves against Metz and paid the price. As well as removing the distraction of the European competition, the defeat was a very salutary lesson for the players and gave me a useful stick to beat them with, whenever they became complacent or self-indulgent. As I held an inquest into the defeat next morning Bernd Schuster announced 'It's very difficult to play with ten men' – a dig at Steve Archibald, who had not played particularly well. 'Don't be too hard on yourself, Bernd,' I replied. 'You weren't that bad.'

The Spanish players have a little bit of the matador in them, an inclination to show off, which was one of the traits we were trying to get them to play down. Unlike footballers, matadors do not always survive their bad displays, however, and when we played in Seville, immediately after the match against Metz, we attended the funeral of Baccheri, one of the best bull-fighters in Spain. He had gone to fight in a small town just outside Seville to commemorate the centenary of the local *plaza de toros*. There were a few hundred spectators and a big, fat bull who had trouble breaking into a trot, with the contest shown live on Spanish TV.

In England, when we played some of the lower division teams, we used to say that we would give a player a dummy and he would not even buy it, he would just stand there and you would run into him. Baccheri made the same mistake. He feinted with his cape to the left, but the bull just lumbered straight ahead and knocked his stomach out, spilling his guts all over the screen – hardly family viewing.

Despite the matador's injuries, the bull-fight equivalent of a *Match of the Day* post-match interviewer charged into the ring and started asking him questions like: 'Well Baccheri, what went wrong?' He started to give the standard reply: 'I suppose I went in there and thought it was going to be easy. I feinted to the right and tried to move swiftly to the left, but the bull just came straight down the middle into me.'

While the interviewer was still plying him with questions, Baccheri keeled over and died, live on Spanish television. All the Barcelona players and officials attended his funeral as a mark of respect, and in the light of the Metz game, his death provided me with a useful motivational tool before our match with Seville: 'Don't believe your own publicity and don't underestimate the strength of the opposition!'

Shortly afterwards, we had dinner with another bull-fighter, Camacco, who had suffered a similar goring, but lived to tell the tale. The bull's horn went into his groin and tore his stomach open. He had to push his intestines back in, and as his blood seeped into the sand, Camacco was certain that, even if he was not about to die, he would certainly have waved his love-life goodbye. He woke up in hospital, however, and when a beautiful nurse walked past the end of his bed, he discovered that everything was going to be all right after all . . .

Had things turned out for the worse, he might have found himself on the menu at a local restaurant called the Triton, which specialises in authentic Spanish dishes. When I took my girlfriend, now my wife, Yvette, to the Triton a couple of years later, I called the *maître-d'* over to explain the house specialities, one of which was *Cojones de Toro* – bull's balls, collected after the bull-fight the previous day. As he described it he looked at Yvette for a reaction, but she was equal to the challenge. She just stared back at him and said, 'What do we get if the bull wins?'

After being bombarded in the Bernabeu, we faced another barrage of missiles when we played at Valencia, but they were relatively harmless compared to the ones at Real Madrid. Valencia is the heart of the orange-growing region of Spain and the fans bombarded us with them before the game. By the time they had finished, the ground looked as if it had been hailing oranges.

We all stood in the centre circle, as you do, but the fans behind the Valencia goal kept throwing them.

The ground is almost circular, more like a bull-ring than a football ground in shape, and there is a sizeable gap between the goal-line and the stand behind it. Even to reach the six- or eighteen-yard box was pretty good throwing, but there was one guy who kept reaching the halfway line. We were in hysterics watching this guy hurling oranges seventy or eighty yards. If they ever hold the Olympics in Valencia, I have a pretty good idea what the demonstration sport will be.

The return game against Real Madrid was a predictably bitter and bruising affair. The Nou Camp was packed with a record crowd of 123,000, who began gathering five hours before the game, and tickets were changing hands on the black market for £200. Three men from each side were booked and our defender Victor Muñoz was sent off in the thirtieth minute for a foul on Sandis, who had just equalised Gerardo's opening goal.

Despite that handicap, we went on to complete the double over them, winning 3–2. Miguelli scored our second with a header from Esteban's corner and Esteban himself made certain of victory with a goal of dazzling brilliance twelve minutes from time. Julio Alberto put the ball into space and Esteban's accelera-tion and close control took him past three defenders on a diagonal run which ended with an unstoppable shot from ten yards. Butragueno's volley for Madrid right on the final whistle was just a consolation. As the players trooped off the field, the stale, sulphurous smell of flares and fire-crackers hung in the air, mingling with the smoke from Madrid flags being ritually burnt by the Barcelona fans. Another battle in the never-ending Spanish civil war between Barcelona and Madrid had been won.

We clinched the League title in an away game at Valladolid, winning 2–1, after Jose Urruti saved a penalty in the eighty-sixth minute, and we flew back into Barcelona airport that evening with the trophy, for the short drive to the Nou Camp stadium. A million people were waiting to greet us, lining and often blocking the road from the airport, and the journey, which normally took twenty minutes, lasted seven hours. As we drove into the city on the team bus, people were holding babies up to us so that they could one day tell their grandchildren that they had watched the champions come home. Other people were strewing the road with flowers and crossing themselves as we passed, and one old lady, in black Spanish lace, kneeling at the side of the road, raised a crucifix to me, as if I were a pope instead of a football coach.

Time and again, the sheer weight of numbers would bring the motorcade to a halt and the fans would swarm around the coach, pressing their faces to the windows, desperate for even a glimpse of the trophy, which was more precious to them than the holiest relic. Many of the faces at the windows were streaming with tears, the intensity of emotion overwhelming young and old alike. I have never seen scenes like it in my life. It was as if the Republican army was returning in triumph from war. We finally reached the Nou Camp at midnight, but there were still 100,000 people there, waiting to see us go out on the pitch with the trophy.

The club officials and all the players' wives and families were also waiting for us at the stadium. Yvette and my daughter Nancy were there and both stood out a mile because they were dressed up to the nines as if they were on their way to Royal Ascot. They had spent hours getting ready, assuming that everybody would be looking their best to welcome home the conquering heroes, and were a bit fed up to discover that all the other players' wives and daughters had turned up in T-shirts and jeans.

The celebrations continued at our next home game, against Sporting Gijon. The kick-off was delayed for twenty-five minutes as the Catalans celebrated their triumph under a cloudless sky. The stadium was packed and it seemed as if every one of the 120,000 people was waving a red and blue flag, banging a drum and blowing a whistle.

As I led the players out of the tunnel, the noise trebled in volume and so many fire-crackers exploded that the smoke took minutes to clear. When order was eventually restored, we kicked off. Ninety minutes and a 2–0 victory later, the final whistle was the signal for a repeat performance from the crowd.

We ended the season ten points clear of the runners-up, and nineteen clear of Real Madrid, while our total of fifty-three points equalled the Spanish record. We had not turned the Barcelona players into more skilful footballers, nor made them fitter, for they were already tremendously fit and supremely skilful when we arrived. What we had done was to change the way that they saw their role in the game. Instead of wanting to shine as individuals, we had taught them to play as a team.

We had also destroyed a couple of myths along the way. The Spaniards – and Bernd Schuster – had learned that not every English coach is a believer in kick-and-rush, and we had also exploded the English myth about the suspect temperament of the Latin footballer, for our players showed plenty of 'English' guts and character alongside their 'Latin' football skill.

If I could do no wrong with the fans at that stage, I was pretty popular with the board too. The president even bought me a present. I had gone home for the weekend, and when I came back, he presented me with my gift, a new player from Zaragossa. He turned out to be very average, but it is the thought that counts, after all.

With no Spanish equivalent of Tommy Docherty around to veto my extra-mural activities, I also finally made it big in showbiz. A group called La Trinca, who used to play as pavement buskers, telling jokes and singing up and down the Costa Brava, were eventually 'spotted' and became big stars in Spain, with their own television show. One of the regular spots on the programme showed high-profile people in a different light, just like Morecambe and Wise used to have serious actors and newsreaders in their sketches.

La Trinca tried to get me on their show to appear in a sketch and sing a song. At first I refused, because it was a long time since I had done any singing in public at all, but they were incredibly persistent. When I went to lunch with Julio Alberto, our left-back and a mutual friend, it proved to be a set-up, because La Trinca turned up as well, and kept badgering me until I eventually agreed. My daughter Tracey was coming to Barcelona the same day, but did not know anything about the show until I took her to the studio and sat her in the audience. I sang with a big band and gave 'I've Got You Under My Skin' the full Frank Sinatra treatment, which seemed to go down pretty well.

My other appearances on television were more long-lasting, for I became a summariser for the BBC in 1985, a job that I have continued, England duties permitting, to the present day. I saw it as an extension of what I was doing as a coach anyway, explaining my ideas on football to an audience, the only difference being that, instead of eleven players in a dressing-room, the audience for this was counted in millions. I never thought about it as anything but a bit of fun, talking about something that I know, but all of a sudden people started describing me as a 'television pundit' and that sounded a bit more serious.

I was also a whisker away from a less welcome television appearance in 1985, coming perilously close to being given 'the big red book' on *This Is Your Life*. I had always said that I would not do it if it came up. Luckily I found out that they were planning to surprise me and was able to knock it on the head before it went any further. There must be something about footballers, because Danny Blanchflower would not go on the programme either, although he did not find out about it until they thrust the red book in his face. They did the show live in those days and Bill Nicholson and the rest of the Spurs team were all sitting out the back, waiting for their moment of televised glory, when Danny walked away from it.

Some intrusions into your privacy cannot be so easily shaken off, however. When you are in the public eye, you quickly learn that even your private life is considered fair game by tabloid reporters and photographers. I soon realised that I was being followed around Barcelona by a photographer and a reporter, and could see them hiding in the bushes outside my apartment at night. I had to get used to it, but after following me for a few days, they suddenly disappeared. I realised that they had got what they came for – pictures of me out on the town in Barcelona, with a very attractive brunette, half my age.

They were so delighted with their scoop that they went straight from Heathrow airport to my home in England. The breathless reporter was on our front doorstep within minutes, confronting Christine with the evidence.

'What do you think of your husband escorting a beautiful woman around Barcelona while you are stuck back here in England?' asked the hack.

'She is beautiful, isn't she?'

'Yes, but what do you think of it?'

'I don't mind at all.'

'Your husband's with another woman and you don't mind?'

'Why should I? She's our daughter, Nancy.'

That incident gave us all a laugh, but it was symptomatic of the change in the English press that I had already noticed during my time in Barcelona. It was a change that spread from the news and feature pages right through to the sport, altering the reporters from relatively passive news-gatherers, into the relentlessly aggressive and often prurient bunch that they have become today.

The euphoria in Barcelona over the League title lasted for weeks, but by the start of the next season, 1985–86, we could already feel the public beginning to change. We had given them exactly what they wanted – the League – but, like football fans everywhere, what they had wanted was now no longer enough; now they wanted the European Cup as well. So did we, but we were to be disappointed, reaching the final only to lose in the most disappointing way possible.

We beat Sparta Prague and Porto in the early rounds, despite a massive dirty-tricks campaign by Porto, who pulled every stroke in the book to try and unsettle us. They put us on the top floor of a high-rise hotel, and as soon as we arrived, the lifts stopped working. For two and a half days we had to walk up all the flights of stairs. When we asked why, they said there was a power-cut, but when we looked out of the window everyone else's lights were on. There was another 'power-cut' when we went to train at the ground the night before the game. There was apparently no one around but five minutes after we got out on the training pitch, the lights went out I had to make a quick decision: should we carry on in the dark or give up? I did not want them to get one up on us so we carried on as if nothing had happened, training in the dark for three-quarters of an hour.

We had the last laugh, since we won, but then faced the toughest opponents of all, the European Cup holders, Juventus, in the quarter final.

We won the home leg against Juventus 1–0, through a Julio Alberto goal, but nobody gave us much chance of surviving the return leg in Turin with such a slender lead. On the night the team put up a tremendous performance, however, one of the best by any team I have ever managed, to get a 1–1 draw and take the tie on the away-goals rule. Steve Archibald scored the goal, and if that had been the only one he scored all year, he would still have been worth his money. The Italian papers' triumphant headline on the morning of the game: 'JUVE OLE!', was replaced by 'JUVE ADIOS!' the next morning. Things were even tighter in the semi-final against Gothenburg. The pessimists gave us even less chance, after we went down 3–0 in Sweden in the first leg. A hat-trick from Picho Alonso tied the match at 3–3, however, and we then won through to the final after a penalty shoot-out.

The European Cup final on 7 May 1986 could have been the crowning moment of my career. Had Barcelona lifted the European Cup, they really would have built that statue of me in the city centre! A score of charter aircraft, a dozen special trains and 300 coaches transported the Barcelona fans to Seville, but they were to return home disappointed. This time it was our turn to be beaten on penalties. A game in Seville should have been like a home match for us, but somehow the tension, which would not have paralysed the players at Nou Camp, struck them down. Steua Bucharest seemed to have little greater ambition than to play for a draw and hope for the luck of the penalty shoot-out, and Barcelona, choked by nerves, failed to perform.

I had brought Archibald back, even though he was struggling with an injury, because he was our best player. On the eve of the match, Steve flew to see a Dutch physiotherapist who had worked miracles on Bryan Robson. I had to overrule the club doctor to get him there and it paid dividends in that he got Steve fit enough to take the field, but he was some way short of his best. Our other star performer, Bernd Schuster, had a dismal game. I subbed him near the end of the game, because I did not think he was giving half as much as he could, but when I brought him off, he walked straight off the pitch and straight out of the stadium. It was to be his last appearance for Barcelona for over a year. The substitution made little difference, however, for we could not find a way through Steua's defence, even in extra time.

Playing in Seville was to our advantage until it came to the penalties. When we had the penalty shoot-out at the Nou Camp in the semi-final, after coming back from 3–0 down, everyone wanted to take one, and the players were so high that they just blasted them in. Even the goalkeeper took one. In the Cup final, having drawn o–o against a side we should have beaten, when we reached the penalty shoot-out, none of the players wanted to take the penalties. They were all scared, which may help to explain why we did not score from a single one of them. When Steua goalkeeper Helmut Ducadam saved the fourth penalty, the European Cup was gone. I do not think I have ever been so depressed after a defeat in my life.

Having tasted the euphoria of success at Barcelona, Allan and I now got a look at the other side of life there. We were virtually ignored at the post-match banquet, but we understood the situation. When you win, they shower you with gifts and adulation, but when you lose, you are snubbed. The fans were exactly the same; when we flew back into Barcelona this time, there were no crowds thronging the streets, not a soul turned out to greet us back.

Oddly the defeat made me more determined to stay on at Barcelona. Had we won the European Cup, I might have thought that there was nowhere left to go at the club, but I could not think of leaving after a disappointment like that. Bernd Schuster was no longer a part of my plans, however, and had finally burnt his boats. He had told me that he wanted to leave halfway through the season. Although he did not give a reason, I think it was for money. I asked him to get the season out of the way and see if we could win the European Cup, and then I would do the best I could for him, but I never felt happy with his attitude. He had been magnificent in my first season, but let me down after that. His wife was also unhappy with my attitude. One day she appeared in the dressing room, striding past the ranks of naked players getting changed after practice, to reach my office and argue with me about my treatment of her husband.

Despite our differences, I liked him, and admired his footballing talent, and we had got on very well, but there could be no way back for him after his walk-out. Apart from the indiscipline and the insult to the club, he could have cost Barcelona a huge fine or even disqualification from future European competition. Two players are chosen at random to be drug-tested after a game, and if he had been chosen as one of them, his absence would have given us very serious problems. It was the final straw.

When I had swallowed my disappointment over the European Cup, and came to look back over the season, we had a record that in almost any other club would have been a matter of pride. We had lost in the final of the European Cup on a penalty shoot-out after extra time. We came second in the Spanish League, lost 1–0 in the Spanish Cup final, and we won the League Cup. Yet a lot of people in Barcelona were saying that we had had a poor season. That was the pressure that we faced.

The League Cup and even the Spanish Cup are regarded as very poor relations to the League title in Spain. Football fans there, and throughout Europe, do not have the same interest in cup competitions as they do in Britain. The FA Cup is the most special cup competition in the world, and its magic reaches right back to the early rounds, but in Spain they only really care about winning the League, and in European competition, they are only interested in the European Cup. The fans do not even start showing up until the quarter-final stages of the other cups, but the Nou Camp was packed for the European Cup right from the start.

I had intended to leave Barcelona at the end of my second season and had already signed an agreement to join Arsenal. I had turned down the Arsenal chairman, Denis Hill-Wood, when I was at Crystal Palace. Ten years later, his son, Peter, who had taken over as chairman, came out to see me in Barcelona, and I agreed to go to Highbury.

I liked both Peter Hill-Wood and Ken Friar, the managing

director, a great deal. I have continually been impressed by Ken, and I rate him as one of the top administrators in the game; he has certainly not had the credit he has deserved. He is Arsenal to the core, and has been there from the age of twelve, when he used to lick the stamps, through to today, when he is managing director. He always has a joke for you, warmth and a smile; if you had your ideal club, you would have him with you.

I had signed a contract that when I finished at Barcelona, I would go to Arsenal ready for the start of the 1986–87 season, and I was very happy about it. My only concern was over Don Howe, who was the Arsenal coach at the time. I never really knew Don well enough to pick up the phone and chat to him, but his coaching was impressive and he was very underrated. The press used to say that he was defensive and boring, but while he was good at setting up a team's defence, to stop them leaking goals, that is not the same thing as being 'defensive and boring'. He was very good and I had a great admiration for him.

I did not want him to think that I had been manoeuvring behind his back and insisted that Peter and Ken tell him immediately what had been agreed, and how it had come about. When I received a call from Don a couple of weeks later and discovered that no one at Arsenal had spoken to him, I was deeply embarrassed. Peter Hill-Wood had mentioned to someone that I might be going to Arsenal, that had been passed on to a journalist and the first Don had known about it was when he read it in the newspapers.

I sat down and thought about what I should do. Arsenal had not handled things the way I would have hoped, but I did not want to cut off my nose to spite my face. I would not have enjoyed going there with Don in that situation, but managers are in a cut-throat and insecure business, and though, in the main, everyone tries to do the right thing, as a professional, you have to do what is best for you. It was still a great job, I would have loved to work with Ken and Peter Hill-Wood, and in the end, had everything else stayed the same, I am sure that I would have gone to Arsenal.

I was now facing a domestic problem, however. My marriage had only recently ended, and for my own, but particularly for my family's sake, I did not want to expose us to the trial by tabloid that would have followed, with reporters door-stepping us, trying to get stories about the break-up. In those circumstances, I felt that it might be better to spend another year or so abroad before coming back to London.

I rang Ken Friar to explain both my disappointment at the way news of our agreement had come out, and to tell him of my domestic problems. I did not renege on our agreement, but I did ask him if Arsenal would excuse me from it. If they did not want to, I told him that I would understand, and would come over to discuss it. Ken was a real gentleman about it, however, and said that he understood my problems and that in the circumstances, they would not hold me to my contract.

It was the second time that Arsenal had failed to land me. The first time, I turned them down because I had a verbal agreement with someone else; the second time, they even had a written agreement and it still was not enough. Some things are obviously fated not to be. It is the best service I have ever done Arsenal, because George Graham ended up going there instead of me and he has won so much silverware that they've had to buy a new trophy cabinet to house it all. George has done so well since joining Arsenal, that any thoughts the board might have had of a third approach to me would swiftly have been forgotten.

The break-up of my marriage had been as amicable as these things ever are, but inevitably I was worried about the effects it might have on my daughters and was determined that I would not let it sour my relationship with them. Happily we have remained very close.

There is now another generation, too: Nancy's son Sam,

who is now four, looks like he might make a good footballer. He certainly has a hell of a left foot, but I cannot take any credit for that, for his father Paul Dobinson, a footballer himself, who had spells at a couple of clubs, is responsible for his son's coaching.

I had already told Barcelona that I was leaving, and that I had a club to go to, though I did not tell them which one, but when my situation changed, Barcelona had still not lined anyone up to replace me and were happy to re-sign me for another year. Juventus had made moves for me, and Tottenham Chairman Irving Scholar also contacted me, but after the Arsenal job fell through, I was happy to stay in Spain.

I had not bought a house when I first went to Barcelona, largely because of the gloomy predictions of everyone I met, who would happily tell me, 'You won't be here long enough to make it worth buying a house.' Instead I rented an apartment not far from the Nou Camp, just off the Diagonal – the six-lane highway leading south from Barcelona towards Cadiz and Madrid. In the morning and evening rush hours four or five lanes of the Diagonal switch with the traffic flow, the cars weaving crazily in and out of the lanes, yet miraculously straightening out into parallel tracks every time they pass a motorcycle policeman. With such exuberant driving, crashes are frequent, each one bringing the traffic to a complete standstill, not because of the number of cars involved, but because everyone simply parks in the road and strolls across to inspect the wreckage. After football, car crashes are Spain's most popular spectator sport.

The apartment ran the length of the building, with all the rooms opening off a long corridor. It had a swimming pool, a private lift and a spectacular view of the city. There were always people coming to stay out there, including my Dad Fred, and my then girlfriend, now wife, Yvette.

We met in my Dad's pub in Chingford. Yvette had only

been there once before, but it was her friend's local. She was looking at the pictures on the wall, all of footballers, and chatting to my Dad. When someone mentioned the name Venables, Yvette, who knew nothing about football, did not recognise it, which upset Fred a bit, and he snapped, 'That's my son.' When Fred introduced us later on, there was a definite instant attraction on both sides. We quickly fell in love, and when I went back, Yvette soon followed.

To begin with, it was almost like being on a permanent holiday for Yvette. She would spend the morning sunbathing, swimming or exploring Barcelona and when I finished work after training, we would meet for lunch at our regular place, a seafood restaurant down at the beach, owned by a man called Manolo, who was a fantastic friend to me. He found me my apartment and whatever problems I had Manolo could solve, apart from taking penalties in the European Cup final. By now thoroughly acclimatised to the Spanish way of life, we would go back to the apartment and have a four-hour siesta, and then go out again in the evening. We sometimes did not eat dinner until 11:00 p.m., which takes a bit of getting used to – you have to pace yourself. It was really good fun, although I do not think I could keep up the pace now; it was ten years ago, after all.

We did a fair bit of night-clubbing too, usually with a guy called Chow, who looked a bit like Jason Robards, and Paco, who looked like Peter Lorre. They both spoke English and were very funny guys. We originally used them as interpreters, but they soon became very good friends of ours. Paco was quite happy to be out all night, and we would often go to a place called the Up and Down, which had a restaurant and nightclub upstairs for people of my age, where you had to wear a jacket, and a more informal club downstairs for the youngsters in jeans.

Chow was barred from the Up and Down, and kept telling me different stories about why he was barred, but I never got to know the real reason. The rest of us liked to go there, however, and rather than go home, Chow would sit in the car for three or four hours while the rest of us went inside. One night we were going to a fancy dress party there, a once-a-year big occasion. It seemed a perfect excuse to put a mask on Chow, so that he could come in with us.

He wore a big rubber mask with holes for eyes and a slit for the mouth and we sailed in and settled down at our table. Chow wore the mask right through dinner, and every time he asked if he could take it off, we kept saying, 'No, keep it on, someone's looking at you a bit suspiciously.' He was a chain smoker and kept lighting cigarettes, but every time he did, the smoke would get inside the mask and come out of the eye holes. He was in serious trouble, pouring with sweat from the heat inside the mask, and with his eyes streaming from the smoke.

Eventually he could stand it no more and took the mask off at about two in the morning. By that time, his grey hair was so wet with sweat and stained with tobacco smoke that it had turned black, and he was so hot that he must have lost a stone in weight from his head alone. He was just heaving a sigh of relief and settling back in his chair, when one of the staff recognised him, came over and threw him out.

Chow and Paco also played walk-on parts in the 'Bilko saga' – an everyday tale of dog-owning folk – that enriched my life in Spain. It was a lovely sunny day – a normal Barcelona day, in other words – and Yvette and Nancy had gone out shopping. They both loved dogs, and Nancy had been badgering me about getting one for ages, but I had put my foot down and said, 'There is no way I am going to get stuck with a dog.' I was watching the television, trying to improve my Spanish, when all of a sudden the door opened, and this white ball of fur, the smallest, most beautiful dog you have ever seen, came scuttling under the coffee table and sat there looking up at me through the glass. Next moment Yvette and Nancy popped their heads around the corner, to check the reaction.

I said, 'Nancy, I told you not to get a dog.'

'But Dad, it's so lovely.'

'Yes it's lovely, but it's going to be a big dog. Have you seen its feet? They're like saucepan lids, the biggest feet I've ever seen, its going to be a giant.'

'No, I promise you, the man said it won't get any bigger.'

Promises, promises ... We christened it 'Bilko', after Sergeant Bilko in the TV series, though with that name, it should really have been a Dobermann. Instead, I was now the proud owner of a Pyrenean mountain dog, just about the biggest dog in the world, and he just grew and grew and grew. When I stood on the balcony, Bilko would put his paws up on the rail beside me, and we were the same height. I would put an arm round his shoulder and he would stick a paw on mine.

For the first few months, you could pull and push him wherever you wanted, but as he became more powerful, he was the one that was making the decisions about where we were going. Yvette and I were standing on the balcony one day, looking out over the swimming pool and the evergreen hedge to the broad, tree-lined pavement outside. Nancy was taking Bilko for a walk, and we could see her head and shoulders bobbing up beyond the hedge and she gave us a wave. As she went past, she was going quicker and quicker and finally ended up on her knees, with the dog pulling her along, like a six-foot husky towing a sled. We could not help laughing, though it was obviously not funny for Nancy. Bilko almost pulled her under a milk-float and that was the last time Nancy took the dog out on her own.

Worse was to follow. He got too strong for Yvette to hold and in the end even I could not hold him. Whenever Bilko saw, heard or even smelt another dog, he went for it. It was like radar, his ears would prick, his head would turn, and he would be off, dragging me behind him. I would be walking one way, would see a dog, turn round and walk the other way, see another one, turn round again – we were constantly zig-zagging and changing course to avoid aggravation.

I had to get a long leather lead that I would wind round the nearest tree at the first sign of trouble. When the danger was past, he would calm down, and we would start walking again. That was only a temporary solution, however, for in the end he grew so aggressive and powerful that he snapped the lead like a rubber band, as he went for a dog.

I had complaints from the neighbours about Bilko barking and attacking their dogs and he kept peeing on the balcony. It then dripped down on to the balcony of the apartment below, creating fresh aggravation. In the end I was taken to court by my neighbours. All I could think was, My God, what a state I'm in. I'm supposed to be coaching one of the biggest teams in the world and I have this constant daily drama with one of the biggest dogs in the world instead. I'm up early in the morning before training, taking him for walks, I'm mopping up and sweeping up after him, it's a nightmare. I would have got rid of him, but Nancy was breaking her heart because she loved this dog so much.

When I took him out for a walk near a building site, he dived into a big pool of water on the site and came out orange all over. I was walking along, wondering how to clean up the dog, when I met Chow, who said, 'Wait here and leave it to me.' He took him round the corner to a small boating lake where kids took their toy sailing boats. It was an idyllic scene, the kids playing with their boats, watched by their proud mothers, all peace and tranquillity in the sunshine, when suddenly Chow let the dog off its lead. It leapt into the pond, crushing the boats and scattering kids in all directions. The dog was clean, but the cost was a trail of carnage across the boating lake, leaving broken-hearted little boys with cracked boats, which cost me a fortune to replace.

Bilko's adventures in Barcelona were soon to end. By now he was in almost permanent detention, but we took pity on him one day, when Nancy and Yvette were staying with me, and took him with us to the beach club. We left Bilko tied to the fence, when up came one of Maradona's pals, a guy called Nestor, who loved Barcelona so much that he had stayed there even when the maestro went off to Naples. Nestor came posing through the club, wearing nothing but a tiny thong and holding a great big Alsatian on a lead.

Bilko immediately went berserk, broke his lead and attacked the Alsatian. They were both ferocious dogs and most people ran a mile, but Nestor decided to break them up. When he did, Bilko bit straight through his thong right next to his 'Niagara Falls'. Luckily it was only a flesh wound. It did cross my mind that it might have been the 'Bite of God', with Bilko getting revenge for the 'Hand of God' when Maradona cheated a goal out of England, but the incident finally convinced us that Bilko would have to go. I found him a home through one of the waiters in the Princess Sofia Hotel, whose parents had a farm with about twenty mountain dogs on it, and when I go to Barcelona now, the waiter tells me up-to-date stories of Bilko, who is now the leader of the pack.

With Bilko gone, Yvette kept us entertained instead. She has an incredible sense of humour and is an even bigger practical joker than me. She also had a winning way with a passport photo. She had noticed that the small head-and-shoulders pictures used in the tabloids are exactly the same size as passport photographs, and if you cut them out and put sellotape over the top, they look just like passport photos. She got hold of Fred's passport one day and put a picture of Arthur Daley on top of the one of him. No one noticed, including the passport controls at Barcelona and Heathrow, who waved him straight through.

A friend of mine, Brian Euston, was rather less lucky. Yvette stuck Idi Amin's picture in his passport and on his way back into England, Brian was stopped. The officials obviously did not share Yvette's sense of humour, because they kept Brian there for hours and strip-searched him, which did not amuse Brian very much either.

Steve Archibald was another person not to be amused when I signed Gary Lineker and Mark Hughes before the start of the 1986–87 season, relegating him to the reserves. There were not many Spanish strikers about at the time and I signed Hughes, thinking that he and Archibald would work well together, but Steve had domestic problems and a number of injuries. He had done a great job for me at Barcelona, but his injuries looked to be long-term, and when Gary Lineker then became available, I had a lot to think about, and in the end I bought Lineker from Everton, to link up with Hughes. I know that Steve was very disappointed that I bought the two strikers, causing him to lose his position, but I still feel that it was the right decision to make at the time.

The deal with Gary was agreed before the 1986 World Cup, in which he was the top goal-scorer, winning the Golden Boot award and proving that Barcelona's £2.2 million was money well spent. While Lineker proved to be as great a success at Barcelona as Archibald had been, however, Mark Hughes was a sad disappointment. The fans – and the directors – were quick to question my judgement and Mark's ability, but his failure was much more to do with personality and immaturity.

People like David Platt and Gary Lineker enjoy a different culture and are willing to learn the language and adapt to their new surroundings. Players like Mark Hughes and Ian Rush, or Jimmy Greaves from an earlier generation, went abroad for the financial rewards, but did not enjoy the culture, did not learn the language and found it difficult to settle. Typically, Gazza found another way to do it, shipping out some of his pals to be there with him. That may have helped in some ways, but he might have been better off with another English player alongside him instead. But there are no guarantees with Gazza, who even has trouble settling in England, because he cannot sit still for long enough.

Whereas Gary was twenty-six and a bit more mature, Mark may also have been a bit too young at just twenty-two, and might have done better in Barcelona had he gone there later. As it was, he missed his pals and his home-life and his form started to suffer. He also found it difficult to adjust to Spanish football. The things that he got away with in England were frowned on in Spain and he was constantly pulled up by referees. Robbed of the physical side of his game, he had far less impact than I had hoped, and in the end, after he was sent off in a UEFA Cup tie, I was forced to drop him from the squad and recall Steve Archibald as our second overseas player.

Mark eventually left Barcelona to return to Manchester United, but I am delighted both for him and for me, that he has done so well at Old Trafford since his return. Even more pleasing for both of us was the moment when he scored one of United's goals in their victory against Barcelona in the European Cup, making a point to the Barcelona board and the public there in the best possible way.

The contrast between Mark's form at Barcelona and that of Gary Lineker could not have been more pointed. Gary did not depend on physical presence for his effectiveness and the goal-scoring touch he had shown in the World Cup was maintained as he averaged a goal every two games throughout the season, ending with twenty-one from forty-two appearances. Gary played the percentages and rarely wasted a chance. Most strikers like to hammer the ball, but it was rare to see Gary blast a shot over the bar. He liked to concentrate on accuracy, keeping it low, on the target area, to make the goalkeeper work. Nor did he panic when he hit the lean spells that all strikers have. He could go ten matches without scoring and not turn a hair, for he knew that his luck would change if he kept his attitude right.

The third season began brightly. Gary scored his first two goals on his début and then repaid most of his fee in his first game against Real Madrid, scoring a hat-trick in a 3–2 victory, but despite Gary's goals, the season did not go as well as we had hoped. We were in contention in the League all the way, but finished second again, and in Barcelona, second is not good enough.

It was always said that Barcelona would never win the League if there were only a few points in it. The directors and fans were equally paranoid about Real Madrid, and would even claim that they always got an easy draw in the Cup. When I asked how that was possible, they said that there were hot and cold balls in the bag for the draw, they would feel for a cold one and know it was a lowly team and if it was a hot one they would drop it again, because they knew it was one of the better teams. Of course, it was just paranoia, but after a couple of years, I began to share it – about the referees if not the Cup draws.

The directors were convinced that all the big decisions went Real Madrid's way and it certainly did look that way. They nominated two referees in particular as ones to watch out for and sure enough they got them spot on. They told me that year after year when they were second, with two or three games to go, there was always a decision against them that cost them the title.

When we had won the League, we had gone off like an alarm clock and were already fifteen points ahead, before anyone actually realised. The second and third year, I began to see what they meant, because we did have a few problems. Now it has changed, however, and everyone in Madrid says that it is Barcelona that always gets the luck.

Apart from our failure to win the League, our biggest disappointment was defeat by Dundee United in the UEFA Cup quarter-final. We drew 1–1 at home and could not turn it around in Scotland, losing 1–0. I also missed out on one other major event that season, the chance to take part in a private audience with the Pope, alongside club president Josip-Luis Nuñez, who invited me to go with him. Unfortunately it clashed with a friendly between England and Spain in Madrid. Glenn Hoddle was in midfield with Beardsley and Lineker up front. It was a tough choice, but I had to go with my own religion . . . football.

I felt that both Barcelona and I might have benefited from a change at this stage. Had I made one, there was no shortage of offers from other clubs. I would have been happy to return to England by then, but if I were to leave Barcelona, it seemed as if Italy, not England, would be the more likely destination. AC Milan and Roma were both very interested and I later discovered that Roma had been on the point of making me a massive offer when Barcelona told them – incorrectly at that stage – that I had already signed a new contract with them.

I was also offered the chance to coach a national side, one of the top three in Europe, but I turned that down because they already had a coach, and after my experiences with Arsenal over Don Howe, I did not want to be drawn into another cloak-and-dagger operation, with everyone except the victim knowing that he was to be sacked. It is one thing for a club or a country to decide that they want to change their manager, inform him of that and then make approaches to replace him. It was quite another for them to contact me first and line me up to fill the 'dead man's shoes'. It does happen in football, but it is rather like being an accessory before the fact and was not something I was willing to be a party to.

The possibility of taking over QPR, by buying out Jim Gregory, had also once more been raised. Adam Faith, whom I had known since the days when I hung around Tin Pan Alley as a young Chelsea player, was one of my principal backers, but we were beaten to the punch by Marler Estates, who were collecting football clubs around London at the time, like kids collect autographs.

I am not sure whether the interest from other clubs stampeded the Barcelona board into offering me a new contract, but Señor Nuñez duly produced a new agreement. I felt that we had got as much out of the existing players as we could and that we needed some fresh blood, but the club did not have the money to buy players at that stage.

Against my better judgement, I was persuaded to re-sign. I insisted on a release clause in the event of the England managership being offered to me, and then signed a new one-year contract. By doing so, I became the longest-serving manager in Barcelona's history, and the only one at that stage ever to start a fourth season with the club. I started, but unlike Magnus Magnusson on *Mastermind*, I did not finish.

We really stuttered at the start of the 1987–88 season, winning only one of the first five games. As if that was not bad enough, Real Madrid got off to a flyer and had a 100 per cent record at the same stage. In success-hungry Barcelona that was simply too much to bear and the supporters showed their disapproval. The Barcelona fans have a way of signalling to the club president that they want a change of personnel. If you are not doing well, out come all the white handkerchiefs to wave goodbye. Obviously the president is not going to leave, so the coaching staff are the ones to be on their way.

When we played Valencia, and their first goal went in, all the handkerchiefs came out. Allan turned to me and said, 'I think we should book our tickets, because we're on our way out.' We knew then that the writing was on the wall. The end was delayed for a little while, but a bad home defeat against Sporting Gijon was the last straw. Many supporters were staying away, and those who were turning up were waving their white handkerchiefs for all they were worth.

Señor Nuñez first offered his resignation to the directors, but that was really just going through the motions, and they swiftly persuaded him to withdraw it, their eagerness not unconnected to the fact that most of them owed their position on the board to him. Even then, Nuñez could not bring himself to sack me, and instead offered a match-by-match trial, beginning with the trip to Howard Kendall's Atletico Bilbao the following weekend. That seemed to me to be the worst of both worlds, for the players and the club, as well as me, and I refused, saying, 'No, let's finish it now.'

It was all very civilised, with no fierce rows or angry words. We simply agreed that it would be best for the club and me to have a change. I went down to training to tell the players and say goodbye to them, and that was it, I was no longer the coach of Barcelona FC. It may seem surprising that a coach can be transformed from a hero to a villain in so short a time but the margins between success and failure in Barcelona really are that fine.

Luis Aragones was appointed as my successor, but he was replaced by Johan Cruyff before the next season and the board then made an enormous amount of money available to buy some great individual players. Cruyff has done a magnificent job with them and been fabulously successful, eclipsing my record as the longest-lasting Barcelona coach by staying with the club for six years, at the time of writing. He led them to four successive Championships and also became the first Barcelona coach to bring the European Cup to the city – if they put up a statue there now, it will definitely be Johan Cruyff, not Terry Venables, looking out over Barcelona.

If my own stay there ended in anti-climax, however, my time in Barcelona also gave me some of the greatest moments of my football life. In three seasons we won the League once, finished runners-up twice, won the Spanish League Cup and were runners-up in the European Cup and the Spanish Cup. Perhaps the proudest achievement of all, in the eyes of the fervent Barcelona fans, was that in thirteen games against the old enemy, Real Madrid, we had lost only once.

It was not a bad record, by anybody's standards, and the suggestions from some quarters of England, that it was easy to do well at Barcelona, because Spain has only a two-team League, merely reveal the ignorance of those who express them. In the previous ten seasons, Real Madrid and Barcelona had won the Spanish League precisely three times between them. In the same period, Liverpool and Everton had taken the English title eight times. If there was a two-team League anywhere, it certainly was not in Spain.

I learned a great deal about European football during my time in Spain and with luck some of that knowledge will be helpful to England as we prepare for the European Championships and then the 1998 World Cup. I also learned a new language, discovered an entirely different culture and enjoyed a fabulous life style. Barcelona is a great football club and a great city and I will always have a tremendous affection for the place and its people.

# CHAPTER SEVEN

# Tottenham Manager

## 1987–91

CONTRARY TO THE OPINIONS of the Tottenham conspiracy theorists, I did not have the job at White Hart Lane lined up when I left Barcelona. I actually had no job to go to at all, though that did not worry me in the least because I was not in a hurry to do anything. I planned to take the rest of the year off, beginning with a long holiday in Florida and then returning to live in Barcelona while I sorted out my affairs there and considered my next move, but a phone call to Florida from England rapidly changed my plans.

I had only been on holiday for five days when Spurs chairman Irving Scholar called me at around ten in the evening, asking if he could fly out to discuss the possibility of me joining Tottenham. Scholar had been dealing with the football agent Dennis Roach over plans to stage the Bruno–Bugner fight at White Hart Lane and Roach had found out where I was staying and passed the number on. Scholar caught the first flight to Miami the next morning and we had dinner that night at my hotel, the West Palm Beach Resort, home to the American PGA, with holiday homes dotted among the golf-courses.

Scholar, a millionaire property developer, had a house in Monte Carlo as well as one in London, but remained as fanatical a Spurs fan as he had been as a child. His boyish looks belied his years, and he still had something of the child in him, with his obsessive interest in the minutiae of Spurs history and his breathless enthusiasm for trivia quiz questions of the 'How many Spurs goalkeepers had names beginning with Z?' variety.

Scholar had approached me a year before, just after I had decided not to join Arsenal and stay in Spain for another year. I had turned him down then, but now he was back for a second go and he was showing considerable urgency in trying to persuade me to take over at Spurs. He had just sacked the previous manager, David Pleat, after an exposé on his private life by the *Sun*.

Scholar was worried that Juventus or Arsenal might have beaten him to the punch and was eager to install me as Pleat's successor as quickly as possible. In fact, I had already had an offer from Juventus, but although it was much higher than the one Scholar put in front of me, I was ready to go home to England, and Spurs looked the right place to be. I was less sure about Scholar himself, a man full of charm, who looked smooth enough to skate on. I never really knew either then or at any time during my dealings with him over the next four years, what he was thinking behind that well-polished front.

My reservations about Scholar – who had also attracted the nickname of 'Irve the Swerve' – were not enough to put me off the job he was offering, however. I had always been a Tottenham supporter as a young lad, but it was also the only club where I had not done particularly well as a player. Maybe I could make it up to myself by succeeding as a manager there? Had I known what that decision was to lead to, I might have been on the next plane to Italy and Juventus instead.

Scholar had no trouble with me over money, even though it was less than half what I had been paid in Barcelona. The chance to be back home in England in a job that attracted me was enough. I never really discussed the money with him. I hardly ever do. I have always found it easier to negotiate contracts on behalf of players or a club than myself, because it is difficult to put a value on yourself. The argument with Jim

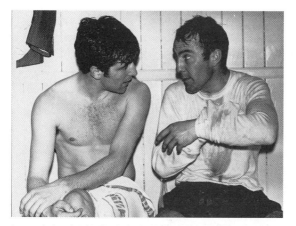

Greavesie looking for a handkerchief up his sleeve

With the great England captain, Bobby Moore, before my début against
Belgium

The daily trek of the District Line from Barking to Fulham Broadway

Spurs player Terry Venables doing his party trick – spot the ball

Carrying the FA Cup, 1967. *From left to right:* Cyril Knowles, me, Joe Kinnear and Jimmy Robertson

*Above:* Reaching the end of playing days and the start of my coaching career. *From left to right:* Ian Evans, Malcolm Allison and me

*Left:* Jim Gregory – Mr QPR – with whom I had the best relationship I have had with a chairman

*Below:* Chris, me, Tracey (left) and Nancy – 'story time'

Whispering one of my deep, meaningful thoughts

First season as coach of Barcelona, 1984, with Steve Archibald, Bernd Schuster and assistant Allan Harris

Sharing a joke during pre-season training in Andorra with Barcelona newboy
Gary Lineker, 1986

*Left:* 'I promise he won't get any bigger, Dad'
　　　'Are you sure?'

*Below:* 'I don't like saying I told you so, Nancy'

Irving Scholar and me in better times

Chief Executive at last. Alan Sugar and me parading the FA Cup after announcing our successful takeover of Tottenham in June 1991

*Above:* Reunited with an old friend in 1991 after one of the most tense and exciting Cup finals of recent years

Gregory was one of the only times I have ever fallen out with a chairman over money, and even that was as much about winning the argument as about the money. I did insist on two things with Scholar: that money to strengthen the team must be made available, and that I would have complete control of buying and selling players. Scholar pledged £4 million, providing half of it was raised through the sale of players.

He wanted me to start straight away, but that was impracticable. There were too many things to attend to in Spain and too many loose ends to tie up first, and I knew that once I began work at Tottenham, it would be impossible to keep nipping over to Barcelona to sort things out. It was eventually agreed that I would join Spurs in early December, with Doug Livermore acting as caretaker-manager until then. In the event, I took over on Monday, 23 November 1987.

I spent the rest of my holiday watching videos of Spurs games that Irving had sent out to me. Tottenham had played in the FA Cup final the previous season, but it was a team that had passed its sell-by date. Glenn Hoddle, a great lad with tremendous skill, whom I had coached in the England Under-21 team several years before, had just been sold to Monaco, which was a shame, for I was a great admirer and would have enjoyed working with him again. Shortly before I arrived, Richard Gough, one of the best centre-halves in Britain, had also been transferred to Glasgow Rangers. Spurs had lost two of their best players, but I found the situation was even worse than that when I got to White Hart Lane.

Ray Clemence had been injured, effectively ending his career, and Ossie Ardiles was reaching the end of the line as well. Spurs had lost Clemence, Gough, Hoddle and Ardiles, not only the best players in the side, but very strong characters, whom you need to build a side around. I also discovered that Steve Hodge, another top-quality player, had already been given an undertaking by David Pleat that he could leave Spurs at the end of the season, Gary Stevens was injured and Danny Thomas had been forced to finish his career by a horrendous knee-injury.

Everywhere I looked, there were more problems. The front players were Clive Allen and Nico Claesen, but while they could both score goals individually, together they were not a blend, and Clive's contract was also up at the end of the season. Apart from Clemence, the other goalkeeper was Tony Parkes, who had done well in their European games but was beginning to lose his confidence. It was obvious that Tottenham needed to buy a lot of players, because although there were some good youngsters at the club, they were not ready for the first team, especially coming into a side that was not doing well. It was definitely the hardest job I had ever had to do, and in the early months, I often shook my head at the scale of the task facing me, and thought to myself: How the hell do I do this?

The one thing that I really felt we had going for us was the loyalty of the supporters. The expectations of Spurs fans are always high, and if the 'Glory, Glory Days' are long gone, Tottenham fans still presume the team will play Glory, Glory football. The older fans could be impatient when the team was struggling, but there was a very considerable difference in the supporters' attitudes from the last time I had been at Tottenham.

Jimmy Greaves and Alan Mullery made the same point. 'When we had been there as players,' as Alan remarked, 'two bad games and the fans were on your back; three bad games and they were rocking your car, trying to turn it over.' Alan could not believe the tolerance of the present Spurs fans, who watched the team go six months without a home win during the 1993–94 season.

It had been a tremendous change. The older generation was still there, but there was a wave of younger supporters coming through, who seemed to have a really strong feeling for their team, supporting them, win, lose or draw. Similarly, on the on the playing side, we certainly had some promising youngsters among the supporters, too. Away from home it was particularly noticeable, because it is mainly the younger element that travel to away games. They really got behind the team, which gave me a lot of hope.

The Tottenham shirt is a proud emblem to the younger supporters. They are living through a tough period of depression and many of them do not have jobs, nor much else to be proud of, but they have their football team and that gives them something in which they can take pride. Local pride is most at stake in the derby matches with Arsenal, and though even the North London derbies cannot match the fervour surrounding Barcelona's clashes with Real Madrid, 'It doesn't matter what else you do, just make sure you beat Arsenal' is a sentiment with which many Spurs fans would readily identify. A season in which Spurs finished second in the League would be counted as a triumph, unless Arsenal finished first, in which case it would instantly become a disaster.

The justifiable pride that supporters take in their team can spill over into something much worse, of course, and we must never again relax our guard against hooliganism. It crippled the image of English football during the early 1980s, but the government are as much to blame as the game itself for failing to take action early enough. The warning signs were there for a long time, but there seemed to be a view that it was better for them to fight on the terraces than on the streets. While it was contained in our own back-yard, no one took any action and it was only when the problem was exported and became an international incident that the government wanted to do something about it. The problem is considerably better than it was, but incidents like the one at Millwall in spring 1994 show that there is still no room for complacency.

There was definitely no room for that at White Hart Lane either, as Allan Harris joined me from Barcelona as my assistant, and our first move was to take the team to Brighton for two or three days' training, which also gave us the chance to get to know the players and staff. I had been away from the English game for three years and immediately noticed the skill gap between the players at Barcelona and those at Tottenham.

European players practise their skills far more than the English do, which explains why we so often lag behind them in technical skills as adult players. It is something we have to improve if we want to match them. Glenn Hoddle was one of the most skilful players in the game and was able to perform those skills at the highest level, but it was not because of the way he had been coached as a child; it was really in spite of that. When I asked him what had made him want to master the ball like that, he told me it was because he had seen the Brazilians on the television when he was very young. They had excited him.

The needs of the professional game are not being answered by the coaching provided to children. There are too many little empires within the game and too much emphasis on winning competitions and cups, rather than on developing skills. We have always overstressed the competitive side of English football at too young an age, with boys being flung into matches instead of being taught the game. Schoolteachers are as much to blame for that situation as coaches.

In Spain schoolchildren are linked to professional clubs, and there are kids of six and seven training at a club like Barcelona. In England they are tied to their schools. We cannot get them early enough, and start to see them only when they are fourteen or fifteen, when the damage has already been done. If the Spanish kids get an hour and a half in the morning, working on their skills in groups of three, the boys will practise heading together, for example, and each of them will get half an hour's practice.

In England, not all schoolteachers tend to want the job, they just happen to have a spare session, so they hang a whistle round their neck, put the ball in the middle and let the kids play for an hour and a half. In those ninety minutes, the best players will only touch the ball for just over three minutes. The others might only touch it for a minute or less. The rest of the time they are all just running around chasing the ball.

Schools may claim that professional clubs might harm young players by paying them money and putting unfair pressures on them, but I do not accept that at all. Martin Edwards's father Louis, when he was chairman of Manchester United, was once alleged on *World In Action* to have broken the rules by paying young lads to go to the club. If it is against the rules, then it is wrong, but let us examine the rules. If we are paying kids at seventeen, what is so wrong about paying them at fifteen or sixteen instead? He did not take money from the kids, after all. Why not make it legal?

My Mum did not want me to become a footballer, because she was frightened that I would not make it, but if I had been paid £1000, for the club's gamble, it would not have been so very wrong. If at the end of a couple of years, the kid does not make it, at least he has got £1000 in the bank. For football's sake, instead of that fear of clubs taking kids away from schools, we should be building on the worship that kids have for the professional clubs and players, using that as the vehicle to increase their skills and involvement in the game.

That is why players and ex-players have got to go back into the schools and train these kids. Happily, the regulations have now been amended so that children as young as nine can now be attached to professional clubs and I am sure we shall see the benefits in years to come.

Back in 1978, we undertook a three-year development plan for boys at Crystal Palace. We told John Cartwright, our youth coach, to take the pressure of winning off those lads for an entire year. You do not have to teach kids to want to win, for the will to win is already in them; if you add to the pressure of winning, you can make kids frightened of making mistakes. You have to teach them to practise with the ball instead. In the first year, we concentrated on breaking down the individual skills like control, passing and heading, to the exclusion of everything else.

In the second year, we tightened up on the physical side, the competitiveness and the endurance, but only after they had been given the confidence to express their skills. In the third year, they trained harder than they had done in their lives. That way, when they reached the first-team coach, there was not a great deal more work to be done on them.

At senior level, mainly through laziness, we are not working at the things we should be, and our football is nowhere near the quality we should be seeking. Too many players are content to play in the little plots of land their coaches tell them they should occupy. There is not enough artistry and invention in our game. It is exciting enough with the ball flying from end to end, but when you look for the extra, special quality, it is not there.

We do not have enough time to spend with our players either. You play Saturday, patch up the injured, play Wednesday, patch up the injured, and play Saturday again. Clubs are happy just to get the game over rather than learn something from it. It is obvious that we play too many games. If we cut back the number of games, then coaches might have enough time to teach the good things and players might have more time to understand them.

Player transfers during the season should also be outlawed – except perhaps for a two-week 'window' in mid-season. That could coincide with a mid-season break from fixtures, giving players, coaches and spectators a chance to recharge their batteries. I would also like to see freedom of contract finally come to mean exactly what it says – not that it will ever happen, for it would frighten chairmen to death. At the moment, when your

contract is up, you are entitled to move, but only after the clubs
or a tribunal have arranged a fee. Yet if a club lets a contract
run out, it is only right that the player should be allowed to
move without payment of a fee. If the club wants to keep him, it
should negotiate a new contract before the old one has expired.

A lot of clubs from the lower divisions might think that the
loss of transfer fees would cripple them, but it is the few
thousand pounds that a small club pays out in transfer fees that
is more crippling – they cannot afford any fees. The game in the
lower divisions would be far better off, for the clubs and the
players alike, as a part-time game.

If you play for a club in the Second or Third Division full-
time, it is because one day you hope that you will be picked up
by one of the giants like Arsenal or Tottenham. For most
players, that dream will never come true, and they would be
much better off becoming part-timers, but a lot of them do not
want to go out to work, because they like the idea of being full-
time professional footballers. They get £200 a week, or whatever, to play full-time, but that means that they cannot have
another job because of the commitment to football. If they were
part-time, they could get a 'day-job' at a reasonable wage and
their footballing ability would then become a bonus, an extra
wage on top of their earnings, giving them a good living now,
rather than feeding a dream that may never happen.

Making Spurs a successful team again was another dream
that would take some time to become reality. All the Spurs
players were working hard to try and impress the new bosses,
but there were one or two areas of discipline that I felt had to
be corrected from the start. The physio, John Sheridan, is a
gentle man and a very good physio, but the players took
liberties because of his gentleness, which they saw as a weakness.
I had to tell John to be firm with them and not let them get
away with things. I made it clear that I thought he was excellent
at his job, so that he would not see it as a criticism of his

expertise, but told him he was too soft with the players, who knew how to get around him.

The next morning, Allan and I were walking along the hotel corridor just as John came out of his room, which was also used as a treatment room for the players. He saw us and turned back into his doorway and started laying down the law to a couple of players, saying, 'I'm telling you, I've had enough. You're going to do what I say from now on. I want to see you back here in half an hour, and I'll work the bollocks off you.'

He slammed the door, winked at us and walked off down the corridor. I managed to resist the temptation to take a peek into the room, but when I went downstairs five minutes later, the two players whom he had apparently been haranguing were finishing their breakfast, suggesting that John might have been giving his command performance to an empty room.

My first game after rejoining Tottenham was on 28 November 1987 against Liverpool, in front of a sell-out crowd. Liverpool were then unbeaten and top of the League, having conceded only eight goals all season. It was like facing Real Madrid in my first match at Barcelona, but the result was not the same. Steve Hodge was sent off in the sixth minute and Tottenham lost 2–0. The next game, again at home, against Charlton ended in another defeat, 1–0. The scale of the task that I had taken on was becoming very evident.

The rebuilding process began at once, but my first signing provoked a row with Irving Scholar. Despite his agreement that I should have complete authority in the buying and selling of players, he violently disagreed with and argued against my choice of Terry Fenwick. Irving was eager to see younger and more glamorous players at White Hart Lane, and I often felt that he wanted a 'Showbiz XI'. I also like talented players, but if you do not stop the goals from going in at your end first, you are in trouble. My own top priority was to replace some of the experience and character that had been lost from the team, and Fenwick fitted that bill admirably.

The row over Fenwick was the first of a succession of arguments with Scholar. When he had come to see me in Florida, I asked him: 'Do you want me to be coach or manager at Tottenham? I don't mind, just as long as I know.'

'Be the manager,' said Scholar.

Yet he interfered from the start, as I was warned that he would. One of the Spurs employees told me, 'Scholar does it everywhere around the club, and he always wants to be there when the photographs are taken.'

Scholar also excluded me from any discussion of the business activities of Tottenham Hotspur, leaving me working in a vacuum, unaware of the pressures building on the club. Like many other managers today, I found myself further than ever from the actual running of the club, and yet stuck in a high-risk structure in which the result on Saturday was everything, without the benefit of knowing how well or badly the club was doing financially. I was not even invited to the first three board meetings after I joined Tottenham, and when Scholar finally did ask me to attend one, I was asked to leave as soon as the discussion turned to business. Perhaps that was just as well, however, for if I had known the true state of Tottenham's finances at the start, I would probably have walked out.

Scholar might have had a great memory for football trivia, but he did not know enough about football to be able to talk about the game itself. He likes to claim that he got on well with Keith Burkinshaw, Pete Shreeves and David Pleat, when they were at Tottenham, but though they have never publicly criticised him, their private opinions portray a rather different version of events, and certainly his meddling in transfers and players' contracts drove me demented at times.

As manager under the Scholar regime, I was employed by the football club, not the plc, and I had limited authority to engage players and discuss their renumeration. I would negotiate the player's signing-on fee and wages and tell him the size of the first-team bonus, but if the player or his agent wanted further benefits, such as help with removal expenses or a relocation payment or a loan, for example, that was outside my responsibilities and had to be referred to Irving Scholar. I did not ask Scholar if any financial arrangements he made with the players on behalf of the plc were in accordance with FA regulations and acceptable to the Inland Revenue, any more than the manager of a branch of a building society would ask his board of directors if a loan raised on the money market by the society was legal and above board. I knew nothing about his dealings until after the takeover.

Scholar liked to be involved in the big deals. He had given the impression that he would allow me to get on with my job, but would try to push me out of the way and negotiate terms with some star players on his own. I did not even know that Chris Waddle was having a change of contract, for instance, for Scholar began negotiating with Chris and agent Dennis Roach without letting me know.

On another occasion, I had done a deal with Jim Gregory to sell Guy Butters to Portsmouth, where Jim was now chairman. Jim and I were always wanting to get one over on each other, but we eventually reached agreement on a figure. At the last minute, Jim rang and told me that Scholar had phoned him the night before and tried to change the price we had agreed. Jim, who could never resist trying to persuade me to go to Portsmouth at every opportunity, asked me if the chairman always interfered with my dealings, saying, 'Do you manage the club or not?'

I was furious with Scholar, both for interfering in the first place and for making me look a fool in front of someone I respected, but he was so thick-skinned that he did not think it was important. I gave him such a 'volley' on the phone that Yvette asked me who I had been having a go at. When I told her it was the chairman she said, 'Oh my God,' and started getting out the suitcases. By the next morning, however, Scholar was acting as if nothing had happened, though it did not stop him from continuing to interfere.

When we agreed to sell Chris Fairclough for £500,000, Leeds did not want any publicity about it. Yet the next morning it was in the papers in a story broken by Harry Harris, Scholar's buddy on the *Daily Mirror*. When I confronted Scholar, he first denied feeding him the story and then admitted it, saying, 'If you put it in the paper, other clubs might want to pay more for him.' Sometimes that can work, but not when you have already agreed a deal and given your word that there will be no publicity. It is like gazumping someone who has agreed to buy your house. In any event, as I told Scholar, 'If you are going to leak a story, it might help if you let me know that you are going to do it first.'

The turnover of players continued through the season. I had obviously been out of touch with the English scene for the last three years and initially I relied heavily on the advice of men whose opinion I respected, like Spurs' chief scout Ted Buxton. Bobby Mimms was signed to replace Ray Clemence, Clive Allen went abroad to Bordeaux for close to £1 million, Ardiles moved to QPR, and Steve Hodge went to Nottingham Forest, being greeted with Brian Clough's announcement that, 'I haven't just signed a player, I've rescued a lad from Hell'.

Hell might have been a bit strong as a description of White Hart Lane at the time – if it was hell then, what was it a couple of years later? – but it was certainly no heaven on earth. The team's results were inevitably poor, given the scale of the exodus, and we were knocked out in the early rounds of League and FA Cups, and ended the season in lowly thirteenth position in the table. The *Sun*, which had christened me 'El Tel' during my time at Barcelona, now renamed me 'El Veg' – Terry Vegetables – instead, giving me the turnip treatment several years ahead of Graham Taylor.

Two signings in particular promised much brighter times ahead at Spurs. Tottenham had kept an eye on Paul 'Gazza' Gascoigne from the time he had broken into the Newcastle first team when he was about seventeen. Liverpool and Manchester United were chasing him as well, but I think that they were less sure about his talent and too worried about his reputation. I have never worried too much about reputations. Great players often tend to have star-sized egos, it is part of what makes them stand out on the field, and I have found that most of the so-called 'difficult' players have responded to me well enough; I give them my respect and try to earn theirs in return. When I later signed Pat van den Hauwe, who was even more 'notorious' than Gazza, he never gave us much trouble at all . . . only now and then.

Because I worked in a relaxed atmosphere, Scholar worried about my handling of discipline, but he did not understand the psychology of it. I think Scholar thought a manager had to be a shouter and screamer, who coached by fear, but the days of the 'Sergeant Major' are over. You can get away with it for a short period of time, but when you lose a player, you lose them for good, and if you rant every day, it loses its impact, and there is no return for you. You have to be more subtle than that in your man-management . . . and if you do need to rant at someone, it has a lot more impact if it is unexpected. I want an atmosphere at a club like you want in your family: discipline combined with laughter and enjoyment, one where the players look forward to coming in to work. They have fun but they know that there is a line drawn, fun is fun, but the work is serious. That is the way I have always worked and I have never had a major problem with discipline at any club.

I have had one or two minor problems with players – not all of them are angels – but you cannot cut off your nose to spite your face. What is the point of banning a player from a Cup game, if you then lose? You have to say that you are not going to make the rest of the team and the supporters suffer; let him play but deal with him in some other way. It is better to make sure that the player concerned suffers and not everyone else.

I had seen Paul Gascoigne on television, and one of Newcastle's greatest-ever players, Jackie Milburn, had raved about him, telling me, 'I can't believe the skills on him, he's the best in the world,' but the first time I saw him in the flesh was when Spurs played at Newcastle. They were building a new stand and had Portakabin-type, temporary dressing rooms. Everyone else was inside preparing for the match, but Gazza was ready to play, half an hour before the game, standing outside, with no tracksuit on, talking nineteen to the dozen to his mates.

I had put Terry Fenwick to mark him, as he was a strong tackler and responded well to a challenge. Early in the game, as Gascoigne took possession, Terry tightened himself right up and really hit him as hard as he could but Gazza just leaned into him and Terry bounced off. We already knew about Gazza's skills, but we now discovered that you could not kick him out of the game either.

Some talented players do not want to know if you give them a kick – I can never remember Rodney Marsh having a good game against Ron Harris, for example – but that is most definitely not the case with Paul. He has tremendous upper body strength as well as skill, and is a player of immense talent. He scored an unbelievable free-kick against us that day as well, showing me his full repertoire in one go. Jackie Milburn had not been exaggerating, this was a very special talent. One or two people were even using the phrase 'the new Duncan Edwards' about Gascoigne, but not me – I had heard more than enough of that one thirty years before.

Initially Paul had a preference for Liverpool rather than Spurs, but with the help of a long chat with his fellow-Geordie Chris Waddle, I managed to persuade him that White Hart Lane was the place he really wanted to be. Newcastle collected a £2 million fee – a British record – and I collected a bundle of hate mail from fans incensed that I had 'blown' £2 million on what one described as 'a fat Geordie yob'.

When Gazza came to the Spurs training ground for the first time, his football reputation had gone before him, and all the players were waiting to see what he could do. They did not have long to wait. When we started a practice game, he got the ball, went round eight players as if they were not there and then smashed the ball into the net. It was absolutely brilliant; just to see him play like that made the hair stand up on the back of your neck. Everybody stood there and applauded him.

We also badly needed a front player at Tottenham. My first choice had been Mark Hateley, but he was not available, and my second choice was Paul Stewart, who was then at Manchester City. I had watched him when he was at Blackpool a couple of years before and liked the look of him. Allan went to see him and liked him too, and we eventually signed Paul for £1.5 million, beating off competition from Liverpool. I felt that he would do well for us and that we would get our money back if he ever moved on, but it took him a long time to settle down at Spurs. He had the misfortune to miss a penalty in his first game for the club, in a game against Manchester United. Lee Sharpe brought Paul down in the box, but he hit the bar from the penalty spot. After that, a section of the crowd seemed to be on his back in almost every game. I could empathise with him, for I had been given the same sort of stick when I was a player at White Hart Lane.

If there is a big crowd, you do not hear the spectators' individual comments and shouts out on the pitch, but you do know if the crowd is against you, and when the crowd is smaller, you can hear the abuse, and it knocks your confidence down. Your own crowd are stopping you from performing when they get at you in that way. If fans must have a go at a player, it is far better if they wait until the end of the game first; then they do not damage his confidence during the game, and hurt their own team's prospects as a result.

The supporters' treatment of Paul Stewart was unusual, because in England, fans normally give a lot of time to a guy you have paid £1 million or £2 million for. The crowd respect that and know that they have to show a bit of patience with him until he settles in. They do not show the same patience with the player who has come through the ranks, because they have seen him come in young and make a few mistakes and have already decided that he is not very good. Those players have really got to work hard to win the crowd over. In Barcelona it is the reverse. The player who has come through the ranks is seen to have the club at heart and is loyal and the fans respect that, whereas the big-money signing has to prove himself to them before he is accepted.

The entrance to the tunnel should really be covered at grounds here, as it is in Spain, because of the danger of fans throwing missiles. At some clubs the fans can actually touch you, which is just asking for trouble. At Tottenham's FA Cup game at Manchester City in 1993, we had a bit of crowd trouble and a guy leaned over, touched me on the shoulder and threw orange juice over me. If they can get close enough to do that, they can do anything – why do they always have to wait for someone to be killed before they build a zebra crossing?

The one thing that is amusing about the abuse from the crowd is that the only person in the stadium who cannot shout his head off is the coach. His job is to tell the players what to do, but he is not allowed to shout at all, because coaching from the touchline is banned. When you are yelling from the touch-line, the referee will come across and give you a telling off, while 50,000 fans in the stands continue to scream their heads off. It does not make sense.

Paul Stewart was not getting the goals, but he was working

hard and knew he could do better – he was very honest about his game, and his faults, which I liked. Some people said he was 'not a Tottenham player', claiming that his touch was not good enough, but although he did work at improving his touch, there was never any doubt in my mind that he was a player of high quality. I thought at the time that Paul would be better in midfield and he won an FA Cup final for us and went on to represent England in midfield, playing some of the best football of his career. By that time, the stick from the White Hart Lane terraces had disappeared, and he eventually became a favourite with the Tottenham crowd.

Stewart and Gascoigne cost us £3.5 million pounds, but we were also picking up some fine young players for next to nothing. We had a good youth policy, and there were some great kids coming through under the guidance of youth-team coach, Keith Waldon; John Moncur and Len Cheesewright, the youth-team scouts, and their team of part-timers, were scouring the country for the most promising youngsters. Any players of potential would be brought in for a trial and we would make a decision on them.

The worst part of being a manager is having to tell youngsters that they are not good enough to be kept on the books. It is hard to tell in the case of an experienced player, but I found it harder with kids of sixteen or seventeen years old, who absolutely live for the game, and if I was in any doubt about their ability to make the grade, I would always try to give them another year to see if they would come good. The pressure from the budget set by the directors makes that difficult, even at a big club like Tottenham, but it is impossible at a small club, where, if you have any doubts, you have to let them go. A Premier League club should have the money to be able to give them a bit more time. You are only talking about £5000 or £6000 a year to keep them on the books. Other clubs, even some of the bigger ones, get rid of youngsters if they are not sure about them.

By hanging on to kids about whom we were in doubt, we found at least three or four good players, like Kevin Watson, who could well have been thrown out at sixteen. Even more satisfyingly for dyed-in-the-wool Spurs fans, I picked up Stuart Nethercott on a free transfer, when he was released from schoolboy forms by the hated rivals, Arsenal, and he became a first-team player. I thought that he would have been a realistic choice for an extended first-team run in 1993–94. Tottenham spent £2 million on two central defenders, when Nethercott, who was already on the books, might have done the job just as well.

One of the best youngsters of all, the sort who only come along once every few years, was Nick Barmby. When our Youth Development Officer brought him in for a trial, Aston Villa, Manchester United and several other clubs were also after him. Nick's friend, Darren Caskey, who plays in the first team now, was already with us, which helped a little, and I had a chat with him, outlined what I thought we could do for him, and he joined us straight away. I was sure from the start that he had the talent to go all the way.

Barmby had intelligence and control, good finishing and knew when to hold the ball and when to knock it off early – a good sign of his awareness. Playing in higher levels of competition did not faze him at all; the higher he went, the better he looked. He needed a good foil and was lucky to have Teddy Sheringham alongside him, in the same way that Andy Cole has benefited from playing alongside Peter Beardsley at Newcastle. Barmby was also very teachable and picked up positional play quickly. With some players, you have to be prepared to spend a long time on the field with them, to make sure they get it right, but with others, like Barmby, you can just tell them and they get it straight away. He looked like he needed an extra yard of pace when he started, but he also worked on that and became much faster.

We faced tremendous opposition when we tried to sign him,

and Alex Ferguson has told me how angry he was that we beat
Manchester United to him. He will never forgive me for beating
him to Gascoigne and Barmby, but as I said to him, 'You've
signed the rest of Great Britain, Alex. You don't mind if we get
one or two, do you?' It is a mark of his professionalism, that
despite all his success in attracting top young players to Old
Trafford, Alex is still bitter about the odd one that got away.

Although Barmby and Sol Campbell – another richly talented
player – were the pick of our youngsters, there were another
five or six who were not far behind; but while the young players
would brighten Tottenham's outlook in the medium term, we
needed a couple more class players to bridge the short-term gap.
I had spent a total of £5 million since coming to Tottenham, the
lion's share on Gascoigne and Stewart, but the money raised in
sales was also substantial and under the terms of my original
agreement with Irving Scholar, there should still have been £2
million available for transfer fees.

Instead, I discovered that the money I had earmarked for
buying players had already been put into buying two women's
clothing companies, Martex and Stumps. Scholar and the other
board members, Paul Bobroff – another property developer, and
Scholar's original partner in the takeover – Tony Berry and
Douglas Alexiou, had set off on a diversification programme,
including these clothing companies, which were hardly natural
partners for football. The companies had been purchased for
around £5 million, but though reportedly profitable at the time,
they very quickly fell into substantial losses. Tottenham had
also done a deal with Hummel, which had been a reasonably
well-recognised sports brand, but was now in extreme
difficulty.

The acquisition of Synchro Systems, which specialised in
stadium ticketing systems, probably sucked in another £1-million
worth of software development. It was a particularly cynical
investment, for at the same time that Scholar was making an

impassioned speech to a parliamentary committee, denouncing Mrs Thatcher's National Identity Scheme for football, Tottenham's computer company was bidding for the right to administer the scheme. In the event, the National Identity Scheme was scrapped, and like the board's other 'outside investments', Synchro Systems was a failure, although ironically, since Tottenham divested themselves of it, the company has become very successful.

Tottenham had neither the management structure nor systems to manage the kind of diversification that had been undertaken, which drained something like £6 million of working capital from the company. The situation was made worse by Scholar's unwillingness to delegate the running of the companies to people with expertise in their fields. Scholar did not see it that way at all, of course.

In addition to these problems, the redevelopment of the East Stand was behind schedule and massively over budget. This was ironic since Scholar and Bobroff had taken power at Tottenham proclaiming their experience in property development as a sure safeguard against the kind of cost overrun that had torpedoed the previous board, which had collapsed under the weight of debt from the redevelopment of the West Stand. As the early 1980s recession had bitten chunks out of the board's optimistic projections of income from the new development, the club's debts had been described as 'the largest in English football', with the bank manager having to give permission for anything more than petty cash to be spent. It was a state of affairs that was to be almost exactly duplicated less than ten years later.

In October 1983 Scholar and Bobroff had produced ambitious plans to transform the club into a 'leisure group' and floated it on the Stock Exchange, making the football club a wholly owned subsidiary of the plc, in a move to get around Football League rules restricting the payments of dividends to shareholders. They then began the diversification programme in which profits from new commercial activities would allegedly subsidise the football club. After they had sold Alan Brazil and Steve Archibald – the latter to a well-known Spanish football club, managed by a well-known English manager – while spending £100,000 on a disastrous TV advertising campaign, and stocking the club shop with everything from Tottenham wallpaper to Tottenham aftershave, coach Keith Burkinshaw quit in 1984, saying 'There used to be a football club over there'. The advertising campaign, devised by 1980s whizz-kids the Saatchi brothers, was designed to boost crowds at White Hart Lane by convincing television viewers that a Spurs game was a great day out for young and old, rich and poor, and men and women. The sentiments were laudable, but the returns were negligible.

Far from subsidising the football, the new commercial activities of Tottenham Hotspur plc, now being described by the *Investors Chronicle* as 'the football club and sportswear distributor', made thumping losses, which had to be covered from football profits. No one could ever question Scholar's enthusiasm for Spurs, for he had been a lifelong supporter, but he was not the person to be in charge when things went wrong. The construction of the new East Stand was a financial and public-relations disaster. Scholar's willingness to accept the abolition of 'The Shelf', an area of terracing that he himself had called 'the best standing view in London', particularly incensed the fans. It led to the formation of a pressure group called 'Left On The Shelf', and when Scholar belatedly altered the plans to incorporate a small standing area, it only added to the spiralling costs of the project. Financed by borrowing, without any protection against delays in construction or escalating costs, the East Stand eventually came in at over £9 million, about twice the original estimate. Scholar and Bobroff showed that they did retain at least some of their old property-developing skills when flogging off Spurs' Cheshunt training ground for housing development for £4.9 million. It was one of a string of asset disposals that would prove necessary as the plc fell deeper and deeper into debt.

Before the start of the 1988–89 season, I parted company with Allan Harris. He had been with me right from the days at Crystal Palace, but after fourteen years as an assistant coach, he was more than ready for the step up to head coach. Espanol had offered him the chance to return to Spain and he left with my thanks and best wishes, but the move was a shambles for him, through no fault of his own.

The president of Espanol, who had signed Allan, suddenly resigned. When the new president was installed, he decided that he wanted to appoint his own man as coach. Poor Allan was let go after just eleven days, without even taking a training session, let alone a game. He returned to England, but ran up against the problem faced by quite a few coaches who have worked abroad – or who have not, in this case – who find that not only does their European experience not impress the 'Little Englanders' running many English football clubs, but that they have also been largely forgotten by possible employers while they were away.

Allan tried his luck as a sports agent for a while, but then left the country again, coaching first in Kuwait and more recently in Egypt, where I am delighted that he has proved a great success, taking his club, Al Ahly, to the top of the League and victory in the African Cup-Winners Cup. The victory that gave him no pleasure was a 3–0 win over Egyptian rivals Ramalek, however. A victory in the local derby would normally be something to celebrate, but it cost Ramalek's coach his job. No coach wants to be responsible for getting another one the sack, least of all when that coach was Dave Mackay.

Allan and I had known each other since we were fourteen and it was a great friendship, in which we trusted each other implicitly. I brought Allan in at Palace, originally to take the youth side, but I soon moved him up to work alongside me and we knew each other so well that he knew what I would want, almost before I did myself. He was also a true confidant; I could discuss anything with him and know that it would go no further, and we only had one argument in thirty-five years.

When the new season began, the cost overruns on the new stand were overshadowed by delays in completing the building work, which made Tottenham the laughing stock of the League. On the opening day of the season, 27 August 1988, Tottenham's home game with Coventry City was called off on the morning of the match, because the new stand had not been finished on time and the ground was still full of builders' rubble. The workers who were supposed to be clearing up overnight had 'got tired and gone home', according to a Spurs director. When the Haringey Safety Officer arrived at the ground, the police, who had been there since 6:00 a.m., advised him that the game should be postponed. When the safety officer inspected the East Terrace, he found far too much rubble to be removed and called off the game. My players and I were not informed of the postponement until mid-morning.

The commercial developments that were supposed to be funding the football were not only draining money away from it instead, they were now damaging the team even more directly. The League deducted two points from Tottenham for that exercise in monumental incompetence, though later in the season their decision was rescinded on appeal and replaced by a £15,000 fine, thanks to the skill of a very fine barrister, Michael Crystal QC. The eventual fine from the League paled beside the costs of the postponement of a game that was not played until the following April, and the reduced capacity at our next three home games. Altogether Tottenham lost somewhere around half a million pounds.

Our next game was not cancelled, but Paul Gascoigne probably wished that it had been. We travelled to Newcastle, where the memory of their hero's 'treachery' in moving to another club, was still fresh in the minds of the fans at St James's Park. Gazza was called 'Rich bastard', 'Yuppie', and 'Judas' and pelted with Mars Bars that the Newcastle fans had bought from a stall specially set up on a garage forecourt near the ground. I brought him off before the end of the match and he was booed all the way to the tunnel. The 2–2 draw we managed gave us one of the few points we had accumulated by the end of October, when after losing 3–2 at Arsenal, we went down 2–1 to Aston Villa to slump to the bottom of the League.

Goalkeeper Bobby Mimms's confidence was proving to be as perishable as Tony Parkes's. After one bad display, Gazza started scrapping with him in the dressing room, which was hardly the right way to promote team harmony. Things became worse as we were knocked out of the League Cup by Southampton, after a mistake by Gazza this time, and dumped out of the ... began by Bradford City. That defeat finally cost ... Mimms his job, though his replacement, Erik Thorstvedt, started in just the same fashion, dropping the ball into his own net on his début against Nottingham Forest.

From that low point, however, he and the team began a revival that took us through to the end of the season with only one defeat in our last fourteen games, enabling us to finish in sixth position – still not good enough, but a lot better than bottom. Even more depressing for Tottenham fans was the knowledge that our sixth place was five below the hated rivals Arsenal, who took the title after a thrilling final match at Liverpool. Our revival had begun with a 2–1 beating of Norwich and culminated with a 2–1 win against Wimbledon in the last game of the season. Beating Wimbledon was always a happy event for me, because their style of play then was so depressing and so completely opposed to the skilful and entertaining game that football can and should be. Kicking the leather off the ball was scarcely great spectator sport, as the size of Wimbledon's crowds at the time indicated.

As time has gone by, Wimbledon have improved, to the point where they now play football as good as any, and their chairman, Sam Hammam, and manager, Joe Kinnear, whom I had roomed with when he was at Tottenham, deserve great credit for the transformation from the 'bad old days' of five years ago. People used to travel across London to watch QPR's entertainers play, but I doubt if many in Wimbledon would have crossed the road to see their team then. Wimbledon would point to their survival in the Premier League and say that their approach to the game paid dividends, but though it was sometimes effective, it was the unacceptable face of football. As I said at the time, 'Wimbledon are killing the dream that made football the world's greatest game. I could take any non-League player and turn him into a Wimbledon player in a matter of weeks.'

Much of their game was based on intimidation, which in the dressing room, where they liked to have a ghetto-blaster on at full volume before a match. It was part of their gamesmanship, intended to put the other team off their game, and it seemed to work. We had had a taste of trial by ghetto-blaster the year before, grinding out heavy-metal music at deafening volume, which drove everyone mad and, coincidentally or not, Wimbledon had a good result that day. I was determined to reverse that when we next played them and planned a little gamesmanship of my own.

We were told that their players had broken some doors at Arsenal when they played there the week before, and though Wimbledon denied it, we used it as an excuse to ban their ghetto-blaster from the dressing room. They tried to hide it in the bag with their kit and sneak it in, but when they got into the dressing room, we turned off the mains power. They were prepared for that, brought out some batteries and put it on, but by then we had all the connecting doors closed and locked, so that we could hardly hear it in our dressing room anyway.

By now their tempers had frayed so much that their chairman was getting angry with me, telling me I was a bad sport, which I thought was a bit rich, and the police were becoming involved to try and prevent feelings boiling over into a full-scale breach of the peace. It was really quite funny, because they were more worried about their precious ghetto-blaster than they were about preparing for the game. It all worked out well in the end – we won.

If Wimbledon's approach to football then was summed by the figure of Vinnie Jones, his old adversary, Paul Gascoigne, was a symbol of the Spurs approach to football. His talents were flowering, both on the field and off it, where his new tabloid title 'The Clown Prince of Soccer' was earning him money and headlines. It also gave us a few laughs. When the officials wanted one of our players for a routine dope test after a game, I said 'Well, don't do it on Gazza. There's no need, he's definitely a dope.' His international manager, Bobby Robson, was unimpressed by that side of his character, describing him dismissively as 'daft as a brush', but that was just more grist to Gazza's mill; the 'Daft as a Brush' joke book was in production within weeks.

Tottenham were further strengthened before the 1989–90 season by the arrival of Gary Lineker and Nayim in a package deal from Barcelona. Gary was not happy under the coaching of Johan Cruyff. He did not get the best out of Gary, playing him out of position on the wing for most of the season and he took little persuading to join Tottenham. I flew out to Barcelona to clinch the deal; a price of £1.5 million for the two of them, £600,000 immediately, the remainder in twelve months' time, represented one of the bargains of the century. They were quality players and would have cost at least twice as much, if we had signed them from English clubs. On this occasion, the Tottenham board readily agreed to make the money available to buy players rather than clothing companies, even though it later transpired that the club barely had two coppers to rub together at the time.

Unaware of that, Tottenham fans could barely contain their excitement at the thought of Paul Gascoigne, Gary Lineker and Chris Waddle in the same team, as we prepared for the 1989–90 season, but it was to be a very short-lived combination. Within three weeks of the start of the season, Waddle was on his way to Marseille. Irving Scholar came running into my office on the morning of the press conference welcoming Gary Lineker to White Hart Lane, saying, 'You're not going to believe this, but we've just had an offer of £2 million for Waddle.'

'So what?'

'It's from Marseille.'

That gave me pause for thought. Bernard Tapie, the owner of Marseille, seemed to have limitless ambitions and equally limitless resources to back them. I turned to Doug Livermore, who was in the office with me and asked him what he thought. We had just been discussing how to stop conceding goals, because with Waddle's crosses and Lineker's finishing, we did not anticipate having too many problems in scoring them. Scholar, as usual, was uninterested in signing defenders, preferring the 'great box office', as he described it, of signing star attackers. I said, 'Yes, but it is Arsenal who are actually winning things. Getting the defence right first, as Arsenal have done, is absolutely the right way to go about it.'

It occurred to me that if Tapie could be persuaded to 'up the ante' to some very serious money indeed, if we did have to lose Chris Waddle, we could at least use the money to add some commonsense to the 'great box office', by buying two or three defenders to sort out the defence. I turned to Scholar: 'I bet he'll go a lot higher.'

I was right. When Scholar turned down the £2 million, Tapie's agent immediately raised the bid to £3 million. On my advice, Scholar again turned him down, but invited him to London to talk through a possible deal. We met him at the Carlton Tower Hotel, and as we prepared for the meeting, I said to Scholar, 'Tell him the price is £6 million. If he'll pay that much it will be worth a discussion.' The price would have equalled the world-record fee AC Milan had paid for Ruud Gullit a couple of years before, but I saw no harm in giving it a try.

When the figure was mentioned, Tapie did not even blink. 'It's too much,' he said, 'but I'll give you £5 million for Waddle and Paul Walsh.' That deal fell through, but Tapie was willing to pay £4.25 million for Waddle alone. That is still big money now, but then it was unbelievable – Monopoly money. I asked for a time-out and said to Scholar, 'I think we should tell the player now.'

'But it will unsettle him,' said Scholar.

'If it gets back to him that Marseille made an offer that we didn't even tell him about, he will not be the same player for us anyway. Let's find out what he thinks.'

It would have been grossly unfair to have kept the offer secret from Chris, who jumped at the offer, because his share of the fee alone would make him a millionaire. At twenty-eight he had only a few years left in the game and this deal would give him financial security for life. Provided all the money was made available for team-strengthening, I was quite happy for him to go. It would be a wrench, but for that money I could not only fill his position, but buy another top player as well.

Scholar agreed to my conditions, but then changed his mind, with less than a third of the money forthcoming to buy players. I bought Steve Sedgley from Coventry and Pat van den Hauwe from Everton, but the rest of the Waddle cash disappeared

down the plughole of Tottenham's bathtub full of debts, and
within six months, instead of buying players, I was being told to
sell more of the ones that we already had. As I complained at
the time, 'At the moment, I couldn't lay out a fiver on a World
Cup star.'

Gary Lineker was not too thrilled about the weakening of
the team either. Playing alongside Chris Waddle was one of
the big attractions about White Hart Lane for Gary. As he
said at the time of his signing, 'Chris knows my game, sees
my runs and provides the most accurate passes that I have
ever had.' With no Chris Waddle and no money to replace
him, Gary's chances of the medals that he craved had been
severely reduced, but like the rest of the Spurs players, he
buckled down to the task, despite further worrying noises from
the boardroom, suggesting that Gary too, might soon be on his
way.

A new chief executive, Bob Holt, had arrived from Spurs
director Tony Berry's employment company, Blue Arrow, which
had been one of the great success stories of the 1980s boom
years, with Tony Berry one of the darlings of the City, backed
by his 'pet merchant bank', County Nat West. Like many of the
meteoric rises of the period, however, Berry's career burned out
just as fast, his empire collapsing in spectacular style, leading to
a DTI investigation. County Nat West's handling of the issue of
837 million Blue Arrow shares turned out to have been under-
pinned by County Nat West buying many of the shares itself,
and then claiming to investors that the flotation had been a
success. Berry was later to make loans and guarantees worth £4
million to Tottenham, using Blue Arrow money, but without
telling the Blue Arrow board.

Holt's first action as chief executive was a significant one.
For the first time ever, the value of Tottenham's players was
included in the club's assets. It made the accounts produced for
the 1989 AGM look better, but it sent a cold shiver through me,

for assets are only worth what they can be sold for, and 'asset disposals' was a term being heard increasingly often as Spurs' debts mounted.

Tottenham's financial troubles were becoming too serious to conceal and a public feud broke out in September 1989 between the erstwhile 'saviours' of Spurs, Irving Scholar and Paul Bobroff. Bobroff felt that as a public company, Tottenham Hotspur plc's first duty was to its shareholders, not its footballers, and supported subsidising the loss-making subsidiaries out of football profits, a view not shared by Scholar.

Bobroff first resigned from the board and was then reinstated within a week. A statement described his resignation as being 'due to increasing outside business interests' and his return a week later as due to 'representations from board members'. The *Daily Telegraph* printed a more convincing explanation, saying that: 'Bobroff left after feuding with Scholar . . . You cannot have two Popes in Rome' – if only I had remembered that comment when I was negotiating with Alan Sugar. Bobroff's departure alarmed the Midland Bank, who were nursing the club's spiralling overdraft, and their intervention got him straight back on the board.

Despite the gathering storm-clouds, it was a successful season on the pitch. After a poor start, in which we won only one of our first six games, we put together a tremendous charge up the table, finishing the 1989–90 season in third place. Gascoigne was at the heart of the revival, emerging as a truly great talent, though his talent for practical jokes was developing just as fast. We were getting ready to set off to play a game at Nottingham Forest, leaving on the Friday and staying overnight before the match. We met at Chase Lodge, Mill Hill, the sports ground that doubles as Tottenham's training ground since the sale of the original training ground in Cheshunt. Most of the lads were waiting in the coach, but as usual, Gazza could not sit still for more than ten seconds and had to find something to do. He disappeared from view, and ten minutes later, Gary Lineker got on the coach, killing himself laughing, having just seen Gazza's idea of 'something to do'.

There was a camper-van in the car park, one of the ones with a ladder coming down the back. Gazza put a traffic cone on the top of the van and then sat in the driving seat. When John Coberman, a supporter who was always willing to do odd jobs for his heroes, appeared, Gazza asked him to get the cone down for him, because he had to nip out in the van. As John climbed up on the roof and reached out for the cone, Gazza revved up the van and drove off through the gates with John still on the roof. He slipped to the back and was hanging off the ladder with his legs trailing behind him in the slipstream, while Gazza drove off down the road, on to the A1, up to the next roundabout, back down the other side of the A1, and back up the road, racing back into the car park and screeching to a halt. John got off the van, as white as a sheet and very shaken up.

The next day we thrashed Forest, with Gazza absolutely outstanding. We were in the dressing room after the game, in high spirits, when John Coberman stuck his head round the door and said, 'Gazza, you can do it again next week, if you play like that.'

He did, week after week, with the sceptical Bobby Robson forced to acknowledge his importance to England's World Cup chances. Gazza and Gary Lineker set off to Italia '90, and despite the disappointment of the semi-final defeat, they returned from the World Cup with their reputations considerably enhanced. Gazza's 'Tears of Turin' had made him world-famous and would bring him hundreds of thousands of pounds in off-field earnings alone during the 1990–91 season. His exploits had also pushed his transfer value through the roof, and given Tottenham's parlous finances, that could only increase the pressure to sell him. Pressure was something that Gazza was going to have to learn to live with, even more than before. From being just the most expensive player in England, he was now one of the most famous players in the world. Fans from Spurs and every visiting team would expect heroics from him every week, while the media sharpened their pens and waited to pounce on any indiscretions.

Tottenham's merchandising arm could have learned a trick or two from the World Cup organisers, who cut the pitch at the Olympic Stadium in Rome into 300,000 pieces at the end of the tournament and flogged them for £50 each. After plastic pitches, this was another prophecy from *They Used to Play on Grass* coming true, for we had described a similar scene in that book, twenty years before.

The summer that made a superstar of Gascoigne was a time of desperate sadness for me, for my Mum died of cancer in August. She had kept her illness hidden from me for quite some time, but when Yvette and I went to see her, she admitted that she had not been very well. We went down to see her again the following weekend and found that her neck was red and swollen. I was really frightened and worried about her. When I left her that day, I thought I was going to crack up. I spoke to her doctor and discovered that she had cancer, but he did not yet know to what extent. Yvette and I talked things over on the way home and decided that we wanted her to come and live with us. When we visited my Mum again, I put the plan to her. We would have a downstairs room for her and arrange nursing and all the care that she needed.

She was very keen on the idea, which both delighted and surprised me, because she had always wanted to live out her days in Wales; but she was very enthusiastic, and I was just as excited as we made plans about what we would do. Yvette and I went home, planning to complete the arrangements as quickly as possible and bring her up to London the following week.

Instead, we had a call to tell us that she had to go into hospital straight away.

Fred, Yvette and I raced down there, a terrible journey in which we barely spoke, all too frightened and upset to want to talk about anything. My Mum had been taken to a huge hospital at Penarth, overlooking the sea. After we had been in to see her, looking so small and frail, and so unlike the vivacious and strong person we knew, we spoke to the doctors, who told us that it was just a matter of time.

We went and sat outside the hospital, on a bench at the edge of a cricket pitch. I sat there for ages, sobbing, while Yvette tried to console me, despite the tears pouring down her own face, and my Dad, in tears as well, walked away to be alone with his grief. There was a cricket match being played while we sat there, and now every time I drive past a ground somewhere and see people playing cricket, it reminds me of that day while my Mum lay dying.

There was a guest-house in the grounds, and I asked if we could stay there for a couple of weeks, with no one expecting her to live even that long. We saw her every day and suddenly we began to see an improvement. It was quite incredible, even the doctors could not understand it, and I could not believe this one-in-a-million chance. The prognosis had changed now; with care and the right treatment, there was a possibility that she might recover.

It gave us all such a boost, but it proved to be the cruellest of false dawns. We had gone back to London for a few days, when we were again summoned back to Wales. Yvette stayed behind this time and my Dad and I went down together. We stayed in the room opposite my Mum's in the hospital, and were there all through the day and night, as my Mum grew steadily weaker. The end came at about two o'clock in the morning. I had been trying to snatch some sleep when the nurse called me. I sat on the bed and held my Mum's hand as she gave up the struggle. Her last breath was like a long, quiet sigh, and then she was gone.

Her strength, her wisdom, her principles and her encouragement had sustained me throughout my life. Now, like all sons, I faced the morning after my mother's death, knowing that my life would never be quite the same again.

Bereavement puts football problems into their proper perspective, but I had to pick up the reins at Tottenham and get on with my life, and the day-to-day distractions of the job were welcome. With the UEFA ban on English clubs, imposed in the wake of the Heysel disaster, now lifted, there was every incentive for Tottenham to do well in the 1990–91 season. We began by thrashing Manchester City 3–1, with the Gascoigne–Lineker axis sharing the goals, the start of a ten-match unbeaten run, the best since the Double year of 1960–61. Gascoigne scored his first hat-trick for Spurs in a 3–0 beating of Derby County and in a foretaste of even better to come, later on that season, the hat-trick included two free-kicks, which left Peter Shilton helpless, as they flew into the net.

Spurs' debts were, meanwhile, leaving Irving Scholar equally helpless. So strapped were Tottenham for cash that Scholar had been forced to go, cap in hand, to the 'Bouncing Czech', Robert Maxwell, at the end of July, borrowing £1.1 million to stop Barcelona recalling Gary Lineker for non-payment of the remainder of his transfer fee. News of that episode did not filter out until later, which was just as well, for it made Scholar's Tottenham Hotspur plc look even more shabby.

At the same time that he advanced Scholar the £1.1 million loan, at Scholar's invitation, Maxwell also began secretly negotiating with him to buy a stake in Tottenham, by underwriting a £13.2 million rights issue on a 'one for one' basis at £1.30 a share, doubling the number of shares by issuing one new share to the holder for each existing one. Scholar gave assurances that his colleagues and he would not take up all their allocations, leaving Maxwell with a guaranteed stake of 26 per cent, roughly matching Scholar's own. Maxwell was unlikely to have accepted that situation for long, even with Scholar, who had been his close friend and faithful supporter since they had served together on the Football League's television sub-committee in 1984.

Maxwell insisted on absolute secrecy, even from the Tottenham board, and it was only later that details began to emerge, ironically as Maxwell's chances of making the deal started to evaporate, as the worldwide slump began to unravel his fragile business empire. Scholar first put the deal to a board meeting consisting of only two people: Scholar himself, who had a direct interest, and finance director Derek Peter. They approved the arrangement and Scholar next took it to a meeting that did not include the chairman of the plc, Paul Bobroff, but did have directors Douglas Alexiou, Tony Berry and Frank Sinclair present. They were told the details of the deal, but not the identity of Scholar's 'fairy godfather'. The meeting gave Scholar the go-ahead to proceed with negotiations, but the way that the Scholar/Maxwell plan had been handled led to a furious row between Scholar and Bobroff at a board meeting on 14 September – coincidentally, just after our home victory against Maxwell's Derby County. The Stock Exchange also intervened, unamused to see a public company negotiating loans and rights issues without informing either the chairman of the company or the shareholders.

Scholar's comments at the time the proposed deal was made public, 'Many people will have mixed feelings about Mr Maxwell but they don't know the man ... Mr Maxwell's record in football is exemplary,' must have struck many as cynical, but in my view they were naïve. His confidence was not shared by his fellow board members, when they were eventually appraised of the identity of their 'white knight', and the rows led to an irrevocable split between Scholar and Bobroff.

Maxwell's involvement led the Stock Exchange to suspend dealings in the shares of Tottenham Hotspur plc at 91 pence on 19 October 1990, on the grounds that 'there was insufficient public information to determine their current value' – or, in layman's terms, until the Bouncing Czech's intentions towards the company were clarified. The club that had been the first in the history of the Football League to become a public company seven years before was now on the brink of collapse.

Despite the fact he was still the major shareholder, Irving Scholar was forced to resign from the board of the plc, though he kept his chairmanship of the football club. His dealings with Maxwell breached both the Stock Exchange Regulations and Football League regulations – which banned direct financial dealings between club chairmen.

In Scholar's place, Midland Bank, who by now had put their dealings with Spurs in the hands of their 'Intensive Care Unit', had effectively installed their own man as the new chairman. The brief for Nat Solomon, formerly head of the Pleasurama casino group, was to conduct 'asset disposals' – also known as 'player sales'. The Midland had also brought in an insolvency practitioner, David Buchler of Buchler Phillips, and were pushing ever harder for the company to resolve its problems – to the point where they were coming very, very close to putting Tottenham into receivership. Scholar's 'cheap' loan from Maxwell was to prove to be an expensive mistake.

The news of Maxwell's involvement was alarming, for his previous record in football was scarcely designed to promote confidence. After taking over Oxford United, he had attempted to force a shotgun marriage with Reading, in which he held a minority stake, flogging off both grounds for development and building a new one at Didcot, a place in no man's land, notable mainly for a particularly ugly power station. The move would have netted Maxwell several million pounds, but the Reading directors unexpectedly rebelled, throwing Maxwell's tame chairman off the board. Foiled of his master-plan, Maxwell contented himself with blackmailing Oxford Council by threatening the closure of the club if they did not provide a quarter of million pounds for ground improvements. The Council, like so many others when dealing with Maxwell, gave in. The Oxford floodlights found particularly good use, being used as landing lights for Maxwell's helicopter as he commuted from his nearby home.

Maxwell next turned his attentions to Manchester United, but after being rebuffed by Martin Edwards, he bought control of Derby County for a knock-down price of £850,000, transferring the chairmanship of Oxford to his son, Kevin, after the Football League raised objections to his ownership of two clubs. Apart from making enormous amounts of money through deals that were at best dubious, Maxwell's other favourite hobby was self-aggrandisement. A successful football club would bring him not only kudos, particularly in the Maxwell-owned *Daily Mirror*, but also cash through the lucrative television rights in European competitions. That income would become a cash avalanche for those teams involved in a European Super-League, which Maxwell believed to be inevitable. His only problem was that his teams did not look likely to qualify for Europe, and he was unable to buy into the ones that might.

While keeping one eye on the situation at Tottenham, Captain Bob set out to turn two moderate football clubs into one good one. Deciding that Derby was the more plausible vehicle for his ambitions, Maxwell systematically stripped Oxford of its saleable players, who were flogged off or transferred to Derby. Dean Saunders went direct to Derby, Mark Wright arrived there via Southampton, while John Aldridge and Ray Houghton were sold to Liverpool. The Oxford fans could but sit and watch the demolition of their once-promising team. Their only consolation would be that Derby would suffer the same treatment when Maxwell tired of them too.

The Football League could do nothing but wring its hands, while Maxwell abused his position at Oxford to wreck one of their member clubs, but they were able to intervene to stop him paying £2 million to add Watford to his football portfolio. From then on Maxwell knew that he would have to sell his other clubs, before they would accept a takeover by him at one of the giants of the game which he coveted. Tottenham or Manchester United were the only two plausible candidates among the Big Five, for the owners of Liverpool, Everton and Arsenal showed not the slightest intention of selling at the time.

United had been for sale, but after the farcical takeover bid by Michael Knighton, during which Maxwell's *Mirror* had vilified both Knighton and United owner Martin Edwards, Maxwell knew that Edwards would only consider selling out to him if he paid well over the odds. The cheaper and weaker target was Tottenham, and despite his fall from grace, Maxwell's friend Scholar remained the major shareholder in the plc and the chairman of the football club, and still attended the plc board meetings.

The thought of Maxwell and Scholar together at Tottenham chilled my blood. I had little confidence in Irving Scholar and even less in Maxwell. As I said at the time, 'The role of managers in English football is being diminished by amateur directors who want to play at professional football. If we had Maxwell as well as Scholar, we would all move one step closer to the boot-room, myself included.'

The collapsing Stock Market forced Maxwell to put his Tottenham schemes on the back-burner for the moment, though typically Maxwell blamed the decision on Football League opposition, demanding an apology for its comments on his proposed involvement at Spurs from what he called the League's 'mismanagement committee' – a tedious joke shared by Maxwell and

Scholar, which had grown whiskers on it since it was first aired a few years before. An apology was never likely to be forthcoming, but gave Maxwell the excuse to step back, while he attempted to shore up his paper fortune.

The decline in the Stock Market made no direct difference to Tottenham, but it made the likelihood of a rights issue or another 'white knight' rescuing them even more remote. The desperate state of Tottenham's finances was demonstrated when admission prices, already the highest in the League, were abruptly raised again halfway through the season. The minimum price of a main-stand seat was now £17, further alienating the supporters, who after our bright start, also had less to cheer about on the pitch, where a run of three successive defeats in December began a slide down the table.

The board members could no longer disguise the fact that Tottenham was in severe financial crisis, and they were beginning to panic. It was clear that there would have to be a substantial cash injection, but the existing directors obviously had great difficulties in raising new money. After watching helplessly from the sidelines as the club sank deeper and deeper into the financial mire, I began to have the idea of forming a consortium to buy the controlling shareholding of Irving Scholar and Paul Bobroff. I was motivated partly by my own ambition, obviously, but I also felt a desperate need to do something to help save the club from the increasingly real possibility of extinction. For every ounce of personal pride, there was also a pound of passion for a great club and for the game of football itself.

Although I had a general ambition to move into the boardroom at some stage of my career, I always imagined that it would be at a small club in the lower divisions, buying players, improving them and moving them on, and hoping that I could make the club stand up financially. I certainly did not join Tottenham with the aim of buying the club, and when the chance came it was not by design at all, but events develop their own momentum.

I began looking for partners in November and the first news of my plans leaked to the press just before Christmas, when the *Sunday Times* ran a story about my involvement with a group, including boxing promoter Frank Warren, which was looking at a takeover of Spurs. Scholar's original demand was for £1 per share, which valued the company at about £11 million and his own holding at about £3 million. He also wanted a contractual guarantee that I would pay off the debts to the Midland Bank and keep Gascoigne at White Hart Lane. Those conditions effectively pushed up the financing costs to over £20 million, an awfully large sum for a company with as dismal a financial record as Tottenham Hotspur plc.

In any event, Scholar was at best ambivalent about his reaction to a sale to me. We had fallen out badly over his failure to make funds available to buy players and he made his preference for another buyer clear as our negotiations went on. His fellow-directors Paul Bobroff and Douglas Alexiou were equally vehement opponents, because they knew that a condition of my takeover would be that they leave the board. The only member in support of me – at that stage – was Tony Berry, who would remain on the board if I took over.

My earnings as a manager had made me comfortably off, but I was far short of the millions that would be necessary to enable me to purchase the shares and clear the debts, and I had to find a substantial backer. I was going to introduce Jim Gregory to Scholar, but Jim, who was very keen initially, went cool on the idea. Through Frank Warren, I was then introduced to a man called Larry Gillick, whose business address was a reputable solicitor's office in Harley Street. He seemed to have access to considerable funds, and for a period of about three months, Gillick came forward with a series of different propositions for the purchase of the shares.

Tony Berry, who was very anti-Scholar, had a meeting with Gillick and me, at which Gillick proposed that I would get 25 per cent of the shares for leading the consortium and taking the role of chief executive. That was obviously appealing, because it would have given me the chance to turn Spurs around, without having to find an enormous sum of money to do so. The other two shareholders would have been Berry and Gillick.

Tony Berry would often come to our meetings as we worked to put a deal together, and in the latter stages, Ian Gray, then the managing director of Tottenham, would also accompany him. It was never really clear whether he was there as a friend of Tony and a supporter of the bid, or something else. Certainly his position was frequently blurred. At one stage an agreement was signed with some property developers, who agreed to procure a mortgage over the ground at White Hart Lane. Along with my own funds, it would have produced enough money to complete the purchase, but though Larry Gillick did his best, the deal, like all his subsequent attempts, fell through.

I do not let things like that get me down; I rarely get low about anything. You have to control pressure or it will control you. That applies if your team is playing in front of 120,000 people in the Nou Camp, or two men and a dog in a park. It is the way that you respond to pressure – what is in your head – that counts. If you can control yourself, you will also control stresses that might break another person. After Barcelona, I was certain that I would never have to face so much pressure again – which just shows how wrong you can be. I had demonstrated that I could live with the pressures of arguably the biggest football club in the world, but I now faced those of a collapsing football club, with a hundred years of history, hope and emotion invested in it.

When I began trying to put a bid together, the pressure was something else again. I have never worked as hard in my life, spending the mornings with the team and the afternoons and evenings in meetings as I sought a way to put together a deal to save the club. Sometimes I would get home in the early hours, sometimes I would not get home at all, as again and again I met with potential backers and thrashed out the details of a package to buy the club. As I told a reporter at the time, 'Many managers have cracked up in the past. I've gone past that stage; I've been there and I'm coming back.' There were so many red herrings along the way that it was simply unbelievable. Every day, people would be coming in and offering money, only to back out again at the last minute. I did not know from one day to the next if it was really going to happen.

The shortage of cash and the uncertainty about Spurs' future was beginning to have an impact on the field as well as off. By early in the New Year, the team was knackered, cut apart by injuries, and with no money for signings, there were no quality players to replace the injured. Our League form went to pieces, the most bitter blow being a 5–1 hammering by Wimbledon, after we had taken the field without five top players and with the rest of the side little more than walking wounded. Joe Kinnear, a former Tottenham player, who was the only member of his Spurs side not to have been signed for a large fee, remarked after the game, 'We are talking about one of the biggest clubs in the land, but all you ever hear is talk about them selling, not buying, which was never the case in my day.'

On a cold January night, we met Chelsea in the League Cup quarter-finals. The game was a yawn from start to finish and ended goalless. It was due to be televised, but almost mercifully for both sets of armchair supporters, the Gulf War had broken out the same night. It made much more exciting television viewing than the drab 0–0 draw at Stamford Bridge, and the football was hastily dropped from the schedules.

Still without the benefit of television coverage, we lost the replay to Chelsea, ironically on the same day that the *Evening Standard* broke the news that the Tottenham board were considering selling Paul Gascoigne to ease their financial worries. The start of my attempts to put together a deal for the purchase of Tottenham had coincided with the beginning of the Tottenham board's covert attempts to dispose of Gascoigne. Initially, an agent, Dennis Roach, was retained to scour Europe for clubs interested in purchasing him, but the board's willingness to sell Gascoigne was not communicated to me or the fans until the AGM in February, when director Douglas Alexiou admitted in response to a question, 'We have a duty to our shareholders. No asset is bigger than the club; players are assets and if the circumstances were right and we could not raise money except by selling star players, we would have to consider letting them go at the right price.' In case anyone had missed the point, chairman Nat Solomon added, 'If someone came in for Gascoigne and the price was right, we would obviously have to seriously consider it.'

These were less than completely open replies at a time when Tottenham had already been hawking the player around Europe for some time, and in any event, for most Tottenham fans, there was no such thing as a 'right price' for Gascoigne. I was equally opposed to selling him and it was also a particularly insensitive time to make such remarks, unsettling the team in the week before a vital FA Cup tie. I had tried to keep the players insulated as much as possible from the financial turmoil at the club, but the problems in the boardroom had now been brought right into the dressing room.

It was obvious that our only hope of qualifying for Europe would be to enter the Eurovision Song Contest or win the FA Cup. Neither looked particularly likely at the time, but our Cup hopes rested more and more on Gazza's broad shoulders, and our Cup progress was destined to run in parallel with the saga of his transfer.

Gazza was carrying an injury and I had to nurse him from game to game, often resting him in League matches to keep him at least half-fit for the Cup games. With several other players also struggling because of injuries, we began the FA Cup trail at Blackpool, where Paul Stewart scored on his return to his old haunts, to give us a 1–0 win, after a match played in some of the most appalling conditions I have ever seen at a football game. A howling gale blowing off the Irish Sea sent torrential rain, sleet and snow driving across the ground, half-blinding the players and turning the pitch into a quagmire. The draw for the next round gave us a home tie in a warmer location, against another of the Maxwell fiefdoms, Oxford United. Gascoigne put on a display to savour, scoring two goals and making the others in a 4–2 win, showing the strength and skill of Maradona and the hunger for the game of Dave Mackay at his best.

Even Gascoigne, Maradona and Mackay could not have sorted out the off-the-field problems. The mood of the shareholders attending the AGM in February 1991 was understandably angry. Astonishingly, no up-to-date accounts were available, but the information that was revealed was bad enough. Total debts stood at £13.6 million and liabilities were £22.9 million. As a placard at the AGM put it: '£22 million in debt – It's Hummeliating'. Another placard was even more humiliating for Scholar; under pictures of Gascoigne and Scholar was the caption: 'Should Tottenham dispose of its assets or liabilities?' There was no doubt in anyone's mind about which was which, for all the Scholar regime's money-making schemes – the East Stand, Hummel, Martex, Stumps and Synchro Systems – had produced the same result: massive losses.

In the fifth round of the Cup we were given a tough-looking trip to Portsmouth. We stayed in a hotel overnight and though the players should really rest and put their feet up before a big game, as in everything else, Gazza makes up his own rules. On the morning of the Portsmouth tie, Doug Livermore came over to me with a long face and said, 'I've got some bad news. Gazza was playing squash for an hour last night.'

'I'm not really worried about him, he's got so much nervous energy, he could play squash all night and still play football the next day, but find out who he was playing squash with, he's going to be shattered.' I never did find out who his opponent had been, but Gazza showed no ill-effects at all. We were losing 1–0, but he scored two cracking goals to give us the game and a match with Notts County in the quarter-finals.

We had cleared the first three hurdles on the road to Wembley, but that was the only good news around White Hart Lane. Progress in the Cup went hand in hand with a further deterioration in our performance in the League. We were to win only two of our last twenty League games, one of those at Derby, where the home fans, who had recently read newspaper accounts of Derby chairman Robert Maxwell's loan to Scholar to keep Lineker at Spurs, were less than delighted to watch Gary score the winning goal. Maxwell's popularity in Derby, already at rock-bottom, plunged off the graph after that.

I did what I could to stop the club's financial problems affecting the players and repeatedly warned them, 'Don't use them as an excuse. I know you're reading the stories in the papers and wondering what is happening, but you're still getting paid, and I am not going to accept bad performances because of this. Don't fall for the trap of taking the easy way out. Keep your attitude right and uphold your standards, I won't accept anything less.'

Even worse was in store for the club, however, for Tottenham were again in trouble with the League and were fined £20,000 after turning up late for a game at Stamford Bridge. In a situation of near-farce, the team coach was towed away by police from outside the Royal Lancaster Hotel, where we were having our pre-match meal. At any moment I expected Jeremy Beadle to appear from behind a tree, but it was no joke. We eventually had to call a fleet of cabs to get the players to the ground, while one of our officials hot-footed it to the police pound at Camden Town to retrieve the kit from the coach. A defeat and the subsequent fine made it even less of a laughing matter. Tottenham were also threatened with court action by Southampton over a £20,000 debt and by Chelsea over a claim for £45,000 as Spurs' financial situation grew steadily worse.

Crystal Palace and QPR asked the Football League to intervene to secure payment of their share of gate receipts and in the most embarrassing moment of all, mighty Tottenham had to pay lowly Tranmere Rovers £500 compensation after failing to pay them their share of League Cup gate money on time. An even worse PR disaster was threatened by reports in the press about delays in paying money owed from Danny Blanchflower's testimonial at the end of the previous season.

Selling Paul Gascoigne would also have been a PR nightmare for the club's supporters, but it would have pleased the Midland Bank, and by March, the efforts of Dennis Roach seemed to have borne fruit. Italian club Lazio saw the capture of Gascoigne as a signal that they were ready to join the élite of Italian football, and after negotiations over the previous few months, their officials had flown into England in March to try and conclude a deal, landing at Southend instead of Heathrow, to throw any waiting reporters off the scent.

A meeting at Claridges between Irving Scholar, Nat Solomon and Dennis Roach for Tottenham, and Gian Marco Calleri, Carlo Regalia and Maurizio Manzini for Lazio, ended with Lazio firmly believing that Gascoigne was theirs, as was evident in the statements they made back in Rome. The certainty was not shared by Gascoigne's agents, Mel Stein and Len Lazarus, who complained that they had not even begun discussions with the Italians, and Scholar also back-pedalled. Stein and Lazarus lost no time in repairing their omission, however, and Solomon, under pressure from the Midland to cut Tottenham's debts, and losing patience with Scholar's delaying tactics, decided to take charge of the Gascoigne sale himself.

Meanwhile, I was also being frustrated in my attempts to take over the club, through Larry Gillick's failure to put together a realistic package. In March 1991, I could allow him no more leeway and was forced to drop Gillick. I could – and perhaps should – have abandoned my plans at the same time, for the appalling financial problems made most businessmen shy away from Tottenham. The hype was going, however, expectations were high, and as well as my own desire to rescue one of the greatest names in football, the club I had supported as a kid, I was also swayed by the passion of the letters from Spurs supporters urging me to save the club. If my involvement, despite the problems, put a question mark against my business sense, I was led by my heart as well as my head, and by my love of football.

That does not make me special, for I can think of a dozen people from Bonham Road, Dagenham alone, who would have done exactly the same thing, if they had been in my position. Gillick's father, Torry, had been a noted player in Scotland, and Gillick was at least partly motivated by his father's memory. Gillick failed to achieve his aims in putting together the finance to fund a takeover, but he was a genuine football man.

Without Gillick, it was clear that if I was going to be part of a bid for Tottenham, it would only happen if I could raise an enormous sum of money. I raised a huge sum in the end, but in doing so, I put a rope around my neck with the capital and interest repayments. Yet my confidence that Tottenham could be turned around was so high, I thought: If I am going to take one big risk in my life, why not do it in something I have always done, the thing that I do best?

I still needed an ally who knew the City, and turned to Eddie Ashby for help, asking him if he would have a look at the possibilities of acquiring the company. From then until the successful completion of the purchase in late June, Eddie worked to put the deal together that saw Alan Sugar and I jointly acquire control of Tottenham Hotspur plc.

I had been introduced to Eddie by a friend at the time, Paul Riviere, with whom I had been working on a football board game, The Manager. Paul had split up with his wife, who had left him only a couple of weeks after their wedding, and he was really low. I was worried about him, and sat him down one night with a list of things that I thought might keep his mind occupied. He showed no interest in any of them until the last one, which was the board game. Gordon Williams and I had originally had the idea, but had never got round to doing anything about it, and when I spoke to Gordon, he was too busy right then, so Paul and I went ahead with it.

We had been working on it for some time, but it was still at a rudimentary stage when Eddie got involved. All we had to show for our efforts was a plastic bag full of table mats and napkins, odd scraps of paper, cigarette packets, and cardboard models of various bits and pieces. In that condition, it was not something that would have impressed the buyer at Harrods.

We wanted to see if it could be commercially launched, and Eddie's considerable experience, together with the fact that he was a likeable and helpful guy, made him a natural person to turn to for advice. He had been at school with Paul, but had not seen him for twenty-six years until they bumped into each other in a London hotel. Paul introduced him and he agreed to help us. It was the beginning of a working relationship between Eddie and me that continues to this day.

Within a few months, Eddie ran into very serious problems in his own business. He told me how he had had trouble with a business partner, which in a way, was a preview of what was to come for me. As a consequence, he effectively had to bring his own company down, by settling a winding-up petition upon it. Eddie spent from June 1990 to March 1991 managing the board-

game business, before switching to the search for a deal that
would give us control of Tottenham.

We looked in turn at various methods of making the deal.
The acquisition itself was not the problem, for I already had the
resources to purchase enough shares from Paul Bobroff and
Irving Scholar to gain a controlling interest – around 30 per cent
of Tottenham Hotspur plc would have given me effective control, but we had to have the ability not only to acquire a
controlling stake in the still-suspended shares, but also to cope
with the much bigger task of completely refinancing Tottenham.
The company was massively in debt, and heavily loss making,
losing £3 million in the year we took over, and several million
more over the previous two years.

Tottenham's problem was both the over-borrowing itself
and the nature of the borrowing, which was all overdraft. There
had to be a serious restructuring plan to put the debt on to a
more stable, long-term basis. That could have been done comparatively simply, by using the most valuable asset, the stadium,
which was valued at approaching £20 million, as security for a
long term mortgage or a sale and lease-back of the stadium
itself, with a buy-back option after ten or twenty years. Both of
those routes would have adequately financed Tottenham, provided that we could reverse the trading losses.

Tottenham's involvement with the Hummel brand had required a huge investment to prop up, and continued to be a
bottomless pit. Mail-order sales were virtually non-existent,
retail sales were sluggish, partly because the margins offered to
retailers were well below the norm, and distribution was so
atrocious that Coventry City, Aston Villa and Sunderland, which
had all agreed to sell Hummel kit, pulled out of agreements
because stock was not supplied. Coventry, for example, had no
stock for Christmas, the most lucrative trading time of the year.
Synchro Systems was equally troublesome. At the start of the
season a number of clubs like Crystal Palace, which had

contracts with the company, found that their season-ticket holders had not even received their tickets.

Against this increasingly chaotic background, with rumours sweeping the club on a near-daily basis, we resumed the Cup trail, with what should have been a relatively easy home quarter-final against Notts County. In this season, however, nothing was remotely easy. At half-time, we were 1–0 down and my team-talk had more than a little urgency about it. Only the possibility of a trip to Wembley was keeping the board from beginning an 'Everything Must Go' sale that would see Gascoigne and Lineker shipped out immediately, along with any other saleable players. My own departure would follow and the only prospect for the rest of the side would be relegation. I spelled it out for them: 'They are beating us in every phase – they are first to the tackle and first to the ball. We've got to show the same attitude. What's worth having is worth fighting for. You have no choice, you just have to go for it. Forty-five minutes, that's all it is. If you don't do it, you're out and that's the end of it.' They went out grim-faced and pulled the game round, Nayim scoring the equaliser and Gazza again netting the winner to send us into the semi-final and give us another stay of execution. Gazza was far from fully fit, and I had 'spelled' him in attack to give him a break from the donkey-work in midfield a couple of times during the game, but the risk had been justified. Had it gone to a replay, he would not have been able to play, but a half-fit Gascoigne had still made the difference.

The semi-final draw was a disappointment, because we got Arsenal, the toughest nut to crack. The game instantly became 'the real final' in the eyes of every Londoner, while Nottingham Forest played West Ham in the other semi-final. With the Hillsborough disaster still fresh in everyone's mind, for the first time, the semi-final was to be played at Wembley.

I had gambled on sending Gazza for a double-hernia operation after the quarter-final. The injury was growing steadily worse and though he might have been fit to play in the semi-final without an operation, I took the chance on it, praying that he would recover in time for the game. Though short of match fitness, he had come through a tough test against Norwich four days before the semi-final. I had intended to play him for the first half only, but he showed such energy and appetite for the game, quite apart from his skill, that I left him on for an hour.

The team doctor had been forced to knock Gazza out with an injection the night before the semi-final, to let both him and the rest of the team get some sleep, but in the coach and the dressing room, Gazza was even more hyper than usual, talking ninety-three to the dozen and oozing with determination and will to win.

When we reached the dressing room, I decided to wait until half an hour before kick-off, let them have a warm up and then really get to work on the players, reminding them what they had to do, but Gascoigne was so hyped up, going from player to player, that I could hardly get a word in. I was talking, but he was drowning me out and I did not need to do any motivation on the team, because Gazza did it all for me. I could not have got a word in edgeways, even if I had wanted to. He knew he was playing in a top-category match and he was really up for the game and dying to get out there. I do not think I have ever seen a player so hyped up for any game. Gazza is always revved up to some extent, and is great in the dressing room before a game, but he was another octave above normal. The other boys caught the fever from him and we were really flying in that dressing room, like nothing I had seen before.

With a parsimonious defence that would have made George Graham's Scottish ancestors proud, conceding only eighteen goals all season, Arsenal were formidable opponents. They were chasing the Double, while we were rank outsiders, but after looking at the video tapes of many of the games we had played against Arsenal before, I felt that I had found a chink in their armour. The key to the game would be to try and pull their full-backs forward. To do it, we had to change the way that we were playing and there was a bit of a problem convincing the players of the need to do it, because, as David Howells had said at the time, 'We've already got to the semi-final and now he's changing it all round. We don't know what the boss is doing.'

In the end I had convinced them, and they worked hard in training to get it right. I had decided to push David Howells out on the left, up against the Arsenal right-back and Paul Allen up against the left-back, leaving Gary Lineker central on his own. We had three midfield players, Stewart, Samways and Gazza. When we started the game, I got the wide players to withdraw slightly, which drew their full-backs up on to them. I could hear George Graham shouting to his full-backs to get tighter and I knew that it was working. We got them coming up even further, which left the gaps behind them for our midfield players to run into.

We were causing them a lot of trouble, and we also had a flying start when Gascoigne struck one of the finest free-kicks I have ever seen. Curling or bending a free-kick is easy if you do not put much pace on the ball, but when he really concentrates, Gascoigne has this terrific ability to put bend on the ball, but still hit it with great power. The free-kick was about thirty-five yards out and I could see he was concentrating hard. It looked a little bit too far, and I thought that for him to score from there, the shot would have to be something special. It was. The ball flew past Seaman into the net. To strike it from thirty-five yards with such ferocity, bending it at the same time, was incredible. A number of people criticised Seaman for the goal, which was unfair; though it was hit from a distance, it was superbly struck, very fast and accurate. Gazza set off on a circuit of the stadium in celebration, while Arsenal's players just stood and gaped at each other. As he reached the bench, Gazza put his arms around my neck and and laughed in my ear: 'The silly bastard only tried to save it, didn't he?'

Gascoigne was also heavily involved in the build-up to an even better goal, which saw us 2–0 up after twenty minutes. A brilliant piece of skill by Gazza pulled Michael Thomas out of position and sent Paul Allen away down the right. David Howells, coming from the left, nearly got on the end of Paul's low cross from the by-line, but it rebounded from an Arsenal defender to Gary Lineker, who flicked it in. If we kept our heads, the game was ours.

Alan Smith pulled one back for Arsenal right on half-time, with a header after we did not clear our box well enough, but when I went into the dressing room, and managed to stop Gazza from talking for a few seconds, I said to the players, 'If someone had told you a couple of days ago that you would be winning 2–1 at half-time, you would have been happy to settle for that, wouldn't you? Don't let your heads drop because of that goal.'

Arsenal threw everything at us early in the second half, but I always felt that we looked in control, and as they pushed forward, desperately looking for an equaliser, they left themselves open for the killer blow. Fifteen minutes from the end, Gary Mabbutt intercepted and put Lineker away on the half-way line. Vinny Samways, to his right, made a diagonal run across the back of the Arsenal defence and as the defender went with him, Gary took it to the hole that Samways had left for him and rode Adams's lunging tackle to put in a shot that someone of Seaman's class should have saved, but which slipped through his hands into the net.

I had already substituted Gascoigne midway through the half, when he ran out of steam, having knocked himself out putting so much energy into the dressing room before the game as well as into the match itself, but he had already done enough. We were through to the Cup final, where we would face Nottingham Forest. To beat Arsenal in a semi-final was one of the biggest thrills our supporters had had for a long time. They had spent so much time in the shadows of an Arsenal team that had enjoyed a terrific run, and the Cup victory seemed to make up much lost ground. We had not only reached the Cup final, but had beaten the 'old enemy' to do so.

The Midland Bank believed that they had a firm commitment from Tottenham to dispose of Gascoigne, but on the Monday after the FA Cup semi-final victory against Arsenal, the board met and resolved to withdraw their agreement to the sale. That decision was communicated to the bank, which further heightened its nerves about the general position at Tottenham, at a time when interest charges alone were running at between £40,000 and £50,000 a week.

The debts of the company had now reached such proportions that even the windfall from the FA Cup run was, in the words of one City analyst, no more use than 'giving half a sandwich to a starving man'. It was inconceivable that the Midland Bank would put the company into receivership when the team was due to play in the FA Cup Final, so the board at least had a breathing space.

Three days later, Nat Solomon, with the full backing of the board, sent a message to Maxwell, asking him to make a new bid. Maxwell did not reply immediately, either because he simply did not have the cash, or because he was biding his time, knowing the weakness of the Spurs board's position. The Midland returned to the attack, insisting on the speeding-up of moves to sell Gascoigne. Three weeks before the Cup final, in the absence of any response from Maxwell, Nat Solomon flew to Rome with agent Dennis Roach. In Rome they linked up with Gazza's advisers, Mel Stein and Len Lazarus, and sat down to conclude a deal with Lazio.

The meeting in Rome, held in the house of Lazio's lawyer, began at lunchtime and continued until 3:30 a.m., with Lazio officials Manzini and Regalia scuttling between Solomon and

Roach in one room and Lazarus and Stein in the other. Gascoigne agreed his personal terms over the phone, leaving his own contract to be signed when Stein and Lazarus returned to England, but Solomon put pen to paper straight away. The price agreed was £7.9 million, payable on safe delivery of Gazza to Rome after the Cup final.

Details of the deal were swiftly leaked to Maxwell's papers and Captain Bob was immediately thundering from the pulpit of the *People* that only he could stop the sale. The news that our top player had been sold could scarcely have broken at a worse time, right in the middle of the build-up to the FA Cup final. I pointed out at once that whatever deal had been agreed by the Spurs board, though Gazza had verbally agreed terms he had signed nothing, and still had the right to refuse to go. I begged him in private and through the press not to leave, telling him that if he waited for a couple more years, until after the next World Cup, instead of settling for second-best now, he would be in his prime and would clinch a deal with one of the giants of the game. Joining Lazio would be like Pavarotti singing in the Copacabana Club in Cleethorpes. It was a reasonable comparison at the time, but to be fair to Lazio, they have shown the ambition and determination that they promised Paul, and with his help, they have now become one of the leading Italian clubs.

I also warned him of the personal problems a relatively young and immature lad would face, including the difficulty of settling in a foreign country and the constant fouling he would have to take from cynical Italian defenders. While I was urging him not to go, his former team-mate Chris Waddle, and his adviser Mel Stein, who had originally met Paul through Chris Waddle, were telling him the opposite. Chris told him that life on the Continent was pretty good and that Gazza should grab the chance while it was there, saying, 'Why wait to break a leg?' – a comment Gazza might have wryly recalled a few weeks later.

Stein had also built up an unanswerable financial case for a move, after first taking advantage of Tottenham's financial weakness. Stein would certainly argue that he was only doing his best for his client, but my respect for him did not increase at that time. He initially demanded a £1 million payment from Tottenham for his client, as the price for Gazza agreeing to the move, while simultaneously turning the screws on Lazio. The demand was withdrawn only when Lazio agreed to meet all the player's financial demands themselves.

Even with the Gazza transfer fee, £4 million over four years in prospect from a new shirt deal with Umbro and the extra income from the FA Cup run, the club still needed a cash injection that the board were unable or unwilling to supply. With the Gascoigne situation unresolved, I made a fresh bid for the club, 29.9 per cent of the shares in Tottenham, based on a price of 60 pence per share. All that I was prepared to guarantee the Midland Bank was that the interest payments would be met, while we negotiated putting the debt on to a long-term basis, to be paid off in instalments.

I was convinced that the bid would be successful, but after hours of negotiations, the Tottenham board rejected it on the evening of 29 April. I was forced to cancel the press conference scheduled to announce the deal and put the champagne back on ice. It was a bitter disappointment, but I did not give up the fight, though I did take steps to secure myself an alternative career, in case my attempt to take over Tottenham finally failed.

I had no intention of remaining there under Scholar's chairmanship beyond the end of the season, when my contract expired, and had bought into Scribes West, a dining club in Kensington, which I thought might make a worthwhile business, post-Tottenham. I had done three years at Spurs and that often seems the right length of time to stay at a club – leave them laughing rather than wear out your welcome.

By now relations between Scholar and me had grown even

icier. They had not been helped by his offer of a renewed managerial contract that was worth considerably less than my previous one. Scholar had just described me as 'the best coach in the world', which was a fatuous comment anyway, but having done so, to then offer me £25,000 a year less was ridiculous and we had a furious row. Scholar's temper was not improved by a demonstration by supporters at the last home game of the season against Nottingham Forest. Reversible placards spelled out 'S-C-H-O-L-A-R O-U-T' and 'V-E-N-A-B-L-E-S I-N'.

Forest were also the opposition in the next, and rather more significant match – the Cup final. The bookies' favourites to win the Cup, having scored a hatful of goals in their recent games, playing the good football that was always the Brian Clough trademark, Forest were the emotional favourites, with most neutrals hoping that Clough could add the one trophy that had eluded him to his remarkable record. One of the few people to back us publicly was George Graham, who tipped us to win: '1–0 in normal time or 2–1 in extra time. I'm convinced it will be as close as that.' It was.

On the Monday before the final, I arranged for the players to come to Scribes for a relaxing lunch before we began the build-up to the game. Gazza had to go for a photo session, which had been arranged weeks before. I pulled his leg, saying that he was a 'Big-Time Charlie' now and would not want to be one of the lads any more, which made him upset, because all he wanted to do was be with the team. While he went to do his photo session, we started lunch. The wine was flowing and by the time Gazza arrived, everyone was singing and having a laugh. He took a look in the dining room, then walked up to the bar, determined to catch up as quickly as possible. He asked Nick, the barman, for a quadruple Drambuie and drank it straight down. He had another – straight down in one – and another, and another. Nick came over and told me that Gazza was getting pissed.

I did not see how he could be drunk, because he had been in the place for less than five minutes, but I told him not to serve Gazza and to send him through to join the rest of us in the dining room. When Nick told Gazza, he said: 'Never mind that, get me another drink.' Nick – a South Londoner who has not been north of Watford in his life – refused. 'You'll never work in Newcastle,' said Gazza, but Nick told him he thought he could live with that, and still refused to serve him.

Gazza made sure that he would never work in Newcastle again either, or at least would never have to, for the night before the Cup final he signed an agreement on personal terms with Lazio, which would bring him an immediate £2 million and a salary of £1 million a year on top. Gascoigne signed subject to a medical examination, to be carried out the following Wednesday. Suggestions that it was his injury the next day that finally persuaded him to accept the deal are not true, for he was already committed to Lazio when he took the field.

I had been to see Mel Stein and Len Lazarus earlier that day, to try and persuade them that if Gazza remained at White Hart Lane, we could build a team round him to win the League title and boost his value even higher. I made them an offer that, if my takeover of Tottenham went ahead, would have made Gazza better paid than anyone in the British game, but Stein and Lazarus remained unimpressed. The only way to keep Paul at White Hart Lane was to match the millions that Lazio were willing to pay him, and that I could not do.

While Gazza was signing his deal with Lazio, I was close to concluding a deal with Scholar to take over the club, for despite the chill between us, negotiations had continued. We had a long meeting on the night before the Cup final, but once again I was frustrated, because, at the last, Scholar set an impossible condition. We had reached agreement to buy his shares at a price of 75 pence, or 70 pence if Gascoigne stayed at the club. The five-pence 'Gazza discount,' worth £250,000, would have impressed me more if I were convinced Scholar had not known that a binding contract to sell the player had already been signed.

Scholar then insisted our deal had to be signed that night. As he well knew, I could not agree to that, for I had told him that I first had to meet the Midland Bank, who held the club's enormous overdraft, to satisfy myself that my refinancing plans were acceptable to them. I could not have gone to the Midland before reaching agreement with Scholar, for the bank would not reveal confidential information about clients without their express approval. To sign a contract to purchase the club, without first ascertaining the Midland's position, would have been financial suicide. I might have bought a company on Friday that was put into receivership on Monday. The deal was once more dead.

We were staying at the Royal Lancaster Hotel that night, and for once the team doctor was not required to fire his usual 'tranquilliser darts' into Gazza to put him to sleep. As events were to turn out, the doctor might have done better to have tranquillised Paul just before the game, though there was no way of knowing that at the time. Irving Scholar's later suggestions that I had hyped Gazza up before the game are laughable and I think the players who were in the dressing room would say the same. Gazza never needed anyone to hype him up, and all my conversations with him before any games, and the Cup final in particular, were designed to calm him down, not wind him up.

He wanted the Cup and he was ready to go, but it looked like his mind was somewhere else – he was a little distant. The transfer might well have been on his mind, and that is certainly what I thought afterwards, looking back on it. In any event, he was not as hyped up as normal and certainly nothing like he had been before the semi-final. That might have been just as well, because everybody was keen to go, without any extra motivation. The officials called us out and I led the team up the tunnel, walking alongside Brian Clough.

The tabloids had been doing their best to wind up Brian Clough and me in the week before the final, playing on the supposed hostility between us. In fact, there was none. I got on fairly well with him, without really knowing him, and he is always amusing. He was great for the game, being such a character, and the teams he put out were good footballing sides. I had great admiration for Brian's ability as a coach and I think he also liked the football that my sides played.

There is often banter between the coaches in the dug-outs and that can sometimes escalate into a furious row. Kenny Dalglish and I had a blazing row during a Liverpool–Tottenham game, when he called Nayim a cheat. Nayim had this reputation for 'diving' and he had a particularly nasty moment at Liverpool where the whole crowd got against him. He was a sensitive lad and it really hurt him. It was a part of his Spanish football culture. Where we would be proud of the fact that we would get fouled and not let anyone see that we were hurt, it is the Spanish culture to make the most of the situation and also to punish the guy for a bad tackle. That is the way they look at it: you made a rash tackle, why should you get away with it?

Kenny has always been passionate about his own team and quite rightly so, but I took exception to his comment and we ended up having a blazing row in the middle of the game. That is not that unusual, especially when you have two dug-outs very close together. Graham Taylor and I had our moments too, especially when he was at Watford and I was at QPR. There was an intense rivalry between us, partly because of local feelings, but mainly because of our differing views on the game. Graham criticised 'tippy-tappy' football, and I always criticised the long-ball game, saying that he had put football back ten years. On reflection, I think that was a bit unfair . . . it put the game back much more than ten years.

I never had any rows with Brian Clough at Nottingham

Forest, however, for one very good reason. Forest avoided the problem by having Cloughie's dug-out right on the half-way line and a strategically placed away-team dug-out near the corner flag. There was never any chance of rowing with Cloughie during the game, but neither did you get a good view.

We were chatting in the tunnel at Wembley, before we went out, and he said to me, 'I hope I don't trip over with all the world watching. I'm always worried about things like that.' Whether through insecurity or mischief, when the time came to walk out side by side, he suddenly grabbed my hand. We were now walking out of the tunnel in front of hundreds of millions of people watching on television, holding hands. He was looking straight ahead and would not let go, so I made him laugh, which at least made it look as if we were joking and not a couple of lovers. We had just reached the edge of the sand, and were about to go on to the pitch itself, when I reached my hand up as if waving to someone, and brought it down so fast that he had to let go.

If Paul Gascoigne was hoping to make a big impact in his last game in a Tottenham shirt, he was not to be disappointed, but not in the way that he would have wanted. If he had set fire to the stadium, he could not have earned more column inches. He made a reckless challenge on Gary Parker in the opening minutes, hitting him in the chest, with a vicious-looking tackle. I thought to myself, Christ, that's him booked, but the referee did not book him, and just gave him a severe talking-to. It was early in the game but Gazza was still looking wild. I do not know whether he was angry or what the reason was, but he did himself no favours.

Undeterred by his near-miss with a booking or worse, Gazza then launched himself at Gary Charles a few minutes later, on the edge of our own penalty area. Gazza was chasing the ball and was outside his own box, so he only needed to stay on his feet and give Charles a problem by staying on him, but he went

wild again and lashed out with a bad tackle in a dangerous area
for us. Charles fell heavily on top of him, leaving Gazza rolling
around in agony, and to make matters worse, Forest scored
from the free-kick. Stuart Pearce is one of the most powerful
strikers of a free-kick there is and when a Forest player, Lee
Glover, pushed Gary Mabbutt out of the Tottenham wall,
Pearce's shot went thundering straight through the gap and into
the net. It was a foul on Mabbutt, but it happens and it was
something we should have been aware of.

Gazza was stretchered off and it was obvious that he was
seriously injured, but all I knew at that stage was that he would
certainly not take any further part in the game. I was too busy
reorganising the team to spare time thinking about the implications of Gazza's injury, but the ghouls and money-men up in the
boxes were no doubt all busy with their pocket calculators,
working out what Tottenham was worth without its most
valuable asset.

Out on the pitch, we had lost our best player, who had
played the major part in getting us to the final, not only
scoring the goals, but putting in the effort and inspiring the
others by his will to win the competition. We were one-down
and things were looking grim, but I still felt quite good, thinking that there was a long way to go. We began to look like
we were going to take over and Gascoigne's injury did have
one side-benefit to the team. Until Gazza went off, I had
actually not got the balance of the side quite right. I had
worked out the way we were going play, and how we were
going to cut out the supply to Nigel Clough. Forest normally
played wingers so wide that it drew the full-backs out with
them and left big spaces through the middle, so I took David
Howells from the left side, to play in front of the two centre-
halves.

I have always had great respect for David, who is very
teachable and bright. We arranged that when Clough came in

deep, as he likes to do, David would take him and we would play Sedgley and Mabbutt against the centre-forward.

I had a problem about whom to leave out of the side, however, because in midfield there were too many players, all of whom were playing well. I wanted two central-midfield players out of three – Gascoigne, Stewart and Howells – who were each very good, and Howells was a must because he was going to do a specific job that the others would not have been able to do. Samways and Nayim were battling for the left side. Nayim gave better balance, but Samways was in particularly good form and in the end I went with him, putting Nayim on the bench. My difficulty was that Samways did not really like playing on the left, and as soon as the game started, he began to follow the ball and vacate his position.

We were getting trouble from their right-back because Samways had gone into midfield. It could have cost us the game, because Gary Crosby got through from that and was one-on-one with the goalkeeper. If he had scored, I do not think we would have been able to come back. Apart from the goal, it was virtually the only chance they had all game, but Eric Thorstvedt made the save that we needed from him.

When Gascoigne came off, I sent Nayim on as substitute and just thought, Well, I'll put Samways into Gazza's position, he and Stewart will play midfield right and forward and with Nayim on the left, it will give us a lot better balance and stop the threat from the Forest right side. Even if Gazza had not been injured, I might have had to make a change anyway. I knew we would miss what Gazza could give us, but it seemed as if everyone else raised their game that much more.

Gary Lineker almost got us back on level terms, timing his run perfectly on to Paul Allen's cross, only for his goal to be disallowed for offside. I am pretty good at judging offsides from central positions by the angles the players run and I could not see that it was offside, but Forest had a free-kick and we were still 1–0 down. The TV replays later confirmed what nearly everyone in the stadium, apart from the linesman, had already decided: that the goal should have stood.

No matter, Gary Lineker then won a penalty, latching on to a perfect through ball from Paul Stewart, before being brought down by Forest keeper Crossley, as he rounded him. A penalty, just what we needed, but the story again went wrong, as Gary missed it, Crossley making amends by throwing himself to his left to tip Lineker's shot around the post, leaving us still 1–0 down at the break.

My mood at half-time was not improved by the reports from the hospital where Gazza had been rushed. I called them by phone on the way to the dressing room and discovered that Paul had torn his cruciate ligaments and faced an operation. I even spoke to him on the phone and he was understandably very low. It was one of the most serious injuries a footballer can face, similar to the ones that had recently ended Danny Thomas's career and finished Brian Clough's many years before. If Gazza could play again at all, it would certainly not be for at least six months. As I wound up my half-time talk, I told the players, 'Gazza played a big part in getting us to Wembley, but it's up to us to show that we can carry on and do it without him. I've seen nothing in the first half to say we can't carry on and get this goal back.'

Their answer was not long in coming, Paul Stewart getting on the end of an Allen–Nayim move to hit the equaliser seven minutes into the second half. From then on, there was only one team in it. Time and again we were almost through the Forest defence and only a brilliant save from Crossley stopped David Howell's last-minute header from removing the need for extra time; we had reached the end of the ninety minutes locked at 1–1.

I was quickly out on the pitch after the final whistle, giving the players instructions for extra-time: 'We can't go wrong if we keep going as we are, because for all the odds against us, we are back in this game and it's got "win" written all over it. The only thing that can stop us is if we stop ourselves. They're on their heels, they don't know if they have got anything in them at all. Just keep it going and going and we'll win.' Surprisingly, Brian Clough decided to leave the talking to his assistants and stayed on the bench, chatting to a policeman.

We kept pressing and pressing in extra time, and though there was a bit of good fortune in the goal that settled the game, in reality Forest buckled under the pressure that we put on them. Paul Stewart, playing the game of his life, was again on the spot, flicking Nayim's corner across the goal, towards the on-rushing Gary Mabbutt. Under pressure, Des Walker could only head it into his own net.

It was a cruel blow for Walker, who had been at the heart of the creaking Forest defence, but it must have been the sweetest moment for Mabbutt. Four years earlier, Tottenham had lost the FA Cup final against Coventry, after Gary had put through his own goal; now he saw the other side of the coin. Tottenham had won the Cup, and after the year we had been through, it ranks as one of their finest achievements.

Although I may be biased because I was involved in it, it was the most action-packed, incident-filled Cup final that I can remember. There have been a few good ones and a lot of disappointments over the years, mainly because the anticipation of the Cup final is so high. It seemed as if it needed something to go wrong – Gazza's injury – to bring it to the boil.

The first thing that we did in the dressing room was to call Gazza up to tell him that we had won the Cup; he was thrilled. We were due at the London Hilton for the Tottenham Cup-final banquet, but there was a call that we had to make first. We all piled on to the coach, wives and everyone, with the FA Cup and Gazza's winning medal and drove to the hospital to see him. When we got there, it was a wonderful scene, everyone was laughing, except Gazza, who was crying. Part of him must have been happy and yet it had been the biggest match of his life and he had missed it. He had been at the peak of his game and his own rashness and this horrific accident had wrecked things for him. Lazio officials felt almost as suicidal as Gazza, but there was no sign that they had given up the idea of signing him; the move to Rome was to be deferred, not cancelled.

There was no sympathy for Gazza in the media, however, with an almost hysterical reaction to his 'red mist'. Yet none of the critics jumping on the bandwagon to savage Paul appeared to give even the slightest thought to the pressures that he had been under throughout the season. I do not believe that any player has ever had to bear so much pressure in so short a time, carrying not only Tottenham's FA Cup hopes, but the whole financial future of his club on his shoulders. George Best's attacks on Gascoigne were particularly hard to take, for the pressures that had ultimately blunted Best's extraordinary talents were far less than Gascoigne had to deal with.

The only visible sympathy for Gazza came from Italy, where a former Lazio star, Giorgio Chinaglia commented, 'I know people have been screaming about the tackles he made, but so what? That sort of tackle happens in Italy all the time.' Lazio president Gian Marco Calleri was quick to contrast the reaction in the two countries, accusing the British press of writing 'a lot of lies about him. We consider him still in our family and we will not abandon him'.

After flying to London to check on Gascoigne's condition and watch a video of the operation on his knee, Lazio's medical expert Claudio Bartolini pronounced himself completely satisfied that Paul would make a complete recovery. Lazio reinforced the point by visiting him in hospital bearing gifts of a £5000 gold watch and a Lazio shirt.

Any hopes that I had harboured of keeping Paul at White Hart Lane evaporated. Gazza would be going to Italy; all that remained in question was the price that Lazio would now be prepared to pay. With the Midland Bank pressing the Scholar regime to reduce its debts, Lazio held all the cards, and the original offer was swiftly reduced to £4.825 million. Gazza might have missed most of the FA Cup final, but he now had what he wanted. He would go to Lazio on a contract that would make him a millionaire.

To lose a player of the quality of Gascoigne, having already lost another one in Chris Waddle, was obviously deeply disappointing, but there was also a feeling of satisfaction for them, because they wanted those moves for what they would mean for their futures. I am sure Waddle and Gascoigne would have been happy to stay at Tottenham for the rest of their careers if nothing like the offers from Marseille or Lazio had come along.

When they did, it was like a British actor, happily doing repertory work and the occasional television appearance in this country, who suddenly gets the chance to go to Hollywood and sees all those noughts on a contract. When players see those noughts, and an agent is whispering in their ear 'No matter how hard you try, you are never going to earn that sort of money staying here', you can understand why they leave. I knew from the meeting I had with Chris Waddle that he wanted to go and I do not blame him – how could I? – for I went myself, to Barcelona, when the offer came to me.

Both the manager and the supporters are unhappy to lose the player after bringing him on, improving him, and getting the best out of him, but you really have to take a positive attitude towards it. First you want the player, but if you cannot have him, you must have the money instead, so that you can strengthen the team.

If you keep a player against his will, you do not get either, because he does not perform for you the way he was doing and you end up with the worst of all possible worlds – you do not have the player, you do not have the money, you have nothing.

The quicker you – and the supporters – come to understand the realities, the better.

It is not all one-way traffic, either. While we have lost players like Waddle and Gascoigne to Europe for a while, we have benefited from a stream of players travelling in the opposite direction. If we no longer have Gascoigne or Platt playing here, we do have Cantona and Kanchelskis.

# CHAPTER EIGHT

# The Takeover: Tottenham Chief Executive

## 1991-93

TOTTENHAM'S SEASON WAS OVER, but the club's financial crisis continued. I began a final attempt to mount a successful takeover bid for Tottenham, this time with a new partner – Amstrad multi-millionaire Alan Sugar. Before the appearance of Sugar, there were in effect four players in the takeover battle. The Tottenham board was obviously one. At one moment, they were apparently unable to raise the monies to keep the company afloat, the next they were so confident of their position that they were backtracking on the multi-million pound sale of Paul Gascoigne. The second player was the Midland Bank, who were certainly conveying the message that their patience was wearing very thin. I was always left with the impression, from discussions with a representative of the Midland, that much of their disillusion arose from their dealings with the board. The Midland appeared unimpressed by any of them.

The third player was me, constantly seeking to put together the financial package that would allow me to buy the club, a process contemptuously described by Robert Maxwell as 'Venables trying on another pair of knickers, and none of them seems to fit'. The last element was the shadow – and I cannot put it any stronger than that – of other bidders. There was always talk of other bidders, such as the Baltic Finance Company or Hambros, but no bid package was produced that had even the remotest chance of acceptance. The only other apparently genuine bidder to emerge was Robert Maxwell, with or without Irving Scholar as his bedfellow, and it is hard to know how far Maxwell's bid was real or illusory.

There seemed to be a genuine wish on Maxwell's part to distance himself from Derby County, where he was intensely disliked, but whether he had any real intention of taking control of Tottenham, or had the funds available, will probably never be known. The pages of the *Daily Mirror* predictably championed his bid, but it was never formulated in terms that could have been successful.

Maxwell's past record in football guaranteed ferocious opposition from both the Football League and the Spurs supporters, who had seen plenty of evidence to suggest that Maxwell's oft-proclaimed love of football was pretty spurious. In any event, Maxwell was desperately strapped for cash, with only the fear of his battery of libel lawyers keeping some City journalists from blowing the whistle on his disintegrating financial empire.

The critical issue on my side was the raising of the finance, and that was repeatedly referred to in the press. What was less prominent in the press coverage, however, was how willing Scholar and Bobroff actually were to sell their shares. It was always assumed that if the right bidder came along, they would sell, but that was far from certain, and the position would change, sometimes from hour to hour.

Scholar would arrange meetings and then fail to show up, offer agreements with impossible conditions attached and take a step back for every halting step forward. It is my sincere belief that Scholar never had any real wish to sell Tottenham, despite the appalling mess he had made of running the company, and that he dragged out negotiations and put obstacles in my way in the Micawberesque hope that something would eventually turn up, allowing him to retain at least some of his shareholding and his place on the board.

Scholar knew that he could only be forced out if the Midland pulled the plug, and had gambled that they would not risk the negative public-relations impact of putting a national institution like Tottenham Hotspur out of business. The Midland would have had to weigh the PR consequences of calling in the receivers very carefully, but I do not doubt for one minute that if we had not been able to produce the financial rescue package, they would have done so. David Buchler, their insolvency practitioner, has since admitted as much to me, saying, 'Had your takeover not succeeded, the Midland would have sent the receivers in.' Yet only at the very last, when Scholar realised the implacable opposition of everybody, including the Midland and his fellow board members, both to him and his knight in shining armour, Robert Maxwell, did he accept that there was no option for him but to sell out.

Despite the Scholar regime's diversification and development disasters, the football club was always potentially very profitable and by concentrating on what Tottenham should always have been focused on – the football business – I never had any doubts that it could swiftly be turned around. The only problem with our plans to use the value of the property to refinance Tottenham, was the City's potential reaction to rescuing an already heavily indebted plc by further borrowing, whatever its nature. We talked to many, many individuals who claimed to be able to come up with the substantial sums, of the order of £5–7 million, that we needed, but the only investor who actually delivered the money that he promised was Alan Sugar.

Alan Sugar is of a similar age and background to me. Like me, he is also often described as an 'East Ender', but the similarities end there. Sugar's main skill lies in amassing wealth – and even the fortunes he has already accumulated are apparently not enough to satisfy him. Sugar left school at sixteen, and began his business career selling car aerials and radios out of the back of a car, but made his break into the big time with hi-fi, devising the Tower System, which he typically described as 'a mug's eyeful', aimed at his chosen market, 'the truck driver and his wife'. He cashed in on a succession of consumer-electronics crazes, using a simple philosophy 'If there was a market for mass-produced nuclear weapons, we'd be making them too'.

His Amstrad personal computer revolutionised the computer market, making him an enormous fortune. He set up Amstrad in 1968, and floated it on the Stock Exchange in 1980. At one time the company was worth well over £1 billion, but fortunes have been less easy to come by in recent years as the computer market has grown more and more competitive. Sugar's ill-advised launch of a poorly designed and produced computer range in 1988 almost sent the company to the wall. The banks were persuaded not to send in the receivers, however, and Amstrad revived, helped by a deal to produce satellite dishes for Sky TV, signed in 1988 and now worth millions a year to his company. At one point Amstrad were knocking out satellite dishes at the rate of 70,000 a month, and you do not need a degree in accountancy to know what a substantial contribution to Amstrad's turnover and profits that represents.

I remain fairly sceptical of Sugar's claim to be a lifelong Spurs fan. Anyone who comes out with a remark like 'Double? What Double? Is that something from the 1950s?', can scarcely be described as a Tottenham devotee, and conspiracy theorists have been quick to point to Sugar's vested interest in the success of Sky Television as a powerful motive for his involvement in Tottenham, just as Sky were about to bid for television rights to Premier League football. He is a personal friend of Rupert Murdoch, and is also friendly with Sky TV boss Sam Chisholm. Soon after the takeover, Sugar introduced me to them in Harry's Bar, and on behalf of his friends and himself, he was certainly not shy about lobbying for the acceptance of the Sky bid.

His interest in Tottenham may equally have been that of a

man who saw a first-class opportunity to increase his already massive fortune. If so, he saw something that no one else had seen, for I had been negotiating with three or four businessmen in particular, who had the money, loved Tottenham and wanted to become part of it, but when they looked at the figures, they told me that it did not stand up as a business proposition. Sugar looked at the same figures and immediately wanted to be involved.

Although Amstrad will never again reach the dizzy heights of the 1980s, Sugar's personal holding was still worth in excess of £100 million at the time of the Spurs takeover. His personal cash mountain was almost as high, and on 15 March 1991, he added another £33.8 million to it from the sale of 42,750,000 ordinary shares in Amstrad plc. If Sugar was interested in buying into Tottenham, there was not the slightest doubt that the money was available.

I had known Sugar slightly for several years, but had taken an instinctive dislike to him, even though he recruited me for an Amstrad advertisement when I was managing QPR, with the strapline 'The best player I ever signed'. He also paid another player and me £50 in cash to attend a party he was holding at the White Elephant on the River, to provide, as he put it, 'a bit of celebrity glamour'. Eddie Ashby first brought him to my notice in connection with the Tottenham bid, asking if I would at least talk to Sugar, who had read about my various attempts to put a deal together, and was badgering Eddie about getting involved. I met Sugar for talks and, with my other options narrowing, I threw in my lot with him. In the end he was the only game in town. I was always wary of Sugar, but I began to think, Perhaps I've been a bit hard on him, he seems to want to do well, and he's a good family man. Despite my reservations, I felt that the working relationship would somehow be all right. I have made plenty of mistakes during my career, but that one has proved to be the worst.

Thoroughly exhausted, Yvette and I had gone away for a brief holiday after the Cup final, but had to fly back for yet another meeting with Scholar, with Alan Sugar alongside me for the first time. This time we required Bobroff's 11 per cent stake as well as Scholar's 26 per cent. Even though, under City regulations, that would trigger an offer for all the remaining shares as well, it had to be done to block any threat from Maxwell. With Tony Berry also on our team, we would hold 45 per cent of the shares, and with the guaranteed support of Spurs supporter-shareholders, that would be enough to repel even a last-ditch, full-scale takeover bid from Maxwell, should one be mounted.

The deal was agreed at 70 pence a share and Sugar and I left the meeting certain that the takeover would take place. The next day, however, the *Sunday Times* published the full story, including the first public acknowledgement of Sugar's role in the takeover bid. Maxwell, stampeded into action by the news, immediately contacted Scholar and Bobroff and made a secret offer to buy their shares at a higher price, with the deal to be confirmed at a special board meeting two days later.

Maxwell's mouthpiece on the *Mirror*, Harry Harris, was immediately recalled from covering England's tour of the Far East and Australasia to trumpet the bid for Tottenham. The *Sun* responded with a phone poll that showed 5205 votes for a Venables takeover and 236 for Maxwell.

Neither Sugar nor I was aware that Scholar and Bobroff were talking to Maxwell, but we upped our offer to 75 pence per share anyway, so that they would have something to show for turning down the Bouncing Czech. The Football League also leapt to Tottenham's defence, insisting that Maxwell must sell his remaining stakes in every other football club before they would allow a takeover of Tottenham to take place. The next morning Harry Harris had another 'world exclusive' in the *Mirror*: 'DERBY SOLD', incorrectly claiming that Maxwell had sold his shares in Derby County to a consortium. Three days later, Maxwell claimed that he had sold his shareholdings in Reading and Manchester United – a relic of his attempted takeover some years before – but through his son Kevin he still controlled Oxford, the club that he had brought to its knees.

Tottenham's Independent Supporters' Association had no doubt which of the two bidders they would prefer to see succeed. 'If that's the choice, then it's no contest,' said a spokesman. 'One safeguards the future of the club, the other doesn't.' The thought of Scholar remaining in charge, backed by Maxwell, was seen by many fans as almost as bad as Maxwell alone, for he was regarded by supporters as the person who had presided over the club's devastation.

Fans were further incensed by the club sending out demands to season-ticket holders at yet higher prices. Lifelong Spurs fan Maurice Keston summed up the anger: 'It's a disgrace. For me and many like me the club has been our lives, but we are kept in the dark while several of the directors fight to look after their own interests. Why should we pay advance money when there is a good chance that we won't even have a club in a few months' time?' The threat to the Tottenham cash-flow of a boycott of season-tickets must have been a factor in forcing a decision in our favour at the special Tottenham board meeting on 20 June. The fear of more weeks of uncertainty while Maxwell attempted to clear the obstacles that the Football League had put in his way, and the opposition of the other directors to Maxwell, persuaded Bobroff and a reluctant Scholar to change their minds about selling to him. There was a unanimous vote from the Tottenham board to accept the Venables–Sugar bid, with the legal formalities to be completed the next afternoon, Friday 21 June, at the offices of merchant bankers Henry Ansbacher in the City. Sugar's PR man, Nick Hewer, announced the deal to the press.

The next day Nat Solomon and Paul Bobroff went to

Ansbacher's, flanked by their advisers, but Irving Scholar was not present. He was represented by a solicitor and was keeping in touch with developments by phone from his apartment in Monte Carlo. Alan Sugar and I had sent our lawyers to sign the necessary documents on our behalf, and I was at Scribes, waiting for a call to confirm that the deal had finally been done, but there was to be yet another twist in the tail. A few minutes before the deadline for signature of the agreement, a call came through to Nat Solomon at Ansbacher's. The voice on the other end of the phone was unmistakable, booming, 'This is Robert Maxwell. I am making a bid for Irving Scholar's and Paul Bobroff's shares.' Solomon told Maxwell that what he was proposing was impossible, because they had already agreed to sell to Sugar and me, but Maxwell swiftly disabused him: 'I have just spoken to Irving, who has changed his mind and agreed to sell to me.'

Pandemonium broke out in the room as Henry Ansbacher director Bernard Jolles rushed out to phone Sugar and tell him what was happening. Harry Harris had evidently been on the phone to Scholar, telling him that it was wrong for him to leave the board while Tony Berry, who should have taken equal responsibility for Spurs' financial chaos, remained a director.

Scholar promptly offered to sell to Maxwell, providing he could complete the deal that day. While Harris prepared his latest Maxwell 'world exclusive' and held the front page of the *Mirror* to receive it, Maxwell's lawyers and advisers descended, in a mob, on Henry Ansbacher's offices. Scholar was constantly on the phone from Monte Carlo, talking in rotation to Harris, Maxwell, Solomon and Bobroff. All Maxwell wanted, according to Scholar, was a 29.9 per cent stake, just below the threshold that would trigger a full-scale takeover bid under Stock Exchange rules. Maxwell wanted to be a passive investor, claimed Scholar, or as Maxwell himself put it, referring to Sugar and him, 'Spurs will have two sugar-Daddies instead of one'.

Such thoughts did not impress Alan Sugar, who arrived shortly after Maxwell's lawyers, screaming 'What the fuck's going on?' as he stormed into the room, abusing Bobroff, Maxwell's lawyers and Solomon in turn. It was language that seemed out of place in the austere offices of Henry Ansbacher, but it was to become commonplace in the Tottenham board-room over the ensuing months. I had also raced to Ansbacher's and more and more people arrived during the evening, contract lawyers, teams of financial advisers and even some small share-holders, who were diverted into another room, to keep them away from Maxwell's minions.

Following a ferocious confrontation with Sugar, Bobroff agreed to sell his shares to us. He had wanted us to match Maxwell's offer, to which the answer was an emphatic and expletive-filled 'No'. More phone conversations between Bobroff and Scholar ensued, with Bobroff complaining 'It's all right for you. Over here, they're all shouting at me,' before capitulating and signing his shares over to us.

After further frenzied consultations between the parties in the room at Ansbacher's, Scholar in Monte Carlo and Maxwell in his penthouse at the *Daily Mirror*, Maxwell was unable to give an unconditional guarantee that he would go ahead with the purchase of Scholar's shares. He wanted it to rest on the sale of his holding in Derby, which had not gone ahead, despite his claims, and approval of his takeover of Tottenham from the Football League. As midnight approached, at last, and for the last time, Scholar again changed his mind and gave instructions to sell his shares to us. My dream had become a reality; the working-class kid who had wanted to see how high he could reach in football, had now become co-owner of one of the greatest football clubs in the game. With the deal done, Scholar spoke to Sugar on the phone, telling him 'I hope you get as much enjoyment out of it as I did, without the aggravation.' Sugar replied, 'Don't worry about me, I'll get no aggravation,' which proved to be an optimistic assumption.

Scholar's representative suggested to Sugar that he might like to pay his air fare to take the documents down to Scholar, so that they could be executed more quickly, to which Sugar responded, 'You can fuck off.' Despite his language, I was very impressed with the way that Sugar had handled the situation at Ansbacher's, and it did make me feel that things might work out well for us. I knew I could handle the football business and here was clear evidence that Sugar could handle his side of the deal.

Back at the *Mirror*, Harry Harris's latest world exclusive, BOB'S YOUR UNCLE – MAXWELL SAVES SPURS, was spiked, replaced by the marginally more accurate £9 MILLION SPURS DEAL IS OFF, SAYS MAXWELL, I'M PULLING OUT – it looked like Maxwell's knickers did not fit either, and he did not have a spare pair. The collapse of Maxwell's empire following his death five months later and the subsequent revelations about his crooked dealings, show just how lucky Tottenham was not to fall into his hands.

The fall of the Scholar regime at Tottenham also left questions to be answered. How did a project like the East Stand, budgeted at £4.5 million, come in at over £9 million? It was, after all, only a refurbishment. They could probably have knocked it down and rebuilt it from the ground up for £6 million. Worse still, even after Scholar had departed, the problems continued. In late 1992, we discovered a fault with the flooring in the East Stand, which was rotting. We had to close off a section of the stand and faced having to close the whole of it because of safety risks. The immediate cost of repairs was £100,000 and rectifying the faults eventually added another £400,000, putting a further half million pounds on the cost of the Scholar regime's most fitting memorial.

For all that he cared passionately about Tottenham and football, in the end, Scholar messed up the job. He had the nerve to talk about 'the horrendous financial problems' created

by the previous board at Tottenham, completely ignoring the
scale of debts accumulated under his own management. As well
as the all-too-visible debts, Scholar had also left an invisible
time-bomb ticking under Tottenham, ensuring that his legacy to
the club after his departure was as financially damaging as his
regime while he was there. Details of Scholar's tangled web of
secret, and irregular loans and deals would later emerge during
the 'war' between Alan Sugar and me.

The first meeting of the new Tottenham board followed
immediately after the signing of the documents transferring
ownership of the club. As a result of the takeover, Alan Sugar
became chairman of Tottenham Hotspur plc, I became a director
and chief executive of the company and Tony Berry and Nat
Solomon were retained from the previous board, Solomon as
vice-chairman – a move to reassure the Midland Bank. Jonathan
Crystal, brother of Michael and also a barrister, was a friend of
mine and a keen Tottenham supporter who brought his legal
expertise on to the new board as an unpaid, non-executive
director. Sugar's associate from Amstrad, Colin Sandy, also
became a director at the same time, the beginning of August.

Just before completion, we drew up a shareholders' agreement between Sugar and me, allaying my fears of a subsequent
power grab by him, using his far greater personal resources. I
had been the driving force in rescuing Spurs and I had no
intention of allowing Sugar or anyone else to rob me of the
fruits of victory. The agreement stipulated that the voting balance between us would be maintained and perpetuated, we
would 'preserve each other's positions', and any disposal or
purchase of shares would only be with the agreement of the
other partner.

The purchase of Spurs took practically every penny I owned.
I was in the Royal Garden Hotel the following night, where a
syndicate of pools winners were being fêted by the pools company before collecting a cheque for £1.2 million. As I passed on

my way out, one of them called out to me, 'This time tomorrow, I'll have more money than you, Tel.'

'You're not wrong there,' I said. 'Well done and good luck.'

Sugar and I were equal partners in the takeover, each investing an initial £3.25 million. Sugar merely dipped into his personal cash-mine; through what was now my company, Edennote, originally set up by Larry Gillick, I ultimately invested £1.3 million of my own resources and raised the rest by borrowings, £2 million from a finance company called Norfina and £250,000 from architect Igal Yawetz, who became a director of the football club, rather than the plc. It was later claimed by Sugar that it was not my own money that I put in, but that is a ridiculously hair-splitting argument. It is like saying someone does not own his own home because he has taken out a mortgage to help him buy it. I borrowed part of the money to buy Spurs, just as other businessmen would do, but the borrowings were my responsibility – I was paying the interest, not Tottenham, and there was plenty to pay. Every penny of my salary as the new chief executive of Tottenham and more besides would be going on interest and repayments for the next couple of years.

After the share purchases, the remaining borrowings were quickly swallowed up as I soon had to find even more money. Sugar and I had jointly purchased 26 per cent of the equity of Tottenham from Irving Scholar and a further 11 per cent from Paul Bobroff, which gave us about 37 per cent. Under Stock Exchange rules, that triggered off a compulsory 'Rule 9 Offer' to the rest of the shareholders. The rule requires any party acquiring 30 per cent or more of a company's shares to make a bid for the remainder. We appealed to them not to accept the offer, because we already had control of the company and every pound we had to spend on acquiring additional shares was a pound that we could not use to reduce the company's debts, but we were forced to buy another 17 per cent between us. Despite our pleas, every single financial institution chose to accept the share offer and bail out of Tottenham. Bearing in mind that we had begged them not to sell to us, it was a stinging rebuff.

Not long before buying into Spurs, Sugar had done his own notorious deal, selling a substantial block of Amstrad shares to institutional shareholders for almost £34 million in cash. Sugar announced his intention to make a 'cheap and unrepeatable' investment in 'commercial property' in North London. The description certainly fitted White Hart Lane.

Sugar's Amstrad sale was made without a formal profit forecast, which he refused to give, and on the strength of his statement that while he was chairman of Amstrad, it would never make a loss. At the time of the sale, the share price was approaching 80 pence. In less than a year, Amstrad had posted a loss of almost £80 million and at one stage, the share price fell below 20 pence.

With Sugar's Amstrad share deal still fresh in City memories, Tottenham began to feel the negative impact of Sugar's involvement. Apart from forcing me to borrow more money to acquire the extra shares, the institutions' hostility had one other important side-effect. If an investment in a plc is to grow, there has to be a free and active market in the shares. It came as quite a shock to me to realise that no institution would invest in Tottenham. Partly as a result of that, the market for Tottenham shares was severely limited and their value problematic. One of the main reasons for my going ahead with what looked to many outsiders to be a risky investment, apart from my love of the club and the game of football, was the potential growth in the value of my shareholding, but that growth already looked stunted.

By this time, late August, all we had done was to acquire shares. We had not even begun to refinance Tottenham and the new season was just starting as we invested or lent the balance of our mutual package of funds to Tottenham. The division of responsibility between Sugar and me was clear-cut. As chief executive, I was responsible for all aspects of the day-to-day running of the company. Sugar's role as chairman was largely confined to chairing the monthly board meetings, and sorting out the Tottenham debts. As he said at the press conference to announce the takeover, 'Terry will look after the eleven on the field and I will look after the eleven in the bank' – the £11 million debt. The theory was fine, the practice would prove rather different. Our formal working relationship began on 21 June and we had our first disagreement on 22 June about the price we would accept for Paul Gascoigne.

If Paul had to go to Lazio, I at least wanted to bring in the money as soon as possible and from the moment that Sugar and I took control, I had been working long and hard, with Eddie Ashby's help, to find ways to persuade Lazio to release the money to us. This we achieved, giving them a cast-iron guarantee that if the transfer did not ultimately take place for any reason, their money would be returned. The Lazio money was duly deposited with Midland Bank in August 1991.

So much has been written and said, and so many false allegations made about the sale of Gazza, that it is worth setting out in detail the truth about the transfer. On 30 April 1991 the transfer of Gascoigne from Tottenham to Lazio was provisionally agreed by Carlo Regalia for Lazio and James Perry for Ashurst, Morris, Crisp, the lawyers representing Spurs. After Gazza's injury in the Cup final on 21 May, the original deal was off, dead in the water, but Lazio and Spurs remained eager to reach agreement and negotiations began again on a new deal at a lower price, conditional on Gascoigne's return to full fitness. Had Gascoigne never been able to play again, Tottenham would have received an insurance pay-out of £5.5 million.

On 17 June, Lazio made a fresh offer of £4.825 million, but with strict conditions about Gascoigne's fitness. Unbeknown to me, three days later a fax was sent from Lazio's solicitors to Ashurst, Morris, Crisp, making a conditional offer of £5.5 million. The header page on the fax was marked for the attention of Irving Scholar and Nat Solomon. Neither Eddie nor I saw this fax, dated 20 June 1991, nor was it ever referred to by any of the parties to the transfer and it was not to resurface until over two years later, when it became the heart of allegations of corruption against me, made on the *Panorama* and *Dispatches* TV programmes.

On 21 June 1991, Alan Sugar and I completed the purchase of Tottenham and a few days later, Tony Berry and I met Lazio's representatives at the Hyde Park Hotel. No one can explain why, when both sets of solicitors were in a meeting with Tony Berry and me to discuss the Gascoigne transfer, a few days after the date of that fax, they never mentioned it. I was discussing a deal at £4.825 million – why was one or the other not saying to me, 'Why are you discussing £4.825 million, when we have a letter offering £5.5 million?' The Lazio representatives made no mention of a higher offer, which might be understandable, but nor was it raised by Ashurst, Morris, Crisp, who were acting for Tottenham.

I never received the fax from Scholar, who also refused to hand over most of his other Tottenham documents and files to us. We wrote to him frequently, requesting and finally demanding that he return his files from Tottenham, but all he ever sent were three small cardboard boxes full of scrap paper – not much from a nine-year reign at the club.

In any event, though, the 'mystery fax' was something of a red herring, for it was conditional on a 'performance warranty' – a guarantee from Tottenham that Gascoigne would play as well after his injury as he had done before it. That was clearly an impossible condition, you could never guarantee that any player would perform for one club as well as he had for another, injured or not. It was a demand that Lazio were later persuaded to drop.

Lazio offered a deal at £4.825 million, which I refused. My intuition told me to lever the deal higher, because they were trying to pull a fast one. Their doctor had seen Gascoigne and he had obviously told Lazio that Paul would make a full recovery. I instinctively knew that, because if Gascoigne was finished, they were not going to offer me £100,000, never mind nearly £5 million. If Gascoigne was fine, however, why were we discounting the price? So I dug my heels in and said 'No, we want more money than that,' and in the absence of a higher offer, I called off the deal.

Sugar had been insisting that we needed the money and should take it with both hands, but I would not budge. Tony Berry and I went out into the street to talk it over and he said, 'What are you doing? Sugar will go mad.' While we were standing there, the Lazio people came down the stairs, ignored us completely and marched off up the road. They were furious, but I knew that they were trying it on and still wanted to do the deal. Otherwise they would have just said, 'It's your problem, not ours.'

Lazio duly renewed contact and, on 28 June, the first item on the agenda of a board meeting chaired by Sugar was an instruction for Tony Berry and me to renegotiate with Lazio. Discussion centred on how to get them to improve their offer of £4.825 million. Ian Gray, the managing director under the Scholar regime, and Nat Solomon were both present but made no reference to the fax and the alleged offer of £5.5 million. When questioned about this curious omission after the television programme had been aired, two years later, Solomon replied, 'I can't remember the fax. It's a long time ago. I'm far too busy to go through my files to find it.'

On 5 July, while I was away on holiday, and despite the instruction from the board that Tony Berry and I should renegotiate the deal, Sugar fired off a fax to Lazio director Maurizio Mancini, accepting £4.825 million and offering White Hart Lane as security for the deal, in case Gascoigne failed to recover from his injury, saying, 'You will get a second charge over our stadium.' Three days later, the impatient Sugar faxed Mancini again, claiming that Marseille were now interested at a price of £5.5 million, and demanding an answer by 10:00 a.m. on 9 July.

Lazio, who were changing ownership, ignored Sugar's deadline and the Marseille offer – if it had been a genuine one – came to nothing. Furious that he had not only been negotiating behind my back, but was also prepared to accept an offer that I had already turned down two weeks before, I phoned Sugar from Bermuda and exchanged angry words with him. He finally agreed to my suggestion that Gino Santin should be instructed to negotiate an improved package from Lazio.

Much has been made of the involvement of a millionaire London restaurateur in a football transfer. Sugar had earlier called Santin an 'Italian café owner' and asked why I wanted him involved, but Santin has had considerable experience in international transfer negotiations. He was involved in the deals that took Luther Blissett, Ray Wilkins, Mark Hateley and Ian Rush abroad. Santin was originally involved purely as a translator in the Gascoigne transfer, but when we reached the impasse, I called him in to broker a deal. Before this, Santin had been helping us without charge, but he contacted me to say that he would want a fee and also required written confirmation that he was representing the club. This was arranged, but the amount of the fee was left open for future discussion.

On 12 July Santin received a fax from Tony Berry, confirming that Santin was the official representative of the club, while Sugar simultaneously informed Lazio of the arrangement. Over the next few weeks, Santin gradually pulled together the deal. The initial gap between the two sides had been pretty wide, with Lazio managing director Lionello Celon's insistence on strict guarantees of Gascoigne's fitness a major stumbling block. Laborious negotiations ensued, but Santin eventually made a deal with Lazio that secured Spurs a fee of £5.5 million, without any question of having to give Lazio the second charge on the stadium that Sugar had offered. The more onerous performance warranties had also been dropped. In addition the money would be immediately deposited in Spurs' account at Midland Bank, and held in escrow (frozen until completion), allowing Spurs to collect the interest on completion – in effect, Lazio paid a year in advance. That gave validity to our financial recovery plans, for the Midland could smell, see and touch the Lazio money.

Santin also secured agreement on the methods of determining the player's fitness, the insurance cover, and the division of the gate and television-rights income from the two friendlies between Lazio and Tottenham that were part of the deal. Tottenham's total return from the transfer amounted to over £6.3 million.

Both sides were equally happy with the deal and Santin's role in it. I thought that he had done a fantastic job for us, while Lazio's Lionello Celon, remarked, 'He carried out a complex and delicate negotiating role. Without Gino, the whole transfer could have fallen through.' Lazio's respect for Santin's abilities was further demonstrated when they retained him to act as go-between, as they themselves contemplated the sale of Gascoigne two years later.

The question of Santin's fee was first raised at a meeting between Jonathan Crystal, Alan Sugar and me at the Grosvenor House Hotel on 24 July 1991. His appointment was confirmed and his fee fixed at a maximum of 2½ per cent. I have a memorandum to that effect with Alan Sugar's signature on it. It was again discussed at a board meeting on 12 September. The minutes report: 'There was a general discussion about fees payable to Mr Santin in connection with the Gascoigne disposal.

Mr Venables was given authority to negotiate further with Mr Santin. It is hoped that the fee can be limited to approximately £150,000.'

In the event, the fee agreed was £200,000, paid almost exactly twelve months later, in a cheque signed by Sugar and finance director Colin Sandy. Santin had asked for 5 per cent of the deal, but I haggled him down. As Santin had to wait a year for his money, he was perfectly entitled to claim reasonable interest. Rates at the time were around 10 per cent and interest was added to his 2½ per cent payment to reach the final figure of £200,000.

In addition, Santin continued to work throughout the rest of the year, shuttling backwards and forwards at his own expense with results of fitness tests and medical reports. When the infamous Gazza night-club incidents took place, one of which left him with a fractured knee, putting the transfer under a fresh cloud, Santin was forced into a further frenzy of activity to soothe and reassure Lazio and keep them from pulling out. Later, the size and method of Santin's payment was to be queried, but there was no question in my mind that he had earned his money. In the end he got Spurs an extra £1.5 million and saved us having to mortgage the ground as security for the deal, which is what Sugar had been offering. I would do the deal again with Santin tomorrow.

Part of the deal was that Lazio would take care of all payments to Gascoigne and his agent Mel Stein. Having tried to hold Spurs to a £1 million ransom before he would advise Gascoigne to agree to the transfer in the first place, Stein had also held a similar pistol to Lazio's heads. I have always had a very good relationship with Gazza, but I found relations with Mel Stein rather more strained. He resents being called an agent and prefers to describe himself as an 'adviser', and his advice certainly earned a crust for himself as well as Gascoigne. Information passed to me by Lazio, at the time of the Gascoigne transfer, was that Stein's own fees, paid by the club, came to a cool £400,000. Stein also charged Gazza £50,000. The deal with Lazio was set to go through at the end of the season, subject to fitness tests in England, followed by a final medical examination in Rome.

While Santin was pulling things together in Rome, back in London, Sugar and I were beginning to pull apart. I may not have known my way through the business jungle as well as Sugar, but football was one business that I did know. I knew who to buy, when to buy and when to sell, and I had made my reputation, and a lot of money for the clubs that I had been involved with, through getting the best out of players and showing a profit on buying and selling them. I devoted myself whole-heartedly to improving Tottenham Hotspur, both as a business and a football club.

As I told the press at the time of the takeover, 'I'm good at football, not property-developing or selling pork sausages, like some other chairmen. Not that there is anything wrong with those trades, but more and more modern-day chairmen seek a degree of involvement in their club for which they are not strictly experienced. I know every job there is to be done. I'll have a coach, someone who looks after the team and is off home by 1:00 p.m., and I'll do the rest.'

Sugar accepted that view without demur at the time, but rapidly grew restive. I was reminded more and more of the exchanges between our fictional counterparts in my football novel, written more than twenty years before:

'Work together? Do it all your way, you mean!'

'As far as the playing side is concerned – yes. You know about business and I know about football.'

The chairman shook his head.

'It's the same old story, isn't it? You remember when Len

Shackleton wrote his book – the chapter entitled, "What the Average Club Director Knows About Football"? And underneath it just a blank page. You pros – you think nobody knows the slightest thing about the game except yourselves.'

In Sugar's case that was absolutely right, but no one could say that he did not know anything about business.

The negative vibes caused by Alan's Amstrad dealings were partly responsible for making the soft option of property finance more difficult, and although Eddie was able to obtain a couple of mortgage offers on the stadium, they were comparatively expensive.

Sugar lost little time in demonstrating his unique style of man-management. Shortly after the takeover, the managing director under the old regime, Ian Gray, claimed that he had been dismissed by Alan Sugar in a telephone conversation. Sugar denied that he had done so and Gray's departure became the subject of litigation. For fifteen months, Sugar maintained his denials, right up to a board meeting held at the start of December 1992, when after meeting with counsel, and with the trial only a few days away, he said that he had been advised that the more prudent course was to settle the litigation. The board was reluctantly persuaded to go along with Sugar, even though he had earlier rejected the chance to settle for £100,000, but the settlement of the litigation now cost Tottenham over £250,000.

Ian Gray was not the only Tottenham employee that Sugar wanted out. The shareholders' agreement between us that was drawn up on the night of the takeover had never been signed by Sugar, and I suspect that by October 1991, instead of a true joint venture, he had already decided to force me out and go it alone. The start of the irrevocable breakdown between Alan Sugar and me can be pinpointed exactly. At eight o'clock on the morning of 21 November 1991, Eddie Ashby and I met Sugar for a breakfast meeting at the Grosvenor House Hotel in Park

Lane. Eddie was with me to give the details on the plans to refinance Tottenham using the value of the stadium. Despite the board's formal agreement to use its property assets to refinance the company, Sugar was pushing very, very hard for a rights issue, underwritten by himself. I was against it, because without the resources to match his potential share purchases, I would be helpless to prevent him from increasing his own holding and taking control of the company.

It was a typical November day, cold, grey and gloomy, but the meeting between us generated plenty of warmth. For two hours we argued and then shouted at each other, while the other people in the restaurant gazed at us in a mixture of fascination and horror. Finally, at ten o'clock, Sugar said, 'Okay, you've won, have it your way.' He agreed to give us eight months to conclude a satisfactory property deal. If we failed to do so, we would proceed with a rights issue. It had been an often bitter and bruising argument, but I had no reason at the time to believe that Sugar would not stick to his word.

As confirmation of the agreement, Eddie produced a hand-written note on Grosvenor House notepaper, covering the heads of agreement. It read:

> I confirm the content of our agreement this morning, concerning the refinancing of Tottenham.
>
> We adopt a strategy as follows:-
>
> a) Gascoigne monies received from Lazio
> b) You provide a commercial mortgage/loan of £4 million against the stadium
> c) We secure bank overdraft facilities of £2 million
> d) If by 31 July 1992, you are unable to realise your mortgage/loan plus the 'Scholar' loan [the loan from Maxwell, which Sugar had taken over when we bought the club], I will fully support a Rights Issue by Tottenham at your discretion.

The agreement is signed by Alan Sugar and countersigned by

me, and a copy of it remains in my possession. Eddie and I had achieved the result that we wanted, and we had eight months to fulfil the agreement, yet within forty-eight hours the rights-issue plan had been resurrected and agreed, after Sugar returned to me with a new proposal for a new shareholders' agreement.

My most important reason for allowing the 'quantum leap' from the Grosvenor House agreement on refinancing the company through a mortgage on the ground, to Sugar's preferred option of a rights issue was that Sugar's acceptance of the shareholders' agreement removed my worries about him acquiring extra shares and using their voting power to unseat me. In addition, we needed to persuade the Stock Exchange that the company was adequately refinanced so that they would lift the suspension of the shares and reinstate them, though either method would have achieved that end.

At a meeting held in Scribes on 26 November 1991, between Sugar, Jonathan Crystal and me – a meeting that Sugar was later to claim that he had not even attended – the revised agreement was thrashed out by the three of us. At the time both Sugar and I held an equal number of shares in Tottenham, and Sugar agreed that he would give me the proxy voting power over half of any further shares that he acquired, maintaining the balance of power between us. He further agreed to use his best endeavours to place those additional shares on the market, and in any event to dispose of them within five years. This was particularly important, for quite apart from the financial institutions' hostility towards Sugar, if his ownership of shares as a result of the rights issue grew to around 50 per cent, it would act as a block against anyone investing in the company. In that eventuality, the free market in the shares would only be restored when Sugar's holding was reduced. The agreement was subsequently reflected in the Rights Issue Document – a document of public record. My deal with Sugar enabled him to present his plans for a rights issue at an asking price of £1.25 a share, and with Tony Berry's support, the plans were accepted by the board on 28 November.

The rights issue went ahead little more than a week later, on 6 December 1991, with Sugar telling me, 'Trust me, even if I pick up all the shares, we have a shareholders' agreement,' but the agreement still remained unsigned. Like a mug, I over-ruled Eddie Ashby's warnings to me not to allow the rights issue to go ahead until we had Sugar's signature on a legally binding document. Events have proved how foolish I was.

Under the rights issue, which went ahead on a four-for-seven basis, putting 5,820,313 shares on the market, Alan and I each found another £800,000 to take up our own share options, putting £1.6 million in cash into Tottenham. The theory was that the other shareholders would also subscribe for their allocations, but in the depths of a recession, and with no institutional shareholders, it was always likely that the underwriter would finish up with the bulk of the shares.

You cannot launch a rights issue without an underwriter to guarantee that it will succeed, by buying any surplus shares. In normal circumstances, a bank or other financial institution would have been the underwriter, but none of them would risk putting any money into Tottenham, having just been taken to the cleaners over Amstrad. As a result, Sugar personally under-wrote it. While he and I both took up our full entitlement of additional shares, virtually no other shareholder did. As under-writer, Sugar accordingly picked up another £3.85 million worth of shares. The company was nicely refinanced, thank you very much, but Sugar's shareholding had become twice as large as mine. Without a signed agreement not to vote his additional shares, he immediately began to play that power position for all it was worth.

I was reduced from an equal partner to a pawn. I might not be the cleverest man in the world, but I am not so stupid that I would put £3.5 million into a business – especially a football business – where I am not even going to have a 50 per cent stake. I had been naïve, and should not have allowed it to happen, but I believed Alan Sugar's promise that it would be 50–50. From that moment, my days at Tottenham were numbered.

Eddie, Jonathan and I all raised the subject of the shareholders' agreement with Sugar several more times, Eddie even pursuing him down the stairs with the document in his hand on one occasion, saying, 'Alan, you still haven't signed the agreement.' Sugar just turned and looked at him and said, 'Oh, fuck off.' Although the end did not come until May 1993, Sugar's control of the club had already effectively been achieved by January 1992.

I had brought in Eddie Ashby as my personal assistant to run the day-to-day administration of the company under my authority. Eddie had been made personally bankrupt just before the takeover was completed, but had not informed me of that fact immediately. When I confronted him about it, he admitted that not to have told me straight away had been an error of judgement on his part, but said that he was really enjoying working with me, was excited by the possibilities that lay ahead, and was afraid that his bankruptcy might have led me to sever my connections with him. I was angry with him at first, but I was also sympathetic to his plight. While I valued his abilities highly, it was not now just a matter of what I thought, but what other people thought, too. I told Eddie that I would have to inform Sugar, and that Eddie would have to accept the consequences, whatever they might be. I could not consider keeping him on as my personal assistant at Tottenham, without the approval of the other board members.

I made Alan Sugar aware of Eddie's bankruptcy in the first week of August 1991, within twenty-four hours of finding out myself. One of the allegations that Sugar has since repeatedly

made against me is that I was negligent in engaging an undis-
charged bankrupt to do such a high-profile job at Tottenham.
Yet knowing of Eddie's bankruptcy, Sugar agreed to him continuing as my personal assistant without objection. Had Sugar's
attitude been different, I would have had to let Eddie go, but
Sugar just said to me, 'Don't worry about it, it happens to most
businessmen at some stage.' He was very supportive of Eddie
and in no way censorious, effectively telling him to get on with
the job and praising him to me, saying, 'I'm pleased that you
have Eddie there guiding you.' Just over a year later, by a
specific minute of a board meeting on 5 September 1992, at
which the auditors Touche Ross were present, the board of
Tottenham Hotspur plc, including Alan Sugar, reaffirmed
Eddie's contract.

The allegations flying around since then have made it appear
as if Eddie Ashby conned me in some way, but that is not the
case at all. I had to have somebody who knew the business
world, to watch my back. I knew no one else who could do that
job, and was in a situation where I had to put my trust in Eddie.
He has done nothing to betray that trust. Eddie's acute business
brain was also the reason why we managed to do the Tottenham
deal at all. It could not have happened without him. Eddie has
put in four years' unremitting effort for very little reward, but,
for his pains, he has had to take more than his share of
vilification and abuse from Sugar and others. His loyalty to me
has been as great as mine to him and I owe him a lot, not least
because he has kept every scrap of paper ever to come out of all
this – the documents that prove my innocence.

Eddie's biggest crime in Sugar's eyes was the same one Sugar
had earlier praised him for – to give me good advice. Had I
heeded his warnings about Sugar outflanking me a little earlier,
I might still be behind my desk at Tottenham. Eddie's other
crime was to stand up to Sugar. When Sugar gave him a burst of
foul-mouthed abuse over something he did not like, Eddie told

him, 'I don't have to take that from you or anybody. I'm not infallible and I'll accept criticism made in a proper manner, but I won't accept that.' Sugar equally does not accept anyone talking to him like that, and there was a marked change in his attitude to Eddie from then on.

It is true that Eddie has been associated with a lot of companies that have gone bankrupt, but working in the highly speculative field of venture capital for so many years, that is scarcely surprising. The nature of the business is that it is high-return, but high-risk. There are successes and failures, not always of the companies' own making. Several companies had also been put into receivership by Eddie himself, who, having had bad experiences with some of his business partners, wanted recompense.

Eddie worked alongside me as my personal assistant through-out my time as chief executive of Tottenham. He was under my control and direction, and would never make decisions without checking with me first. His role was to ensure that all the things that I wanted done were carried out. My days were largely taken up with football matters, and in other areas I laid down the broad outlines and Eddie attended to the details. We were in constant communication and met every Monday morning, when I would give him my instructions, and met in the evenings, two or three times a week, to discuss progress.

At the same time as Eddie's appointment, Sugar's man, Colin Sandy, had become finance director, with my agreement. Sandy is a diminutive, balding, ginger-haired, bespectacled former tax inspector – a Woody Allen-type character without the charm. Sandy succeeded in falling out with Eddie very shortly after joining Spurs, and they were involved in daily battles on behalf of their respective principals, which may explain, though not justify, some of Sandy's subsequent conduct. His official function was simply to monitor the finances of the company. His unofficial function rapidly became clear, when in

April 1992, he produced a dossier on the companies of which Eddie had been a director that had gone into receivership. An article appeared on the front page of the *Independent on Sunday* at the same time, headlined: SPURS USE BANKRUPT IN GAZZA DEAL. Sandy also made untrue allegations against Eddie, including the false claim that Eddie had set up a bank account in Japan to divert the company's proceeds from the sale of a Gary Lineker video in Japan.

Sandy alienated many of the staff who had to work with him by wielding the big stick of his authority as a director. Nor was I particularly struck by his efficiency. I frequently had to criticise his work to Alan Sugar, pointing out that management accounts were often late and board minutes only produced at the last minute. The computer system for stock control was not in operation fourteen months after Sandy began the project and at one stage no reconciled merchandising accounts had been produced for nine months.

In all the time I was a director, Sandy never voted against Sugar on any issue, however slight. They were a double-act in which Sugar would put forward some proposal, and Sandy would then pause for a moment, before greeting it with great enthusiasm. Sugar, in his characteristically foul language, argued that Jonathan Crystal was equally supportive of me, but Jonathan was a non-executive director and, as a barrister, he took a very correct and professional approach to his duties.

Sugar would often ridicule Sandy in front of others, insulting him to his face at board meetings when information was incorrect or insufficiently detailed. I had not come across this kind of behaviour towards subordinates before; I have always believed that you have to give respect to get it back, but Sandy meekly took whatever was dished out to him. Sandy's dossier became a prime weapon in Sugar's war to remove Eddie from the administration. His aim was obvious. By parting me from my chosen

and trusted assistant, he would have made my working life
enormously more difficult.

There were several other very gritty problems to face. Tottenham had fallen foul of FA rules before my time as chief
executive, with irregular loans and all sorts of other breaches of
the regulations. As early as July 1991, Ossie Ardiles had begun
pressing for payment of money purportedly owing under contracts signed with the Scholar regime. Investigations revealed
that several other loans, totalling a huge sum of money, had
been made to players. In most cases, Irving Scholar's stamp was
all over them. Not only did the loans represent a loss to the
company, because in many cases they were irrecoverable, they
were also a source of continuing friction.

Paul Allen, now at Southampton, had been given what was
described as a 'loan' of £55,000 when he joined Tottenham in
1985, but the way it had been structured, even though it was
called a loan, it was nothing other than a disguised payment to
the player. If it had been a straightforward payment, Paul Allen
would have been taxed once on the original £55,000, but he
found himself being taxed every year on the 'beneficial interest
on the loan'. Because Scholar had not bitten the bullet and paid
the tax on it in the first place, the player had to pick up a tax
bill on the 'loan' in perpetuity. Paul had already repaid £20,000
in tax on this notional interest, and the Inland Revenue could
simply carry on taxing him on it for ever. It was not just the
existence of the loans and the breaches of League regulations
that caused great problems to us, it was how the loans would
actually be dealt with. We were faced with writing off more
than £400,000, and both Jonathan Crystal and I felt that legal
action should be taken against Scholar and other past directors.

Sugar went along with that initially, but his claim that he
was behind the original investigation is completely untrue. Documents shown on the *World In Action* programme about the
affair, in 1993, prove that it was Jonathan Crystal who had

identified the arrangement with Ardiles as being unacceptable. The Tottenham board minute of 12 September 1991, 'Mr Sugar is very clear that a report must be sent to the appropriate authorities. In this respect, the board instructed Mr Jonathan Crystal and Mr Colin Sandy to meet with leading counsel to consider the resulting ramifications of disclosure and any actions that can be taken against Scholar in particular' gives a false impression of what was discussed. I was pushing hard for the 'loans' to be disclosed to the League and corrected, but no report was made to any authorities until December 1993. We were soon to discover that the Ardiles and Allen loans were only the tip of a very large and damaging iceberg.

While the boardroom battles steadily escalated, the main business of Tottenham Hotspur, playing football, provided sweet relief. I had appointed Peter Shreeves as first-team coach, with Dougie Livermore as his assistant, and Ray Clemence as the reserve-team coach. I felt that as chief executive of the plc, I had plenty on my plate to turn the club around off the field and the club would be better placed, in the beginning at least, if I took more of a back seat with the coaching. I was there if Peter Shreeves wanted me, but otherwise, I kept away.

Peter had done extremely well as a coach at Tottenham before. They had won the European Cup-Winners' Cup under him and a lot of the players at Tottenham spoke very highly of him. He was very unfortunate to have had to leave the club, not because of football, but for other reasons, and my idea was to bring him back and see if he would do well in the Premier League. He took the job on a one-year contract so that we could both see how the arrangement worked out.

We met Arsenal in the Charity Shield at Wembley, the traditional pipe-opener for the new season, and the game ended in a draw, which meant that both clubs held the trophy for six months. That was only the dress rehearsal, however, and when we set off to play the first League match at Southampton, I was as excited as a kid on an outing to the seaside, except that the kid from Dagenham had now become the chief executive and part-owner of one of the greatest names in football.

Although there were other ex-players in club boardrooms, like Terry Cooper, who was a director at Bristol City, or most famously, Sir Matt Busby at Manchester United, it was unheard of for a former professional footballer to have gone through management and ended up running a club like Tottenham Hotspur. The game at Southampton was the moment when the new era really began, and it got off to a winning start, with Gary Lineker and fresh signing Gordon Durie both scoring.

It was to be the last season of Gary Lineker at Spurs, for Gary was to sign for the Japanese side Grampus 8 in November, but as with the Paul Gascoigne transfer, we managed to make a deal that gave Tottenham the money immediately. This deal, like much else at Tottenham, was later to be used against me, but the facts are perfectly clear. Lineker was sold to Grampus 8 for a fee of £850,000 and in addition Gary agreed to waive a fee of £166,650, owing to him from Tottenham as part of his original contract with us, in return for our agreement to the transfer. That effectively made the fee up to over £1 million, close to what we had paid for him three years before and exceptionally good business for a man who was fast approaching thirty-two years old, especially as we were paid in advance and had the use of him for the rest of the season as well.

Sugar was later to imply that Lineker had been worth far more and that part of the fee paid by the Japanese club had been diverted, a claim ridiculed by both Lineker and his agent, John Holmes. Sugar also complained that his experience in negotiating with the Japanese over electronic components was not used in the Lineker sale, but it would have been completely superfluous. Grampus 8 employed a trusted English agent, Christian Flood, who as the man who organised Margaret Thatcher's tours of Japan needed no help from Sugar in dealing with either the English or Japanese ends of the transaction.

With Gary still a part of the team, we began well in the European Cup-Winners' Cup, beating Stockerau in the opening round. The away leg in Austria also provided a reminder that there are greater misfortunes in life than defeat on the soccer field, for Stockerau had offered a temporary home and a staging point for children who had been affected by the Chernobyl disaster. The Tottenham directors went to see the children, bearing gifts from the club. It showed all of us how lucky we were to be fit, healthy and well paid for work we loved. Whatever future these Chernobyl kids faced, it was unlikely to be bright, and I was touched and proud at the way the players responded to our request for donations.

We received incredible hospitality throughout Europe in the away legs of our games and the home legs always required us to provide hospitality in return. We entertained several of the visiting sides to dinner at Scribes, but Alan Sugar never once showed up.

He has subsequently suggested that I exploited this situation to put business the way of Scribes, yet I provided facilities at a cost of around £20 per head, against a cost of a comparable meal at a hotel or restaurant of around £40–50 per head. Alan Sugar was kept fully informed and raised no objections to the arrangement at any stage. It would be amusing, if it were not so annoying, that Sugar, who could be miserly in the extreme, got the best and cheapest deal that he could possibly have had, and then later went on to accuse me of lining my pockets at Tottenham's expense.

Sugar's preferred form of hospitality was a competition called 'King for a Day', involving expensive pre-match entertainment – an attempt to bring people to the ground an hour and more before the kick-off so that they would spend more money on refreshments and merchandise. It was fine in theory, but a disaster in practice. People did not come to see the performers – Chas and Dave, for example, played to an empty stadium an hour before kick-off time – and the money that had been expended was wasted, but as his brainchild, it was above criticism.

The 'gate' could be improved only by success on the field. Crowds would not increase in response to advertising, especially for a team with Tottenham's already high profile. Sugar's attempts at such pre-season promotion in 1992 cost £65,000, without any discernible impact on attendances, but until I put a stop to it, Colin Sandy wanted to spend a further £100,000 monitoring supporters coming through the turnstile, to count the 'new' fans.

I felt a sense of tiredness at times at having to argue with Sugar about these things. The one thing Sugar has is great forcefulness and the dynamism that goes with it, and to have a board meeting where every single item is a matter of dispute is wearying. In the end, over a relatively trivial issue like that, people just went along with it. That may be a sad reflection of the commitment of the people who were there, but having fought hard to achieve results on the important issues, we reached a point where we seemed to be fighting over every single item. Sugar would happily keep a board meeting going all night if necessary and that is how some of those decisions got through.

He was not wrong about everything, of course, and I should not have stood up to him on virtually every issue. He might have had a bit more respect for me if I had let him have his way without a struggle on some things. I never argued with my other chairmen the way I did with Sugar, nor spoke to them the way I did to him, but then none of them ever spoke to me the way Sugar did either.

We got safely through the early rounds of the Cup-Winners' Cup, but our League form was poor and off the field there were more problems, as three of our players had simultaneous worries about their kids. Gary Lineker and Gordon Durie's sons and Paul Allen's eldest daughter all fell seriously ill. Gary Lineker faced an awful situation when his son, George, contracted a rare form of leukaemia. I obviously gave Gary permission to miss the next few games to be with his family until the crisis was resolved, and happily George made a full recovery and is now fine again.

Gary felt ready to resume playing in December, in the away game against Leeds. Jonathan Crystal and he were due to fly up on the Saturday morning, but Heathrow was fog-bound and the flight was delayed and then cancelled, forcing them to miss the game. I missed it as well, because I was in Barbados on honeymoon. Yvette and I had married on 6 December 1991, a quiet register-office wedding with just ten guests, only two days after Bobby Moore and Stephanie had got married at the same register office. We wanted to keep our wedding low-profile, and only the guests at the actual ceremony knew that we were getting married. Yvette had secretly taken my mother's wedding ring to a jeweller and had it 'stretched' so that I could wear it on my own wedding day, which touched me beyond words. Fred was my best man, because they say you should have your best mate as your best man, and that is my Dad.

Afterwards we went back to Scribes where about sixty people were waiting. They thought that they were just going for pre-Christmas drinks, for we had not told any of them that they were going to a wedding reception, and George Graham was mortified, after turning up in his jeans. We had a terrific party and then went off on honeymoon, spending a week in Barbados relaxing in the heat, and six days in New York, where it was snowing and bitterly cold, but we had a fabulous time.

I had asked Jonathan to phone me in Barbados at five o'clock in the afternoon local time, to tell me about the game. The theory was to have a few days' complete break from football, but when I left Yvette sunbathing and wandered into the

hotel bar and discovered it had satellite TV and was showing
Leeds versus Tottenham, I could not believe my luck and settled
down with a beer, to watch the game. Jonathan phoned up as
arranged, but said, 'I can't tell you anything, I didn't make the
game.' 'Never mind, Jonathan,' I said, 'what do you want to
know and I'll tell you about it.'

Gary Lineker returned to the Spurs side in time for the
third round of the FA Cup in January 1992, at Aston Villa,
but it was not a happy return. Paul Walsh had a great chance
to win it for us in the last few minutes, but he missed it and
we went on to lose the replay. Paul had little chance to make
amends, for he committed an unforgivable sin later in the
season and had to be sold. To be fair to Paul, he always did
want to play and was a super footballer, but he did not score
the amount of goals I thought he should have. So often he
was a sub or started a game and then came off, and he
would be angry if he was substituted. On this occasion, Ray
Clemence brought him off in a reserve match at White Hart
Lane, because I wanted him fit for a mid-week game, but he
lost his temper and punched Ray in the face, in full view of
the crowd and the press. If it had happened in the dressing
room behind closed doors, we may have been able to handle
it discreetly, but Walsh's public attack on his coach could not
go unpunished, and he was moved on at the end of the
season.

After the Cup defeat, our only hopes of a trophy rested on
the League Cup and the European Cup-Winners' Cup, and in
the space of three days in March 1992, Tottenham had the
home leg of a League Cup semi-final against Nottingham Forest,
followed by the away leg of the Cup-Winners' Cup quarter-final
against Feyenoord. The Forest tie was a televised game on a
Sunday afternoon. As I drove up to the ground with Jonathan
Crystal, my mobile phone rang. It was Peter Barnes, the club
secretary, to tell me that there had been a bomb warning. The

ground had been cleared and spectators were not being admitted.

We parked the car and pushed our way through the crowds locked outside the stadium. Once inside, we went up to the police room, and looked out on a bizarre reversal. On a normal match day the ground would be packed and the streets outside deserted; now the ground was completely empty, but every inch of road for hundreds of yards around was jammed with supporters milling about. Both the team buses were stuck in the crowds, unable to get through.

The senior police officer from Tottenham and an officer from the Anti-Terrorist Branch were among a mass of uniforms in the police control room. They told us that this was no ordinary hoax call. The previous day there had been a coded warning, followed by an explosion on the Tube, and the same coded warning had been given with this threat. The police said that they had used sniffer dogs and searched the ground from top to bottom. While the senior officer was saying this, a nervous look spread across his face. 'I've just realised,' he said, 'the only place we haven't searched is under here.' All of us looked down in absolute horror at the floor beneath our feet for half a second, and then there was a rush for the door.

'It's all right,' said the policeman, 'if we had made a mistake, we would have known about it by now – we'd have had our legs blown off, or worse.' Just the same, I saw over my shoulder that he was the first policeman out of the door, with only T. Venables and J. Crystal ahead of him. I showed a turn of speed that had not been seen since I hung up my boots, and was halfway down the terraces before the last policeman came spilling out of the control room. No bomb was found, even under the police room, and eventually the match went ahead. There was no happy ending, however. We lost both that game and the Cup-Winners' Cup tie against Feyenoord.

Smiling faces had not been much in evidence at a sharehold-

ers' meeting chaired by Sugar either. The question of paying a
dividend had arisen, and some shareholders were asking questions about whether they could waive their dividend payments. I
was in favour of a dividend – I needed one to help me meet my
commitments – but I was appalled at the way Sugar dismissed
their suggestions, and the people making them. His position was
effectively: I've got more shares than you. If I vote my shares for
a dividend, your views don't matter a hill of beans. After the
meeting, Nat Solomon, Jonathan Crystal and I had to go round
soothing shareholders, many of whom had come a long way for
the meeting and were upset at the way they had been treated.
The shareholders would have been even more horrified if they
had heard Sugar's comments at a board meeting, during a
discussion about buying players. Sugar turned to Jonathan Crystal and said, 'You've got to be fucking joking, if you think
you're going to spunk my money all over the wall.'

I had told Sugar a number of things about football over a
drink in Harry's Bar one night, but I might as well have saved
my breath. I warned him that he had little chance of taking a lot
of money out of Tottenham for a long time. We had to get a
successful team first, which required an investment of money to
bring in new blood and an investment of time to bring our
young players through. He just looked at me and said, 'Bugger
off. If you think I'm in it for anything other than money, you
can ask my family.' 'I don't need to ask your family, Alan,' I
replied, 'I can see for myself exactly why you're in it.'

My aim at Tottenham had always been to assemble a squad
of players that would give us a realistic chance of the Premier
League title. In the short term, that would have necessitated
capital investment, but in the long term, the potential rewards
were enormous. If you do not have enough good players in your
team, you must improve every deficient position and more to
cover for injuries. I told Sugar that we had the best batch of
youngsters Spurs had had for many, many years and that five or

six would eventually make the first team, but we had to buy ourselves some time, while the young players came through. Sugar could not bear to see 'his' money spent on anything that did not carry a direct financial return, however, and had his own theories on developing players: 'They never come through.'

Manchester United have one of the most successful youth policies in the country, but they are well aware that you must also be willing to reinvest at least part of your profits in established players to keep your team at the top. They made £4 million profit in their Championship year of 1993, for example, but instead of resting on their laurels, they went out and invested it in Roy Keane, strengthening the squad even more, to keep ahead of the rest. They are simply following a lead set by Liverpool, who were the first club to realise that, although good coaching is very important, buying top-quality players is absolutely imperative. Spurs, Arsenal, Everton, Manchester United and Aston Villa are always cited as being 'moneybags' clubs, but Liverpool have spent the most of all, though, remarkably, they are never referred to as big spenders.

You have to generate the profits first to be able to invest in players, of course, and I worked with all the sector heads, like the commercial manager, Mike Rollo, and Peter Barnes, the secretary, to make sure that Tottenham's commercial activities – box sales, perimeter advertising, and the rest – were as profitable as possible.

I was also involved very closely in the design and redevelopment of White Hart Lane. I always felt that people wanted to be in the West Stand, because that was the heart of the action, where the players' entrance and the directors' box were sited. The Legends Club, a concept borrowed from Barcelona, gave members the chance to rub shoulders with great players from previous eras. We sited it in a special enclosure and it proved to be very successful.

We also introduced the idea of an overseas members' club at

Tottenham, alongside the existing members' club. In Spain and Portugal, clubs have an enormous overseas membership. Benfica, for example, have two million members, paying an annual membership of £4 a head, which is huge money for the club. The idea is big already and can only grow bigger. Other sports come and go, but football just grows bigger as the world gets smaller through television.

Television brought the 1990 World Cup to millions and millions more people than ever before, particularly in Third World countries. When Yvette and I were on holiday in Phuket in Thailand in 1993, we thought we would go out for a nice quiet evening, but we were mobbed in the street. Everyone was chanting 'Lineker' and 'Gazza' at me; they are football-mad out there, it is like a forest fire. The 1994 World Cup accelerated the process even more.

Twenty years ago, expatriates living in Australia and California could not even find the football results; now they can not only see the results, they can watch the games on television as well. A Spurs supporter, living in Chingford, who had stopped going to the games and watched on television instead, could be in Australia and still see just as much of the club.

He would often have seen as much of it as Alan Sugar, whose attitude to Tottenham as a football club was never more vividly demonstrated than the day that he pointed to Nick Barmby and said, 'Who's that geezer out there?' I told Sugar his name, and said that he was the most promising of our young players, with a glorious future ahead of him. 'Well, flog him,' said Sugar. 'That'll pay for the South Stand.'

He saw nothing wrong with stating at a board meeting, 'I'm happy if we finish halfway up the table and go a few rounds in the FA Cup.' He wanted to make money and make a profit, which was the aim of us all, but he had made his investment in Tottenham and now wanted to take money out, not put any more in. Flog Barmby, flog the lot if necessary, and then 'just get a few more geezers in'.

If one good thing has come out of all the troubles at Tottenham, it is that Sugar has now come to accept the idea of spending money on players, as the heavy expenditure before the 1994–95 season confirms. A piece in the *Sunday Times* in spring 1994 even suggested that Sugar was a changed man and is now '80 per cent football and 20 per cent money'. I find that hard to believe, for he was certainly never that in all the time I spent with him at Tottenham; the percentages then were very different.

Following our Cup defeats, our League form went from bad to worse as we slid dangerously close to the relegation zone. I was never truly worried that we would be relegated, but we did not guarantee our safety until a victory over Luton, in which Gary Lineker scored two goals. He ended his Tottenham career with a flourish, scoring seven goals in his last four games as we pulled away from the bottom of the table.

We had already played the whole of the 1991–92 season without Paul Gascoigne and would now have to go into the next one without Gary Lineker as well. Gazza made his comeback in the last week of the season, appearing for the reserves in a friendly match against the youth team. He showed that he had lost none of his skill or his appetite for clowning around, scoring a brilliant goal in front of a battery of press photographers and then bellyflopping into a puddle on the pitch. There was nothing I could do to keep Gazza at Tottenham, though. He remained on schedule to go to Lazio, once he had proved his total recovery from the knee injury sustained at Wembley the previous May and aggravated in the two incidents in his native Newcastle during the year.

At the same time that Paul was facing his fitness test at the Tottenham training ground, the newly formed Premier League committee was meeting at the Royal Lancaster Hotel to decide

between the competing offers for television rights, a subject very
close to Alan Sugar's heart. I had been involved in the negotiations that led to the setting-up of the Premier League, representing Tottenham at every meeting, usually with Jonathan Crystal
or club secretary Peter Barnes. Alan Sugar only ever attended
one Premier League meeting, the one at which the television
deal was to be discussed.

I felt that we had a duty to make changes, so that the
Premier League was distinct from the former Football League,
and I was initially very concerned at the name the League would
have. By conceding the name 'Football Association Premier
League', I thought that we would give too much influence to the
FA, in addition to the 'golden share' that they would hold,
allowing them a right of veto in some areas.

I also felt that the Premier League should signal a radical
change in all sorts of areas, including a transfer embargo and
an increase in the number of substitutes, to bring us into line
with the rest of Europe. When it came to a vote, however,
only the increase of substitutes was approved, from two to
three. The lack of enthusiasm for radical change was unsurprising, for of all the people around the table, apart from me,
only Derek Dooley of Sheffield and David Stringer, the ex-
manager of Norwich, were real football people, the rest were
businessmen and club directors. As a result, the bulk of the
meetings were not taken up with footballing matters, and I
often sat through hours of commercial discussions, just as at
Tottenham, when footballing matters would scarcely be
mentioned.

On the day of the vote on the television deal in May 1992,
Jonathan Crystal and I attended the meeting with Alan Sugar.
Jonathan kept dashing out to phone the training ground for a
progress report on Gazza's fitness test. The reports coming back
from the physio, John Sheridan, were not encouraging and
Gazza's transfer looked to be in doubt. As the vote on the

television deal was approaching, Jonathan came back into the meeting and told me, 'It is not looking too good at the moment, John Sheridan thinks you should go out there.'

I left immediately for the training ground before the vote was taken to award the television contract to Sky. The financial deal from Sky was undoubtedly very attractive to clubs, but whether it was in the best interests of football is another question. I personally felt that it was a financial decision not a footballing one. Several newspapers later speculated that I had cast the Tottenham vote, but it was actually Alan Sugar who voted in favour of Sky.

The way the bids had been made and handled was a shambles. Final bids were supposed to have been handed in the night before, but the ITV companies upgraded their offer on the morning of the meeting, a fact communicated by Sugar to Sky in a call from a pay-phone in the foyer. It was overheard by Trevor East of ITV, who was giving out details of the ITV bid and claims that Sugar was shouting down the phone that Sky 'had better get your act together, if you don't want to lose the contract'.

The meeting, due to start at 10:00 a.m., was delayed until an improved bid from Sky was received, allegedly scrawled in longhand 'on the back of a fag packet', as one chairman put it to Trevor East, indicating the last-minute nature of the bid. Sugar lobbied to get the deal accepted and voted for it himself. It is not true to say that Sugar's was the casting vote, but it is true to say that if Tottenham had voted the other way, the deal would not have achieved the necessary two-thirds approval. While Sugar apparently did declare an interest to the Premier League committee, he certainly did not do so in discussions at Tottenham board meetings before the vote, where he was a great champion of Sky. He had very close contacts with the people who ran the network, particularly Sam Chisholm, and felt that Tottenham should throw their weight behind the bid.

That led to great friction with Arsenal, who had similarly close ties with ITV. After the contract was awarded to Sky, there was a period when relations between the two clubs were strained.

Sugar stood to gain in two ways from the deal. Spurs would receive a far larger pay-out from Sky than that promised by the ITV companies, but there was another indirect, though very substantial, benefit to him. What Sugar failed to disclose to us at any stage, though I suppose if anybody had sat down and really thought it through, they might have worked it out for themselves, was that the greatest beneficiaries of the Sky deal would not only be Sky Television, but the suppliers of satellite dishes. Alan Sugar's company, Amstrad, was then, and remains now, one of the prime sources of those dishes.

Gazza's problems with his fitness test proved to be less serious than was feared and he was passed fit to try and clear the final hurdle before his transfer, the medical at Lazio's ground. Jonathan Crystal and I went with him to Rome and Paul also had two bodyguards to prevent any further incidents or disasters. The drive to the ground was completely maniacal as the Italian driver put on an even more terrifying display than Gazza at his worst. I thought that, for once, Paul could not be blamed for that, as he was only a passenger, but I later discovered that he had told the driver to give me a fright . . .

The Lazio training ground has a lovely pitch and Paul went out and successfully did a full test, running up and down, sprinting and doing zig-zag runs. We felt that Paul had proved his fitness completely, but it was clear that Lazio's doctor, Claudio Bartolini, was scared of committing £5.5 million of Lazio's money on his own authority. He was relying on an American doctor whom Lazio had also brought in for the final verdict, perhaps so that he would have someone to blame if things went wrong later on.

The American doctor led us back to a little treatment area.

Apart from Paul, the two doctors, Jonathan Crystal and me, there were also several representatives from Lazio, all jammed into an area no bigger than eighteen foot by twelve. The American put two shoes on the floor and told Paul to hop across the room between them. He did it a couple of times, but I was growing increasingly worried, not that Paul would be unable to do the test, but that he would slip on the polished floor and suffer a fresh injury while doing it.

I immediately stopped the tests and said, 'That's enough. He's proved his fitness. Either he signs up now or we're leaving.' Jonathan and I then walked outside and waited. After much muttering in Italian, with an occasional plaintive word in American, the Lazio officials finally signified their approval and the deal was completed.

I watched Paul complete the formalities with very mixed emotions. He was one of the most talented footballers I had ever coached, and had taken us to Wembley almost single-handedly twelve months before. Yet although I was very sad to see him go, I was pleased for him that, after an agonising year, he would be back on a football field, playing the game he loved, even though it would no longer be at White Hart Lane. I could only hope that the pressures of Italian football would make and not break him.

Sugar was determined that Sky should televise the two friendlies against Lazio, one in each country, that were part of the Gascoigne deal, despite Jonathan Crystal's specific warning that we would be offending against Article 14 of the UEFA regulations. The rule prohibits clubs from signing TV deals with companies who broadcast across national borders, since that obviously affects the ability of the other club to deliver exclusive coverage to their own chosen broadcaster. Sugar then insisted that Jonathan, rather than himself, should sign the contract.

Minutes before the kick-off in Rome, there was still no

indication of whether Lazio would let the game go ahead, because of the satellite coverage. I spoke to Alan Sugar by phone from the tunnel, with the players already in the warm-up area, and Sky waiting for a decision on whether to transmit. Sugar's response was characteristic: 'Get it on, fuck the FA, I'll deal with that later.' When Sky did show the match, Tottenham paid the price for his decision – the club was charged with a breach of UEFA regulations and fined 100,000 Swiss francs.

That was not to be Sugar's only assistance to Sky. In the pre-season Fiorucci tournament at White Hart Lane, we had secured the involvement of two top Italian clubs, with Tottenham keeping the gate and British television revenue. Sugar helped secure the rights for Sky, assuring Jonathan Crystal that they would simply film the matches and show highlights at some later date. Over the weekend preceding the game, Sky then advertised it as live coverage and, though we managed to get that stopped, they still went ahead and showed highlights at 10:00 p.m. on the evening of the match. The attendance at White Hart Lane was unsurprisingly under 10,000, and Tottenham received no fee for the coverage.

We began the 1992–93 season under a new coach. If Peter Shreeves had done well, his one-year contract would have been extended, but the results were very poor towards the end of the year. He did not run away and I did not sack him during the season, when times were particularly difficult, but when we got to the end of the year, I felt I could not offer him another contract. It was a hard task because I liked him and he was a good coach, but I felt it was the right business decision to make. In fairness to him, he walked into a very difficult job, perhaps more difficult than either of us had realised at first, because the players were not such a professional group as the last time he had been at Tottenham.

I took on a more active role as 'over-manager', giving me closer control of team affairs, and before the start of the season

replaced Peter Shreeves with Doug Livermore, who had originally been brought to Spurs as a reserve team coach by
Peter. I had approached Doug before I appointed Peter, but
Doug felt that it was too big a job for him, too early. One year
on, I spoke to him again and this time he agreed to do it, but on
two conditions; one was that Ray Clemence could be his assistant and the other was that I would be on the training field with
him every day. I was delighted with that, for I had missed the
direct involvement with the team and the thought of getting
back into my tracksuit was great. I was equally happy to
promote Ray Clemence from reserve-team coach to Doug's
assistant.

I also had another serious problem to face, finding a goal-
scoring replacement for Gary Lineker. The player I decided on
was Teddy Sheringham, then at Nottingham Forest. Halfway
through pre-season training, Teddy came to London and made
contact through his agency, First Wave, run by Graham Smith
and Frank McLintock. We met at the Royal Garden Hotel in
Kensington, and Sheringham told me that Forest were prepared
to let him go and that he was interested in a move to Tottenham.
Ted Buxton, who knew the player from their time at Millwall
together, sounded out Brian Clough's assistant Ronnie Fenton,
who came back with a price of £2.1 million.

Negotiations continued for some considerable time, and I
was getting sick of the never-ending delays in completing the
deal, caused mainly by Forest chairman Fred Reacher demanding
an extra £100,000 on top of his original price of £2.1 million, so
that Forest would get back all the money that they had laid out
on the player, including the signing-on fee paid to him at the
start of the previous season, 1991–92.

Sugar and the Tottenham board had been kept fully informed
of the progress of negotiations. After the initial contact by Ted
Buxton, most of the dealings had been done through Frank
McLintock and Ronnie Fenton. Cloughie just did not become

involved in the deal, and I never spoke to him during the entire process. In fact, I had not talked to anyone at Forest at all, until I finally lost patience and spoke to Fred Reacher direct, telling him it was now or never. He got back to me within an hour and said, 'Okay, the deal's done.'

First Wave had been working for us on and off for a year or so on various other matters. Frank McLintock was mainly involved in transfer dealings, while Graham Smith had done a lot of work negotiating marketing opportunities on our behalf. With Forest's fee at last agreed, I met with Sheringham and McLintock at our training ground to negotiate Sheringham's personal terms, which proved to be fairly straightforward, but Frank then turned to me and said, 'Tel, what about our money? I've told you we want paying today. Tottenham have been saying they'll pay us for months, and I'm not waiting any longer. Either we get paid today, or the Sheringham deal doesn't go through.'

With that ultimatum hanging over me and not wishing to sour the deal, I phoned Sugar and Sandy and told them that the deal was agreed, but that we had to pay First Wave immediately. The payment of £50,000 in cash, made that day, was to be the subject of further allegation and innuendo after my sacking by Sugar, even though he himself had co-signed the cheque with Colin Sandy to withdraw the cash. Neither Frank nor I asked for it to be in cash, I simply asked for it to be 'paid today'. Frank would not take a cheque, because he wanted the money immediately, but a banker's draft would have done perfectly well.

Instead Sandy and his deputy, Nick Jacobs, brought cash in for him. I was not even aware of that until a couple of days later, when Eddie reported to me that Frank had been overpaid. The deal we had agreed was for £50,000 including VAT, but Frank had been paid the VAT on top. I insisted that he repaid the £8750 VAT.

The *Panorama* 'exposé' of me, broadcast in September 1993, would suggest that there was something funny in that, but if I had wanted to steal that money I would have said, 'Bring it back to me'. Instead I told him to go to the club and give it back. He took it to the club secretary, Peter Barnes. I thought no more about it until my court action against Tottenham a year later, when I was told that the £8750 was apparently still in the safe. I have no idea why Barnes did not pass it directly to the accounts department.

The innuendo about the reasons for McLintock's cash payment was to resurface in court a year later, when Alan Sugar would also make even more sensational allegations about the ultimate destination of some of McLintock's money, but the mere involvement of agents in our transfer deals was also made to sound as if it was part of some web of corruption at Tottenham.

The use of agents is, of course, contrary to FA regulations, in certain given circumstances; it is also commonplace for managers and clubs to negotiate with agents, whatever the regulations might say. Even the FA itself has used an agent, John Smith. It is the way the football business works. When a player says, 'Talk to my agent,' what are you going to do, tell him to get lost? However, when a club is making a payment to an agent, it should always be on behalf of the player involved, part of the benefits he receives from the club. As such, it should be reported to the Inland Revenue on that player's P11D form – it is a benefit in kind. The Premier League Inquiry has now accepted this form of payment and the Premier League are amending their rules accordingly. Chief Executive Rick Parry told the *People* newspaper in June 1994, 'What is really important is that procedures are drawn up which say what agents can and cannot do. Penalties also have to be brought into force if an agent breaks the rules. These guys are here to stay, we have to accept that. It's now up to the Premier League and FA to draw up a set of proposals that are workable and achievable.'

Invoices received from agents were incorrect only in so far as they were worded to comply with the FA's rules as they then stood. Instead of invoices charging us for work involving transfers, which breached FA regulations, agents invoiced us for commercial work, which did not.

The media have led the barrage of criticism of agents, but there is a hidden agenda, another reason why some of the press are so strongly anti-agent. Before the advent of agents, reporters used to act as intermediaries between players and clubs. Players would tell a reporter that they wanted a move, and the reporter would then talk to clubs. The reporters were agents of sorts themselves, but they did not get paid in money, they got paid with an exclusive story, and that useful lever for later on, 'You owe me one'. That is why a few of the press have such a down on agents.

I certainly do not subscribe to the widely held view that agents or personal managers are a blight on the game. The mere word 'agent' seems to offend people, whereas if they are called 'accountants' or 'lawyers', there does not seem to be a problem. Players should have representation when negotiating contracts, because without it, they can be taken for a ride. Talented people are noted for their talent, not their wisdom in other areas. If you could do it yourself, you would not need an agent; they exist because there is a need for them. No one complains about actors, writers or even competitors in other sports having agents, so why should footballers be singled out and expected to negotiate their own contracts, while being forbidden the services of an agent?

People think that agents have just appeared in the game, but thirty years ago Jimmy Greaves, Denis Law and all the greats from that era who went to play in Italy were represented by a guy called Gigi Peronace. Clubs had better get used to them because agents are not going to go away.

Apart from working on transfers of established stars, agents also have a vital role to play in finding the stars of the future, for no club can afford to employ scouts in every country of the world. How do we find Cantona in France, Kanchelskis in the Ukraine, or Roger Milla in Cameroon as young players? We have got to have a wide network of people searching for players, which costs money. You try to convince some directors that you want to look for players overseas, and they say, 'Why do you want to spend all that money, when we can get Billy Smith from down the road?' but in all fairness, Billy Smith is not Eric Cantona. The Barcelonas and Milans spend a lot of money making sure that if great players like Gullit and Stoichkov become available, they know about them in advance, and they are in to sign them double-quick.

Quinton Fortune came to Tottenham by a fluke, purely because of my friendship with Barry Bridges, who knew a guy called Colin Gie. Quinton, from Cape Town, is an outstanding talent, a player that I always felt would be one of the youngest players ever to play for Tottenham. He was fifteen when I left Spurs, and had Tottenham done better in the 1993–94 season, I am sure he would have made his début then.

If Barry Bridges had not been living in South Africa, and Colin Gie had not known Barry, and Barry had not been a very good friend of mine, we would not have had the opportunity to sign this boy, and who knows how talented he may be? We cannot afford to rely on the coincidence of knowing people who know people. We have to know what is going on, not just in our own back-yard, but throughout the world of football.

'Monster' agent Eric Hall played no part in the Sheringham deal, but I dealt with him over another couple of players and our business dealings rekindled a friendship that dated back to the time I used to hang around Tin Pan Alley as a young player at Chelsea. Eric was then a 'gofer' at Mills Music, but he went on to become one of the most successful promotions men in the record business, working for some of the biggest names in music, including representing Frank Sinatra in this country.

He is well accepted in show business, but Eric offends the sporting world, because he is really a showbiz agent. He is a rough diamond and a very much larger than life character – loud clothes, loud voice, big cigar and plenty of razzmatazz. Yvette has frequently told him to tone down his showbiz image, but it is just the way he is. Players like him, but some club directors are rather less enthusiastic, though he has a heart even bigger than one of his trademark cigars.

He got into the business of being a football agent almost by accident after Steve Perryman, then captain of Spurs, asked if he would represent him. Steve liked what he did and Eric's circle of contacts widened rapidly. Eric knew virtually nothing about the football business then, but he is a very quick learner, not afraid to ask for advice, though willing to bluff his way through, if he has no other option.

He doesn't have a clue about football – you mention 'flanks' to him and he will say, 'What, like a flank of wood or something?' – but he is good at his job and very honest. He is also honest in admitting that he does take a percentage. His biggest kick, however, is that the client thinks that he is the best there is. His ego has to be comforted more than anything else. His only problem is that he cannot take 'yes' for an answer, he will keep talking nineteen to the dozen, as if he has hinges on his jaw. You say, 'Okay, Eric, you've got the deal,' and he will say, 'Yes, but you don't realise there's another thing . . .'

Not long after he became a football agent, Eric had phoned me up in Barcelona, to ask for advice. I helped him out then, but it did not do me much good; he still does me absolutely no favours when we are doing a deal, and he no longer needs advice from anyone. Eric is a friend of my family and me, not my agent. I have never had an agent negotiating for me.

Eric's friendship was once thoroughly tested by Yvette. He

was having a drink at Scribes one night when she decided to set him up with an exploding cigar. She sabotaged one in his cigar case and we sat back to await the explosion. Eric stayed for several hours, lighting a succession of cigars from the case, but the firework display never happened, and Yvette wrote it off as a dud. The next day Eric met Manchester City chairman Francis Lee to negotiate a deal. They haggled long and hard, but eventually reached agreement. To celebrate, Eric gave Francis a cigar. Later that night, Eric received a somewhat irate call from Mr Lee about a cigar that had exploded in his face at the end of a formal dinner . . .

Teddy Sheringham made a hesitant start at White Hart Lane, as players often do at a new club. It takes them time to find their feet and establish a rapport with their team-mates, but fans – and directors – often conclude that the signing has been a mistake and rubbish both the player and the manager who signed him, only to be the first in line with the plaudits when the player starts to show his true worth.

Tottenham's current and former chairmen were both guilty of that over Sheringham. Sugar expressed his opinion in his customary forthright way, while Irving Scholar, who still came to Tottenham away games, carrying a torch for the club like a jilted lover, whispered to a Manchester United director, 'This Sheringham will be Terry Venables' Achilles' heel.' The remark said much about Scholar's attitude towards me and his football wisdom, for Sheringham went on to become the top scorer in the Premier League, the winner of the Golden Boot, presented to the game's highest goal-scorer.

Darren Anderton also got a rubbishing from the directors' box after his transfer from Portsmouth. Jim Gregory had bought control of Portsmouth after selling QPR, but had lost none of his relish for haggling over deals with me. Anderton was not on the transfer list, but I liked the look of the player and asked Jim to name a figure for him. When Jim told me his price, I said, 'No, not that one, give me another one.' After he had named about twenty different prices, we finally agreed on one that was a bit nearer to my valuation.

The critical remarks about Darren Anderton and Teddy Sheringham from Sugar, Berry and co., continued for some time after I bought them, and I could sense that the fans were not too sure either, because both lads did start off slowly. It was natural that the fans would have a go, but the directors should have known better. When we played in the Cup at Norwich, who were top of the League at the time, a great ball in from Anderton was met by a superb header from Sheringham, for a brilliant goal. There were few complaints about Anderton and Sheringham after that.

Not every signing I have made has worked out, of course. I am no more infallible than anyone else. I will spare my own and the players' blushes by not naming the signings that did not work out, but strangely enough I do not consider the one that is most often held against me to have been a mistake at all. I sold Neil Ruddock soon after joining Tottenham and then re-signed him two or three years later for a much bigger fee. On the face of it, that may seem a pretty stupid thing to have done, but there had been a change in the circumstances of both the player and Tottenham. We had originally bought Ruddock for about £50,000, but were trying to get money together to make a quick buy, and my feeling, reinforced by the other coaching staff, who had known him much longer, was that while Ruddock would be a good player, it would take two or three years. He had some rough edges and was not the finished article at that stage. We felt that things were so bad that we could not afford to wait and had to do something immediately, so in the end we felt that both Ruddock and John Polsten, who was a similar case, should go.

They were both players that needed a bit of experience, and Neil also needed to learn to calm down. Polsten went to

Norwich, and we sold Ruddock to Millwall for about £300,000. What happened at Millwall and Southampton, where he went next, vindicated our opinion of the player at the time. He did not really play at centre-half and was not in the team much at Millwall, and got moved on to Southampton.

He then started to improve, but still had a disciplinary problem, and was out for a few weeks after head-butting someone. I believe the Southampton coaches then worked with him in the afternoons, getting his weight down and his thinking improved. When his contract was up, we bought him back. We needed a player in his position and I was quite happy to re-sign him; I would have been pretty stupid not to have done so, if he was the best available in his position, just because we had sold him a couple of years before.

Sugar said that he realised I was a bad businessman when we bought Ruddock for £750,000, after I had told Sugar he was only worth £350,000, but Sugar had misunderstood what he was told. I had explained on several occasions to him that, through the process of the tribunal system, we would offer the lowest price that we could justify, while Southampton would ask the highest figure that they could justify, and the way the tribunal works, the final price would be somewhere in the middle.

We could genuinely offer £350,000 against Southampton's valuation of £1.6 million, because of his bad disciplinary record, which is why I also put Ruddock on a lower contract than he could have expected, but told him that if he proved over the year that his discipline was better, I would give him a better contract. Neil went along with this and did respond very well. Sugar learned a little, but not enough, from this, for when Calderwood came up the next year, Spurs also offered £350,000 for him; however, without the excuse of a poor disciplinary record, the tribunal effectively said that Tottenham were 'taking the mick' and made them pay £1.25 million.

Despite all the problems between us, there were plenty of

things that Sugar and I saw eye to eye on in the early stages of our working relationship. We were in complete agreement on the need to end the practice of making payments to directors, for example. To have a good board, the directors should be giving something to the club instead of just having the perks of being a director. I looked to Jonathan Crystal to help out on the legal side of things, for instance, and he never received a penny for doing this.

Nat Solomon, who had been brought on to the Scholar board in 1990, at the suggestion of Midland Bank when they were contemplating putting the company into receivership, was on a salary of £40,000 a year from Tottenham at the time of the takeover, but in Spurs' overall interests, he generously agreed to accept a much lower figure. Sugar took charge of negotiations with Solomon, and by September 1992 he was gone from the board altogether, although Sugar softened the blow by allowing Solomon to keep his tickets in the directors' box. Solomon's departure was a serious weakening of the board, however. He was well respected in the City and could have been counted on to make impartial and correct decisions, in line with business ethics and City regulations. He also balanced the board, between the increasingly hostile factions of Sugar and Sandy on the one hand and Venables and Crystal on the other, with Berry an enigmatic floating voter in the middle. When Solomon was removed, he should have been replaced by another non-executive director, but when asked about it, Sugar, whose dislike of non-executive directors is well documented, would only reply, 'Not just yet'. David Buchler, the insolvency practitioner brought in at the same time as Solomon, could also have been relied upon to take a correct and impartial view, but Sugar wanted him off the board, and he too was removed.

Sugar was not entirely consistent in trying to eliminate payments to directors, because in December 1992, without informing the other directors, Colin Sandy drew up a 'company to company' contract with Sugar's Jersey company, Amshold, on behalf of Tottenham, awarding Sugar £50,000. Amshold provided Sugar's services to Tottenham, yet as a non-executive chairman, there was no reason for Sugar to be paid at all. It provoked a furious boardroom row when it was eventually disclosed in January 1993.

The 1992–93 season went really well for Spurs, not in trophies won, but in the continuing development of a side that could challenge for them the next year. There was a buzz about the place that I had not known since I had rejoined the club. Former Spurs winger Cliff Jones said he thought it was the best football Tottenham had played since the Double team, which made me very proud. It is easy to say, but I do believe that the Spurs side would have been in contention in the Cups the following season and could even have been a Championship side. We shall never know now.

We had high hopes of repeating the FA Cup win of two years previously when we once again found ourselves drawn against Arsenal in the semi-final. I had a pretty good record against Arsenal, which is the first essential for anyone involved with Spurs. In the first season after the takeover, we did not lose to them, and in the second year, 1992–93, we beat them twice in the League, but lost the most vital game of all, the Cup semi-final, 1–0 to a Tony Adams goal, headed from a free-kick. Everybody on the bench could see Adams moving up and we were all on our feet together, screaming at the Tottenham wall to mark Adams. We could see what was going to happen, it was like watching the whole thing in slow-motion, Adams moving down the field towards the goal, the free-kick coming over and Adams rising, unmarked, to head the only goal of the game.

It is interesting to speculate whether the events of May 1993 would have happened had Tottenham won that semi-final and been in the FA Cup final once more. Would Sugar have levelled the allegations that he did at the time that he did? As it was, I was sacked on the day before the Cup final. I will always believe that it was the crowd that finished Sugar with me. The team was successful, the younger players like Darren Anderton and Nicky Barmby were playing well, Teddy Sheringham was scoring the goals, but when the crowd chanted 'Terry Venables' blue and white army', I saw Sugar clearly discomfited. He subsequently said in an interview in the *Sunday Telegraph*, 'Venables ain't put in as much money as me, why are they chanting his name and not mine?' He was a kind of frustrated celebrity, or that is certainly the way he came across. He was a very wealthy man, but scarcely a household name. His question reminded me of a famous occasion when Don Revie's Leeds United were sweeping all before them, and a Leeds director, the owner of a laundry, demanded to know, 'Why is it that Revie gets all the credit?'

Sugar apparently no longer wanted to share the limelight – or the profits – with me, and once we had lost to the Arsenal in the Cup, he felt that he could do better on his own. Tottenham's fortunes had clearly prospered under our joint regime, and initially there had been a healthy dialogue between us, but Sugar now wanted no dialogue at all.

The specific issues over which we fell out were computerisation and merchandising. All the rubbish about 'back-handers' and everything else has appeared long after the event; there was no mention of any of it at the time. It is a huge task to run a big football club, for even the core business – the football alone – is a full-time job. The peripheral activities at Tottenham included the catering, which was franchised, and the merchandising side, which should have been franchised, too, because initially it caused us a lot of problems. But we carried on doing it ourselves, very successfully, so that by pre-Christmas 1992, we were achieving record sales.

The October 1992 management accounts included a £75,000 provision against stock loss, however, which was suddenly inserted and, when translated to the profit-and-loss figures, made it look like an enormous loss had been sustained. The November sales figures were then understated, with sales that should have been included in that month's accounts, held over to December. Mike Pay, who was in charge of the department, and his assistant, Ivy Calvino, were then summarily dismissed by Colin Sandy. The sackings could have laid the club open to serious compensation claims, and only the goodwill between Pay and Calvino and me resolved that.

The departure of Pay and Calvino enabled Sugar and a millionaire friend of his, Harvey Gilbert, to take over the running of the department. Sugar saw it as the basis of a much wider mail-order scheme, once bragging, 'One of my mates has made a fortune out of egg-timers and carriage clocks.' In the annual financial statement, published in autumn 1993, there was a paragraph praising the contribution of the merchandising department to the overall figures. Yet you can have as many wonderful hats and shirts and badges as you like, but if the team is not successful, the merchandising sales will reflect that lack of success. In addition, the contribution of merchandising to the total operating income was less than 10 per cent, and the operating profit it produced was very small. Despite all the marvels of the modern age, the real money is made, as it always has been, in getting people to come through the turnstiles on a Saturday afternoon, and they only tend to do that to watch an attractive, winning team, not a bunch of 'other geezers'.

During the time I worked with him at White Hart Lane, Sugar surrounded himself with friends, acquaintances, associates and relatives. His friend Harvey Gilbert said at his interview that he did not want to be paid for working on merchandising, which was a considerable point in his favour. When the board minutes recording this were circulated, however, Sugar insisted on deleting the reference to Gilbert not being paid, and shortly afterwards, Gilbert was receiving £40,000 – twice as much as

Mike Pay, whom he had replaced. When protests were made, Sugar's response was: 'It's not your fucking business, keep your head out of it.'

Nick Hewer, a public-relations man who also represents Amstrad, was put on the pay-roll by Sugar at a fee of £1500 per month plus expenses, despite the existence of a highly efficient Tottenham press department. Hewer's company, Michael Joyce Consultants, obtained £42,000 from the club in 1991–92. Touche Ross, Sugar's accountants, replaced Peat Marwick on the pay-roll and received £72,000 in the same period. Sugar had sold us the idea of the change because he said that they would be cheaper, but they turned out to be more expensive. Sugar's lawyers, Herbert Smith, were also paid £41,000 from Tottenham by January 1993, of which £4,112.50, though paid by Tottenham, related to Sugar's legal costs in underwriting the rights issue. The bill had been mailed to him at his home address, a matter raised at the board meeting on 25 February 1993.

Sugar's brother Derek – who oddly has the different surname of Shaw – worked at Tottenham for a while. Colin Sandy's services, and those of his secretary – Sugar's daughter, Louise – were provided through Amsprop, another Sugar company, for £4000 per month, plus £1000 per month in expenses. Amsprop received £96,000 of Tottenham's money in 1991 and 1992. Claude Littner, an Amstrad man, is now managing director and Sugar's son Daniel has also joined the Sugar 'team' at Tottenham.

Sugar's power within the company further increased with the introduction of a new computer system. Tottenham was a comparatively small plc, but was structured into several departments, which had different operating systems. Apart from the football-club administration and accounts, there were sizeable departments such as the ticket office – where the control system was of paramount importance, for obvious reasons – merchandising, a developing membership scheme involving over 20,000 members, and commercial activities including advertising, sponsorship and television.

Early in our partnership, we had agreed to revamp the computer system at Tottenham and a committee was set up consisting of Eddie Ashby, Colin Sandy and Richard Simmons, a systems analyst from Amstrad. The committee agreed that we should get a decent central computer, located at White Hart Lane, and a series of sub-systems for the departments, linked to the central computer. From September 1992 onwards, however, Sandy and Simmons took to meeting without notifying Eddie and the computerisation plan was changed. Instead of developing an indigenous system at White Hart Lane, a modem link was to be introduced connecting Tottenham to Amstrad in Brentwood, with all the Tottenham systems becoming nothing more than an extension of Amstrad. I was alarmed at this discovery.

While it is true that the board minutes of 29 October 1992 actually refer to a discussion of the linkage to Amstrad, the discussion only covered merchandising, not the linkage of the whole system. Surprisingly, that was not accurately reflected in the minutes of the meeting issued by Colin Sandy. After a free and frank discussion of Sugar and Sandy's minutes – a constant source of friction between us – I commissioned an independent report into the idea of the computer linkage from Creative Project Management, since my own knowledge of computers is as short as Sugar's temper.

Meanwhile, the work was apparently still going on to set up the previously agreed central system at White Hart Lane, just across the corridor from Eddie's office. We only discovered this was not the case after Eddie was reinstated on the computerisation committee in February 1993, when Richard Simmons casually dropped a systems diagram on to the table at a meeting. Eddie picked it up, and after studying it for a moment, discovered that the supposed central computer at Tottenham had already been by-passed by a direct modem link to Amstrad at Brentwood.

When raised at board level, it was described as 'the cheapest option'; not only was that incorrect, but, irrespective of the cost, the fundamental point was that the administration's information system had been removed from White Hart Lane and my direct control, to Brentwood. That is the beginning of the end in terms of how you control your business. It is like trying to fly a jet without having any instruments. If all the information is being diverted to a remote facility before you clap eyes on it, or is not available to you on demand, you are completely powerless to act.

That was the position in which I found myself early in 1993. On more than one occasion, I was told that information I required urgently could not be obtained, because other Amstrad projects were ahead of Tottenham in the queue. 'We might be able to get to it in two or three days' time' was the response when I phoned Amstrad about the delays. On top of that, without obtaining the necessary approvals under public-company regulations, all of the hardware and software supporting this system, and the income relating to it, had effectively been siphoned off to Amstrad. Sugar was also demanding a service charge for the facilities provided.

At my instruction, Eddie fired off four or five memos to Colin Sandy, requiring details of how much had been spent on computerisation with Amstrad. When Eddie finally cornered him in his office, Sandy told him that he was under orders from Alan Sugar not to reveal the information. I then summoned Sandy to a meeting in my office, with Eddie also present, and Sandy repeated his earlier refusal to disclose the information – requested, lest we forget, by the chief executive of Tottenham Hotspur plc – saying, 'It's more than my life's worth.'

The purchase of computer equipment had been the subject of a friendly conversation between Sugar and Sandy at a previous board meeting, in the course of which Sandy said that he had acquired some hardware for Tottenham. The fact that it was actually a mixture of unsaleable stock and used equipment from Amstrad was not revealed to the board and was only uncovered later, by which time we had no other choice than to accept the link to Amstrad's mainframe.

Incidents such as these further increased the friction between Sugar and me, but the beginning of the end came at a board meeting on 6 May, at 4:25 on a Thursday afternoon. We met in the Spurs boardroom on the fourth floor, with its windows looking out over the entrance to the ground. The meetings were routinely held on Thursdays, starting at 1:30 p.m., and for almost three hours we had been covering the agenda without any more than the normal acrimony.

We were once more discussing the White Hart Lane computer system, when I tabled the report that I had commissioned from Creative Project Management. It cast substantial doubts on whether the link to Amstrad's mainframe was an appropriate system for Tottenham, suggesting that it was not the labour-saving, cost-cutting dream scheme that was being suggested. I put it to Sugar that the costs associated with the link to Amstrad were unjustified and that there was a more cost-efficient way forward. Jonathan Crystal, who was pouring himself a cup of coffee at the time, supported me. Sugar immediately lost his senses, and rather than confront me directly, rose to his feet and charged across the room towards Jonathan, screaming, 'You c**t, you fucking c**t, you arse-licking fucking c**t.'

I put myself between them, because I was afraid that Sugar was going to hit him. Sugar then ran back to his seat, tipped the contents of his briefcase all over the table and stormed out. As he left, he threw a letter at me, saying, 'You'd better read this.' The letter told me that I was fired. There had been no advance warning of what Sugar was planning, but the letter was obviously premeditated. It was like carrying a knife in your pocket – you do not arm yourself with a weapon like that unless you intend to use it.

Even when he tossed the letter at me, Sugar still could not meet my eyes. He evidently did not have the guts to take me on head to head and instead displayed his aggression towards Jonathan, attacking me by proxy. The end result was the same, however. In football you can take a broken leg better than you can take spit in your face, and what Sugar had done was the equivalent of spitting in my face. There could be no backtracking now, this was war.

In the initial stages of our partnership, Sugar had been prepared to listen and implement ideas other than his own, but later, particularly after the rights issue, he regarded his money as being the casting vote, the trump card, and his patience with people who put up a contrary argument began to diminish. It was like a game of Monopoly to him: he who had the most money won. If you went along with Sugar, that was fine, there would be some peace and quiet, but there were some decisions, like Sugar awarding himself money without telling the board, that any director acting in the bona-fide interests of a football club, particularly a club that was not flush with cash, would have had to query. It should have been cleared with the directors, but when it was finally discovered and raised at a board meeting, it led to volcanic eruptions from Sugar. It was his money and his club, end of story. Sugar hated the fact that we would not just nod our heads and do what he said. He always thought that he knew better.

In throwing a letter of dismissal at me, Sugar had acted unilaterally without reference to the board – his money, his club. The letter had no legal force and Sugar would have to call a further meeting of the Tottenham plc board to legitimise his actions. Surprisingly, I felt pretty calm, thinking, What do I do now, what have I got to sort out? I was not expecting it at that particular time, but I was not wholly surprised, because we had spoken once or twice about buying each other out, but Sugar had said, 'It shouldn't have to come to that at all. The only reason would be that there can only be one boss. You want to do things your way, I want to do things my way, and I'm the biggest shareholder.' When I asked him how he would feel if someone tried to take Amstrad off his hands, he did not respond.

It is comparatively easy to replace a chief executive, but having the right coach is the most vital ingredient in building a successful football team, and the skills of player-trading and player development are rare. When I asked Sugar whom he would get to replace someone with my football knowledge, his reply was, 'I'll just get another geezer in.' Sugar, like many other chairmen and directors, is completely ignorant of the quality of the people employed as coaches. They seem to take the attitude that there are always people out there in the marketplace who will do the job cheaper, but that does not mean they will do it better.

What made my sacking even more frustrating was that we were on the verge of great things. I am sure that, at the minimum, we would have qualified for Europe the next season and I thought that we would have won a domestic Cup, if not the League itself. We had got it right on the field, and it is so hard to get right that when you do, you do not let it go, whatever happens – if it works, for God's sake, don't try and mend it. To see all the promise turn into the shambles after I was sacked, with the team struggling to avoid relegation most of the season, was a bitter disappointment. I felt that I had completely wasted my time and effort. My emotions were a bit like seeing your worst enemy driving over a cliff in your brand-new car. To be honest, I found it hard not to enjoy Sugar's discomfiture, but I was saddened to see Spurs in the doldrums. The year before, the club's prospects had been good in the short term and tremendous in the long term. I told Sugar and the board that all we needed was two more experienced players, who might have cost £4 million. Sugar would not countenance spending that sort of money to build a potential Championship side, but then spent more than that trying to avoid relegation.

Running a football club is a common-sense matter for the most part; things fall into place if you use your head, but the most difficult things are the results on the field. You have to get the best out of the players that you have and while the tactics and coaching are very important, the most vital thing is the atmosphere at a club. Buying players like Gazza and Gary Lineker helps enormously, but when you find Lineker watching the kids training after he has finished his own training session and Gazza actually joining in with them, that creates a spirit which is appealing to everyone at the club.

No one can put a value on that aura that surrounds a club, the hardest thing to create and the easiest thing to destroy. We had that atmosphere at Tottenham. Star players could sense it and were attracted to it, and we were also beating Manchester United, Arsenal and Liverpool to the best young players. When you are trying to attract young talent, mums and dads can smell that atmosphere and want their children to be part of it. They want them to be happy and fulfilled, as any parent does, not just going somewhere for a few extra quid. If the atmosphere is bad, however, then everything starts going wrong. The atmosphere now has changed and if they do not get it back, the young players will stop going to White Hart Lane.

Youth-team coach Keith Waldon, sacked by Sugar in May 1994, told the Daily Star that it was already happening: 'Morale is the worst I have ever known at any club. I can't believe things have slumped so dramatically, so quickly. It's not just the immediate future that's a worry. We have to be concerned about the long-term prospects. I know for a fact that kids lined up to come straight here from school are having second thoughts, in view of what has been going on.'

All the time that the feud with Sugar had been raging, the football – and the profitability of the club – was improving in leaps and bounds. An annual loss in May 1991 of just under £3 million, had been converted to a profit of £3 million in my first year as chief executive. In the year ending May 1993, although the company did not subsequently return this profit, the April management accounts of that year showed a forecast of £5 million, and reported that Tottenham had already made in excess of £4 million.

Balance sheets deal largely in tangible assets. Football teams are not quite so easy to sort out, but the rich crop of young stars like Barmby, Walker, Hill, Watson, Turner and Nethercott from the youth policy that I had put in place was starting to pay enormous dividends – in financial as well as playing terms. The estimated value of this home-grown talent increased the value of the company by another £10–12 million from the date of the takeover.

In that time, Sugar had hardly shown his face, except to attend board meetings. He never appeared at the training ground, nor visited the dressing room. His later allegation against me that I was not up to managing the club is absolutely refuted by the success I achieved. The 'product' of the company – the football – was beginning to look fabulous, and the financial performance was equally impressive. Under my guidance as Chief Executive, Tottenham had actually improved its worth to the tune of approaching £20 million.

Yet Sugar fired me. Never once had he had cause for complaint about my conduct as chief executive, nor of Eddie Ashby's performance as my assistant. All the mud was thrown in retrospect. In my view, it is clear that he saw the massive potential value of Tottenham, when it had been put right. I must have stood in his way.

After my sacking, I had the company independently valued by Coopers & Lybrand, who put its worth at around £30 million. At the time of our purchase, it was valued at £7.5 million, and the shares were suspended – arguably worthless.

Had I wanted to sell out, I could therefore have reasonably expected three to four times the value of my investment in May 1993. Yet Sugar's reportedly 'generous' offer for my shares, made at the time of my sacking, was less than I had actually paid two years earlier. He also offered me a derisory sum for the termination of my contract, which had more than three years to run.

The next stage in Sugar's campaign came at 'the board meeting that never was', held for the first and only time in Tottenham's history at the home of Arsenal, Highbury Stadium, on the evening of Tuesday, 11 May, when Spurs were meeting Arsenal in a League game. I arrived at Highbury with Jonathan Crystal at 6:35 p.m., and went to the dressing room, while Jonathan went upstairs to the Arsenal boardroom. Sugar, Berry and Sandy were already there. At about 6:50 p.m., Berry left the boardroom with Jonathan, to go to Berry's car for a telephone number they needed. They returned shortly after 7:00 p.m., when there was no indication that any meeting of the Tottenham board had taken place.

The 'minutes' of the meeting, signed by Alan Sugar, claim that it took place at 7:00 p.m. in the presence of Alan Sugar, Colin Sandy and Tony Berry, which is demonstrably false. Whatever discussions the three men may have had, a board meeting never took place, as Berry admitted to Jonathan in a telephone call at 12:50 p.m. on 13 May, when he acknowledged that the board minute did not reflect what had taken place and told Jonathan that the best thing was that the matter should all 'just be forgotten about'. The company secretary, John Ireland, also sent a letter to Jonathan on 13 May, in which it was implicitly accepted by Tony Berry that 'the board minute is a sham'. Sugar himself, while insisting that the meeting had taken place, later admitted that it was not validly convened, because no notice had been issued to two directors, Jonathan Crystal and me, nor to the company secretary.

The alleged board meeting at Arsenal was probably one of the darkest moments in Spurs' history, the ultimate sell-out, held at the ground of our greatest rivals. While I was down in the dressing room with the players, three of my fellow-directors were conspiring together to create a situation where I could be outvoted at a genuine board meeting, held at White Hart Lane two days later. I was sickened and felt that not only I, but also the club had been betrayed.

To get rid of me altogether from White Hart Lane, Sugar had to sack me from both Tottenham Hotspur plc and Tottenham Hotspur Football and Athletic Club. To sack me from the plc, Sugar only needed a majority of the board to back him, but under the Articles of Association of the football club, you have to call an Extraordinary General Meeting, giving twenty-one days' notice, before you can sack a director. There is a loophole, however. If all the shareholders consent, you can dispense with the twenty-one days' notice. Tottenham Hotspur plc owned 99 of the 100 shares in Tottenham Hotspur Football and Athletic Club. The only share missing was the one held by the former managing director, Ian Gray, the recipient of a £260,000 settlement from Tottenham. The sole purpose of the Highbury 'board meeting', was apparently to legitimise the transfer of his share into Colin Sandy's name, effectively giving it to Sugar, since Sandy was hardly known for his fierce independence.

Once the share had been transferred, Sugar could issue what is called 'A Consent to Short Notice' and hold an EGM immediately. All the members of the football club – Tottenham Hotspur plc and Colin Sandy – being present, it was unanimously resolved to alter the Articles of Association of the Football Club and remove two directors from its board: Terry Venables and Jonathan Crystal.

That final showdown came at the plc board meeting held on 14 May 1993, which, on this occasion, was properly convened. I knew that I faced a long, hard and bitter struggle, with very little likelihood that I would be at Tottenham the following year. I told Doug Livermore, Ray Clemence and Ted Buxton what was about to happen, but the players were not informed at that stage.

A couple of days before the meeting, Sugar spoke on the telephone to Eddie Ashby. Tony Berry had already made contact with Eddie twice and offered him 'a year's money to go'. Sugar now reaffirmed that offer: 'I think that Terry is getting a load of bum advice from fucking Jonathan Crystal, who doesn't know fuck-all about financial affairs and keeps giving Terry a load of shit about all this. You are a bloke that understands these things and I want to tell you so that you can tell Terry what this is all about. Do you understand what I am talking about?'

'I'm trying,' said Eddie.

'I'm going to give to you on a "one to ten" so that you understand and can make Terry understand,' Sugar continued. 'One – the fucking game is over. There is no fucking compromise. Two – I've made a diplomatic offer, so Terry wipes his face. Three – Friday's board meeting will terminate his contracts. He'll be given the name and address of the lawyers to sue for his money and he'll be asked to leave the premises.

'I want you to understand that I don't need these fucking shares. I swear on my children's life, I don't need these fucking shares. What do I get? Another fucking 20 per cent and I'm £3 million out. I swear by all that is holy to me, I'm trying to find a way out for him. I've made him a generous offer.'

'Terry is not an idiot,' said Eddie. 'He can do his own arithmetic for himself.'

'I haven't spoken to you for a year,' went on Sugar. 'I made my point and that's it. You've been part and parcel of talks with Terry. Tony offered you a deal . . . the deal is still open to you.'

'How much?'

'When you started, you got Ian Gray's money, £50K or something like that. You can have a year's money.'

'I bill £7K per month, what are you saying?'

'The car and expenses are another matter, but we can talk about that. If you're his friend, tell him there will be a fucking big hoo-hah in the press. If it has to get dirty, then okay. Tottenham is a big name, it will last 140 years after I've gone. Terry Venables will be forgotten five weeks into the new season. I wish to avoid confrontation, but if it has to be, it will be. Friday is a foregone conclusion. There will be no debate. It will last ten seconds. As a plc, we will be forced to make an announcement. Do you understand?'

'I understand. I will pass all you have said on to Terry.'

Eddie came to see me immediately to tell me what had occurred. On the Thursday, the day before the meeting, Sugar again tried to get through to him and left messages for him all over the place, but Eddie did not respond.

Sugar was not content with tying up Gray's share and trying to buy off Eddie. He rang Jonathan Crystal on the Thursday before the plc board meeting and warned him that if he did not go along with what Sugar wanted, his name would be splashed all over the newspapers and he would be ruined. Jonathan refused to play ball and Sugar did his best to live up to his threat.

Having failed with their attempts through Eddie to get me to 'go quietly', both Sugar and Berry now tried the direct approach, asking me to walk away from Tottenham and not complain about my sacking, and telling me, 'You're the best coach there is, you could go abroad and get a job,' as if that made everything that had gone on quite all right. I found their belief that I would take it lying down, scarcely credible.

The meeting on Friday, 14 May 1993, was a fiasco. Five directors were present, Sugar, Colin Sandy, Tony Berry, Jonathan Crystal and me, and the company secretary, John Ireland. There were also three sets of lawyers – my own; Peter Leaver, a barrister who was advising Tony Berry; and Margaret Mountford of Herbert Smith. Since Herbert Smith were by now both Sugar's and Tottenham's lawyers, I was uncertain who they were actually advising at the meeting, Sugar as an individual or the Tottenham board. As usual, Sugar sat at the head of the table, I sat to his right, with Tony Berry next to me, and Jonathan Crystal sat at Sugar's left, with Colin Sandy next to him.

As soon as the meeting started, Sugar proposed a resolution terminating my employment as chief executive of the plc, and acted to block me from voting on the grounds that I had an interest. The shareholders' agreement would also have prevented Sugar from voting, of course, and should even have prevented Sugar from proposing the resolution in the first place.

The votes of Colin Sandy and Jonathan Crystal were predictable – Crystal would vote for me, Sandy for Sugar. Tony Berry's vote thus became the pivotal one. If he voted in favour of me, I stayed; if he voted against me, I was gone. Strangely, when the vote came, Berry did not even cast his vote himself, but gave his adviser, Peter Leaver, his proxy. Leaver abstained on his behalf, and Sugar, whether constitutionally or not, made the decisive vote in favour of his own resolution. Berry's abstention, via Leaver, shocked me, for I had thought that he would be on my side. He later said in court that, had it been necessary, he would have voted against me. Now firmly in the Sugar camp, Berry remains a member of the Tottenham board.

Berry, a bald-headed guy, who looks like a 6'2" Max Wall, had also been a member of the previous board, but despite his passionate interest in the club, he claimed to have no knowledge whatsoever of the improprieties carried out by that regime. Berry had also been the subject of a DTI report into his personal involvement in the Blue Arrow scandal. While Sugar has been quick to use Eddie Ashby's bankruptcies against him and me, he was happy for Berry to remain a director, despite the serious criticism of him by the DTI inspectors. They had been investigating among other things, a £25 million loan from

Blue Arrow that had been made to a company owned by Peter de Savary.

I pointed out to Sugar how wrong it was to treat Eddie Ashby differently from Tony Berry. Some months later, Berry expressed the opinion that Eddie Ashby should leave Tottenham because of his business history, an astonishing comment in view of the DTI's views of Berry's own business record. Things came to a head one day when Berry was trying to argue the merits of one of Sugar's latest brainwaves with Eddie, who would not accept it and told him, 'You're all Sugar-lumps – Sugar's clones.' Not long after that Berry announced that he wanted Eddie out.

Berry had initially been supportive of my attempts to acquire the club and had actually been part of the consortium put together by Larry Gillick, with the three of us to be equal partners. Berry remained a supporter of my attempts to take over Tottenham, but when the original bid fell through, he walked away, leaving me with all the legal costs of the bid, including his own share – £50,000. At some point, he had clearly shifted to the Sugar camp, which was a surprising state of affairs, because before October 1992, Berry never had a kind word for Sugar, considering him, among other things, to be ignorant about football matters. That Berry in the end contributed to the assassination in the Roman forum that was White Hart Lane is beyond argument because of the way his vote was cast.

Peter Leaver's role as Berry's adviser was not his first involvement at Tottenham. He had been a director in 1983–84, at a time when the board was beginning its irregular dealings with 'loans' to Ossie Ardiles. Leaver came off the board shortly afterwards, but was retained as counsel by Tottenham in 1992, specifically to advise on whether the club should make disclosure of all loans and misdemeanours to the authorities. He advised Tottenham that there was no need to make disclosure, as from June 1992 they had become members of the Premier League and were no longer responsible to the Football League. The argument is ingenuous, as opposed to ingenious, for the Premier League, like the Football League, comes under the overall authority of the FA; saying you are now married to one daughter instead of another, does not protect you from the wrath of the angry parents.

Having removed me, Sugar's next move was to announce that Douglas Alexiou, a relic from the Scholar board, would be re-elected back to the board of the plc. I was shocked. Alexiou was married to the daughter of the former chairman of Tottenham, Sidney Wale, who had been ousted by Irving Scholar's boardroom coup seven years previously. Alexiou had remained on the board, however, and as a director under Scholar, he shared responsibility for what had gone on at that time.

The old Scholar board had now virtually been reconstituted under a different chairman. Peter Barnes was still club secretary, two of the directors under Scholar – Tony Berry and Douglas Alexiou – still had their feet firmly under the boardroom table, while Irving Scholar and Ian Gray also apparently enjoyed complete immunity from legal action to recover the losses to Tottenham incurred during their tenure.

As I drove away from White Hart Lane, one of my grandfather Ossie's sayings came into my head: 'What's right is right, and what's wrong is no man's right.' I thought, We'll see if you're right, Ossie, your bloody saying is really going to be put to the test this time.

# CHAPTER NINE

# The Long Road Back

### 1993–94

IF SUGAR THOUGHT that he had seen the last of me, he was quickly made aware of his mistake. The board meeting ended at 11:50 a.m. and I left the ground through throngs of Tottenham supporters, who had gathered to cheer me on and vent their anger on Sugar. When he emerged a few minutes later, the fans left him in no doubts about the strength of their feelings. Until that moment, I am sure that Sugar did not understand the emotions that football supporters invest in their club. He had never understood that football is not like a computer business, dealing with inanimate objects, but a people business, dealing with human beings and their emotions. His comments to the press at the time said it all: 'I feel like the man who shot Bambi . . . I don't know what all the fuss is about, managers always come and go.' That is not true – only the unsuccessful ones go – and in any event, how many managers have put up £3.5 million to have that happen to them?

Apart from my own feelings, the reaction of the fans and the public was equally instrumental in persuading me to fight it through the courts. People do not always believe that, or feel that it was naïve of me, but the amount of popular support that I was getting at the time was a powerful influence. It was heartening for me, but it would take more than demonstrations by Tottenham supporters to force Sugar to change his mind, and within an hour I was closeted with my lawyers. Their advice was to seek an injunction to reverse the Tottenham board's decision to sack me, pending a full court hearing. The case was in court by late afternoon, but it was not until after nine o'clock that night that the news came through that the judge had granted the injunction.

It was my first bit of good news in quite some time. Yvette and I cracked a bottle of champagne, but we both knew it was only the initial battle in what would be a long and bloody war. Had I known then just how long and bitter it would become, I might have thought harder about the course on which I was embarking.

The sacking was timed for after the final game of the season, preventing the embarrassing possibility of anti-Sugar demonstrations at Spurs games, but 2500 turned up at a testimonial match at Enfield that evening to stage a demonstration in support of me. The Tottenham Independent Supporters' Association, set up to counter the threat of a Robert Maxwell takeover two years before, rallied behind me against another overbearing tycoon, and Neil Ruddock and Teddy Sheringham led the support from the dressing room.

The battle-lines in the press were quickly drawn. The sports pages were largely sympathetic to me, the business pages to Sugar. Apart from *Today*, the Murdoch papers – part of a media empire including Sky Television, the *Sun*, the *News of the World*, and the *Sunday Times* – were uniformly hostile to me, however, a pattern that continued for some time. Within two days, the focus of attention had been broadened, to include Eddie Ashby and Jonathan Crystal as well as me. If I could not be damned directly, then it would be done by association. Mihir Bose, a friend of Irving Scholar and author of his biography, wrote an article in the *Sunday Times* dwelling on Eddie's business failures on the same day that the Sunday morning LBC radio programme of then *Sunday Times* editor, Andrew Neil, gave Sugar a platform for a character assassination of Jonathan Crystal, in which he stated: 'I blame Jonathan

Crystal for everything that has happened to this company in the past two years – I firmly blame him for everything ... Terry will reflect in years to come how his dream to run and own part of a football club was destroyed basically by Jonathan Crystal and nobody else.' It was a bizarre accusation against a non-executive director who had never taken a penny out of the club, but Sugar's next verbal assault on Jonathan Crystal was to be even worse.

Sugar lost no time in removing anyone tainted by their links with me from Tottenham. Eddie Ashby's consultancy was terminated on Monday 17 May, and my secretary, Penny Sawford, who had been promised by Sugar that nothing would happen to her after my departure, was then sacked within a week, along with Eddie Ashby's secretary. Spurs physiotherapist Dave Butler and chief scout Ted Buxton went the same way, and my daughter Tracey, who ran Spurs' international members club, was also sacked.

In the months following my sacking, a relentless newspaper campaign continued against my associates and me. They dumped so much garbage that while I was answering one set of false allegations, another load would be heaped on me from a different direction. I was so busy defending my goal that I could not mount any attacks of my own.

A stream of pro-Sugar stories appeared in the papers, while journalists trying to file stories countering the blizzard of allegations found that their copy was spiked. I showed documents and papers in support of my case to two senior reporters on one newspaper. They went out punching the air going 'What a story we've got' and the next day they came back embarrassed, because not a word went in.

Almost every day there seemed to be fresh allegations doing the rounds, many dusted off, reworded and trotted out for the second or third time. We began to refer to Scribes as 'The Bunker', evoking the wartime spirit we were starting to feel.

Even 'The Bunker' was not beyond the reach of my enemies, however. A friendly journalist on one of the tabloids rang to warn me that he had overheard a plan by some of his colleagues to 'plant' two girls carrying drugs in the loos at Scribes. A photographer had been sent to get the pictures. We immediately doubled the 'guards' on the front door and the photographer returned empty-handed.

I was surprised about the difference in treatment given to the two sides of the argument in two television programmes with Jimmy Greaves. I did not expect any favours from Greavesie, even though he was a team-mate from way back, but equally I did not expect him to give Sugar an armchair ride in the first programme and then attack Eddie Ashby and me.

I have since heard that Sugar decided right at the last minute that he was not going to go on the programme, a question-and-answer session with a studio audience, chaired by Jimmy, who had to ring him and persuade him to change his mind. When he reached the studios, Sugar objected to the presence in the audience of two guys from the Tottenham Independent Supporters' Association, and would not agree to appear until they were ejected. After all that, Jimmy then lobbed him some extremely soft questions. It was quite amazing how his attitude changed on the next programme, when Jimmy became very aggressive, especially towards Eddie, who was in the audience. I am sure that Jimmy was only acting under instructions from his producer, however, and I suspect a truer indication of Jim's own feelings came in a newspaper column in which he said: 'It's a sad day for soccer when someone with Terry's love for the game is turned over by a hard-nosed typewriter salesman from Hackney. Terry has football in his blood and I would question whether the same applies to Sugar.'

Harry Harris at the *Mirror* lost no time in joining the attack and was prepared to throw brick-bats at the drop of a hat. Harris, a great friend of Irving Scholar – he was one of only

The last supper – Gino Santin (right), Jonathan Crystal and me saying our
goodbyes to Paul Gascoigne

Gazza on cracking form as usual at a farewell presentation to Lineker and
him in the last home game of the season, 1992

One of my all-time great pictures

Grandad with the
great-grandson of Fred

Toots and Tel on our wedding day

With my daughter Tracey the day I left Spurs

Support for me at the court battle

For what we have already received; Dennis Roach, apparently seeking divine guidance on how to keep the peace in the midst of our court battle, while announcing the Makita international soccer tournament.
I'd have preferred to sit anywhere but here

I was far happier to be at this press conference in 1994 when I became England coach

Nothing changes, only the faces – and more of them. *Above:* Now we know where Gazza got it from

The first photograph before my first game against Denmark.
*Back row, left to right:* Stuart Pearce, Des Walker, Gary Pallister, David
Seaman, Tim Flowers, Darren Anderton, Paul Ince, Rob Jones. *Middle row,
left to right:* David Butler (physio), Bryan Robson (coach), Mathew Le Tissier,
Tony Adams, Les Ferdinand, Alan Shearer, Graeme Le Saux, Dr John Crane
(team doctor), Alan Smith (physio). *Front row, left to right:* David Batty, Paul
Parker, Paul Gascoigne, me, Don Howe (coach), David Platt, Ian Wright, Peter
Beardsley.    The result, 1–0.

Well, isn't that the Spitting Image?

four guests at his wedding – had been one of Robert Maxwell's principal confidants on the Mirror, and through him Captain Bob's pronouncements on football would often be made. I had sued Harris and the *Mirror* for a false story during the takeover and had won substantial damages, which obviously did not improve my relations with him. Harris continued his attacks on me during the FA's deliberations over the England coaching job, in a series of pieces expressing his view of the reasons why I could not possibly be given the job. Luckily for me, but unluckily for Harris, the FA did not agree.

Harris's most recent attack came in his biography of me, co-written with Steve Curry. At the press conference to launch it, Harris was asked if the book was not just part of a long-running vendetta against me. Curry hastily intercepted the question, but then scored a spectacular own goal. As the football fanzine *When Saturday Comes* pointed out, Curry '. . . explained that the publishers had brought him in specifically so that it wouldn't be a vindictive smear on Venables. The race to point out that he was implying that a book by Harris alone would have been just such a malicious work, was won by the man from the BBC.'

While the media blitz against me continued, Sugar still had other weapons up his sleeves. On 1 June 1993, just over a week before the date set for the full hearing of the court case, Jonathan Crystal was telephoned at home by Sugar. Shortly afterwards, Jonathan phoned me in a terrible state. When I asked him, 'What the hell's happened?' he said, 'I've had a threat from Alan Sugar. He told me that if I care about my future and my family, I should meet him today, since he had something to show me, which could affect my family and my career.' Jonathan was particularly concerned by the threat to his family, since, as Sugar knew, his father was in his late seventies and in frail health. Sugar wanted Jonathan to meet him in Brentwood at Amstrad, which Jonathan refused, but he eventually agreed to meet him at White Hart Lane that afternoon.

I was chairing a Tottenham management meeting that lunchtime and Sugar sat in on it, something he had never done before. It was a tense meeting, for he just sat there with a face like thunder, staring at all of us. The staff did not know which way to look. In the end I just decided to defuse the tension by getting everyone laughing, but the more they laughed, the angrier Sugar became. After the meeting, I went up to my office and I was there around ten to five, when Jonathan came in, white-faced and looking like death. When I asked him what had happened, he said: 'I'm not saying anything here.' I arranged to meet him up in town later that evening, when he told me what had happened. Jonathan had arrived at White Hart Lane at twenty to five and was met on the stairs by Sugar, who led him into the deserted Dave Mackay Suite.

Sugar said to him, 'I've met your mother and father, they're nice people.' In normal circumstances that would have been a friendly remark, but in the context of this meeting, Sugar's words had a sinister undertone. 'If you go against me,' continued Sugar, 'if you give evidence against me, I'll make sure I damage your family and your future.' He then accused Jonathan of being blinded by loyalty to me and said that if Jonathan produced an affidavit for the court case that Sugar did not like, he would swear an affidavit of his own, making serious allegations about Jonathan's professional conduct. I do not propose to repeat Sugar's allegations here, for that would merely be to give them wider currency.

Sugar claimed that two people, Nick Hewer of Michael Joyce Consultants – the Amstrad PR man whom Sugar had brought in to do work for Tottenham – and Margaret Mountford – a partner at Amstrad's, and now Tottenham's, lawyers, Herbert Smith – had witnessed the alleged misconduct, and were prepared to swear affidavits about it. Jonathan heard him out in silence, and Sugar then said, 'That's it,' but as Jonathan went downstairs to leave, Sugar followed him to the door and said, 'This conversation never took place.'

Jonathan went straight to his car and wrote down the details of the conversation. After coming to see me, he immediately contacted his own lawyers and informed the Professional Conduct Committee of the Bar about the allegations. On the following day, 2 June, Crystal's solicitors received a letter from Sugar's lawyers, Herbert Smith, suggesting that '. . . if and insofar as Mr Sugar may have seemed to suggest, in the course of that conversation, that Mr Crystal should refrain from filing evidence in the above case because of evidence which Mr Sugar would file concerning his (Mr Crystal's) professional conduct, that would be a misunderstanding of Mr Sugar's intention'.

However, Mr Sugar had already made his intentions abundantly clear and his actions led to committal proceedings against him, in which he acknowledged his contempt of court. Sugar could have been imprisoned, and the judge told him that but for the 'physical intimidation, abuse and threats' against Sugar by Spurs fans, he would have been punished far more severely.

In the whole course of our two-year working relationship, despite the near-daily reams of faxes on almost every topic that Sugar would send to my house, I never received a single one from him criticising any aspect of my transfer dealings for the club, nor the manner in which they were conducted. Yet those were precisely the issues cited by Sugar in the courts as the reason why matters came to such a head, and by the time of the first full court hearing of the case in early June, he was ready with a string of allegations of wrongdoing.

The allegation that caused most sensation during the hearing was Sugar's claim that I had told him 'Brian Clough likes a bung'. The suggestion was made that the £50,000 payment to sports agent Frank McLintock at the time of Teddy Sheringham's transfer from Nottingham Forest to Spurs included a cash bribe to Brian Clough. Sugar went on to claim that I 'explained that Mr Clough wished to receive a payment personally for selling Mr Sheringham . . . Mr Venables mentioned this to me once more and told me what usually happened in these cases was people would meet Mr Clough in a motorway café somewhere and Mr Clough would be handed a bag full of money'.

The 'bung' story and a series of other allegations and innuendos about my part in transfer dealings were enough, if true, to justify my sacking and blacken my name throughout football. I vigorously denied the allegations. I knew that I had absolutely nothing to hide and my lawyers immediately proposed that a 'forensic accountant' be brought in to investigate all player transfers at Tottenham, a proposal that Sugar rejected.

Sugar did not report this alleged offence to the police until November 1993, six months after the court hearing and eighteen months after it was supposed to have occurred. A full investigation by the Fraud Squad failed to uncover any evidence to justify the allegation and the Crown Prosecution Service announced that the case was being dropped in August 1994.

Astonishingly, by the time Sugar came to give evidence to the Premier League Inquiry into Tottenham's affairs – not long after he had made the formal complaint to the police – his recollection of events had changed completely. Sugar then told the inquiry that he had never claimed that I had mentioned the alleged 'bung' to Clough on the Sheringham transfer at all. The members of the inquiry pointed out that he had said quite clearly in court that I mentioned the 'bung', but Sugar said that he had been misquoted, and that I had actually said to him, over dinner with our wives several months before, that Clough had a reputation of liking a bung. 'Bung' is not an expression I ever use and I never made the remark.

There were further hints, both in the court case and afterwards in the media, that in some way I had also benefited from transfers, with much attention focused on the role of Gino Santin in the sale of Paul Gascoigne to Lazio, and my dealings with my close friend, football agent Eric Hall. Innuendo was once more enough: Eric Hall is a football agent. Eric Hall is a friend of Terry Venables. Eric Hall was paid money by Tottenham. Therefore Terry Venables must have been doing a crooked deal. QED.

Yet Sugar also told the Premier League Inquiry that he was now satisfied that I had never made money out of any transfer deals. He claimed that Tottenham had just paid Gino Santin too much money, which in the inquiry's view was simply an internal problem at Spurs. If it was a problem, it was one that Sugar had known about since the day the deal was done, for he was the man who signed Santin's cheque. The mud thrown at Gino Santin and me over the Gascoigne transfer had already had plenty of time to stick, before Sugar's comments to the Premier League Inquiry, however. It was only one of an endless series of allegations thrown at my associates and me in the months following the court case.

On the advice of my lawyers I had brought a complex action in the courts, known in the trade as a 'section 459 petition', in which I sought the court's ruling that I could not be dismissed from Spurs, and that because of Sugar's breach of the agreements that he had with me, he had demonstrated his unfitness to continue as a director of Tottenham. I asked the court to order that I be able to buy Sugar's shareholding from him. In retrospect, I should have chosen my battleground more carefully, for the costs of pursuing that particular action proved to be too great, and the potential chances of success too slim.

I neither won nor lost the court case for it never went to trial. I ran up against the wall erected to ensure that only the very rich can afford to enjoy the fruits of 'British justice'. We are all equal before the law, but since we are not all equally able to pay for it, British justice becomes all the justice you can afford and no more. The men with money can use the legal system to their advantage, and whatever else may be said about him, Alan Sugar does have an awful lot of money. Secure behind the bastion of his unbelievable resources, Sugar brought an action against my company, Edennote, the official owner of my Tottenham shares, for what is termed 'security for costs', requiring me to deposit £300,000 with the court. In the event that I lost, Sugar and Tottenham would be able to recover the costs and would not be at risk.

It would not have ended there. To take the matter to trial, Sugar would almost certainly have sought further orders of another half a million pounds. I would then have faced risking £800,000 on my chances in an area of very complex and difficult law. If I had lost, I would have been bankrupt, absolutely penniless, and for the sake of my wife and family, who had already suffered enough, that was not something that I had the right to risk. After further advice from several sets of counsel, it was decided that I would drop that action and bring simpler contract law actions against Tottenham and/or Sugar for damages. It was a terrible decision to have to make, because it effectively meant that I had to withdraw from Tottenham and sell my shares, but I bit the bullet and took the decision immediately.

Depressed at the court reverse and weary from the months of battles, Yvette and I went to the USA for a short holiday, to recharge our batteries and plan the next move. We flew to Boston and drove up through Martha's Vineyard, towards Cape Cod. The countryside was as beautiful as everyone had told us and we simply drove where the mood took us, stopping the nights in small guest-houses.

By the time we got back to England, my shares in Tottenham Hotspur plc had been sold. Most of my holding went to a number of investment institutions, through Japanese brokers Yamachi. The rest went to one of my creditors in lieu of repayment of the loan taken out to buy them originally. I retained a nominal 100 shares. It crossed my mind, of course, that some of my shares could eventually find their way to Sugar, but it made no real difference what their ultimate destination was. It did not bother me if he got hold of any, for my priority was to restructure my finances, and selling my shares was a necessary first step on what would be a long road.

I was out of Tottenham, but there was no let-up in the media war against my associates and me. Journalists have told me that during this period, Nick Hewer, Alan Sugar's PR man, not only telephoned newspapers on a daily basis, but also turned up at their offices with negative stories. My companies and I were also the subject of formal inquiries by various different government agencies, such as the Department of Trade and Industry, Customs and Excise, and the Serious Fraud Office, all arising from complaints and information supplied to them. When such formal complaints are made, government departments are bound by statute to make inquiries, even if the complaints are completely groundless. Meanwhile, the media were informed by 'persons unknown' that an investigation was taking place. At the time of writing, no complaints of any wrongdoing have been received, but the belief that there is no smoke without fire, helps to build an impression of dishonesty or double-dealing on my part irrespective of the lack of evidence to support it.

*Panorama*, broadcast in September 1993, was the lowest point in these months of allegation and rumour. The most awful thing, sitting watching it with Yvette, was to think that millions of people who did not know me, would also be watching and might believe it. I felt as if I had been tried and found guilty. It was like Franz Kafka's *The Trial*, or a film in which a man is found standing over a dead body with a smoking gun in his hand. I knew I was innocent, but who was going to believe me now?

*Panorama* always goes out on Mondays. The only time that they do a 'Special' is for something momentous like a General Election or the assassination of a president. The last one that I could remember was for the sinking of the *Belgrano* during the Falklands War, yet here was a *Panorama Special*, going out on a Thursday night, about Terry Venables.

Parts of the programme were laughable, but it was far from funny, for *Panorama* was probably seen as the most damning indictment in the whole trial by media. I always thought of *Panorama* as being gospel; it is, after all, the flagship current-affairs programme of the BBC. Yet when we analysed the transcript of the programme, we found that there were some ninety defamatory allegations, innuendos and inaccuracies against me, many of which were easily disproved by basic documentation in my possession.

The implications of the programme were obvious – that I had taken a 'back-hander' from Gino Santin, after the Gascoigne transfer, for example. It was a slur that was to be repeated on the Channel Four *Dispatches* programme three days later, which turned the screw even further, by producing as a key piece of evidence the mysterious fax of 20 June 1991 to Spurs' solicitors Ashurst, Morris, Crisp, from Lazio's lawyers, stating Lazio's willingness to pay £5.5 million for Gascoigne, long before Gino Santin became involved. Once more, the implication was crystal-clear. If the price was already £5.5 million, Santin's involvement was unnecessary and must have been part of a crooked operation to 'skim off' some of the money.

When the *Dispatches* interviewer produced the fax with a flourish in front of me, I could only truthfully say: 'I've never seen it before.' As I said it, I saw him turn to the cameraman and wink, as if to say 'Got him'. When the fax was shown to Sugar, he did not react like a man seeing it for the first time, and his response, 'You've shown me a piece of paper that indicates to me that £5.5 million was on the table in the beginning . . . I'm absolutely shocked that I've been such a mug,' also struck me as far from spontaneous.

The second part of the attack was to query the ultimate destination of Santin's £200,000 fee. The programme pointed out that the invoice came from what was alleged to be Santin's Swiss company, Anglo-European Market Research & Consulting Company. Santin reportedly has said that he was advised to set up the company by his accountant, rather in the way that Sugar's accountants might have advised him to set up a Jersey-based company called Amshold, so that the £50,000 a year he had arranged to pay himself from Tottenham could be tax-free.

The two signatures on Santin's cheque were those of Alan Sugar and Colin Sandy, in breach of a board minute that cheques over £100,000 could only be jointly signed by Alan Sugar and Terry Venables. The programmes traced the money to the Swiss company and then, with much nudging and winking, wondered where the ultimate destination of the money could have been. The clear implication was that part of it was being 'laundered' for me, a surprising suggestion, given that I was not consulted over the treatment of the payment, did not approve the invoice and did not sign the cheque.

Gino Santin was as incensed as I was by the allegations, and his solicitors immediately wrote to Sugar, asking him to exonerate their client from any suggestion of 'impropriety'. 'All I want to do is clear my name,' said Santin. 'The fight between Sugar and Venables is nothing to do with me.' Sugar's response was to invite Santin to a meeting with Sugar's lawyers, Herbert Smith, to which Santin's reply was: 'Why should I? I'm the one who has been slandered.' On 29 September Santin informed Sugar that he was making his side of the story public, and his libel actions against *Panorama* and *Dispatches* continue.

*Panorama*'s last smear against me was that I had 'refused to accept the BBC's normal terms and conditions of interview', and had therefore not appeared on the programme. The truth was rather different. I had expressed my complete willingness to be interviewed on the programme, provided that the makers of *Panorama* would give me certain assurances about the extent of the 'chequebook journalism' they had been pursuing. On 12 September, I sent them a fax:

Thank you for your letter asking me to appear on *Panorama*. However, before I agree to answer your questions, I need written assurances signed by the programme producer and the programme editor, that you have not:

1) Paid or agreed to pay any person any money for copies or access to copies of the private and confidential ledgers of my company Edennote plc.

2) Paid or agreed to pay directly or indirectly any money to accountant Richard Theobalds for information about me.

3) Paid or agreed to pay my former business partner Paul Riviere any money or expenses for assisting you in your enquiries.

4) Paid any person more than the normal rate of interview.

If you are able to give me this written assurance, I am of course quite happy to answer any of the questions you have put to me. However, if you are not able to give me this written assurance, I am unable to go on the programme.

Mark Killick, the senior producer of *Panorama*, replied the next day: 'I cannot discuss the details of any arrangements between the BBC and any programme contributor or consultant and am therefore unable to give the undertakings you seek.'

It was unsurprising that he could not give me those assurances, because he knew that *Panorama* had been paying their sources. *Panorama* have admitted that they retained Richard

Theobalds as a 'consultant' on the programme, for example. Theobalds had been a business associate of Eddie Ashby for a number of years and had been engaged at my office in Princes' Gate, London, for a short while, but was sacked in 1991, following his unauthorised removal of £1200 from the cash register at Scribes, which he claimed he was owed for expenses.

Shortly after the programme I wrote to the FA and the Premier League, inviting them to look into all the business dealings of Tottenham while I was associated with the club. I also made an offer, broadcast on *Dispatches*, to any media organisation: 'Prove any of the allegations that you have made and I will pay a quarter of a million pounds to charity. Fail to do so and you pay a quarter of a million pounds to charity.' No organisation has ever offered to take me up on the invitation.

Throughout all the troubles, Yvette never wavered in her support; she was always at my side, always encouraging me to fight on. Yvette is everything I am not – slim and beautiful, to name but two things – but we share quite a few characteristics, including the determination not to be the victims of a miscarriage of justice, and we are true soulmates for each other. She is so calm and, like me, retains a sense of humour, even when things go wrong. We were able to laugh when maybe we should have been crying. There are fifteen years between us, but we are never aware of any age gap and never happier than when we are together, especially in the house that we bought when we came back from Spain. The house is only just off Kensington High Street, but on a Sunday morning, with the birds singing, it is so peaceful that you could almost imagine you were in the country.

Yvette was a rock to cling to when a few friends began to have their doubts about me, as the mud-slinging reached its peak. I could see in their eyes sometimes, that they were beginning to doubt me. Friendships are like business partnerships – easiest to maintain if things are going well, when friendships blossom and businesses make profits. When the tough times start, or the losses begin, that is when partnerships and friendships are broken, but for every friend who just stopped calling, there were a hundred people calling after me in the street to say 'Good luck'. Cab drivers would refuse payment for fares, and the support and kindness of ordinary people, not just in London but throughout the country, was incredible.

My first involvement in football since the sacking from Tottenham was to manage an International XI against Liverpool, in autumn 1993, for Steve Nichol's testimonial. An awful lot had been said about me in the meantime, and I was worried about what sort of reception I might get, but the crowd gave me a great welcome, which was a terrific boost. I felt that the people in the street were on my side. I do not think that was just because they thought I was good at the job; I am sure there was more to it. Was it because I had stood up against the hierarchy, or because they are fed up with money always winning?

There was never a time when I felt I should just give in and walk away from it all, because when your conscience is clear, nothing, not even the dreadful events of 1993, ever really seems that bad. You have to live with yourself in the end and I knew that I had done nothing wrong. Together with Yvette's support, that knowledge gave me the strength to fight the injustice and not just hide away to lick my wounds.

The avalanche of media allegations against me was begun by a freelance journalist called Tony Yorke, who wrote the first 'exposé' but the key sources for most of the stories about me included Richard Theobalds and Paul Riviere, who used their knowledge of my associations and business affairs in the 'exposé' articles and television programmes in those early months of autumn 1993, which culminated in the colossus of the *Panorama Special*.

In 1992, a year after his sacking, Richard Theobalds had gone to see Eddie, and said, 'I'm sorry, my fault, let bygones be bygones. I would like to work with you if it's possible.' Eddie told him that could not happen, but Theobalds also mentioned that his wife, Gillian, had just been made redundant from a very good computer-programming job with Thorn Data Systems. By coincidence we were developing our computer management systems at my offices and needed a programmer on a short-term basis, and as a result of that conversation, Theobalds' wife worked for me on a consultancy basis, for a total of eight or nine days over a period of six weeks. Giving her the work proved to be a disastrous mistake. Her brief was to carry out the initial set-up of accounting management systems for several of my companies and in the course of that, it was obviously necessary for her to input data like opening balances on various accounts. A package of that documentation was on Edennote, which was the company through which I purchased my Tottenham shares.

When Gillian Theobalds finished her work with us, we had a minor fracas, because she had walked off with the software manual that was essential for operating the system, and we withheld her last two days' money until it was returned. She eventually brought it back and was paid off. What became clear a year later, in about July 1993, was that she had also removed copies of the Edennote documentation. The police have established that she took the documents from my office.

The documentation dates back to early in Edennote's life, June/July 1991, and the attraction to any purchaser of these documents is that he suddenly gets a very close insight into how I financed the purchase of my Tottenham Hotspur shares – how much I had had to borrow, who held the debts, and on what terms. There were also entries referring to transactions with Landhurst Leasing, a company from which I obtained a £1 million unsecured loan.

Landhurst was run by a man called Ted Ball, who was a bit outlandish and a real character, but his firm specialised in

lending money to 'names'. He had also lent money to Spurs
director Tony Berry and a number of other prominent sporting
and City figures, and I had no reason to query the loan. I had a
meeting with Ball who said that if I wanted £1 million, he could
get it for me. I asked him a couple of questions about it, but he
just said, 'Do you want it or don't you want it? Don't mess
around. There's no problem, I've done deals far bigger than
this.'

Ball's approach to making loans was clearly rather less
rigorous than that of a bank, but that was scarcely my concern;
it is the lender, not the borrower, who needs to make inquiries,
to satisfy himself that he will get his money back, just as a bank
does when it makes a loan. I put Eddie Ashby together with
Ball's man and they sorted out a no-strings loan. The money
was not used to purchase Tottenham shares – they had already
been bought by the time the loan was made.

When Landhurst Leasing later went bankrupt, I began to
negotiate settlement of my debt with the receiver, Arthur Andersen. This became more urgent by mid- to end July 1993,
when I was under pressure from Sugar's side in the 'security-for-
costs' application for £300,000. Without a settlement of the
Landhurst loan, there was a £1-million question mark hanging
over Edennote, making it appear that the company might even
be insolvent. I was offering advanced settlement of the five-year
loan, and haggling with the receiver over the amount, but my
efforts to reach agreement were stalled by another party offering
to buy the debt from Landhurst and as a result I took a
whacking at the hearing of the security-for-costs application.

All was not lost, for I still had twenty-one days to settle the
Landhurst debt or to appeal the verdict of the hearing, but
another new factor was then introduced. On the day before the
security-for-costs hearing, Alan Sugar's PR man Nick Hewer,
together with Alan Watts, a solicitor at Sugar's lawyers, Herbert
Smith, were at the offices of the *Daily Mirror* with journalists

Tony Yorke and Peter Hounan, examining the documents removed from my offices by Gillian Theobalds. After Hewer and Watts had examined them, however, Watts declared that it was clear that the present owner of the documents had not come by them in a legal fashion and he and Hewer left empty-handed. The *Mirror* also refused to purchase the documents.

The documents next appeared on the desks of Reid, Minty, the solicitors acting for Landhurst Leasing. They were sent anonymously, coupled with a set of audited accounts of Edennote, which had been produced for the security-for-costs hearing, to show that the company had sufficient resources to meet the costs. Only two copies of these particular accounts were ever produced by my auditors, Crouch, Chapman: one was presented to my lawyers, Kanter Jules Grangewood, and they passed a copy to Sugar's lawyers, Herbert Smith, for the purposes of the court case.

Those accounts were unique because they contained one tiny error: the shares of Tottenham were described as '£1 ordinary shares' and in fact they are 25 pence ordinary shares. That was quickly put right and the accounts properly filed with Companies House, but by an extraordinary coincidence, the 'unique' set of accounts, including the error, together with copies of the stolen documents, found their way to Reid, Minty.

Accompanying them was a threatening memo, suggesting that the Landhurst receiver, Arthur Andersen, would be unwise to accept settlement of my debt to the company on the basis of accounts which the memo claimed did not reflect Edennote's true financial position. The effect of the documents, if accepted at face value, could have been to frustrate settlement of the debt and prevent me meeting the requirements of the security-for-costs application within the twenty-one days allowed. It might seem unimportant that these documents, whether stolen or not, were circulated, unless they showed wrongdoing on my part, but they were damaging to my case because of the false interpretation that was put upon them, showing a very different picture of my finances than the true state of affairs.

The stolen documents also found other uses. I have evidence of Nick Hewer reading extracts about Landhurst from the documents to a journalist and saying, 'It must never be said that this comes from me, we are in breach of legal process, we are in contempt of court, I shouldn't have a copy of these accounts.' The package of misappropriated documents and the unique set of accounts were also distributed to various newspapers, including the *Sunday Times*. The documents also found their way to Diverse Productions, producers of *Dispatches*, and to *Panorama*.

Apart from the Theobalds, *Panorama* also relied heavily on information supplied by two other people, Paul Kirby and Paul Riviere. Paul Kirby is the representative for Oceania (New Zealand, Australia and the South Pacific) on the FA's General Council, and an estate agent, who found me the house in Kensington, which I bought on my return from Spain, and still have today. He befriended me and we became co-directors in a pub-owning company, Transatlantic Inns, one of a number of businesses in which I invested my earnings from Barcelona. I had 50 per cent of the company and Paul Kirby, Colin Wright and another guy called David Brown had the other 50 per cent between them.

I never had any executive responsibility at Transatlantic Inns, and had left Kirby to run it, which I later regretted. On becoming chief executive at Tottenham, it was clear that I would have even less time available for other business interests in the future, and having also received a damning accountants' report in May 1991 on the performance of Transatlantic Inns, after due consideration and advice, I resigned the following month.

At the same time, I negotiated a deal with Kirby and Wright

to break up the business, and shortly afterwards, I purchased the assets and liabilities of two of the pubs – at way over market value in anyone's terms – giving me a way out of the company and effectively recapitalising Transatlantic Inns. Kirby and Wright simultaneously undertook to purchase my shareholding in Transatlantic for £1 and release me from the bank guarantees associated with the business.

Despite our agreement and the indemnities given to me by them, they left me to pay off the creditors, including the bank, at a personal cost of half a million pounds. The 'shell' of Transatlantic eventually went to the Official Receiver, because the company failed to respond to a winding-up petition from a disputed creditor. My associates and I have fully complied with our duties to the Official Receiver, who expressed his complete satisfaction in a letter to us, at the same time confirming that, in breach of their statutory obligations, neither Kirby nor Wright had even filed Statements of Affairs with him.

Unfortunately, it was only after I had gone into business with him that I discovered more about Paul Kirby. As the saying goes, those who do not learn from their mistakes are condemned to repeat them, and I had obviously not learned from mine. Paul Kirby supplied *Panorama* with documentation purporting to substantiate his allegations that, in September 1991, without the knowledge of the directors of Transatlantic – Paul Kirby and Colin Wright – Eddie Ashby and I had fraudulently sold the company's assets to Landhurst Leasing, and then leased them back, thus generating £1 million. I am suing Kirby and Wright for some £150,000, the figure that they indemnified me for with Transatlantic Inn's bankers.

The documents produced by Kirby bear no resemblance to any genuine Transatlantic Inns or Landhurst Leasing papers and his allegation is simply not true. Eddie Ashby and I have both been interviewed by the Serious Fraud Office who, on submission of our evidence, have confirmed that both of us are potential witnesses and neither of us is under investigation for any wrongdoing. They also confirmed that they do not recognise any of the Landhurst 'documentation' shown on *Panorama*. Ray Needham, the police officer who investigated the Theobalds affair, after I had asked for a police investigation, later told the *Sunday Mirror*: 'I am satisfied that Mr Venables has not been up to any mischief. He has been accused of improperly obtaining a £1 million loan. That is simply not true ... Although I was called in by Mr Venables and asked to investigate the theft of documents, I had to be satisfied that Venables was not simply trying to cover up a £1 million fraud. We could find nothing wrong.'

*Panorama* should have checked the accuracy of their information before broadcasting it. Astonishingly, in view of the importance of his 'evidence', Kirby was neither interviewed on the programme, nor cited as a source, being granted anonymity by the producers.

The other main 'witness for the prosecution' on *Panorama* was Paul Riviere, the man who I had involved in the board game, The Manager. He was described on the programme as running 'a highly successful financial-services company', but the reality is that the financial-services company, Elite First Ltd, which he was reported to be running, had collapsed in a welter of claims and disputes two years before and he had then been made personally bankrupt in July 1991. He had been engaged by me at Scribes until that time, but resigned by mutual consent.

His allegation on *Panorama* that he was never paid for his work on the board game The Manager is ridiculous; I have documents from my company, Glenhope, showing his monthly payments. His claim that there was no money in the company bank accounts is exploded by the bank statements in my possession, showing in excess of £100,000 on deposit. He claimed that money was moved from various companies, in illegal transactions to support other companies, yet our audited accounts have confirmed that no such money was ever transferred.

Paul later claimed in a conversation with me that he had never done anything to harm me, only Eddie Ashby, but that was not a distinction that anyone watching *Panorama* was likely to make. He also admitted that he was paid to dish dirt on us, and he sold himself very cheaply. I am told he got £1000 from *Panorama* and a similar amount from elsewhere. Having befriended him and given him a helping hand when he was down, I was deeply shocked at his actions.

Apart from further damaging my credibility, the *Panorama* and *Dispatches* programmes had another immediate effect. Gary Lineker had been trying to persuade me to go to Japan as coach to Grampus 8, his Toyota-backed team in the new Japanese League. The money was spectacularly good – a three-year contract at £600,000 a year, plus up to £500,000 a year in bonuses – but Japanese businesses do not like bad publicity or suggestions of misconduct, and after the *Panorama* programme, Japanese interest froze.

Simultaneously, I had to turn down Real Madrid, who had approached me about a return to Spain. Barcelona were doing very well, Real Madrid were not and had problems with their coach. They were thinking of a change and asked if I was willing to consider it, but at that time I did not want to do anything except clear up my horrendous situation in England.

The allegations being made for money by Riviere and Theobalds were given wider currency by the efforts of Nick Hewer and Colin Sandy. Like Hewer and Tony Berry, Colin Sandy was also peddling stories to journalists and providing them with documents. The cumulative effect of all these individual allegations, was to make the apparently authoritative 'exposés' on *Panorama* and *Dispatches* possible.

As the wall of lies begins to crumble, however, more and more information is forthcoming to Eddie Ashby and me, and our lawyers. *Dispatches*, for example, having realised how seriously astray they were in the programme vilifying me, based on evidence they now know to have been false, have agreed to open their files to us and have made statements to our lawyers. Tony Yorke, the freelance journalist who 'broke' the original story, also now realises how he has been used, and has written a series of articles for the *People* newspaper, exposing a truer, and very different state of affairs.

We are subpoenaing police material gathered in the course of their investigations into the removal of the documents from my offices. Some police officers expressed their frustration at criminal proceedings not being brought against the Theobalds, because in criminal law, the value of the proceeds of the crime is assessed as the value of the goods stolen, in this case paper at 50 pence a sheet – fifteen sheets, £7.50. You cannot bring a serious criminal prosecution on the basis of that, and the criminal law does not consider the damage. That is a civil matter, and I am considering pursuing the Theobalds for damages instead.

Ultimately I intend to pursue legal action against every party who has attacked me, whether they are deliberately guilty or have been duped. I have not yet served a writ on *Panorama* at the time of writing but it will be served. After my previous expensive forays into the courts, I have been persuaded, against my own instincts, that the sensible course of action is to pick off the lies one at a time, until the whole carefully constructed house of cards comes tumbling down. Eddie and the lawyers have often had a battle to convince me to stick to that course, because of my frustration at the time the law takes to grind its way through each case, but by the time we get to *Panorama* – and if necessary, the law allows us three years to do it – our case will already be largely proven.

After all the money I have already spent – and I have

already incurred some £1 million in legal costs and other expenses – I need more court cases like a hole in the head, but I am determined to clear my name whatever the cost.

Apart from legal costs, the payments to creditors pushed me very close to personal bankruptcy. My experiences with the 'gentlemen' of the City run counter to everything I have previously experienced in life. My Mum always taught me that my word is my bond and that a handshake is as good as a legal contract. My Dad always told me, 'Out of debt, out of danger'. Yet the morality that my parents taught me and that I have tried to adhere to throughout my life, seems to be completely alien to the businessmen, bankers and professional people with whom I have had to deal.

One of my companies, Venables Venture Capital Limited, not Edennote, was responsible for the £1-million debt to Landhurst Leasing. When I was in personal financial difficulties, the run-of-the-mill business judgement would have been: 'Let's dump the creditors'. I had two opportunities, in June and December 1991, and could simply have allowed the company to fold and walked away from the debt.

What I owe I pay, however, and I have not just paid my own share of the debts, in some cases I have paid everybody else's share too, because I feel it is immoral to allow a company with which I am associated to go bankrupt, simply to avoid paying creditors. I would not like that to happen to me and, with one exception, I have not allowed it to happen to anyone else. My businesses suffered enormously from the loss of credibility arising from the tidal wave of allegations against me, but we have stood the test and survived.

Every undisputed creditor of every company, has been paid, except for Herbert Smith, the lawyers representing Sugar/Tottenham/Amshold, who succeeded in having my company Edennote wound up in a court judgement reached in May 1994. That proved doubly damaging to me, for it made my breach-of-

contract and wrongful-dismissal cases against Tottenham much
more difficult to pursue, since Tottenham's agreement to employ
me was with Edennote, but I eventually reached an agreement
with the liquidator of Edennote that allowed me to revive the
claims.

Footballers kick lumps out of each other out on the pitch
and then have a drink together in the bar afterwards. Perhaps
businessmen think they are the same, sitting down for a gin and
tonic after twisting and conniving to screw their adversaries in a
business deal, but there is one basic difference: in football you
always know who is on your team and who is with the opposition. I have always thought that football is a tough and cut-
throat business, but it is kids' stuff – just a playground –
compared to the jungle of the City. Although it has cost me a
fortune, I can at least face myself in the mirror and know that I
have done right.

On top of the campaign against me in the media, there was
also a campaign to conceal the irregularities perpetrated by
Irving Scholar at Tottenham before the takeover by Alan Sugar
and me. The man ultimately responsible for blocking disclosure
of the Scholar regime's actions and for protecting Scholar from
legal action is none other than Alan Sugar.

An investigation by Eddie Ashby in July 1991, shortly after
the takeover, revealed the first evidence of irregularities under
the Scholar regime. Eddie's investigations continued and in
October 1991, Eddie and Jonathan Crystal arranged a consulta-
tion with eminent QC, Anthony Grabiner. Also in attendance
were Colin Sandy and Bryan Fugler, the club's then solicitor.
Anthony Grabiner's advice was unequivocal. He stated that
Alan Sugar and I should 'meet with a representative of the
Football League ... to make a full disclosure as quickly as
possible'. Grabiner added that it would be better done after the
loans had been discussed with each of the players. Bryan Fugler
wrote to us on 11 October 1991, noting the content of the

meeting with Anthony Grabiner and recommending 'that you each attend to this matter with the utmost priority'.

Eddie Ashby was detailed to talk to each of the players and in January 1992, he wrote to Jonathan Crystal: 'I refer to our discussions of a couple of weeks before Christmas and reaffirm that I have spoken to all the players individually and now have the basis for an overall settlement.' Eddie advised the January board meeting that 'piecemeal' disclosure did not seem possible. The payments had been made throughout the previous regime and full disclosure was required: 'The matter must be resolved and a policy agreed by the Board.'

Soon after the Grabiner opinion, I proposed legal action against Scholar because of the emerging evidence of his wrongdoing, but at that stage, we had barely touched the surface. Bryan Fugler wrote to Sugar and me on 3 February 1992, suggesting that the Board might take legal action against Scholar:

> There seems to be a constant theme relating to these enquiries and indeed other matters with which I am dealing, namely that there appears to be misfeasance by a former director of the company, Irving Scholar. I think it is only right that I bring this matter to your attention, although I appreciate that it may be distasteful to sue a former director and there may in any event be difficulties in pursuing Mr Scholar, who I believe is resident abroad. Be that as it may, I do believe that the board ought to consider whether or not it wishes to pursue a claim against Mr Scholar.

In June 1992, a routine check of Tottenham's PAYE files by the Inland Revenue revealed serious irregularities. As the taxmen probed deeper into the club's affairs over the previous decade, more and more irregularities were uncovered and a full-scale Inland Revenue investigation began. At my instigation, we commissioned the City accountants, Touche Ross, to undertake a thorough review of the club's affairs. The report, presented to the board in late 1992, confirmed and expanded upon the scandalous irregularities under the Scholar regime. Among the new breaches discovered by Touche Ross were ex-gratia payments to players and a former manager that were likely to cost us £140,000 in tax and National Insurance contributions. Nico Claesen had been given a secret payment of £42,000 when he joined Spurs in 1986, for example, and it appears that PAYE deductions had not been made. Icelandic defender Gudni Bergsson also benefited from a payment, which was, like Claesen's, made via his former club. The payments were authorised by Irving Scholar.

Pension papers relating to Paul Gascoigne and Chris Waddle were also backdated by two years and loans to Gascoigne and Waddle to buy houses in the south-east were also likely to cause tax problems. Scholar had also given secret undertakings to both Gascoigne and Waddle guaranteeing them ex-gratia payments of up to £120,000 after they had left Spurs. A letter from Scholar to Gascoigne's agent Mel Stein promises to pay the player '£70,000 net of all UK taxes up to a maximum of £120,000 gross'. As the Touche Ross report commented, the discovery was 'like having a gun held to the club's head'.

The Inland Revenue have launched several separate investigations into tax irregularities surrounding the game of football. The Special Office inquiry at Tottenham began in earnest on 17 July 1992. Colin Sandy wrote a memo to the board stating, 'The Special Office of the Inland Revenue, a unit specialising in negligence and investigation . . . have decided to carry out a full-scale investigation into Tottenham's tax affairs.' In November of that year, the Inland Revenue demanded a payment of £500,000 from Tottenham on account, and the final cost to Tottenham of all the Scholar regime's irregular dealings is likely to exceed £3 million. Were the FA's punishments of Tottenham to result directly or indirectly in relegation, that figure could easily be multiplied by a factor of three or four.

Even more disturbingly, after an investigation by the *People* newspaper, it later emerged that Scholar and Stein, together with Gascoigne's other adviser, Len Lazarus, had gone into partnership together in June 1988, in a limited company called Junior Brain of Football. Scholar, who remained a director of the company until 31 December 1991, never divulged this to the Spurs board. Yet as a director of a public listed company, Scholar was compelled to disclose his relationship, particularly when Stein's law firm, Finers, began to do commercial work for Spurs. Scholar was in clear breach of Section 317 of the Companies Act.

The transfers of Chris Waddle to Marseille and Paul Gascoigne to Lazio both involved payments to agent Dennis Roach, who, as the *People* reported, was being paid by both sides in the deals, in breach of FIFA, UEFA and FA regulations. Roach had been brought in by Scholar and despite being 'paid off' with a £27,500 payment when Gino Santin was brought in to finalise Gascoigne's transfer, Roach continued to receive monies from the deal. A Spurs document states: 'It would appear that Mr Roach has been on the pay-roll of the club, unknown to Mr Solomon and Mr Berry, having been paid £64,400 in the year ending 31 May 1991. It would also appear that Lazio may also be paying Mr Roach in connection with the Gascoigne sale – this is forbidden both under Football League and FIFA regulations.' It appears that Spurs have not reported Roach's involvement in the deal with Spurs and Lazio to the FA and it is hard to see why not. The wild allegations against Gino Santin have provided a convenient smokescreen to conceal this.

Scholar's other legacy to Spurs was the most explosive and potentially damaging of all, for the £250,000 transfer of Mitchell Thomas from Luton to Spurs in 1986, the £425,000 signing of Paul Allen from West Ham in 1985 and the £387,500 capture of Chris Fairclough from Nottingham Forest in 1987 have all been exposed as irregular. The Touche Ross report submitted to the

Special Office Inquiry for the Inland Revenue revealed that
Thomas had been given a £25,000 loan when he joined Spurs,
but papers forwarded to the Football League's tribunal at the
time of the transfer, omitted any mention of the loan. A letter to
Thomas outlining a parallel agreement whereby the loan was in
effect never to be repaid, was given to Thomas by Irving
Scholar and the submission to the tribunal was signed by club
director Frank Sinclair. On the information received, the tribunal
decided that £250,000 was a fair fee, against West Ham's
valuation of £650,000, but had they known the true level of
remuneration, the fee would have been substantially increased.
Luton chairman David Kohler is contemplating suing Spurs for
damages, which could run to several hundred thousand pounds,
and West Ham and Forest could take the same action.

Like Thomas, Allen and Fairclough also received loans
before joining Spurs – of £55,000 and £25,000 respectively –
which were not disclosed to the transfer tribunal. Thomas's ex-
gratia 'loan' was actually paid to him a full three weeks before
he even became a Spurs player. A memo from Colin Sandy,
written on 27 November 1992, reveals that the letter agreeing
the payment was dated 11 June 1986, even though Thomas did
not become a Spurs player until 1 July. Sandy went on to warn
that it would be difficult for Spurs to emerge unscathed from
the Inland Revenue's tax investigations because 'Through the
working practices, or the lack of them, of Derek Peter (Tottenham finance director for much of Scholar's regime) and particularly the dominance of Irving Scholar, who had scant regard for
financial controls . . . I doubt that there is any area where some
errors in procedures have not been made, either deliberately or
by default.'

Despite this open admission from Sandy and the direct
knowledge of Sugar and his co-directors of Scholar's responsibility for Tottenham's troubles with the Inland Revenue, Sugar has
consistently tried to portray me as the man responsible. Yet as

Tottenham manager under Scholar, I was not even a director, and was employed by Tottenham Hotspur FC, a wholly owned subsidiary of Tottenham Hotspur plc, with each organisation having its own board of directors. The FA have examined the evidence and exonerated me from any involvement in the irregularities and breaches of regulations that occurred under Scholar's regime.

Shortly after assuming control, I discovered documents that revealed the details of the Maxwell loan and Jonathan Crystal and I made a serious attempt to instigate legal action against Scholar over it. We also urged full disclosure to the FA and the relevant authorities. Sugar for reasons of his own was opposed to it, preferring to sweep it under the carpet, at the same time altering the minutes, with Colin Sandy's help, to make it appear that he was not only in favour, but the instigator of attempts to make full disclosure.

The reality is shown by Sugar's failure to send the Touche Ross report to the Inland Revenue until March 1993. In Touche Ross's presentation to the board on the report and accounts for the year ending 31 May 1993, the accountants also pointed out that any liabilities over £120,000 should be disclosed. Yet despite a reminder from Touche Ross about the board's responsibilites as laid down in the Companies Act, neither the Inland Revenue's Special Office inquiry and its potentially massive costs to Tottenham, nor the improper payments, were disclosed in the 1993 company accounts, in clear breach of the board's duty to the shareholders and the City authorities. Sugar also only handed over details of some of the player loans to the Premier League Inquiry – as *World In Action* producer Charles Tremayne explained 'when it became clear to him that *World In Action* was about to reveal it anyway'.

Sugar was interviewed for the programme some time in advance of *World In Action*'s transmission in December 1993, and realising its drift, he immediately released transcripts of the interview and other information to the rest of the media, but his tactics backfired. As another producer on the programme, Steve Boulton remarked, 'I am sure he (Sugar) thought that he would minimise the damage to Spurs by putting so much material, including our uncut interviews, into the public domain. I am not sure that what he has got is what he wanted. The phrase "own goal" comes to mind.' Sugar's response to the programme was that '*World In Action* are amateurs playing in a professional's world'.

A legal opinion from lawyer Elizabeth Gloster in autumn 1992 advised us that we should sue all the directors at the time of Scholar's previous irregular dealings – Scholar himself and his co-directors, Bobroff, Alexiou, Berry and Gray. 'Prior to July 1991 ... some payments were falsely characterised as "loans" in order to evade payment of tax,' said Gloster, 'but in reality, such "loans" were understood both by the company and the recipient to be non-repayable.' A total of over £2 million was claimable, in Gloster's opinion, including £400,000 in written-off 'loans' to players, £200,000 in irregular payments to Paul Gascoigne and Chris Waddle, £260,000 to Gray, and £500,000 in payments on account to the Inland Revenue. She went on to warn us that if we did not sue, we would lay ourselves open to legal action. 'The board itself will run the risk of action at the suit of the company's shareholders, if no steps are taken to recover losses caused by such directors.'

When this was raised at a board meeting, my reaction and that of Jonathan Crystal were identical: 'We've got to sue them.' But despite the legal advice, Sugar blocked any attempt to institute legal action – and at the time of writing, none has been taken. Scholar is a multi-millionaire and both Elizabeth Gloster and another legal opinion commissioned by Spurs have told Sugar that the money is recoverable, yet no attempt has ever been made to do so. Instead Eddie Ashby and I have been portrayed as villains, rogues and even thieves.

There are a series of great unanswered questions. Why pay Ian Gray £260,000 instead of suing him? Why keep Tony Berry on the board, and welcome Douglas Alexiou back on to it, rather than sue them? And why would Irving Scholar, the chief architect of Tottenham's financial plight in 1990–91 and the tax evasion and irregular dealings over several years, now be welcome at White Hart Lane once more?

When Scholar was removed as chairman and director, he lost all the benefits that are normally extended to former officers of the company. He was a pariah at Tottenham then, but is now back at White Hart Lane, not yet in the directors' box, but sitting close enough to chat across the wall. Despite being informed of Scholar's links with Mel Stein, at the time of writing, Sugar has still not initiated any action against Scholar nor attempted to make full disclosure to all the relevant authorities.

Scholar, Berry, Alexiou and Gray: Sugar has them all back on board in one way or another and has not sued any of them until now, yet Sugar's pitch, as it was throughout the 'war' between us, has incredibly been to try and stake the claim to the moral high ground. He may be a foul-mouthed, rough diamond, runs his publicity, but he is an honest man. As Sugar himself said in an interview, 'I'm no angel, but I've always run things straight and honest.'

Perhaps Sugar should tell that to the Amstrad shareholders. Sugar offered them 30 pence a share in December 1992 to take Amstrad back as a private company, after it had plunged to a £70.9 million loss in 1991–92. Sugar told the shareholders that the position of the company was hopeless, saying, 'I am your receiver. I am your liquidator.' His pessimistic forecasts were backed up by independent advisers, who also recommended acceptance of Sugar's largesse. The shareholders were sceptical of the offer, however, and questioned why Sugar was so eager to buy their shares. Led by a small shareholder named Gideon Fiegel, whose name is probably now as painful to Sugar as that of Terry Venables, the shareholders revolted and threw the plan out.

The half-year results, returned just five weeks after Sugar's 'crisis meeting', showed a dramatic improvement, and by the next shareholders' meeting, Amstrad was firmly back in the black. Unsurprisingly, Sugar had a very rough ride at the meeting. Fiegel once more led the interrogation, asking Sugar, 'If you didn't know five weeks before the half year-end what profits were likely to be, what are you doing as chief executive?'

In an interview with the magazine *Business Age* in March 1994 Sugar claimed that the 30 pence offer had been an opportunity for the shareholders to have taken a big dividend. He said the fact the share price went up was for one of two reasons: for hype or through results. As Amstrad had not made any profits it could only have been sentiment that pushed the price up.

Sugar's business dealings are in my view accurately summed up by the attitude he displayed in the same interview in which he winningly remarked, 'retailers are prostitutes and the City are still assholes.' The City must reciprocate his feelings, for Sugar's Tottenham board contains two men who cannot do much for City confidence – Alan Sugar and Tony Berry.

For some reason neither the City nor the retail trade have much of a liking for Sugar any more. As he himself admitted, in a rare moment of self-abasement, 'We're getting paid back in the manner we treated the retailers in the mid-1980s, when we had a very arrogant and contemptuous attitude.' The only things that I would query in that assessment are his use of the word 'we' and the past tense.

Sugar's business ethics remained less than sparkling when he set off in search of 'another geezer' to replace me. Having decided that the return of Ossie Ardiles might pacify the Tottenham fans, he lured him away from West Bromwich Albion, without worrying too much about the legal niceties. As West

Brom chairman Trevor Summers complained, 'The way the deal was conducted was absolutely scandalous. This is a matter of principle. It is clear there was a contract and the rules have been broken.' The Premier League clearly agreed, for Tottenham were fined £25,000 for their breach of the rules.

The only evidence that the 'straight and honest' Sugar can produce in support of his position against me comes from board minutes at Tottenham. The most serious error I made in this whole business – apart from linking up with Alan Sugar in the first place – was to underestimate the importance of those board minutes in a plc. By the time I realised the way that Sugar was exploiting that situation, several lots of inaccurate and misleading minutes had already been produced.

With Sugar as the chairman, and Sandy, his own man, producing the minutes – one of the company secretary's tasks – the minutes would always read exactly as Sugar wanted. The trick – and I protested regularly about this – was that those minutes would always appear as part of the package of papers tabled for the next board meeting. Until my protests, there was never pre-circulation of the minutes. We would arrive to start the next board meeting, with an agenda already set to run for four or five hours, and there would be ten or fifteen pages of minutes of the previous meeting. Sugar's first remark would be: 'Can we approve the minutes from the last meeting?' My invariable reaction was: 'How can we approve them? We haven't even read them yet.'

For the first few board meetings, however, both Jonathan Crystal and I decided to save time and avoid embarrassment by just assuming that the minutes would be accurate and agreeing them without studying them first, and the first four or five sets slipped through on that basis. It was a serious error of judgement on my part, but I was not then aware of the real nature of Alan Sugar, nor the use to which those minutes would later be put.

In those first few meetings there were some critical issues, particularly over the loans made by Irving Scholar, a matter of vital importance. Sugar and Sandy's massaging of the minutes was blatant. The comment in the minutes was: 'Mr Sugar is of the firm opinion that this must be disclosed as soon as possible.' Yet that is completely untrue; his attitude in discussion had been the exact reverse of that . . . and two and a half years later, he had still not disclosed it. He had slipped that into the minutes and was later able to use it in evidence.

After one or two occurrences like that, I then insisted that there was pre-circulation of the minutes. Two or three days before the next board meeting, Eddie or I would ring up Sandy and say, 'Board meeting in two days, Colin, where are the management accounts, where are the minutes?' Sandy would then waffle through a few excuses, and finally, if we were lucky, we would have a day to go through the minutes and possibly even the management accounts.

At the board meeting, we would try to raise five or six points on which we did not agree. Even that turned into a drama and we would find ourselves spending an hour talking about the last board meeting all over again. Sugar would get more and more aggressive, saying, 'What the fuck is all this about, we had all that at the last fucking meeting, I ain't talking about this no more.' Jonathan Crystal and I stuck to our guns, however, which created great friction with Sugar.

When John Ireland was brought in as 'in-house solicitor', primarily at Jonathan Crystal's instigation, he also took on the role of company secretary. As a legal professional, Ireland wanted things specific and correct and therefore would not change the minutes. They would come out much earlier, within two or three days of the board meeting, which is what should happen, so we had three weeks to think about it. The draft minutes would be circulated and 'a war of memos' about the minutes would break out, with Sugar claiming, 'No, I never said that.' Jonathan and I never deliberately fostered the antagonism and the 'us and them' situation that developed; we just wanted it right, but that brought us into head-on collision with Sugar.

There is some very specific evidence over things like the Cadbury Report, which recommended among other things that companies should have non-executive directors, an audit committee of directors and/or senior executives reviewing the accounts and the way that they were presented, and a remuneration committee, looking at the payment of senior executives. Sugar wanted the minutes to show that he publicly supported the Cadbury Report, even though he was vehemently opposed to it, and he tried to manipulate the minutes to achieve his aim.

These apparently trivial sort of issues turned into major battles and it became impossible to get the minutes agreed. All that did was throw into sharper focus the manipulation of the minutes that had been happening all the way down the line. The fundamental reason for Sugar's attention to what the minutes said is that, particularly in a plc, the board minutes are a matter of public record. They are available to every shareholder and must be kept indefinitely. As lawyers and journalists search for evidence to support one side or the other, they go back to the minutes, which is why it was so very important to Sugar that they 'read right'. Sugar wanted a public position which often did not reflect the views that he had forcefully argued in the meetings. It became increasingly important to us not to allow him to get away with any further exploits of this kind, and the minutes became another running sore, another reason why he did not want Venables, Crystal and Ashby around, asking awkward questions and exposing contradictions.

Sugar continues to present himself as the 'Mr Clean' of Tottenham and I am the one who has been under the cloud of suspicion, yet despite all the pro-Sugar propaganda since then, I was the person to instigate the inquiries conducted by the Football Association, the Premier League and the police. I am the man who tried to bring the full story out into the open, before the courts.

The FA Commission of Inquiry set up to investigate Tottenham's catalogue of irregular deals charged that Spurs broke the 'regulations dealing with the avoidance and evasion of fees' from transfer tribunals in the three cases. In total, forty charges were considered by the Commission of Inquiry, twenty of which related to breaches of transfer regulations.

When Swindon were found guilty of cheating rival clubs in 1990, they were demoted. Tottenham faced the possibility of the same punishment as the result of Scholar's dealings and Sugar's cover-up. When the Commission of Inquiry announced its findings on 14 June 1994, however, the punishment fell short of demotion, though it was still harsh enough. Spurs were fined £600,000, had twelve points deducted from their Premiership total in the next season, 1994–95, were banned from the 1994–95 FA Cup and ordered to pay the costs of the inquiry.

The members of the Commission spent almost nine hours listening to Sugar's six-man delegation pleading their case, but as the *Independent* reported the next day:

> In the event the mitigating circumstances pleaded by Spurs in a 1,000-page presentation appeared to amount to very little. The five-man commission found them guilty as charged of breaches of transfer regulations and were apparently unmoved by Spurs' protests that they were the crimes of a previous regime; perhaps not previous enough for the FA's liking, since two directors, Douglas Alexiou and Tony Berry, and Peter Barnes, who had been club secretary throughout, remain from the earlier one.

Among Sugar's reported comments was the statement that 'I was always brought up to believe honesty is the best policy, and have followed that throughout my career ... in view of the Inland Revenue inquiries into most Premiership clubs, my suggestion to the chairmen of other clubs is to follow my lead and disclose any irregularities.' As the *Independent* pointed out, however, 'The FA also seem to have viewed unfavourably the fact that Spurs, though fully co-operative, did not bring the irregularities to the attention of the FA until some two years after they came to light in 1991.' In addition, Paul Allen, the recipient of one of the 'loans' from Scholar, made a statement to the Premier League Inquiry that 'I was surprised to receive on Tuesday 17 May (1994) a telephone call at my home from Sugar, who said he wanted me to come to his office at Amstrad's headquarters at Brentwood and sign a statement to the effect that the money I received from the club was a loan. He also said that it would confirm that I had not defrauded West Ham when my fee was decided at the tribunal.' Allen did not respond to Sugar's request.

After my experiences over the previous twelve months, it came as no great surprise when some sections of the media immediately associated my name with the punishment for Tottenham, and in some papers allegations already made a year before and considered and rejected by the Premier League Inquiry were dusted off and aired again as if they were new. As an FA spokesman remarked, 'The FA is aware of the story. It is also aware of the coincidence of its timing. The matter the story refers to has already been addressed by the current Premier League Inquiry.'

Just as predictably, Sugar's public statements on the affair pointed an accusing finger at me and accused the FA of 'a vendetta against the club, if not me', claiming that 'they are paranoid that I want to discredit them in some way over their choice of manager'. The FA was unable to comment on the Commission of Inquiry's findings in case an appeal was lodged, but after Sugar's outburst, a brief statement was issued:

Allegations of any personal vendetta defy all logic. Mr Venables has had nothing whatsoever to do with the investigation into

Tottenham Hotspur. His position as England coach is unaffected. On Tuesday (14 June 1994) Tottenham Hotspur itself admitted many charges of breaking football regulations over many years. The FA were not prepared to give details of those charges, because proceedings were and remain confidential. However Mr Sugar has seen fit to say that there were 22 charges admitted. The figure is inaccurate, 34 charges were admitted.

The *Daily Star* reported on Friday, 17 June 1994, 'FA officials privately insisted that Venables was not even mentioned during the Commission's hearings.' Colin Sandy's comment, also reported in the *Daily Star* that day, 'The board will be taking advice on possible legal action against past employees and directors' was really carefully phrased. The advice to take legal action had been lying on Sugar's desk, unheeded, for over two years.

Tottenham duly appealed and succeeded in having the twelve-point deduction reduced to six, but only at the price of having the fine increased from £600,000 to £1.5 million, and the club were still banned from the FA Cup. It is a matter of the deepest regret to me that Tottenham Hotspur FC and its supporters had to bear such a heavy punishment. It did seem harsh and a hefty fine should have been sufficient – you do not want the fans to suffer for the misdeeds of club officials – but I also have a lot of sympathy for the predicament that the FA and the Premier League found themselves in. The FA is forced by its own regulations and jurisdiction to penalise the club rather than individuals, a situation that is as distasteful to the FA as it is to the supporters.

The officials of the FA and the Premier League have the thankless task of implementing regulations that do not really cater for this kind of abuse. If coaching England is 'the impossible job', how on earth can you describe the job of chief executive at the FA or the Premier League? I have tremendous admiration for the Premier League's Rick Parry, in particular, who has managed to steer a path through a minefield of problems. He has had a horrendously difficult job to do and has done it admirably.

Until the rules are changed, men compromised by their association with wrongdoing are theoretically free to be involved in running football clubs from here till Doomsday, with the FA and Premier League currently powerless to intervene. The rules cannot be altered retrospectively, and Tottenham will have to bear whatever punishment the FA sees fit to impose, but the regulations must surely be amended, so that in any future case where the officers or directors of a club are found guilty of abuses they will be debarred from ever again holding office at that, or any other club. The guilty men could then be punished and the club left clean and untainted.

Football is called 'the people's game'. That should mean the people that play it and the people that watch and support it, but ever since the game began, it has been the people's game with a layer of the establishment on the top, controlling it. That still applies, perhaps to an even bigger extent. The buyers, the Alan Sugars of this world, believe that it is their game, but they are wrong.

When we took over, I told Sugar, The problem you've got, is that it doesn't matter how much money you put in, how much you make or how much you lose, you will have to leave the real decisions of this business to someone else – you're going to have to leave them to me. Now he is having to leave them to Ardiles. If he wants to buy the best players, he has to lay out a huge amount of money – £3 million, £4 million, or £5 million. In any other business, he would make the purchasing decision himself, but in football it is the manager, not the chairman, who chooses the players, the tactics and the team. This is the problem that all the directors have: they run their own businesses themselves, but in football they have to leave it to someone else – a manager – which is an inevitable source of friction.

The coach is more important than any of them, because he is close to the team; he makes it function or he does not. Sugar will still be sitting there, thinking 'It's my money, this is wrong', but he cannot change it unless he puts a tracksuit on and becomes a manager. Otherwise, he cannot control it, and none of them can; that is their big frustration.

Football in Italy or Spain always used to be talked about as being 'like a religion'. That was never said about the game in this country when I was young. Football here was something else, more than a recreation but less than a religion. I get the distinct feeling now, that for young people, football is replacing religion. After several years of recession, many young people have not got much to be proud of. They are doubting their government, their country, their religion, they are doubting a leadership that cannot do anything to help them. Only their football team does anything for them. It gives them pride in themselves and where they come from.

Football is not just another 'opiate of the masses', however; it is of far more significance to working people than that. If Barcelona FC embodies the culture of the Catalan people, football in Britain is the embodiment of the culture of working people. You do not have to have an old school tie, or have the right sort of accent; if you have the skill and determination, you can play the game, become a coach and a manager and aspire to rise higher – if you have the self-belief.

I hope that the things I have done will persuade other footballers from similar origins, to aspire to bigger things themselves. It was important that I did well in Barcelona, not just for me, but so that kids could see that you could go abroad and do well. I hoped that that they might say, 'I can go to Barcelona, because Terry Venables did it. If he can do it, I can do it.' That is what I have always believed, but it is more an American than an English attitude – the English are just as likely to think, 'Flash bastard'. It was important too, that I owned a club, so that kids could also see that it was possible. They might now be thinking, 'Well, you can't do that one, he got his fingers burned, the man with the money showed him,' but I really do not think that it was a failing of mine – and I would be happy to admit it if I thought that it was.

In all the attacks that have been made on me, nowhere is it suggested that I did a bad job, or that the company was unprofitable. Even two years at Tottenham proved to me that I could do what I said I would do – improve the club, improve the football, improve the finances. I did not do it alone, of course, I had the help of a hell of a lot of other people, but it was not done with the aim of making money for me. Unlike Sugar, who thought that he was going to get a good return on his money every year, I did not go into it for that. I knew that I was going to be well paid for perhaps fifteen years, of course, but most of all, I wanted to put my mark on the club, and that would have been enough for me.

Sugar put several million pounds into Tottenham, which is an awful lot of money, but it is relative. If you have £71 million in the bank, as he once told me, an investment of a few million is not that significant. It is a vast amount of money and more than most people would earn in several lifetimes, but not to him. I put every penny I had and every penny I could raise into Tottenham, because I believed in the dream, Sugar put his loose change into it and then robbed me of my dream.

We did not like each other. That was it. No one could believe that was all there was to it, but that was the top and bottom of it. Our basic problem was that we could not get on, but I was prepared to co-exist to make it work. If I have an ordinary player who is a bit of aggravation to me, he is not worth it, but if I have a player like Gascoigne, he is worth a bit of aggravation. Sugar should have been wise enough to learn the same lesson and say, 'This man is making it work, we've got to have some common sense and find a way to work together.' If he had been in the game longer, he would not have done what he did.

The feud between Alan Sugar and me did have its lighter moments, however. I was invited to Harry's Bar for dinner one evening, but when I entered, the first person I saw was Alan Sugar. Everyone else in the place froze, waiting open-mouthed to see what would happen next. It was like the clichéd scene from a thousand Westerns, where the honky-tonk piano stops dead and everyone falls silent, preparing to dive under the tables, as the gunslinger enters the saloon for a shoot-out. There was a long silence as Sugar and I stared at each other, then both of us turned away, the customers let out a collective sigh of relief – or disappointment – and the babble of conversation started up again.

Sugar may well have contributed an enormous amount to Amstrad and his ways have obviously worked well for him in other areas, but a football club is like a family and families do not survive if they are broken apart. That is the difference between selling computers or satellite dishes and running a football club. We were on the verge of greatness only for it to be thrown away by a man who thinks that human beings can be interchanged as easily as components in a computer. He had been in the game two years and thought he knew it. I have been in it all my working life and I am still not sure I know it.

The ridiculous thing is that it was all so unnecessary. Had he come to me and said, 'Look, it's not working out, I want you to go. I'll make you a fair offer for your shares and compensate you properly for the work that you have done,' while I would not have liked it, I would have accepted it. Instead he took the club from me and then tried to justify his actions by making a series of false statements about me. I have been in football for thirty-five years without a blemish and I have never taken a back-hander in my life. Yet all of a sudden, I was labelled a crook and a fraud.

Even when the last false allegation has been nailed, however, and the last legal battle won, it seems unlikely now that I will ever be able to return to Tottenham. Events have moved on. I now have the England job, while Sugar holds in excess of 50 per cent of the Tottenham shares, and would have to be willing to dispose of his shareholding for any other party to take control. No bookmaker in the world would offer odds on that.

At the time of the court case, Sugar complained, 'Mr Venables says he has suffered a nightmare, but no one spat on him, smashed his car up or called him the names they've called me. No one chanted and shouted abuse outside his house.' They did not have to. I was being abused, slandered and libelled, called a crook, a cheat and a thief, not in front of half a dozen people outside my house, but in front of tens of millions of people in the newspapers and on television.

No amount of damages will compensate me for the theft of the dream that I had worked so long and hard to achieve, but having been defeated only by the obscene cost of British 'justice' on the first round, the second and final battle will be fought on ground that is simpler and less expensive to contest. Enough evidence exists in statements, tape-recordings, affidavits and documents, to prove my innocence. The result is not in doubt: my good name will be restored.

# CHAPTER TEN

# England Coach

## 1994

I THOUGHT THAT EVENTUALLY there would be a let-up in the trial by media, as both the reporters and readers became tired of seeing the same old stuff dragged up, but I had reckoned without the effect of Graham Taylor's resignation as England boss in November 1993. A rank outsider at the start of the race, I did not give myself a cat in hell's chance of taking over his job. If anything, the odds of 25/1 quoted in the papers seemed on the stingy side. If only I had known, I would have had a few quid on myself. My name began to be mentioned more and more frequently as the likely choice and, as my odds shortened, the enemy sharpened their pens for a further series of attacks, typified by the comment from *Sunday Times* editor Andrew Neil, who said in a radio broadcast that if I was made England manager, it would be the first time that the team had been coached from prison. After that remark people might assume that I would be pleased with Andrew's recent move to New York, but they would be wrong . . . it is still too close!

The FA had passed up the chance to interview me four years previously, after Bobby Robson quit the job, apparently not even considering me worthy of a place on the short-list. It seemed obvious that what was wrong with me in the eyes of at least some of the venerable gentlemen of the FA was not my coaching ability, but my personality. People often told me that I was 'not an FA type', which I took to mean that I was too outspoken, too much my own man, and perhaps had too strong a cockney accent to be acceptable to the mandarins of Lancaster Gate. The FA seemed to prefer their managers to be conservative and unobtrusive – Alf Ramsey and Bobby Robson, not Malcolm Allison and Brian Clough. Perhaps I was also seen as too much of a joker, but while I never take myself too seriously, I take my football very seriously indeed and the omission from a short-list of Graham Taylor, Howard Kendall and Joe Royle, who had never coached above the Second Division, still rankled with me. I had said at the time: 'Sod 'em. Forget it, I'll do something else.'

Had the FA kept to its traditional way of doing things, I am sure I would not have been on the short-list this time either, for Sir Bert Millichip, the chairman of the FA, was definitely not a supporter of mine in the early stages. But at the prompting of Graham Kelly, the International Committee broke with its tradition of deciding the short-list and recruited Jimmy Armfield to take wide-ranging soundings among English coaches and players before drawing up a short-list for the England job. Jimmy was a little bit older than me and I had held in him high regard in his playing days, as he always showed the style and ability of an international. Jimmy talked to a host of coaches, including Alex Ferguson, George Graham, Dave Sexton, Bobby Robson and Howard Wilkinson. He also spoke to Johnny Giles and Gordon Taylor of the PFA, and to the men who had just left the job, Graham Taylor and his assistant Lawrie McMenemy.

A further round of consultations followed, with senior players and the men who might be candidates for the job. Apart from me, Trevor Francis, Gerry Francis, Kevin Keegan, Ray Wilkins, Glenn Hoddle and Bryan Robson were possibilities. Some disqualified themselves and others lacked experience, but the name suggested to Jimmy by a large majority of the coaches and players was mine. When he reported back, the FA then instructed him to meet me and open discussions in secret.

The first time we met was a week before Christmas, at the

Royal Lancaster Hotel in London. We sat and drank endless
cups of coffee, while he informed me that he had been up and
down the country, speaking to a great many people, who had
been practically unanimous in recommending me for the job. He
had certainly been thorough in his research. Premier League
chief executive Rick Parry later told me that, while drawing up
a draft contract for the England job with the FA lawyers,
Jimmy had turned to one of the solicitors and asked, 'What do
you think of Terry Venables as a coach?'

The vote of confidence from coaches, players – and solicitors
– was a nice lift after a difficult few months. The press had
already been talking about me as a possible England manager,
but journalists do not really appreciate your qualities in the way
that your peers in the game – the players and coaches – do. I
would always want to be judged as a coach by players rather
than the media, directors, or anybody else, because the others
do not see your work, and even if they did, would not recognise
what you had done. Even if I had not been given the job in the
end, the fact that I was the number-one choice of the footballers,
the coaches and the public meant everything.

Jimmy and I spoke for about three hours altogether, ranging
over all aspects of football, including Jimmy's own career. It
was very relaxed and low-key, and we got on well. By Christmas
Eve, he had held more talks with other people and events had
moved on. He wanted to speak to me again, but could not make
up his mind whether to come to London by car or train. He
called me, discussed it, said he would phone back in half an
hour, when he had made up his mind, and then called me back
to say he still could not decide. If he was having all this trouble
with travel arrangements, I could see the appointment of the
next England coach being settled only just in time for the
European Championships in 1996.

It reminded me of the days when he was managing Leeds
and I was managing Crystal Palace and Jimmy wanted to buy

Peter Taylor from us. We wanted £200,000 for him, which was a great deal of money then. Jimmy had offered £160,000 and kept asking me if I thought Peter was good enough, and would do the job for them. I told him: 'Leave off, I'm selling him, what do you expect me to say?' In actual fact, I did believe he was an outstanding player who, against the odds, had played for England while in a Third Division side. While Jimmy was prevaricating, Peter signed for Tottenham, for the £200,000 we had been asking.

On this occasion Jim eventually did make up his mind to come up by train. He did not like the idea of meeting at the station, in case anyone saw us together. Since the papers had already reported that he had spoken to me, that seemed a bit like shutting the dressing-room door after the team had already bolted and I finally managed to persuade him that it would be perfectly all right to meet at the station and talk in my car. I had eaten a heavily garlic-laced dinner the night before, however, and absolutely reeked of it the next morning. I could not talk to him in the car while I was stinking of garlic, and told Yvette that I would take him to a hotel. Yvette raised an eyebrow, gave me a quizzical look and said, 'What, are you going to sleep your way to the top?'

While waiting at the station, I opened the car window and shovelled down peppermints to try and get rid of the smell. When Jimmy got in, I talked to him while looking out of my window, to avoid breathing on him, and all he could see was the back of my head. In the end, despite Yvette's comments, we went to a hotel.

Jimmy was trying to clarify a few points and mention some problem areas, and he wanted to ask more in-depth questions, both about football and my business interests. I had a clear impression that I was coming very close to being offered the job, rather than just having a general discussion, but the FA were still concerned about the court case against Alan Sugar.

Their concern was entirely understandable, for they had read all the stories in the newspapers, and while I knew that the allegations were completely unfounded, they had only my word for that. Jimmy asked me if I would be willing to take the position on a caretaker basis, but I refused, feeling that it would have left me too vulnerable, giving the 'anti-press' an open season on me, while also preventing me from taking any other jobs that might come up in the meantime.

The FA also wanted to know if there were any skeletons in the cupboard, waiting to be discovered. I said, 'Jim, I've had more inquiries than the Jockey Club stewards. I've seen the Police, the Special Fraud Office, the Inland Revenue, the Customs and Excise, the Department of Trade and Industry, and just about everybody else you can think of. If there was anything to find, they would have found it. For some extraordinary reason, people keep making allegations about me to these bodies, which then have to investigate them, even though they turn out to be false. The press are told that I am under investigation, by the same mystery informants.' When Jim left I firmly believed that the job was mine, but there was to be an agonising wait of over a month before the final confirmation.

My formal interview at the FA was scheduled for eleven o'clock on a grey January morning. I had woken early and ploughed through the newspapers. For the last few weeks they seemed to have been running 'Venables will get the job' and 'Venables will not get the job' stories on alternate days, but even the tabloids' feeding-frenzy appeared to have been sated for the moment. For once there was no rash of fresh speculation on the sports pages and, even more mercifully, there were no new 'Venables ate my hamster' allegations on the news or business pages.

I lingered over the papers as long as possible, but still had two hours to kill. After pacing around the house for half an hour, driving Yvette mad, I decided to walk to the interview, held not in the FA headquarters at Lancaster Gate, but in the Football League's Commercial Department in Old Marylebone Road, in the hope of throwing the football reporters door-stepping the FA building off the scent. I kissed Yvette, told her that, win or lose, we would have a special dinner that night, and set off. I reached the offices in good time and paused for a moment outside the glass double-doors.

Here I was, the only name on a short-list of one, and the only things that could prevent me from becoming the next England manager were not football matters, but the slurs, allegations and accusations levelled at my character and business dealings. Although I knew in time everything would be cleared up, for the moment, my immediate fate rested with a group of men, waiting in a room on the seventh floor.

The last time I had met most of them was in the middle of a furious row over the FA's insistence that Nick Barmby should join an England Youth tour to Australia. Tottenham had a Cup quarter-final match with Manchester City coming up, but the FA were insisting that all players, even if they were in the first team, should go. One of my complaints was that he should not play three games a week, which he was going to have to do in Australia. We were playing him, then resting him for six days before he played again and I did not want him overloaded.

Barmby himself was disappointed with the FA, because he wanted to play his part in the Cup tie, and we really went right up to the wire with them. They were threatening to take us to court because we would not let Barmby go, but by then I was already beginning to think that I had made my point and that no good would come, for the club, the player or me, of going on with it much longer. I saw FA chief executive Graham Kelly, and said, 'Right, the boy goes,' told Barmby and that was it.

The FA Committee was already in session and there was a message to say that my interview might be delayed for a little while. Rather than cool my heels and worry about the reasons for the delay, I grabbed a cup of coffee and wandered down to Lee Walker's office. I knew him quite well socially, and I spent twenty-five minutes talking about football with Lee before I was summoned to the inner chamber on the seventh floor.

The room was small, plainly-decorated and dominated by a large mahogany table. Like the rest of the building, there was nothing in the decor to suggest a link with football, no pictures or memorabilia. It could as easily have been the modest board-room of a rather staid and old-fashioned corporation, like the HQ of a surgical-appliance manufacturer. Sir Bert Millichip presided over an interviewing panel that included Ian Stott, the chairman of Oldham FC, Noel White, the vice-chairman of Liverpool, Graham Kelly and Jimmy Armfield. Sir Bert set the ball rolling by asking what I thought of the structure of the game and the present England set-up, and what qualities I could bring to it. The need for change in the structure of the game in England is a particular hobby-horse of mine, and I outlined my views.

Over the years there has been far too much of a divide between the professional and amateur halves of the game and it is imperative that the two sides are brought closer. Most people in the FA have had a different kind of schooling or upbringing from professional footballers. The traditional 'FA type' of coach came from an amateur background, had not played professional football and was more like a schoolteacher.

For two weeks at Lilleshall every year the professionals and amateurs used to have one chance to get closer. The FA-type coaches and the pros would be out on the pitches, coaching together for a fortnight, and an FA man called Alan Wade used to do a particularly good job in bridging the gap between the two sides. At the sessions I attended, he identified Malcolm Allison as a leader and had a mickey-taking session with him, developing a bit of rapport, and by getting Malcolm on his side, he had everyone.

Something went wrong, somewhere, after that, however. Charlie Hughes, the FA director of coaching, who is still in the post, tried to get on with the pros, and show them what was wrong, but came up against a bit of a wall with the players. He felt he was right about many things, but instead of pursuing it, and convincing the doubters, he decided to walk away from the confrontation, and the split grew wider. It has to be closed. The PFA are now making a big move on coaching courses, and if we are not careful, the FA and PFA will end up competing with each other.

Many of the arguments that have erupted centre on the belief that Hughes is an apostle of the 'long-ball game'. Some dismiss it as 'kick-and-rush' as if nothing had changed in English football for forty years. It is too harsh a description and it is not even true to say that England were playing kick-and-rush in 1953 – Stanley Matthews, for one, was scarcely a kick-and-rush merchant – when the Hungarians' travelling circus rolled into town. England played a style of football that had always been successful for us and so saw no reason to change, but all of a sudden, these Hungarians appeared – like Martians with brand-new weapons that no one had ever seen before – and destroyed us. It made us realise that we were not leading the world any more.

It is tempting to see parallels between that situation and the one forty years later when England's obsession with 'Route One' football was causing us problems. The Route One approach has not done our game any good and it was not the right way to go. It is not a question of believing in short passing as opposed to long passing, it is a question of combining the best of both. We have many good qualities in our game, but our technical abilities have grown worse, if for no other reason than the mere fact that the long ball cut out a lot of work in the middle. It became just a matter of 'Let's get it up there as quick as we can, and catch them out', but when we played against the best teams, it did not work.

As well as damaging the technical skills of players, Route One has damaged the imagination of coaches. They took four or five values from that approach and became fairly successful with them, but the imagination and enjoyment of seeing things that were different, challenging, good to watch, vanished. Fortunately, good footballing teams have now returned to the top.

The game's possibilities are endless, but before they can be fulfilled there has to be much thinking, and many changes. First of all, we have to strip the game of some of the fear, because there are too many managers living from day to day. Before we can give the country its super stadiums, we first need to ensure the basic security of the manager's post. Clubs complain with good reason when managers walk out on them in mid-season, in breach of contract, but you can scarcely blame the managers when clubs have shown themselves more than willing to sack managers part-way through the season as well. Both sides should operate by the same rules.

How often do you see managers who have poured their energies into setting up a youth policy not being allowed the time to exploit that work? At the least, a club should stick with its staff for the whole season – the manager should not leave and the club should not sack him. If a sacking is absolutely unavoidable, because the manager has lost the confidence of everyone at the club, I would like to see a regulation compelling a club to fill the breach from its existing staff, until the end of the season. They should not have the option of picking up another manager from another club, because that is just passing the problem down the line.

A contract should really be for three years, to give the man time to show what he can do. If you give him a cast-iron contract, then he has a chance. At the end of that time, his work can then be reviewed. That is the time when it becomes fair to make judgements. In the meantime, as you broaden his horizons, you encourage him to be bold.

The game has become corrupted by caution. We need to reward aggression and boldness with extra points and sweep away the absurdities like allowing teams to come out of a o—o draw with a point each. How can you give a team a reward when it has failed to score? By one simple device the authorities could bring in a new era of attacking football. Wipe out the points for a goalless draw and the effect would be dramatic, changing the emphasis of the game at a stroke, without introducing any artificial element. It is also absurd to see highly skilled footballers ploughing through thick mud in midwinter. The skill dwindles and the game loses its point. I believe that ultimately soccer will become a better weather game – imagine the incentive to develop skills, playing on thickly grassed, true pitches.

Throughout the interview, the panel members did not once refer to Graham Taylor by name; they spoke only about the previous regime rather than the individuals. Our analysis of where we now stood was very similar, and bordered on the blindingly obvious: at international level, English football was at an all-time low. The World Cup in the United States could have had an even greater impact in England had the team been there and would have generated an enormous amount of commercial revenue to plough back into the game. Having failed to qualify, however, there was no point in wallowing in pessimism; we had to be positive and make the most of this chance to take the game forward.

As I talked, the members of the panel frequently came in with questions, but I felt quite relaxed and not under any pressure at all. It was far from the solemn and difficult meeting reported in the press; Sir Bert was right, it was nothing like an inquisition. It was hard to continue feeling relaxed after Graham Kelly's dramatic intervention, however, when he leapt to his feet, pointed out of the window and said, 'Oh my God, there's a woman on the roof over there. She's going to jump.'

I have to confess that my initial thoughts were not full of

concern for the fate of the woman. I was halfway through the most important interview of my life, and here was a complete stranger, doing her best to blow it for me. All I could think was: Why me, why here, why now? A few moments later normal human sympathy – plus a touch of morbid curiosity – took over, and I joined the rest of the assembled company at the window, saying, 'I don't believe it, every day's a drama.'

Directly opposite us and about twenty yards away, the woman sat on the parapet at the edge of the roof, staring down into the street below, while a few yards beyond her, two policemen awaited developments. We did the same for a few minutes, but in the absence of even a flicker of activity from the rooftop, Sir Bert finally decided to get back to business. He resumed his seat and cleared his throat, calling the meeting to order. Graham Kelly was the last to return to his chair, saying, 'It just goes to show, I bet she's got more problems than all of us.' I smiled and thought: Speak for yourself. If she had my problems, she would have jumped twenty minutes ago.

The remainder of the interview covered more personal territory, in particular the allegations in the media of wrongdoing, and the legal battles with Alan Sugar. The panel's concern was entirely understandable, because it would have been very embarrassing for them to have appointed me, if there later proved to be any substance in the allegations. They had already made their own inquiries into the existing allegations and I reassured them that there was no smoking gun, stinking corpse or anything else left over from my time at Tottenham that might compromise them or me.

They then asked a series of specific questions: 'Would you think about dropping the court case against Alan Sugar?'

'No. It is my right. I had three years left on my contract at Tottenham and my dismissal was wrong. Sugar did it for his own personal reasons – to get me out.'

'Well, would you be prepared to settle out of court?'

'Yes. I don't think either of us wants any more aggravation. As long as it was a sensible offer, I would be happy to get my lawyers to sit down and agree a settlement that was fair to both sides. I would have no problems with that.'

'Are you still a friend of Eddie Ashby, your financial adviser?'

'Yes.'

'Is he still doing any work for you?'

'Yes, as my personal assistant in my private business.'

We finally discussed money. Graham Kelly outlined what the pay for the job was likely to be, and though it was certainly not a king's ransom, I had already made up my mind that I would not haggle over the money, and told them so. The interview lasted ninety minutes in all. There was no definite offer of the position there and then, but while the rest of the panel stayed in the room to continue their deliberations, Jimmy Armfield saw me to the lift and seemed very upbeat and pleased with the way it had gone. He also warned me: 'Whatever happens, don't say a word to anyone about this meeting, because no one knows we are here.'

'It's not in my interests to say anything, Jimmy. The only comment I have made throughout this whole process has been to say that I would be interested in the job, if it was offered.'

When I got down to reception I mentioned to the guy on the desk that there was a woman on the roof threatening to jump off because, after all, you do not see that every day of the week. Apparently you do in Old Marylebone Road. All he said was: 'Oh no, not her again. Last time she was there at three o'clock in the morning, and woke everybody up. It was a right carry-on.'

With Jimmy Armfield's warning still ringing in my ears, I made sure there were no paparazzi hovering in the street before slipping out of the doors. I strolled down the street and picked up an *Evening Standard* on the corner. Right across the back

page was emblazoned the headline: VENABLES IN SECRET MEET-
ING WITH FA. If you jumped off the roof anywhere in London
the press would know about it before you hit the ground . . .

Getting a decision from the FA on the England job was
nowhere near as quick. They blew hot and cold from one day to
the next and kept Howard Wilkinson and Gerry Francis on a
reserve list for the job, just in case. Behind the scenes, they
remained very positive, but kept telling me that they had 'difficulties' and asking me to wait a little bit longer, and then a bit
longer still.

It dragged on and on and my family and friends went
through agonies, waiting and hoping for everything to turn out
right. As light relief, Tottenham Hotspur plc served a winding-
up order on my company Edennote, as they endeavoured to
recover their court costs. Meanwhile, the pro- and anti-Venables
factions carried on with their lobbying. I finally reached the
stage where I began to think, Do I really need this?

I did have other offers of work to consider, with both
Nigeria and Wales offering me the jobs of managing their
national sides. The Nigerians wanted me to oversee their World
Cup campaign, and, unlike England, they had already qualified
for the finals. John Fashanu came into Scribes one day and told
me that they had also approached him about playing in the side.
I was not sure how seriously to take the approach when it was
first made, but the Nigerians were genuine and very interested. I
could not commit myself to anything else while the England job
was still possible, however, and in the end I had to turn them
down.

The Welsh had also made contact just before Christmas,
around the same time that England were beginning to look as if
they were interested. The chief executive of the Welsh FA, Alun
Evans, came to see me at Scribes, and confirmed they were
willing to give me the job there and then. I would have grabbed
it with both hands, if it had come along on its own when there

was no chance of the England job being available. I really fancied managing Wales because of my relations who still lived there, plus the thought of how special it would have been for my mother.

I told Alun quite frankly that there could be a chance of the England job, but asked him to let me have a think about it, and agreed to give him a call on 28 December. I told him then that I wanted to wait for the interview with the English FA the following week, before reaching a decision. Understandably, he said that Wales did not want to look like second-best to England. We met again the next day, at which point he insisted that it was 'make your mind up time'. I had to turn him down, because my curiosity was too much for me, I could not resist waiting to see if I would be offered the chance to coach England.

It was the second time I had turned down the Welsh job, for I had also been offered it on a part-time basis, shortly after I became manager at Spurs. I was keen to take up the offer then, and felt that I could do justice both to it and to my Spurs commitments, but the then Spurs chairman Irving Scholar was hostile to the idea and, as the man who paid my wages, I understood his objections. Perhaps the chance to manage Wales will come again in the future – to have coached two different national sides would be quite something.

There were not many jobs that would have lured me back into football at that stage. I had had a bit of a bellyful of club football after my experiences at Tottenham, although I would certainly have jumped at the Liverpool job, if it had been offered. Graeme Souness did not leave the club until the day that my appointment as England coach was at last announced, so the opportunity never came up.

The FA kept on wobbling. Even Alan Sugar in his evidence to the Premier League inquiry, headed by Rick Parry, Steve Coppell and Robert Reid QC, had no fresh mud to sling, though, having declared to the press outside that I was the man for the job, he then went inside and said the opposite. Despite that, the inquiry could find no reason why I should be debarred from taking the England job. The FA had intended to make the announcement on 20 January, but an article in the *Financial Times*, almost the last shot in the extensive armoury ranged against me over the previous few months, raised questions over the way I had funded my share purchases at Spurs. The announcement was postponed while the FA examined these latest allegations.

Meanwhile, Sir Bert Millichip had so far reversed his earlier opinion about me, that he told the press that I was the FA's chosen one. 'It is well recognised that I did have my reservations about Terry Venables,' said Sir Bert, 'but they have been greatly dispelled. There are many, many accusations against him, but when I have asked, no proof has been delivered. There is no proof whatsoever about these allegations.'

Sir Bert Millichip's conversion may have happened, not on the road to Damascus, but on the way back from Las Vegas, where the draw for the World Cup had been held. With England already eliminated at the qualifying stage, Sir Bert Millichip said that he was 'overwhelmed with humiliation; England felt like poor relations'. Perhaps that was what persuaded him to accept the recommendation to choose a coach on his football ability, not his 'clubability'.

On Tuesday, 25 January 1994, the FA finally called me in to tell me that I had been confirmed as England coach – the only man in history who could actually get less publicity as a result of getting the job . . . Despite all the frustration I had felt at the delays in confirming the appointment, however, in the end I was relieved that the FA had taken the time to investigate the allegations against me and satisfy themselves that they were groundless.

Graham Kelly and I met in the Royal Lancaster Hotel with our solicitors, to finalise the details. Matters were very straightforward and it did not take much time to come to an agreement. The FA did suggest a review in six months, which I was willing to agree to, provided that it applied equally to both sides. But after consulting with his colleagues, Graham amended the proposal. The contract would now run for two and a half years, with a clause allowing us to part company if anything substantial came out of any new or old allegations. There would have to be cast-iron proof, however, rather than some journalist making unsubstantiated allegations. I was more than happy with that, and was prepared to say that if that should happen, I would not want any compensation.

The announcement was scheduled for the next day, but the death of Sir Matt Busby forced a postponement, and the press conference was at last held at Wembley, on Friday 28 January. At 1:30 p.m. I emerged from the shadows of the stadium, into the sunlight out on the Wembley turf. The light was made even brighter by the flash-guns of about seventy photographers and the lights of a battery of television crews. The photographers jostled and elbowed each other and kept up a deafening chorus for half an hour, like crows in springtime, cawing for a mate: 'Terry, Terry, Terry. Over here, Terry. Look this way, Terry. Put your arms up, Terry. Look over here, Terry. Come on, Terry. Just one more, Terry. Terry, mate, over here. Terry, one this way. Terry, Terry, Terry. Terry, Terry, Terry.'

After a thirty-minute photo-session, we all trooped upstairs for the press conference, which lasted an hour and then it was back down to the pitch again, for an endless series of TV, radio and newspaper interviews. By the time we had finished, the sun was setting and everyone was exhausted. I shook hands with Sir Bert and Graham and drove back into the West End. I was too tired to set the corks popping in a big way at Scribes. It had been a very long and hard road from the end of one dream, on a summer afternoon at Tottenham, to the winter afternoon at Wembley, when another one was realised. I would have swapped everything, even the England job, for the chance to be back in control at Spurs, free of Sugar's baleful influence, but the most important job in the English game was a glorious prize.

The next morning I began to plan. My first action at any new club has always been to take a sheet of paper and write down the names of the current players whom I felt were up to the task I had set myself. At a club with a good existing pool of players, that might be eight or nine names, and at Barcelona, I had only to make one signing to complete a Championship-winning side. At other, weaker clubs, there have been as few as two names on the sheet of paper when I took over.

In the England job, the rules are different. In theory, I could write down any names I liked, from any club, as long as the players were English, but whereas I had all season to work with players at a club side, day after day and week after week, developing tactics, and working on individual skills, there is scarcely any time to work with your chosen England side before a game. You must concentrate as much as you can on what you have been planning, for your time with the players is desperately limited. If you want to make tactical changes, you have only two days in which to do it, before the players return to their clubs. It makes life very difficult, but you have to believe that it is not impossible.

The responsibilities of the job have grown disproportionately in recent years, and the media interest alone has grown dramatically and become far more intrusive. Don Howe felt that in the four years he had been away from the England scene, the sheer volume of television, radio and press had more than doubled. Dealing with the media is a big part of the job, but it must not be allowed to distract you from your main function.

The question is how best to get things over to your players in the very short time available to you, especially if you are asking them to do something different from what they do at their clubs. The best way, if you can, is to do it the same; the more positions you can fill with people who can play just like they do at their club, the better, but you cannot get it all like that. Germany's way of playing has been with them twenty-five years. Rather like Liverpool, they stuck to a successful pattern, but England have not been successful consistently enough to assume that we can do that.

I wasted no time in worrying what the attitude of the leading clubs might be. England managers have always bemoaned the problem of getting full co-operation from the leading clubs and I am sure there will be difficulties at times, but as England coach, you simply have to try and get a good relationship going with them. If they say their players are injured, then you have to accept it. It is no good questioning their word, because that is when the relationship suffers. It is difficult for a club to let players go for internationals, when they have their own vital commitments, but we must learn to work together. Eventually the League will be reduced in size, making it easier to get the players that we want.

The first job was to pick my coaching team, rather than my players, however, and I was glad to have some previous international experience to look back on. I had been given a great opportunity to work within Ron Greenwood's England set-up in the late 1970s, when I was still only a novice coach. Ron decided to have a group of people around him that he would feel comfortable with and that would offer a lot of ideas. Working alongside him, he had a coach called Bill Taylor, a Scotsman who sadly became ill and died not long afterwards. Ron brought in Bobby Robson and Don Howe to coach England B, Dave Sexton and me to work with the Under-21s, with Howard Wilkinson to help us, and he also had Brian Clough and Peter Taylor working with the Youth team, which is something that hardly anyone remembers now. We all had a meeting in Manchester one Sunday morning, and as a young coach, I had found it very exciting, listening to the views of all these experienced guys around me.

I had known Dave Sexton since I was about eighteen, when he was the coach at Chelsea, and he was the person who really got me interested and motivated to become a coach. We had a terrific time working with the Under-21s, as over a couple of seasons, they qualified for the European Championships, won through to the final and then beat Germany over two legs. When Bobby Robson took over as England manager, however, he came to see me at Newcastle, where we were playing on the opening day of the new season, to tell me that he did not want any part-timers, to use people who were not already club managers. I understood his wishes, but was very confused when he then brought in Graham Taylor and Howard Wilkinson, who were also club managers.

When I started to pick my coaching team, I had no hesitation in including Dave Sexton and Don Howe. Neither are in the first flush of youth, but they are both still so sharp, and complete football nuts, who have lost none of their enthusiasm for the game. They are very bright, professional and inventive, and with luck we can help Bryan Robson and Ray Wilkins, as Dave Sexton once helped me.

The England job has been called 'the impossible job', and the odds are certainly stacked very highly against you. There are not many weak teams in the world any more. Sides that would once have been mere cannon-fodder are not there just to make up the numbers now; they want to win as well. For some reason we all think that England should be ahead of the rest of the world, but we have to learn to be realistic; we have no divine right to be the best and we have to start from basics. I certainly had to do that at the FA when I settled into my office on the third floor of the stately premises in Lancaster Gate, practically a baronial hall, reeking of wealth, power and privilege. The reception area is oak-panelled and thickly carpeted, with an open fireplace and an ornate ceiling. Portraits of Royals hang on the walls, flanking display cases full of silver, porcelain, crystal and cut glass. Blue and gold moquette armchairs and sofas look too pristine ever to have borne the weight of an FA rump.

Upstairs, the newly refurbished offices are equipped with every aid to office efficiency known to modern man, but when I asked for data on other international teams, there was none to be found. When I wanted to talk tactics with my coaching team, I discovered that there was not even a blackboard, and we finished up down on our hands and knees on the carpet, while I moved Subbuteo players around to make my point. My secretary was treated to the sight of three grown men scrabbling around on the floor like kids playing with their Christmas presents.

There was also not a scrap of paper at the FA giving any information about the experiences and coaching philosophies of any of my predecessors. Alf Ramsey, the most successful England manager of the modern era, who led England to the World Cup in 1966 and was unlucky not to go closer than he did in 1970, when England and Brazil were possibly the best two teams in the competition, might as well never have existed. There is nothing on file at the FA to tell us about his ideas, his tactics, or his thoughts on the job. There is nothing from any of his successors either; the accumulated experience and football wisdom of Ramsey, Revie, Greenwood, Robson and Taylor are nowhere to be found.

When I realised the state of affairs, I decided that if I could not discover anything from the files, I would have to talk to the people themselves. I spoke to Graham Taylor first, as the most recent England coach. He was very helpful, and after I had a couple more games under my belt, I planned to speak to the rest of them. By then I should have had a better idea of the problems I would have to face.

There is some information on other teams at the FA, but it is confined to reports of recent games England have played against particular countries. I do not just want to know about those teams, however, I want to know about Brazil, Argentina and the rest. I want to know why Germany and Holland can keep turning out world-class teams, year after year. How can the Dutch manage to do it, from a population not much bigger than that of Greater London?

It is the sort of basic research on competitors and their methods that any decent League team would do without a second thought. Tottenham know about Arsenal, Liverpool and Manchester United, because they are in competition with them. England are in competition with the rest of the football world and we have to have information on our potential opponents and their methods.

All previous England coaches have had scouts operating in England, so that they know what is going on in their own back-yard, but we have to look further afield as well and the FA have now taken on Ted Buxton, who worked so well for me at Tottenham, to fill that role. His brief is to cover the world, building up a library of information on other countries, which will be available to me, and to my successors.

It is astonishing that the FA and the PFA, through Paul Power and John Cartwright, are only now belatedly beginning to find out what is going on elsewhere in the world. The FA know about youth coaching methods and the development of young players around the world, but there is no information on the competitive side of the game. We can learn from everyone else, just as they have learned from us. For years we felt that we were the best. Everyone came to us, assessed our strengths, and put that knowledge together with the best of their own game to go forward, while we stood still. We have to get our heads out of the sand and see what we have been missing. Obtaining knowledge of what is going on in the world is the first stage, but it could take eight to ten years to implement a development plan fully.

The style of English football may be very different under my coaching, and I hope at least to signal an end to the days when, as I complained myself, 'The way the English game is going, with its packed midfields, it is like trying to dribble a ball through a bus queue.' I do not want simply to swap one style for another, however, but to try and combine the best of the two European styles – introducing more of the quality football played in Italy and Spain without losing the things that are good in our own game. When I was at Barcelona, Bernd Schuster told me that he never liked playing against England, or English teams in European competitions, because our players never gave him much time, and were always snapping at his heels.

We must try to retain that side of our game, but when we get possession, we must loosen up a bit, and play more expansive, thoughtful football. Of course, that is easy to preach and hard to practise, for when you are really aggressive and uptight in defence, it is difficult to lose that attitude and become cool and calm as soon as you have the ball, but that blend of skill and aggression is what we must aim for. We also have to be willing to work. A lot of football followers groan when you mention things like 'work-rate', but as a coach, while you want the skill in a player, you want reliability as well. Very skilful players can win a match with one snatch of brilliance, but if they do not want to work for the team, they have nothing else to offer when the goals dry up. They are not popular with their team-mates either, because they bring nothing else to the party.

You often hear coaches say, 'I'd like to buy so-and-so, he wants to win.' That remark suggests that some of the others do not, which of course is not true. Everybody wants to win, because they want the bonus, the glory or whatever, but what coaches mean is that some players will pay a higher price to win. When they get a stitch, some people give in to it and stop running, thinking: That really hurts, I'll win next week, but others go right through that pain barrier, saying, I want to win and I'll pay any price to win, and that is the attitude coaches love the most. The really great players, like Pelé, Cruyff, or Maradona in his heyday, were supremely talented footballers, but they also wanted to win and were willing to do their share of the donkey-work, even if it was just chasing and harrying and closing down space in midfield. Paul Gascoigne is the same sort of player, willing to graft as well as show his skills.

Naturally talented players like Gazza often think coaching is a very overrated pastime, however, and it was interesting to talk to him after he had spent a couple of years with Lazio. When he was at Tottenham, Gazza was one of those guys who thought that the organisation of the team was okay, but not really important, but he had changed his mind when I went to see him the week after Lazio had played AC Milan. In Signori, Boxic and Gascoigne, Lazio have three of the most dangerous and inventive players in the Italian League. AC Milan do not have any really big names in the team, but they are so well organised that Lazio could not find a way through.

Milan scored a goal just before half-time, and then they simply sickened Lazio off. Lazio grew more and more frustrated, and from playing at a hundred per cent they went down to sixty per cent, which made their position even worse. Gazza admitted, 'They were so bloody organised, you couldn't do anything.' I said to him, 'So all of a sudden, you've decided that you like organised football now?' When you face a well-organised team, you begin to appreciate that it really does count.

My job now was to select a team for my first match in charge, a friendly against Denmark at Wembley on Wednesday, 9 March 1994. The squad I chose for that first match signalled a change of direction, with Darren Anderton and Graeme Le Saux making débuts and Peter Beardsley returning from the wilderness. The selections of Anderton and Le Saux were to be hailed by the press as the harbingers of a new attacking era, but the choice of Beardsley was in many ways the most significant.

For the Denmark game I wanted to introduce a new system, which I called, for obvious reasons, 'the pyramid' or 'the Christmas tree', adopting a 4-3-2-1 formation instead of 4-4-2. Recalling Beardsley immediately solved one problem. Having two front players makes life easy for defences. They put markers on them, have a sweeper and tie them up. If one of your strikers goes off deep, though, which Beardsley does in his natural game, you immediately ask them some awkward questions. Beardsley is really saying to his marker, 'Are you coming deep or are you going to stay there?' If the defender goes deep, he vacates an area for a midfield player to run into, and if he stays, Beardsley is going to get a lot of room to collect the ball and spread it around. We could be much more fluid in our play, just by that one selection. It was something Beardsley used to do at Liverpool, and, in fact, they did it before him with Dalglish, who, like Beardsley, was originally a midfield player.

The build-up to the game began in earnest ten days before the match. I was due to announce my squad on Monday morning and spent most of Sunday trying to track down Sheffield Wednesday manager Trevor Francis to confirm Chris Waddle's fitness. I gave up in the end and sat down to watch the football on television, instantly realising why I had not been able to find Trevor – he was one of the panellists on the programme. When I made contact with him later, I discovered that Chris was not fit enough to be considered. Other than that, I was happy with the look of my first squad; not too many changes from the old regime, but enough new blood to signal a fresh start.

For weeks the only thing on my mind had been to get the first game over and done with and this was one of the steps on the way: Having named the squad, I now began the ordeal that all England coaches face, spending the rest of the week praying that the players do not get injured in training or playing for their club sides at the weekend.

As the week went on, the anticipation was really beginning to build up in me, and I was champing at the bit to meet the players, talk to my coaching staff and get things moving, but all I could do for the moment was continue to plan, finalising the training ideas to put to Don Howe and watching videos of Denmark games.

I was in my office at the FA before nine on the Friday, preparing for a three-hour planning meeting with Don Howe. Later there was an interview to record for *Grandstand* and the first of the injuries to squad members. Gerry Francis phoned to tell me that Les Ferdinand was injured, and I had barely put the phone down, when there was another call to say that Gary Pallister was also doubtful. We had not even got to the weekend matches and it looked like we needed two replacements already. When I called Manchester United, however, it seemed more promising, for I was told that Pallister would be playing against Chelsea. Ferdinand looked rather less likely, with Rangers considering giving him a cortisone injection.

On Saturday I watched videos of a couple of members of my squad, and then went to Loftus Road to check on Les Ferdinand with Gerry Francis. Les was given the all-clear to play. I decided not to stay there for the game, but nipped over to the BBC's Shepherd's Bush studios, to watch live the three games that were to be shown on *Match of the Day* later on: Manchester United against Chelsea, Spurs versus Sheffield United and Sheffield Wednesday against Newcastle.

Trying to watch three screens at once I almost developed schizophrenia, but I caught the injuries to Paul Ince and Paul Parker and was on the phone to Alex Ferguson within minutes of the end of the game. Alex reckoned that both should be fine and would be joining the squad as planned, the following day. Luckily there were no other injury reports. One advantage of being at the BBC was being able to pick up the news as it happened, rather than sitting at home, chewing my fingernails, waiting for the phone to ring.

I went for dinner at Scribes with Yvette and Stephanie Moore, Bobby's widow. Stephanie insisted that I would be too busy to get involved with Bobby's testimonial on the Monday night, but I was just as insistent that, as one of Bobby's oldest friends in the game, I wanted to be there. I had known Bobby since the days when I went training with him at West Ham as a fourteen-year-old kid. Bobby was so friendly, but also had that quality that showed you that he was a born leader.

We were always good friends and grew even closer over his last few years, when we saw a great deal of each other. We could never be stopped from laughing. Bobby was one of the funniest guys you could meet, with a terrific sense of humour, which many people did not realise. As the captain of England's World Cup-winning side, he did have a high profile, and when we went to functions together, he was aware that people might be looking at him. He would be a little bit on his guard to begin with and would do everything absolutely correctly, but by his third lager he had loosened up and was the life and soul of the party.

His illness and subsequent death came as a terrible shock. Bobby and Stephanie had kept the nature of his illness close to their chests and though we knew he was not well, we did not realise how seriously ill he was until quite near the end. Eight of us were due to have dinner together, on Sunday night, Bobby, Bobby Keetch, Jeff Powell, me and our wives. By then we knew the severity of Bobby's illness. He was confined to bed, but he really wanted to go to the dinner and kept saying he would be there, right up to the last minute, when Stephanie rang through to say that he just could not get out of bed. The remaining six of us spent a very sad evening together, talking about the past and wishing that Bobby could have been there with us. Two days later, he had died.

Bobby's testimonial was the chance for all his friends and admirers to pay tribute to him and to help provide for his family and it was not an occasion I wanted to miss, even though we would already be in camp, preparing for the game against Denmark.

I was at the team hotel on the Sunday long before the players and had a dinner meeting with Don Howe, Bryan Robson and David Davies, the FA's new media director. As the players began to arrive, a phone call from Italy told me that Paul Gascoigne had been badly injured playing for Lazio. I was told that he had been 'seen to, good and proper' and had had to be carried off. He was in hospital in Rome, very doubtful for the game. I had been steeling myself for something like this and there was nothing I could do about it. Later in the evening the news was better, however, and Gazza called to say that he was going to fly over in the morning. If the player is with the squad, you always feel that there is a chance. I introduced myself to the players, over some tea and sandwiches, before they turned in for the night. Some I already knew well, others I was meeting for the first time. There was no chance of an early night for me, though because the news of Gazza's injury had every football reporter in the country on the phone to the hotel, wanting a comment.

England's training headquarters are at Bisham Abbey, a leafy suburb on the Berks–Bucks border. On the Monday morning, I had a fifteen-minute meeting with the squad before we began training, just to outline my ideas, my hopes and my belief in their ability. There was not much in the way of formal chat; I prefer to talk to the players one on one, rather than lecturing them as a group. Then we split up, and I worked with the forwards, trying to get over my ideas on adaptability and flexibility, while Don Howe organised the defence and Bryan Robson worked with individuals.

The first training session was open to the media, but the players started early and had an hour on their own without being shadowed by reporters and photographers. Later on, Gazza's appearance led to a few minutes' bedlam as photographers and camera crews jostled for shots of him. I felt much better about his chances of playing after speaking to him. He was sore, but confident that he would make it.

During the session, I gave press interviews and introduced David Platt as my team captain. He had also had a spell as captain with Graham Taylor, when Stuart Pearce had been injured, but I had a different on-field role in mind for him. Graham Taylor seemed to have a problem fitting both Platt and Gascoigne into a balanced formation for England and you must have balance, because the opposition will zero in on a weakness and exploit it.

Previous England coaches had a similar problem in getting the best out of Glenn Hoddle, who seemed to have a fantastic game in only one out of every five matches he played. It was always felt that he had difficulty getting the ball when close-marked, but I would have wanted to have him in my team, because he was so talented, and there should have been a way to get the best out of him more consistently.

I can understand why Graham Taylor wanted David Platt up front, because he is such a good finisher, but I felt he would be better coming into the box facing the goal, rather than with his back to the game. Normally Platt plays 'box to box', but he then has to come from too deep on attack. I wanted him not to drop back so far in defence. If he was only going the shorter distance, he would make more trips into the attacking area, giving us better value from him.

We finished training just before eleven, had a light lunch and an early-afternoon closed training session before returning to the hotel. With Les Ferdinand's injury not responding to treatment, I called up Ian Wright to replace him in the squad. Meanwhile, Stephanie Moore had phoned Yvette and insisted that I should not turn up for Bobby's testimonial. She knew I was struggling to fit everything in and said that it was all under control and there was no need for me to be there. This time, I reluctantly agreed.

On Tuesday, the day before the game, we had our last two-hour training session, apart from an hour to practise set-pieces the next morning. It was still uncertain whether Gazza would be fit to play, but I had two teams in my mind, one with Gazza and one without. I had not told the players at that stage, but they would be the first to know.

The way that England play under me is ultimately a compromise between the system I might want if I had limitless time available to teach the players and the pragmatic approach of finding a system that is not too far removed from the players' normal game. There has to be a starting point and there is very little time to prepare, which is why I had brought Don Howe into the coaching set-up. I felt that if I only had two days and I tried to do the defence and the midfield, I was going to have to do a great deal very quickly and it was going to be confusing. If you try to put a lot of information into someone in one hit, none of it sticks, but if you do a little bit at a time, you need more time, but you get more in.

I effectively doubled the days available to me, by getting Don to organise a defensive pattern and work with the back four and the goalkeeper on defence and defensive corners and free-kicks, while I worked with the front six on the new pyramid pattern, and the attacking corners and free-kicks. Then we put the two halves together, again doing it very simply.

On the night before the game, I went to watch the Under-21s against Denmark at Brentford, knowing that there was now nothing more that I could do to prepare for the match. I had studied the videos, planned the tactics and prepared the players as well as I could, the rest would be up to them.

I had deliberately kept the build-up to the game very light-hearted, because you do not have to pressure people in a Cup Final or international. The pressure is already there; it is in the newspapers, the television and radio, and in the people you meet when you walk along the street. There is no lack of motivation and your job is really to loosen things up instead. On the day of the game, after the players have gone out and warmed up, you can tighten them up on a little motivation, but not too much, and it is done individually not collectively. The dressing room is quiet and insular. Players talk in low voices, preparing themselves mentally, and they do not like disturbance or intrusion. They are wary of intruders, and do not want people coming in or even putting their heads round the door. They are public property much of the time, but this period of mental preparation in the dressing room has to be private.

Each player has a different method of self-motivation and preparation; there is no right or wrong way, whatever works for you is what you must do. Paul Ince, for example, never likes to warm up with the other lads, and Tony Adams already has his face set for battle, long before he goes out on to the pitch. Some players have to be calmed down before the game, others are so laid back that I might have to pull them to one side and try to get at them, but I do it individually, on the quiet, and mainly I just give them little reminders of their specific jobs and then send them out. My last words before the match were to all of them, however. I simply told them, 'Make opponents afraid of England at Wembley again. Don't stand off the opposition, and when somebody goes in for a tackle, make sure that there is another one coming in behind him.'

Outside the dressing room, the buzz begins. As you walk up the tunnel, your vision of the stadium is restricted by the canvas 'tunnel within a tunnel' that protects the teams as they enter and leave the field. From the bottom of the tunnel, all you can see is a small round hole, and then quite suddenly, you are out into the lights and the deafening, nerve-jangling, bowel-loosening roar of the crowd.

I did not go out straight away with the players, but stayed in the dressing room for a couple of minutes, talking to Don Howe and Bryan Robson and finishing off my cup of tea. The cheers for the team had died down, but when we went out, the roar swelled up again, as a personal ovation, a volcanic eruption of noise. I had expected a good reception, but not such an over-whelming one; it was almost alarming in its intensity. If I was overwhelmed by the reception from the crowd, however, I was almost overpowered by the reception from the photographers. All the way along the touchline, I was surrounded by cameras, with photographers and cameramen walking backwards, jostling each other, and then falling over each other, tumbling in all directions. My promise of entertainment for the crowd was being met even before we had kicked off . . .

There was plenty of entertainment after the kick-off too. We could have scored a couple before the first goal of the Venables era arrived. It was to be the only one of the game, a scoreline which did not do justice to our superiority, but it was a goal good enough to grace any game, and I felt that it symbolised the start of the new era.

Once we coaches have laid down our formation and our tactics, the rest is down to the players and the choices they make out on the pitch. Brains and good passing are often as effective as trying to go past defenders, to take them out of the game. The decision on when and where to do it is vital; I do not make them do anything, but the choices that they make show me whether they are good or clever enough to be England players.

We were building up through the team, and Beardsley, instead of playing out wide, was playing inside. The defender did not know whether to go with him or stay back, and one ball put him out of the game. Graeme Le Saux took possession on the edge of our own box and put Alan Shearer away with a perfectly weighted pass over forty yards. Shearer turned from deep and measured a pass into the path of David Platt's diagonal run, and Platt turned and shot in one movement, across Sch-meichel into the far corner of the net. Platt hit it so early that the goalkeeper had not even set himself up, and though the shot was not that far from his leg, he got nowhere near it. To get that angle of shot to the near post would have been unusual, but to get it to the far post was quite exceptional.

At half-time there was little that needed to be put right. I had a few things to say to individuals, and I told the players, 'Don't listen to all of this, because it will be confusing, just listen to whatever comes specifically to you.' I might say eight things altogether and no player would be able to keep all of them in mind, but if only one thing is directed specifically at him, he can disregard the rest. The only remarks I addressed to all of them were to urge the players to believe in themselves and their skills and to want the ball, and to get another player or two forward to join Shearer, because we were making, but not finishing our chances.

There were no more goals, but some good football and few problems for us in the second half. Had Gascoigne and Anderton been able to convert some good chances, we could easily have won 4-0, but it was a highly satisfactory start, both for Darren Anderton and for me. Talking in the dressing room after the game, none of us could remember a more impressive England début. Graeme Le Saux was not far behind him, good at going forward and getting in quality crosses, but with equally strong defensive qualities.

The support from the crowd was heart-warming and I think that we gave them the football that they had come to see. The FA will also not have been displeased with a crowd around 40,000 above what might have been expected in different circumstances, which at least will have paid my wages for the next two years.

All in all it was very promising, but I was keen to rein in some of the wilder excesses of enthusiasm. There were other players and other systems to look at, and it was only one match, after all. The reaction was even more euphoric after a 5-0 thrashing of Greece in our next game, before Norway brought the supporters a bit closer down to earth in a dour goalless draw at Wembley. It should have been a 1-0 win, for in my view the referee incorrectly disallowed a David Platt goal after Alan Shearer's free-kick had rebounded from a post.

The referee brought our celebrations to a premature end by ordering the kick to be retaken, because he said that he wanted the wall ten yards back from the ball in strict accordance with the rules, but in reality, if you are awarded a free-kick and decide to gamble on a quick one, you should be allowed to take the advantage. It was particularly disappointing, because we knew that the game would be tight and in that situation you have to wait for your opportunities. The free-kick was the opportunity we had been waiting for, and the referee really should have played advantage to us.

Despite that disappointment, a record of played three, won two, drawn one, with six goals scored and not a single one conceded, was not a bad start, but the important results would come in the European Championships two years down the track, not in friendlies. Just the same, I am looking to keep on winning, because it is no good saying, 'Well, I'm happy if we lose every game, so long as we win in two years' time.' I am not happy if we lose every game, it would not do the players' confidence any good, and it would make me extremely bad-tempered. I want to win now as well as in two years' time.

It was frustrating that we could not build on the foundations laid against the European champions with a game against the World champions, Germany, but with 365 days in the year to choose from they had to go and pick the anniversary of Hitler's birthday. The FA received a great deal of stick from the Germans for calling the game off, but I think the FA got it absolutely right. Football in this country has suffered enough from crowd trouble in Europe. The last thing we want is to risk another Heysel and another ban because of morons using a football match on Hitler's birthday as an excuse to re-fight the Second World War on the terraces. The game was put back till the following year, leaving us praying that they would not opt for the same date. We had some good news from the Under-21s, however, which, under the coaching of Dave Sexton, Ray Wilkins and Peter Bonetti, won the highly rated tournament in Toulon, beating Portugal 2–1 in the final.

With England failing to qualify, my only involvement in the 1994 World Cup was as a BBC summariser and very interested onlooker. The tournament produced some great surprises, some beautiful football . . . and some atrocious refereeing. Changes and interpretations of the rules promoted positive, creative football. The outlawing of the tackle from behind, for example, enabled forwards to discover new freedom and I am sure that in time it would lead to more skilful defending, too. Unfortunately, while Fifa gave the right lead to the football world, they forgot to tell the players what was required. That, coupled with the inconsistent way the rules were interpreted, littered several games with red and yellow cards, and left players mystified and angry.

It is an admirable principle to select referees from throughout the football-playing world to officiate in the World Cup, but if they are not of sufficiently high standard, you are asking for trouble. The best teams in the world deserve the best referees, and I could not care less if they all happened to come from the same country. Happily, the victims of some of the worst refereeing injustices, such as Bulgaria and Italy, which both had a player sent off in very questionable circumstances, won their games despite the handicap and survived to progress further in the tournament.

As well as complaints about the World Cup being decided on penalties, I heard many criticisms throughout the tournament about goalkeepers moving before penalties were taken and about penalty-takers – Romario, for example – stopping as they ran in to take a kick. Both are against the rules, but it was no real surprise that they were allowed to get away with it.

A referee is under so much pressure when he awards a penalty in the first place that it is even more difficult for him to order a kick to be retaken. Things do now seem to be unfairly weighted in favour of the goalkeeper, however. If he moves early, goes the right way and spreads himself, he has a very good chance of saving the penalty.

My solution to the problem would be to allow the goalkeeper to move, provided that he stayed on his line and did not advance towards the penalty-taker, but I would also allow the man taking the penalty to stop on his run-in. If the goalkeeper knows that the player taking the penalty can check and send the kick the other way, he will not move early, and that will give the penalty-taker a better chance of scoring, returning the advantage to the side that has been infringed against.

A penalty shoot-out was obviously not the ideal way to decide the World Cup, but few would argue about Brazil's right to the trophy. Most people felt the final was an anti-climax, though I personally enjoyed it and found it an intriguing struggle. It was probably too much to expect the classic final for which everyone was hoping, after all the superb football there had been in the earlier rounds. Brazil had their chances – both Bebeto and Romario had what were 'tap-ins' by their normal standards – and if either of those had gone in, we would have seen a different game, but I could not criticise the approach of either team.

Italy clearly felt that their only realistic chance was to defend and break; had they played it differently, they could easily have been beaten by four or five goals, and although Brazil did not entertain as they have in the past, they were there to win a tournament. In the 1970s the opposition was not as tactically aware and well-disciplined as in 1994, and in any event, the game of football is not about entertainment to the exclusion of everything else. If it was, you might as well have teams like the Harlem Globetrotters contesting the World Cup. They are entertaining to watch, but they play exhibition matches, not in a competitive professional league – one is showbiz, the other is professional sport.

Brazil did provide plenty of entertainment in the earlier rounds, as well as winning their games, and their supporters proved that they could also entertain themselves and everybody else within earshot. I was staying in the same hotel as hundreds of Brazilian fans, and they kept up a cacophony from morning to night, all beating out samba rhythms on their drums and blowing bugles. Looking down into the hotel's vast atrium, was like peering down into a bee-hive, with hundreds of yellow-shirted Brazilians buzzing to and fro in a tumult of noise and movement.

They only fell silent for a short while deep in the small hours, and as I lay awake at 6:30 the next morning, I heard the first faint stirrings of the Brazilian dawn chorus. Somewhere in the dark, a lone Brazilian tried a tentative toot on his trumpet, the only sound in the still of the night. Then from another corner of the hotel, came an answering note. One by one, the rest of their fellows awoke, seized their instruments and added their note to the swelling chorus. The drums picked up the beat, gently at first, then faster and louder until the samba rhythm was fully under way. They shortened a few of my nights' sleep, but you could not be angry with people who took such joy in their football.

Apart from noisy Brazilian fans, good football and curious refereeing, the World Cup was also notable for one other thing – the light it threw on the pressures facing the top footballers. The death threats allegedly levelled at the Colombian coach and some of his players, followed by the murder of Andrés Escobar, shot because of his own-goal as Colombia were eliminated in the opening round, were sickening events – the game of football poisoned by murderous criminals.

Maradona's drug-stained departure from the stage that he had once graced and Paul Gascoigne's tear-stained revelations about his personal life also commanded huge headlines during the tournament. There has always been a self-destructive side to

Maradona, as there has been to so many other great sportsmen, but while people like Maradona and Gascoigne are obviously not blameless, having contributed to their own problems, the feeding-frenzy of the media pack surrounding them has also made their situations far worse.

Only those who have experienced the pressures surrounding such superstars can really comprehend what their life is like. Neither the public, nor their managers nor even their team-mates can appreciate the pressure of media expectations and scrutiny. That already massive pressure is increased still further by the ferocious competition between individual papers. If paper X gets a story on Gascoigne, for example, papers Y and Z must instantly try to better it. If paper X has already printed the truth, however, the only way to better it is by exaggeration or invention – a media game of 'Chinese whispers' that continues until the truth has been forgotten altogether. The good things are ignored, the bad seized on, exposed and exaggerated. The concentration of media ownership into fewer and fewer hands has made the media pressure even more formidable. After the ruthless asset-stripping of football clubs by media tycoon Robert Maxwell, FA rules were strengthened to prevent an individual or his family owning more than one football club. Yet there are apparently no rules to prevent a media tycoon such as Rupert Murdoch from owning several newspapers and television stations at once. Such media power in one pair of hands could give a press baron the ability to bring down almost anyone – even a prime minister, or a member of the royal family – and certainly a footballer.

For stars like Gascoigne and Maradona, it must sometimes seem as if the whole world is against them. Of course, Maradona has been very foolish, but I hope the lasting memory of him will not be of his drug-taking, nor of the notorious 'Hand of God' incident in the 1986 World Cup, but of his magnificence as a footballer, epitomised by his electrifying run for his second goal against England in the same game. Paul Gascoigne has the ability to make a similarly glorious impact on the next World Cup, if the media pressures do not destroy him, as they have helped to destroy Maradona.

We now have less than two years to prepare for the finals of the European Championships, and straight after that we will be starting to work towards the 1998 World Cup. When the draw is made for that, I want every other country to fear us. To make that happen is going to take a lot of hard work from everybody involved, but I will also be working hard to make it fun for everybody too. The pressure is there anyway, so the last thing I want to do is add to it, piling pressure on pressure.

Some people say it takes ten years to get a top-class international side together, but it depends how lucky you are. On a good day, you might perhaps get away with just two world-class players, but ideally you must have three or four in your team, with the rest good international performers. At the World Cup in 1966, we had three world-class players – Gordon Banks, Bobby Moore and Bobby Charlton – and the rest were very good internationals.

Bobby Charlton was in a very disciplined side, with good players around him, but he was different. He could change pace and go by people and he could score from thirty-five yards. Gascoigne is different, too; he can do those sorts of things and is that type of player. David Platt has improved greatly and has reached that kind of level, and Alan Shearer is developing into quite a high-class goal-scorer.

In defence, Tony Adams has shown his maturity in the European competition with Arsenal. We have two goalkeepers, David Seaman and Tim Flowers, who have the same maturity. Paul Ince and David Batty have improved, with Batty making great strides since he went to Blackburn, and it has also been interesting to see people like Lee of Newcastle, who seems to have improved a great deal, very rapidly.

I also wanted to look at some underrated players, like Dennis Wise. Because Dennis started at Wimbledon, he has been pigeon-holed as a certain type of player. Clearly, he is industrious, he wants to win, and he will make his tackles, but he is also a very good passer and crosser of the ball with both feet.

Then there are 'tomorrow's men', perhaps people like Jamie Redknapp, Bart Williams, Ray Parlour, Robbie Fowler and Nick Barmby. These boys have been popping in to their club first teams and looking around, as if to say 'What am I doing here', and then all of a sudden they go up a grade, and really look like first-team players. Those boys have now actually earned the right to be in a squad for me to take a look at them. I have them in mind, and youth will definitely get its chance with me, but there also have to be some players in there with experience, who may still be around in two years' time, you never know. Peter Beardsley was written off when he was thirty and is still playing exceptionally well at thirty-three.

Ninety-five per cent of my work is done before the day of the match. If we get to the day of the game, and I am still trying to get things over to the players, I have not done my job properly. My task is to get the team selection, preparation and tactics right and then on the night, it is down to all of us, my coaching staff, the players and me to make sure it goes well out on the pitch.

Preparation comes from training during the week leading up to the game. Things like the team-talk before the match are really useful only as a reminder of what we have been working on in training. The nearer you get to the event, the less can be taken in and I usually confine myself to two or three points before the players go out, just reminding them of what we have been doing.

The important time to talk to the team is at half-time. Before the game, you only know what you expect to happen, you have not actually seen anything. At half-time, you cannot do anything about the first half, which is already gone, but based on what you have seen in that forty-five minutes, you can certainly do something about the second half. It is not going to improve the situation if all you say at half-time is, 'We are not getting our crosses in.' If the crosses are poor because your plan to pull the opposition full-backs forward and create space behind them is not working, saying: 'Make your crosses better' is a complete waste of breath. It is like going to see the doctor with a pain in your chest. If he gives you some embrocation to rub on it, he is treating a symptom, but he has not found the bad heart, the thing which is really wrong with you, and has missed the chance to help you recover. You can sometimes see incredible transformations in the second half, just because the manager knew what he was doing. He will not always be right, but if he can maximise the number of times he is right and minimise the number of times he is wrong, you have a good manager and a good team.

I always prefer to watch the first half of the game from high in the stand, where you have a better overview of the patterns of play, and can make your best observations for the time when you can use them at half-time. In the second half, I prefer to be in the dug-out. You need to be down on the line to get involved in directing the team and supervising substitutions.

I try to avoid talking to the players about the match immediately after the game. I have had a go at players in the dressing room in the past, but in the end, I learned from what Don Revie told me: 'There is nothing for you straight after the game.' When the game is over, you cannot do anything to change a bad result, all you have to do is put it right for the next time. You are not going to do that immediately after the game. The players will also be upset at the result and you could fly at each other in the heat of the moment and then find yourself in an irreparable situation. It is better to let them all have a shower and unwind and then have a meeting on the Monday to talk about where things went wrong.

The one danger for you in that approach is that by Monday, you may have lost your impetus and might not get out of it what you would have done on Saturday, when you were still angry. You have to be yourself and you must keep the anger there, if you need to, and not let it disappear by Monday. You also have to get players to be honest about their mistakes, so that you can solve the problems more quickly. That is easier these days, when you have the back-up of a video to help you to identify and demonstrate mistakes, but in the old days you did not have that, and the players had to take your word for what was wrong.

I hope to use my position as England coach, not only in the obvious way of finding and preparing the best available English team, but also to influence the players throughout the game. Footballers in England still have some way to go before being really professional in their attitudes. They are quite prepared to listen to someone lecturing them on tactics, but if they are consistently mis-hitting the ball when shooting, or putting it over the bar, they do not take kindly to someone saying 'Your non-kicking foot is not close enough to the kicking foot' or 'Your head's not over the ball'. If you look at them, you can see where they are going wrong. It is such a simple thing, yet it seems to offend their egos – 'I'm a footballer, I know how to kick a ball, thank you very much.'

It is not a problem that you find in any other sport. Someone like Nick Faldo or Seve Ballesteros might be playing golf in Japan, but if he is slicing the ball, for example, he will ring back home to his coach and say, 'I'm going wrong somewhere, can you look at it?' and his coach will come out, look at his swing and spend whatever time it takes to get it right. That is how meticulous they are, and that is what professionalism entails, yet most footballers would think a similar technical error in their own game was not important.

Practising everything from the most basic skill to the most complex set-piece is vital, but it has to be the right kind of practice. 'Practice makes perfect' is one of the oldest clichés in the book, but a truer version would be 'practice makes permanent'. If someone is shooting at goal and he keeps missing, is he practising to score or practising to miss? People would automatically say that he is practising to score, but if he keeps missing, until he gets his action right, he is not going to score. All he is doing is reinforcing his bad habits.

If a golfer is slicing the ball off the tee, until he corrects his swing, he will just keep slicing. If he practises ten hours a day, the practice will make permanent – he will become the best slicer in golf. Once someone has sorted him out and said, 'Look, your right thumb has got to come around more to the front, and your left shoulder is too low,' and he has corrected it and is hitting it straight down the middle, then practice makes perfect, but until then, practice makes permanent.

You hear lots of sayings in the game that perhaps have been quoted over years and years, but I usually find that the reverse of the saying is true. If you played brilliantly on Saturday afternoon, for example, and won 4–0, ending up knocking the ball around, you will always hear someone say the following Saturday, 'Let's start how we ended last week.' If you start by knocking the ball around, however, the opposition will just destroy you. What you should really be doing is starting the way you started the week before, because that is what laid the foundations for your victory.

Another opposite comes when you are coaching a team in trouble. If you are at the bottom of the League, as we were at the start of my first couple of seasons at Tottenham, all the players will be waiting for a bollocking from you. If you have had a bad start, however, and things do not look good, the crowd gets on to you and your confidence level diminishes. If I start bollocking you and getting at you as well, I might just finish you off. What I have to try and do in that situation is build your confidence back up again, so I take the pressure off and try to have a bit of fun, even though the players may not understand why I am taking that attitude.

The reverse is true when you are top, because then I always take a much tougher role, as if to say, 'Keep your feet on the floor.' If they are not doing well, footballers tend to think that they are the worst players in the world, and if they are doing well, they think that they are the best. Neither is true, but a big part of coaching is to give people room to breathe and move and, above all, to give them confidence – that intangible, untouchable thing between the ears.

You have to know what type of leader you are. The *laissez-faire* coach lets everyone do what they want, which breeds a lot of confidence and personality, but if you have not got it under control, it can actually end with everyone going haywire. The autocrat rules with an iron fist, and everything relies on him, which can work, but is basically unhealthy, and does not encourage flair from individual players. If the coach is not around, you lose your leadership. The democrat, the leader of the band, is perhaps the most skilful coach, who lets players blossom but is always watchful, ready to nip excess in the bud and keep it under control.

Sometimes it is hard to keep your cool and do the most effective thing, because when it is not going well, it is tempting to go berserk, but you are really just indulging your own feelings, and slating the players is not going to do them any good. You can shout and shout at them and in the end it becomes like a nagging wife, they just think, 'Oh, he's droning on again – get lost.' There comes a stage when the player has had enough and you can then do irreparable damage to your relationship with him. Someone can shout and scream and eff and blind all they want, but if you have no respect for them, it does not mean anything. You do not believe it anyway; you did not believe it before the game, so why should you believe it afterwards?

If you can use a quiet and encouraging voice instead, then when you do need to get tough, the harsh words out of nowhere will have much more impact, especially coming from someone you respect. If I look you in the eye and say, 'It just wasn't good enough today, was it?' that can be far more of a crushing blow than a 'sergeant-major' screaming so loud that his veins are popping in his forehead.

I am not so arrogant as to think that I am the only person who knows how to coach the England side. There are plenty of other good coaches around, and I hope that one of my legacies to the English game when I eventually step down – if I do not get sacked first – is a natural succession, and a smooth transition, with the next-in-line ascending to the throne, after time spent learning the ropes alongside me. That is the way that the West Germans and Dutch have tried to organise their national teams, and the benefits are obvious in their results over the last twenty years.

I want the English side to play in a manner that brings admiration from the public. That means good football, but not fantasy football, because there must be common sense in the approach and tactics. I am looking for imagination, but the pattern needs to be simple and efficient and we cannot afford to alternate systems too much. The quality of players is undoubtedly there, even if it is not yet everywhere that I would want it, and I hope that in the next two years, we can begin to show English football in its true colours.

I do not accept for a moment the suggestion by some people that players are no longer interested in representing their country, unless they are well paid for doing so. Pride plays a big part for players; they always want to play for England, whether or not you pay them. They do it for themselves, their families and their country, not for the money. So do I, although the England job does have a few perks, such as the chance to pick up an easy £1000, as I discovered when Rodney Marsh and George Best came into Scribes with their wives one Saturday night. Both Rodney and George are very good at trivia quizzes and had been to a pub quiz that night. I always told Rodney that all the useless information he accumulated would never do him any good, but he liked nothing better than catching me out on some arcane bit of football lore.

I had not seen Rodney for ages, but as soon as he came into the bar, instead of catching up on the gossip, he went straight into trivia quiz-mode, asking me to name three England internationals with a double 'o' in their surname. I knew one straight off: 'Osgood'.

'Yeah, that's one,' said Rodney, 'but you won't get three.'

Then I guessed, 'Woodcock', which was right as well, but he still insisted that I would not get the last one.

'I bet I do.'

'I bet you don't, whatever you want.'

'Crook of Norwich.'

'I'll bet you £1000 that isn't right.'

'You're on.'

'Well, you've lost then, because Crook isn't an international.'

'He will be next week!'

It is still very early days for me and there is a great deal to learn. Graham Taylor and Bobby Robson both said it took two years to see what the job was about. What I have learned so far is that the FA is a sort of civil service, with meetings planned a month ahead, whereas the League manager's job is fast and furious: quick decisions, the press knocking on the door, players wanting to see you, your staff trying to prepare, the doctor wanting to see you because he has a problem with the physios, and just when you have made arrangements for your training, two players are not going to be able to play. Everything is matching and patching and last-minute. If you lose on Saturday it is a blow, but by Monday you are preparing for a midweek game, and last Saturday is already forgotten.

In the England job the decisions are slower. There is time available and I must take that time, but when the next game finally comes round, the pace dramatically quickens. Your decisions then have to be really fast, and you must be needle-sharp. Things are brought to the boil under tremendous pressure, because the whole country stops for an England game. When it is over, you go on the back-burner again for a while, waiting for the next game to come around.

The profile of the England job makes the highs higher and the lows lower. A win is a cause for national celebration, but a defeat may lead to national despair, and the hangover from a beating can last weeks. Harold Wilson was not joking when he claimed that England's defeat in the 1970 World Cup cost Labour the General Election, and Silvio Berlusconi's presidency of all-conquering AC Milan obviously did not harm his chances in the Italian general election in 1994.

The year 1993–94 was a really tough one for Tottenham Hotspur and me, but with luck, all the troubles are behind us now, and we can both look to the future with confidence. Although missing out on Brazilian defender Marcio Santos, Tottenham's signing of two World Cup stars before the start of the 1994–95 season, Ilie Dumitrescu and Jurgen Klinsmann, players of the highest quality, certainly suggests that Spurs are heading in the right direction. I hope that I will also be steering England on the right course over the next few years, and that the stars everyone will be talking about after the 1998 World Cup will not be Brazilians, Rumanians and Germans but English players. The job is a tremendous challenge, but one I am relishing.

We have made the right beginning, but as I said after the Denmark game, 'It's a promising start, but let's not get carried away, there's a long way to go yet.' It is a long road, but if I do have one advantage over younger guys like Gerry Francis or bright people coming up like Bryan Robson, Glenn Hoddle or Ray Wilkins, it is that I have done the job for a long time and known the best and the worst that it can bring.

I have learned something about myself: I can take a huge disappointment like losing the European Cup final on penalties or being sacked at Tottenham, and not be crushed by it. Football is just like life. You have to give it your best shot, take the best and survive the rest. You have to be resilient above all else, and I have certainly learned to be that.

# Index